The Working Class in American History

A list of books in the series appears at the end of this volume.

Workers on the Waterfront

Workers
on the Waterfront

Seamen, Longshoremen,
and Unionism in the 1930s

Bruce Nelson

To Bob,

fellow worker,
friend, teacher,

with gratitude,
Bruce Nelson
12/98

University of Illinois Press
Urbana and Chicago

Publication of this work was supported in part by grants from
Dartmouth College and the Andrew W. Mellon Foundation.

This book is printed on acid-free paper.

Library of Congress Cataloging-in-Publication Data

Nelson, Bruce, 1940–
    Workers on the waterfront : seamen, longshoremen, and unionism in
the 1930s / Bruce Nelson.
        p.   cm. — (The Working class in American history)
    Bibliography: p.
    Includes index.
    ISBN 0-252-01487-1 (alk. paper)
    1. Trade-unions—Merchant seamen—United States—History—20th
century. 2. Trade-unions—Stevedores—United States—History—20th
century. 3. Strikes and lockouts—Merchant seamen—United States—
History—20th century. 4. Strikes and lockouts—Stevedores—United
States—History—20th century. 5. Syndicalism—United States—
History—20th century. 6. Trade-unions and communism—United
States—History—20th century. I. Title. II. Series.
HD6515.S4N45 1988
331.88'113875'09—dc19   8728749
                                                                         CIP

To:
Bill Bailey
John Gladstone
Bob McElroy
Al Richmond

Contents

Acknowledgments

It is a pleasure to acknowledge the debts I have incurred in the course of writing this book. In many cases, a word of thanks is long overdue.

I'm grateful for the generous assistance of Irene Moran and other staff members at the Bancroft Library, University of California, Berkeley; Bette Eriskin at UC Berkeley's Social Science Library; Carol Schwartz of the International Longshoremen's and Warehousemen's Union, Anne Rand Research Library, San Francisco; and Debra Bernhardt and the staff of the Tamiment Library, New York University. At the Sailors' Union of the Pacific in San Francisco, I am especially indebted to President Paul Dempster and to Stephen Schwartz, archivist-historian of the SUP's hundredth anniversary project.

During the course of my research, I've had the privilege of interviewing many participants in the maritime union movement of the 1930s. All of them have added something of themselves and their life experience to this study; some have made major contributions to my understanding of the events, institutions, and people discussed herein. Joe Stack and Randall B. "Pete" Smith helped me get started. Lew Amster, Al Lannon, Jr., and Stanley Postek made valuable historical materials available for long periods of time. Thanks in large measure to Esther Palazzi's warm and generous hospitality, my research trips to New York were like coming home to a visit with family and friends. Roy Hudson spent many hours discussing the Marine Workers Industrial Union with me, and my knowledge of the MWIU owes much to him. Sam Darcy communicated with me at length and criticized drafts of several chapters. His unrelenting but insightful criticisms are much appreciated. Harry Bridges, John P. Olsen, and Henry Schmidt contributed enormously to my understanding of the development of unionism on the San Francisco waterfront in the early thirties.

A number of people I interviewed have since "crossed the bar." I want to express my thanks, and a final *salud*, to Roy Hudson, Thomas Ray, Ann Rothman, Henry Schmidt, Herman "Dutch" Thomas, and Arno Weissflog.

And I must single out several individuals for a special word of thanks. Bill Bailey has been a generous ally and friend. Not only did he provide me with several engaging interviews; he allowed me to read his thoroughly entertaining autobiography and put me in touch with a number of maritime veterans on the West Coast. John Gladstone has aided my work in ways that are too numerous to mention. Even when we engage in long-distance polemics, I trust that Johnny understands my enduring gratitude. Bob McElroy has been one of my most partisan supporters and, at times, one of my harshest critics. Perhaps no one has attached more importance to my work than "Mac," and I'm deeply grateful for his encouragement and support. Al Richmond, who died in November 1987, was a unique resource and a treasured friend. Not only did he participate in some of the events discussed herein, but he also reflected critically on that experience in a splendid autobiography. Al read and criticized several chapters; he showed extraordinary patience as we discussed the subject year after year; he encouraged me to hurry up and get it done! Along with other maritime union veterans, Al, Bill, Johnny, and Mac helped me understand that "setting the record straight" is both an exacting task and a labor of love. This book is for them.

Henry May, Michael Rogin, and Harry Rubin read portions of the manuscript, and their criticisms were most helpful. Lawrence Levine, my dissertation director at Berkeley, provided much encouragement and penetrating criticism. Paula Fass not only read several chapters; she also provided me with office space at a time when I was very much in need of a place to collect my things and my thoughts. David Brody's editorial skill and unrivalled knowledge of twentieth-century labor history have been vitally important to the development of my work. His criticism, offered generously over the years, has improved the manuscript; his friendship has made the undertaking more meaningful. Finally, there is David Montgomery. His work has been an inspiration to me; his keen criticism has made complacency impossible; his encouragement has helped sustain me.

At the University of Illinois Press, Richard Wentworth was patient and supportive, and Carol Saller, who read the manuscript with a keen eye, gave me a gracious lesson in the elements of style. George Au, Bill Bailey, Ruby Hynes, Irene Moran, and Lisa Rubens provided valuable assistance in finding and selecting photographs. Sylvia Brown, Karen Hairfield, Grace O'Connell, and Helen Reiff typed early drafts of the manuscript with professional skill and a nice personal touch. Gail Patten typed the final draft with all that and more. My wife Donna convinced me to put the work aside on occasion and join her in experiencing the beauty of the Green Mountains and the high Sierras. For that, and much more, I'm grateful to her.

Finally, I gratefully acknowledge the financial assistance of Dartmouth College, especially the Committee on Research and Dean of the Faculty Dwight Lahr, in the publication of this book.

Of course, I alone am responsible for the opinions expressed in this study. Some of the above-mentioned people will disagree strongly with my interpretation at certain points, but I hope all of them will recognize the importance of their contributions.

Introduction

On Working-Class Consciousness and the Mood of Syndicalism

Recently, historians of the American working class have been reassessing the "turbulent years" of the 1930s. A growing number of studies are challenging the notion that the decade was characterized by widespread militancy and ideological ferment and are reaffirming the venerable hypothesis that job consciousness and pragmatism were at the root of the workers' activity and outlook. While acknowledging that the massive strike wave that crested in 1937 led to impressive gains, recent historiography has tended to emphasize the narrow, episodic character of worker militancy and to assert the primacy of a deeply rooted social inertia beneath the turbulent surface of events.[1]

This study examines the insurgent activity and consciousness of maritime workers during the 1930s and concludes that among longshoremen and seamen on the Pacific Coast the thirties were years of major institutional gains, sustained bursts of self-activity, and expanding consciousness. The West Coast maritime industry was convulsed by two major strikes during the decade, and day-to-day labor relations on the waterfront were characterized by a constant state of guerilla warfare. Moreover, the marine workers' struggles increasingly involved politics as well as "porkchops"—not only the walkouts and job actions to transform the world of work, but the strikes to defend workers faced with stiff legal penalties, the refusal to load cargo designed to aid Mussolini's aggression in Ethiopia, and the boarding of German ships to tear down the hated swastika. It is an experience that stands in sharp contrast to the emerging portrait of the thirties as the "not so 'turbulent years.' "

The main focus of this study will be on merchant seamen. In particular, I will attempt to delineate the relationship between long-standing patterns of life and labor in the maritime industry and the distinctive consciousness and subculture that emerged from that experience. The seamen's conditions of life and work were characterized by raw exploitation, a legendary rootlessness and transiency that led to a persistent isolation from the main integrative institutions of American society, and a sense of internationalism deriving from frequent contact with port cities and maritime workers around the world. By itself, no one of these factors was decisive in shaping a subculture that encouraged militancy, spontaneous radicalism, and the mood of syndicalism. But taken together, they provided a powerful impulse in that direction.

In discussing maritime unionism, I will sometimes trace the development of organization in Atlantic and Gulf ports. But the principal focal point will be the Pacific Coast. The great West Coast maritime and general strike in 1934 unleashed many of the forces that shaped the marine unions in the 1930s. Moreover, the strike was followed by a "Pentecostal" era of insurgent unionism and expanding consciousness that was not limited to the Pacific Coast but certainly found its most distinctive expression there.*

Finally, the focus will often expand to include longshoremen as well as seamen. There were many similarities in the experience of these two groups of workers. On the West Coast, many longshoremen were former seamen. When it came time for a seafarer to settle down, he often sought employment on the docks. Thomas G. Plant, an executive of the American-Hawaiian Steamship Company, recalled his earliest impressions of San Francisco longshoremen as "mostly steam schooner sailors" who "when they married . . . wanted to come ashore. So they came ashore and became longshoremen." Although the stevedores were neither as transient nor as isolated from mainstream society as the seamen, they suffered from the same raw exploitation and a similar lack of social respectability. The rhythm of their irregular work schedules made it necessary for them to live near the waterfront and congregate mainly with their own kind. And in spite of its segregated character and unsavory image, the waterfront environment of the West Coast's major ports inevitably imparted to its work force some of the cosmopolitanism that

---

*I have derived the term *Pentecostal* not from normal religious usage, but from International Seamen's Union President Andrew Furuseth, who once called upon the seafarers to make a union anniversary observation a "pentecostal" one and to be "saturated with the spirit of the crusader." Ironically, this call came in 1929, one of the lowest points in the history of maritime unionism. Furuseth's use of religious terminology was usually designed to sanctify and revitalize conventional institutions and commitments. The upheaval of the thirties was Pentecostal in a markedly different sense. It was accompanied by a zealous commitment to new leaders and new, or transformed, institutions and by an apocalyptic sense of urgency.[2]

derived from the constant interaction with cultures and ideas from around the world.[3]

Longshoremen not only shared many cultural characteristics with the seamen, but on the West Coast they played a leading role in the union movement of the 1930s. Their coastwide walkout in May 1934 triggered the wider maritime and general strike, and particularly in San Francisco they continued to symbolize militant unionism throughout much of the Pentecostal era. In 1935 the Maritime Federation of the Pacific Coast brought seamen, longshoremen, and other waterfront workers together in one organization that seemed to be the precursor of an even closer alliance. The federation constituted the realization of an impulse toward organic unity that had resounded in the ranks of the marine workers for decades. But ultimately, in the face of clashing personalities and ideologies, it proved unable to overcome the long-standing legacy of craft separation. Moreover, the federation was overshadowed—and ultimately pulled apart—by the coming of the Committee for Industrial Organization (CIO) and the growing fratricidal warfare between the American Federation of Labor and the CIO. The rise and fall of the Maritime Federation, and the bitter controversy between the AFL and the CIO, provide vivid case studies of both the strengths and the limits of working-class consciousness in the 1930s.

It would seem that any consideration of working-class consciousness is an invitation to polemics. My own understanding of this phenomenon is based on a recognition of the primacy of complexity and diversity over simplicity and unity. Such factors as national boundaries, different time periods, ethnicity, race, and gender have played a major role in creating diversity. Even at the point of production, the simple formula "labor versus capital" has not been an adequate description of reality. For in addition to the above factors, the development of capitalism has led to a continual recomposition of the working class, creating ever new internal divisions and, therefore, a complex and often contradictory consciousness.[4]

In a study of workers in a specific industry and geographic location at a particular historical moment, it is perhaps all the more important to acknowledge that their ideology does not possess normative dimensions that can and should be measured against an enclosed ideal category called "working-class consciousness." On the other hand, it would be equally wrong to take refuge in pure empiricism. For as English historian E. P. Thompson has reminded us, there is a logic if not a law in "the response of similar occupational groups undergoing similar experiences." Without falling prey to notions of historical inevitability, it is possible to affirm that the experience of working people over centuries has demonstrated a tendency toward the development of ideas, institutions, and values that have transcended time periods and national boundaries and have reflected a striving toward a collective affirmation of self.[5]

To be sure, this tendency toward self-affirmation has not always given rise to oppositional movements and ideologies. As Herbert Gutman pointed out, "Most of the time subordinate populations live with their exploitation. They make adjustments. They create institutions to deal with inequality. . . . They do so without seeking to transform the conditions that create or sustain that inequality." Among large sections of the English working class, and among immigrant workers in the steel and textile towns of the United States, the inwardly focused and politically passive subcultures that developed over time seemed almost impervious to the volatile tug of external events. However, ethnic and working-class subcultures do not always promote acquiescence; they can also nourish the seeds of opposition, which in turn can mature into rebellion when the historical circumstances are favorable. At the moment of fruition, what appears to be an alternative but acquiescent way of life can become an oppositional force of enormous power. Even "quiescent" steel had its volcanic 1919; and some textile centers were rocked by recurring explosions of protest.[6]

Among maritime workers, the tendencies toward spontaneous radicalism inherent in their subculture were like parched grasslands waiting for a spark to ignite them. The spark came from a number of dynamic historical factors that were specific to the 1930s: the desperate conditions brought on by the Great Depression, the opportunity and widespread optimism generated by the New Deal, the growing presence and influence of the Communist party, the worldwide rise of fascism and its apparent manifestations in the United States. Although the marine workers' insurgent self-activity reached a peak of white hot intensity for only a brief historical moment in the thirties, it was no aberration. For it drew upon resources that were deeply rooted in a longstanding way of life and work on the waterfront.

In evaluating the consciousness of maritime workers I have drawn upon a wide range of sources, including (among others) the vast archives of the International Longshoremen's and Warehousemen's Union and the Sailors' Union of the Pacific; union convention proceedings and newspapers; leaflets and bulletins published by activists; and the correspondence, oral histories, and memoirs of participants in the events on the waterfront. Since it has become fashionable in some quarters to distrust literary evidence and to posit a necessary gulf between the outlook of the entrenched or activist minority on the one hand and the "inert" majority on the other, we must ask whether the offical press of the insurgent unions, and unofficial but widely read bulletins such as the *Waterfront Worker* in San Francisco, reflected the sentiments of significant numbers of rank-and-file workers. Without denying the existence of complexity and diversity in the mental universe of marine workers, I believe that, overall, the answer to this question is a clear yes. Obviously a few sources represented the views of only a small minority. But in the case of the *Waterfront Worker,* longshoremen demonstrated their commitment to this journal by avidly reading it, raising money on the docks to keep it alive, and endorsing its program. Moreover, its pages included a significant number of letters from stevedores, expressing many concerns and a broad range of political opinion. As for the *Voice of the Federation,* the official publication of the Maritime Federation of the Pacific, some unions initially refused to subscribe to the paper, and it gradually became a pawn in the factional warfare within the Federation. But in the heyday of maritime unity, the *Voice* was received with pride by many maritime workers, and it served as a weekly forum for the vigorous expression of a wide range of views.[7]

The shipowners were quick to blame the waterfront's surge of activism and ideological ferment on the Communist party. To the employers, the Pentecostal era represented a deviation from the "safe, sound Americanism" that allegedly had prevailed before the 1934 strike. They longed for the more congenial unionism of the AFL old guard, even though for more than a decade they had refused to recognize the unions headed by these men. What the shipowners conveniently overlooked, however, was the fact that the consciousness and activity of longshoremen and seamen in the new era had long been an inherent part of the subculture of the marine industry and had been expressed by the workers, episodically if not consistently, during the fifty years that maritime unionism had had a foothold on the Pacific Coast. The tendency to override craft separation and form cooperating federations—at its highest level, the demand for "One Big Union" in the industry—had existed side by side with craft divisions and jealousies and had often swept aside the latter during periods of upsurge. Moreover, the marine workers' internationalism was as much a product of their subculture as it was a reflection of "derived" ideas brought to the men from without. Given the long history of harsh exploitation and the fact that there were few institutions that served to mitigate their suffering and draw them closer to the American mainstream, longshoremen and seamen did not need the Communists to tell them about the reality of the class struggle.

On the other hand, it is undeniable that the Communists were a major force in the maritime industry; and their role will receive a good deal of attention in this study. They provided the workers with a number of disciplined cadres who not only were more able and energetic than the AFL incumbents, but were far more in tune with the sentiments and aspirations of the men. In most cases, these Communist cadres were themselves marine workers of many years' standing. And whereas the Communists did indeed bring ideas to the workers in marine, the ones that took hold were not so much new as they were a more sophisticated distillation of popular experience and of tendencies that were inherent in the maritime subculture. Early in the decade the Party's ultrarevolutionary sloganeering often contrasted sharply with the caution and demoralization engendered among many workers by the stark material conditions of the Great Depression. During the late thirties, the Party line would fly in the face of the marine workers' deeply rooted syndicalist tendencies, emphasizing instead the "final importance" of the "political front" and seeking to harness the union movement to the Democratic party and the legislative agenda of the New Deal. In between, however, there was an extended moment of transition from the flamboyant leftism of the so-called Third Period to the reformist themes of the Popular Front. During this period the line of the Communist party coincided in important ways with the natural propensities of radicalized maritime workers, whose combativeness and class awareness were enhanced by the magnetic pull of a resurgent labor movement and the widespread political ferment that accompanied the New Deal.[8]

The years immediately following the great maritime strike of 1934 saw the development of a "syndicalist renaissance" on the Pacific Coast. The choice of this term may at first seem peculiar. The word *syndicalism* has a distinctly European ring. It is associated with the brilliant but ominous eclecticism of Georges Sorel and the increasingly remote history of trade unionism in France, Italy, and Spain. Historians have generally agreed that for the most part syndicalism passed into oblivion with the triumph of the Bolsheviks in Russia, the crushing defeat of the great strike wave in one country after another from 1917 to 1920, and the subsequent establishment of Communist hegemony on the Left. In the United States, the Industrial Workers of the World (IWW), or Wobblies, were once widely regarded as the American variant of syndicalism, but the IWW was permanently crippled by the wave of government and vigilante repression during and after World War I.[9]

In recent years, however, an increasing number of studies have looked beneath the level of doctrine and have discovered a syndicalist impulse or mood in the workers' movement that was much more widespread and durable than the formal ideas and organizations associated with the anarcho-syndicalist tradition. In its most dynamic form, this mood of syndicalism signified a desire to transform the world by fundamentally reshaping the patterns of authority and organization in the realm of work. More specifically, it was characterized by at least four readily identifiable dimensions: first, the impulse toward workers' control of production; second, the belief that direct action at the point of production was the most effective means for the achievement of working-class objectives; third, the determination to cross traditional craft union barriers in order to build solidarity with other workers—ultimately, the impulse toward One Big Union; and, finally, an apocalyptic dimension, a striving for fundamental social transformation embodied in the Wobblies' exhortation to "bring to birth a new world from the ashes of the old."[10]

Many workers came to believe that the transformation of the familiar but increasingly oppressive world of work held the key to a better future and that their unions were the germ of the new society. As the charter of French syndicalism put it, "The union, which is today an instrument of resistance, will in the future be the unit of production and distribution, the basis of social reorganization." But while stressing the priority of direct action over politics, many syndicalists did not express a dogmatic hostility to political activity. Tom Mann, the famed leader of the British dockworkers and a prominent convert to syndicalism, stated in 1910 that the syndicalist movement must "*be avowedly and clearly revolutionary in aim and method. . . .* Does this mean that we should become anti-political? Certainly not." Likewise, in her perceptive survey of the American labor movement in 1914, Helen Marot noted that "all direct actionists do not oppose political action, and many indorse it." She added, however, that "all object to the *tendency* of political action to rob rather than supply the workers with opportunities to test and exercise their own powers."[11]

The syndicalism that made such spectacular headway in the early years of the twentieth century was one of mood rather than doctrine. Many workers who reflected this mood had little interest in the doctrinal preoccupations of the various organizations on the Left and probably did not even think of themselves as syndicalists. But industrial unionism, the quest for One Big Union, the various moves toward amalgamation and federation among craft unions—all of this made sense to growing numbers of workers for whom the ballot, the union label, and the unabashed class collaboration of labor statesmen had become blunt instruments indeed. The ideological content of the New Unionism was vague and eclectic, but the impulse was nonetheless powerful. As one perceptive labor journalist pointed out, its appeal was "to the profound but still vaguely articulated craving of working men for a new society."[12]

Although there is still no consensus about the breadth, persistence, and exact form of this impulse, it is clear that the mood of syndicalism gathered momentum in response to the process of capitalist rationalization that effectively challenged and disrupted the vibrant traditions of job control that artisans and craftsmen had developed over a period of many years. As this process of rationalization spread and concentrated its forces under the banner of "Taylorism," large numbers of semiskilled workers joined the battle along with the skilled craftsmen. Thus, the second decade of the twentieth century was marked not only by the epic drama of world war and revolution, but also by a fierce and protracted struggle for control of the workplace.[13]

The United States did not witness any upheavals on the scale of the massive Italian factory occupations during the *biennio rosso* of 1919–20; nor did it experience anything as threatening to bourgeois order as the huge shipyard strikes led by avowedly revolutionary syndicalists on Glasgow's Clydeside or the Spartacist uprising in Germany.[14] But American workers did respond vigorously to the onslaught of capitalist rationalization, which reached its highest stage of development in the United States. David Montgomery has identified an era of the New Unionism in the United States, lasting from approximately 1909 to 1922, in which the "direct, mass-involvement challenge to managerial authority and contempt for accepted AFL practice . . . [remained] the outstanding characteristics of American labor struggles, not episodically but continuously" for a dozen years. Moreover, by 1919, the "unprecedented revolt of the rank and file"—as the *Nation* characterized the burgeoning workers' movement—was reaching unprecedented proportions. Among immigrant clothing workers in New York City, the contagion of the wartime rhetoric of democracy and of the postwar revolutionary upsurge in their native lands proved "irrepressibly infectious." One labor-relations specialist noted with alarm that "discipline, production, efficiency, low enough at best, were often shot to pieces . . . in many instances the workers virtually took over the establishments." In addition, the Seattle General Strike, the refusal of West Coast longshoremen to handle arms and supplies destined for the counterrevolutionary forces in Russia, the sporadic strikes and armed conflicts in the coalfields, and the nationwide steel strike of more than a quarter of a million workers—all this and more reflected the mood of syndicalism. As the Interchurch World Movement *Report* on the steel strike concluded, the mass of immigrant steelworkers were largely devoid of any coherent radical ideology. But they had a "vague idea," stemming in part from their perception of the Russian Revolution, that "poor people who have been run for a long time, on farms and in mills, are coming up in the world and are beginning to run themselves."[15]

Although semiskilled operatives in steel and other major industries were often enthusiastic participants in the strikes of this era, it is undeniable that skilled workers were the leading force in the syndicalist movement. During and after the war it was highly skilled metalworkers in the munitions industry who were at the forefront of the working-class upheavals in Turin, Glasgow, Berlin, even Petrograd, and also in Bridgeport and other centers of the munitions and electrical industries in the United States. Their long-standing traditions of job control were most clearly challenged by capitalist rationalization, and compared to industrial workers, they had the literacy, confidence, and organizational cohesion to mount a sustained defense against the ravages of Taylorism.[16]

But especially in the United States, syndicalism also appealed to a markedly different constituency, namely, the rootless and transient workers in agriculture, lumber, metal mining, and maritime who lived and worked on the fringes of the social mainstream. Their oppressive conditions of work, and their isolation from the principal integrative institutions of American society, made these workers peculiarly receptive to a radical critique of capitalism. In their ranks the mood—and sometimes the doctrine—of syndicalism grew like a hothouse flower.

It was among these wandering workers that the IWW found its main constituency. This was particularly true in the West, where Charles Ashleigh noted the existence of "an immense army of unskilled and semiskilled workers, of no fixed abode, who are forever engaged in an eternal chase for the elusive job." Writing in the *International Socialist Review* in 1914, Ashleigh applauded the "phenomenal spread of the propaganda of the I.W.W. among the migratory workers" and declared with joy that "around nearly every 'jungle' fire and during the evening hours on many a job in the great westland, the I.W.W. red songbook is in evidence, and the rude rebel chants are lustily sung."[17]

Although they sometimes found themselves in tactical disagreement with the formal representatives of syndicalism in Europe and America, the Wobblies were indeed the most dynamic representatives of the syndicalist tradition in the United States.[18] However, as Montgomery has suggested, syndicalist tendencies among American workers reached "far beyond the limited influence of the Industrial Workers of the World." The very breadth of the mood of syndicalism made it a larger phenomenon than the Wobblies could contain within their ranks, but the Wobs' own shortcomings also contributed to their limited influence. They idealized the "bindle stiff" and "the obscure Bill Jones on the firing line, with stink in his clothes, rebellion in his brain, hope in his heart, determination in his eye and direct action in his gnarled fist." But this one-sided veneration of the most oppressed workers led them to underestimate the growing combativeness and radicalization among skilled workers. The IWW's well-known contempt for craft unions easily translated into contempt for skilled workers. Moreover, the revolutionary élan of the Wobblies was no substitute for the practical necessity of consolidating organizational and material gains in the wake of a strike. Montgomery points out that in the era of the New Unionism other forces were more successful than the IWW in combining militant, even revolutionary, leadership with businesslike organization, especially among the increasingly assertive immigrant workers.[19]

On the waterfronts of the Pacific Coast, the syndicalist impulse went far beyond the Wobblies' limited appeal, and survived their demise, because it was rooted in the maritime workers' conditions of life and work and was nourished by contact with other workers whose experience gave rise to a similar mood. This is why it is possible to identify a syndicalist renaissance in the 1930s, long after the heroic age of syndicalism had passed. The decade's volatile mixture of hope and despair, sharp class struggle and ideological ferment, not only at home but in the wider world that was peculiarly accessible to the marine workers, brought deeply rooted impulses to the surface once again and recaptured many of the themes of 1919.

To be sure, the syndicalist renaissance was limited in time and ambiguous in its political implications. From the vantage point of the Left, it could be parochial as well as cosmopolitan. From the standpoint of the conventional wisdom in labor relations, it has been judged an era of massive irresponsibility. Viewed from the standpoint of the workers themselves, however, the Pentecostal era represents a long overdue festive upheaval, a search for more humane and just patterns of work relations, and the flowering of an insurgent consciousness that was quite distinct from the bourgeois mainstream. The fact that this consciousness burned brilliantly only for a relatively brief historical moment should not be allowed to obscure its dynamic impact on the lives of the maritime workers, the shaping of waterfront labor relations, and the development of unionism along the West Coast.[20]

1

Foc'sle and Sailortown:
The Life, Work, and Subculture
of Merchant Seamen

The mature working class is a phenomenon of the nineteenth and twentieth centuries. For the most part its development has been contingent on technological advances that made possible the assembly line and other agencies of mass production. But unlike his distinctly modern counterparts in auto, rubber, and steel, the seaman is as old as water-borne commerce and transportation. As long as there have been laborers—under ancient slavery, under feudalism, and in the social systems of the modern world—there have been seamen.

This venerable status has contributed to the image of Jack Tar as a carefree, daring, and riotous adventurer. After all, he sailed the Spanish Main with Sir Francis Drake and guided Columbus to the shores of the New World. He hunted whales in the blue Pacific with grim Ahab and sailed speedy clipper ships to the far-flung cities of Japan and China. He has hoisted a glass and chased a skirt in every port city on the globe. More rapid forms of transportation have dramatically reduced his numbers, but his place in literature and legend will long endure.

All too often, however, the glamorous myth has obscured a grim reality. Jack could indeed be jolly; he much preferred the raucous culture of the "sailortown" to the pious alternatives offered by his self-appointed benefactors; and he was often a far more rational, calculating being than his detractors were prepared to admit. But the fact remains that for centuries the seaman was regarded by law and custom as less than a man and was often treated worse than a chattel slave or a pack animal. He entered the twentieth century bearing the burden of an archaic, semifeudal tradition of the sea and a code of laws that perpetuated his bondage. Along with American Indians, seamen had the dubious distinction of being regarded by law as wards of the federal government. As late as 1897, in the *Arago* case, the Supreme Court stated that "seamen are treated by Congress as well as by the Parliament of Great Britian, as deficient in that full and intelligent responsibility for their acts which is accredited to ordinary adults." The court's ruling affirmed that the provisions of the Thirteenth Amendment and subsequent legislation barring involuntary servitude did not apply to the seafarer. In other words, he was still subject to arrest and imprisonment for desertion and absence without leave. Small wonder that the seamen called the *Arago* case the "Second Dred Scott Decision."[1]

Partly because of the close historic ties between the merchant marine and the navy, and partly because of the separation of seafaring life from the direct scrutiny of the larger shoreside community, workers at sea were subject to a code of discipline that would have been unthinkable even in the worst sweatshops, mines, and lumber camps of early industrial capitalism. Flogging was a traditional form of "correction" in the British navy and it became common and lawful in the American merchant marine. In his review of maritime labor relations in early America, Richard Morris stated that "short-tempered captains had quick recourse to flogging even for relatively minor lapses on a seaman's part." As many as six or seven hundred lashes were by no means unheard of, and sentences of one or two hundred lashes were common. Although flogging was finally outlawed in 1850, Frederick Law Olmsted could still state with no exaggeration that American seamen "are more wretched and are governed more by threats of force than any other civilized laborers in the world."[2]

Olmsted was one of many observers who compared the life of a seaman with that of a chattel slave. And he was unusually well qualified to make this comparison. For not only did he travel extensively through the Cotton Kingdom, but in the 1840s he sailed before the mast for two years. After one plantation overseer told him, "Why, sir, I wouldn't mind killing a nigger more than I would a dog," Olmsted commented that such conversation was "exactly like what I have heard said, again and again, by Northern ship-masters and officers, with regard to seamen." Nor did the sailors themselves shy away from this odious comparison. In 1911, as five hundred striking seamen marched through the streets of New York City, they issued a statement in three languages declaring that "we are held in more abject slavery than the Negroes of the South before the Civil War."[3]

Resistance to shipboard discipline was often deemed mutiny, and it subjected the seaman to harsh penalties. Richard Henry Dana, a Boston Brahmin who like Olmsted went to sea for several years, pointed to the mariner's dilemma: "What is there for the sailors to do? If they resist it is mutiny, if they succeed and take the vessel, it is piracy. . . . If a sailor resists his commander, he resists the law, and piracy and submission are his only alternatives."[4]

The outlawing of flogging in 1850 eliminated the most notorious form of punishment, but it did not end the often sadistic brutality to which seamen were subjected. In 1895 the sailors' union published a short pamphlet, *The Red Record,* which documented the fact that in the previous seven years fourteen seamen had died as a result of shipboard discipline "under circumstances which justify the charge of murder," but that only three convictions had been obtained. The following examples from *The Red Record* are indicative not only of the extremes to which seamen were subjected but of the contempt with which various agencies of government, including the judiciary, regarded their efforts at legal redress.

RAPPAHANNOCK, Captain Dickinson, loaded at Philadelphia, on her maiden voyage, April, 1890. Got aground towing down the Delaware. Crew complained of vessel being undermanned. Captain . . . beat the seamen, then put them in irons and locked them in the forecastle, where they remained with little food for two weeks. A detective got aboard and saw the men, one with an arm broken and another with his head smashed. A United States Marshal boarded the ship and took Captain Dickinson back to Wilmington, where he was examined by the Commissioner. Case dismissed on ground of "justifiable discipline."

T. F. OAKES, Captain Reid, arrived in San Francisco, May, 1893. Captain Reid and First-Mate J. McKay charged with cruelty to seamen, the latter on twenty-eight distinct indictments. McKay's case dismissed on the second trial. In the case of Captain Reid six seamen gave direct evidence of his cruelty and bore on their persons the actual wounds inflicted. Spectators in the court expressed indignation and confidence of a conviction. Reid made no defense. Case dismissed. Jury returned the verdict that "a shipmaster has the right to beat a seaman who is unruly."

The "buckoism," or sadistic brutality, of some ship's officers seemed to know no bounds. In one case a burly mate attacked a seaman with the result that "a piece was bitten out of his left palm, a mouthful of flesh was bitten out of his left arm, and his left nostril torn away as far as the bridge of his nose." In another case, right in front of a ship's passengers, the captain beat "four negro stowaways over their heads with a plank until they bled and pleaded for mercy." In the former instance, the union noted laconically, "Case tried; usual verdict—acquittal."[5]

This kind of experience caused the men aboard ship to develop a deep cynicism about the possibility of legal redress. Nearly half a century earlier, Richard Henry Dana had complained about the judiciary's *"want of confidence in the testimony of seamen."* After an unusually lenient sentence against a captain and mate convicted of murder, Dana concluded: "Sailors are made to feel, that however aggravated may be the cruelty practiced upon them, if there are none to testify to it but themselves, a conviction will hardly be worth procuring." It is not surprising, then, that on the notorious *Rappahannock* (cited above), where "beatings, kickings, belaying-pins and pistols were the order from the day of sailing," resulting in two deaths, the crew refused to go to the law, saying "No use to bother the courts."[6]

Whether such incidents were the exception, as the biographer of the legendary seaman's advocate Andrew Furuseth has argued, or "of the commonest order," as the sailors' union maintained, it is at least highly probable that before 1900 the average seaman in the foreign trade witnessed this kind of sadism on occasion and continually lived in its shadow. Furuseth himself maintained that buckoism aboard ship was a major factor in driving native-born Americans out of the merchant marine, until by the 1890s fewer than 10 percent of the sailors were citizens.[7]

Gradually, with the replacement of sail by steam-powered vessels, which meant voyages of shorter duration and therefore less tension aboard ship, and with the seamen's unions waging aggressive legislative reform campaigns, brutal shipboard discipline became less of a factor in seafaring life. There were still complaints of physical abuse, and even of old-fashioned terrorism on occasion, but the focus of the seamen's grievances shifted to other areas.[8]

Seamen often complained of low wages and bad working conditions, but these issues hardly distinguished them from millions of other workers. It was living conditions aboard ship, and the degraded life ashore, that set the seamen apart. On the ships, where cargo or passenger space was at a premium, the marine worker was relegated to a foc'sle that was cramped, dirty, badly lit, and ill ventilated. Furuseth characterized the sailor's quarters as "too large for a coffin and too small for a grave." Joe Curran, an obscure bosun's mate who was to become president of the largest seamen's union in the world, described his experience in twenty-by-twenty foc'sles with three-tiered bunks that slept twelve men. "I had a top bunk under a dripping steam pipe," recalled the six-foot-two Curran, "and I learned to curl up like a pretzel so the scalding water wouldn't drip on me when I slept." Hugh Mulzac remembered his days as a steward and the infamous "donkey's breakfast" upon which the men slept. There were no linens, he said. "I issued a blue sheet, mattress cover and blanket at the beginning of the trip, and there was a pile of straw on the dock for the sailors to make up their mattresses." Messman Robbie Robinson recalled sailing on ships "where the foc'sle for the messboys was the size of a linen closet, with only one light, so that if one man wanted to cork off the others had to sleep too or else sit in the dark."[9]

The foc'sles were usually situated near paint lockers, chain lockers, and bathrooms, so that noxious fumes and the steam and stench from showers and toilets pervaded the air. The medical officer of the Port of London submitted a report comparing the minimum air space allowed for cattle in cow sheds and for humans in military barracks, boarding houses, and seamen's quarters. He concluded that "cattle are the best off in this respect and seamen worst." The reports of the surgeon general of the U.S. Marine Hospital service showed that "seamen suffer in a startling manner from diseases, most of them springing from the inadequacy of pure air and healthful conditions in which to eat and sleep."

As for food and other conditions aboard ship, Messman Robinson remembered vessels "where the grub served up to the crew was stuff that seagulls wouldn't eat, where there were washrooms without any running water and the bathtub was a bucket, . . . where the bedbugs 'were so big they could toss you out of your bunk.'" A British marine officer described the ship's fare as "of the coarsest and poorest quality, and the amount allowed per man is just sufficient to keep body and soul together, with the aid of a stout belt. It is badly cooked and badly served, and is usually more fit for pigs than humans." Another Briton characterized seamen's accommodations as worse than those provided in a prison, "with the additional risk of being drowned."[10]

In spite of a succession of disasters at sea that caused enormous loss of life, safety conditions in the merchant marine remained deplorable. Bosun Snooky McCune, a U.S. Navy veteran who began shipping as a civilian in 1916, surely was engaging in poetic license when he claimed that "there are ships still in service with hulls so thin that 'if you lean on them hard you'll fall in the drink.'" But the tragedies kept occurring, with mounting casualties. Charlie Rubin, another navy vet who started shipping in the merchant marine in 1921, claimed that "all the written safety rules and regulations could be used as toilet paper as far as the shipowners were concerned," because safety cost money that cut into profit margins. Instead of hiring more and better-trained men, whose knowledge and experience in a crisis often proved to be the vital factor in saving lives, the shipowners continually sought to reduce the number and quality of their crew members. They concentrated instead on prettying up the vessels, slapping so much paint on moving parts that they wouldn't budge. "Life rings had so many coats of leaded paint, there were doubts as to whether they would float."[11]

Occasionally all the evils of cramped, vermin-infested quarters, rotten food, harsh discipline, and low morale came together to create a real "hell ship." Charlie Rubin described one such vessel where "the foc'sle was a mess, with clothes, broken bottles, spilt wine and drink-crazed maniacs all over." He jumped that ship, only to land on another where members of the crew fought like wild animals, and when a vicious bully swung a fire axe at his head, "it came so close I could feel it graze my ear." Joe Curran wasn't quite so lucky. He bore two big scars from a "wild and terrible night at sea" when a shipmate went berserk and caught him square in the back with an axe.[12]

With the end of a voyage the seaman exchanged the confines of the foc'sle for the tawdry world of the sailortown. Every coastal city had its port district where parasitic "land sharks" swarmed over the seafarer and devoured his "payoff," where fleabag hotels, brothels, and bars seemed to define the outer limits of his terrain, and where waterfront missions advertised a spiritual alternative to hungry and homeless men. The linchpin of this network of shoreside "friends" was the boardinghouse keeper, or "crimp," who also played the vital role of shipping agent. The crimp enticed the sailor into his establishment and catered to his appetite for food and drink, until Jack had run up a substantial bill and the crimp could claim a sizable advance on his next wage payment. Walter Macarthur, a Glasgow Scot whose long association with seafaring life on the West Coast began in the 1880s, declared that the crimp "would determine the length of [the sailor's] spell ashore, fix the rate of wages, and generally relieve him of all worldly cares." It appeared that the sailor was "Jack easy." But the other side of the coin was that he was "entirely helpless to do anything for himself." His state of carefree but enforced dependency was the mechanism through which the crimp maintained complete control of the marine labor supply. As Macarthur put it, "Such a thing as 'living private' was out of the question. The seamen were herded under the eyes of the boarding-master as completely as so many cattle in a corral"; and " 'Play the game, or go to hell,' was the order of the day."[13]

Moral reformers regarded the boarding-master as a parasite who ruthlessly victimized an ingenuous and dissolute constituency. With regard to the nineteenth century, however, there is simply too much evidence of the seamen's willing collusion with crimps to sustain this stereotype without qualification. Crimps were often colorful characters, with names like Shang-Hi Brown, Bullfrog Johnson, Whale Whiskers Kelly, Liverpool Mackey, and Black Jack Berendes. Many of them were ex-seamen, and their boarding-houses and saloons were steeped in the familiar ambience of ethnic and seafaring subcultures. Macarthur recalled that upon leaving the "democracy of the forecastle," seamen tended to cluster in boardinghouses on the basis of nationality. Scandinavians, Germans, and Finns flocked to establishments run by their compatriots, where the hoisting of drinks with a hearty "Skoal" and the passing of the snuffbox served as rituals of fellowship. Meanwhile, the English-speaking men, especially the Irish engine room workers, or "black gang," "boarded with their own kind, 'likkered up' on chain lightning, and chewed tobacco [while] they talked Irish-American politics and traced their lineage to Brian Boru." Historian Judith Fingard has pointed out that in the sailortowns of eastern Canada, "crimps and sailors demonstrated a consciousness of their community of interest again and again in the face of interference from 'upper town' society."

In the United States, however, particularly on the Pacific Coast, the crimps' hold on the seamen became an increasingly intolerable burden, and seafaring unionism was born out of the struggle to wrest control of hiring from a united front of shipowners and boarding-masters. The West Coast sailor came to loathe the crimp more than any other of his exploiters. An early issue of the *Coast Seamen's Journal* gave vivid expression to this hatred. While acknowledging that some boarding-masters were ex-seamen ("bucko ships' officers"), the *Journal* characterized others as graduates from the ranks of "played out gamblers," "confidence men," "knocked out prize fighters," and "jail birds." "They generally end up in the work house or prison or by committing suicide."[14]

In the twentieth century a number of factors—the rise of seafaring unions, the spread of government regulation, the shipowners' determination to take direct control of the marine labor market—combined to undermine crimping in many of the world's ports. But the institution survived and even flourished on the East Coast of the United States, and as it became more of an anachronism it also became more parasitic. In 1934 a marine fireman named Harry Alexander offered an indictment that eloquently summed up the seamen's view of the twentieth-century crimp. He charged that whenever a vessel docked,

it doesn't take long for the ship to be filled with all sorts of merchants, tailors, bootleggers, boarding house keepers, barbers, shoemakers, prostitutes, and agents for prostitutes. All these parasites are allowed aboard the ships, but when a seaman tries to board a ship to look for a job or get a meal he will be promptly chased off. . . . Of all the parasites the shipping agent is the most ruthless. He does not even go aboard the ships; he knows that the seaman will eventually come to him to look for a job. . . .

These crimps are not satisfied with what they are getting from the shipowners for shipping men. They have various sidelines. Most of them have rooming houses where they charge the seamen from three to five dollars a week and then in some cases put from three to six in one room. Others have cheap restaurants where the seamen have to pay first-class prices for third-class food.[15]

Self-appointed friends of "Poor Jack" made numerous attempts to develop an alternative to the crimping system. In the early days of the new nation, seamen, along with widows, orphans, prostitutes, and chattel slaves, became the object of charitable attention, in the form of seamen's friend societies, sailors' homes, and other similar organizations. The attention continued for more than a century, but seafarers found it hard to be entirely grateful to benefactors who viewed them as "childlike and irresponsible." The *Coast Seamen's Journal* acknowledged that the women of the Ladies' Seamen's Friends Society were "well meaning" but complained that "religious books and tracts and providing us with a grave for the sum of $2.50" meant "securing our bodies after death, but leaving us while alive a prey to the land-sharks which swarm around us."[16]

Perhaps the most famous of these religious charities on the waterfront was the Seamen's Church Institute (SCI) in New York City, where for a reasonable price a sailor could get a clean bed, a hot meal, and a place to store his baggage. Although large numbers of seamen took advantage of these services, many of them regarded the SCI with contempt and distrust. They nicknamed it the Dog House and the Shipowners' Institute. Perhaps it was the air of paternalism, or the security guards who were sometimes overzealous in enforcing the house rules, or the fact that many a destitute seaman couldn't pay the storage fee on his baggage and had his only personal belongings auctioned off to someone else. There were frequent charges that much of the charitable money intended for the seamen went instead for the "fat salaries" of SCI officials or for religious literature—" 'Come to Jesus' propaganda that the men pitch over the side as soon as the ship sails." Al Richmond, an organizer on the waterfront in the early 1930s, when the marine workers were more destitute than ever, accurately summed up the predicament of seamen ashore when he spoke of "the amazing variety of hustlers and parasites who somehow managed to feed off men who had so little to feed themselves."[17]

Virtually everyone regarded the seamen's conditions of life and work as deplorable. But there was a nearly universal consensus that the seaman himself was not merely a reflection of his conditions but was also in some significant measure responsible for them. Indeed, the reputation of seafaring men and their subculture for instability, turbulence, and decadence has endured for centuries. In the colonial period, seamen were a staple ingredient in the mobs that periodically rioted in the port cities. In the famous Boston Massacre of 1770, two of the four men killed were seamen. John Adams described the crowd as "a motley rabble of saucy boys, negroes and molattoes, Irish teagues and outlandish jack tarrs." Some variation on the term "sailors, boys, and negroes" was a constant in the description of mobs during the colonial period and the era of the American Revolution.[18]

By reputation seamen could be every bit as riotous aboard ship as they were ashore. The log of the brig *Betsy* recorded in 1796 that "at 5 o'clock this afternoon the crew came aboard all drunk and got a fiting with clubs and A hammer. And bruise themselves varry bad. The pilot wanted to heve up the Anchor but we could get no work out of them." Likewise, the master of a vessel berthed in Quebec complained in 1861 that "my crews conduct has become very bad, careless of any orders, constantly running on shore and in every way neglectful of duty by being constantly the worse for drink." After refusing to load the ship, unmoor it, or raise the anchor, the mutinous crew deliberately wrecked the vessel in the St. Lawrence River.[19]

Whether these incidents were typical or not, the seamen's allegedly unruly nature became the rationalization for the harsh shipboard discipline, the absolute authority of the master, and the stringent laws that defined any resistance to that authority as mutiny. A century and a half separated the crew of the brig *Betsy* from the "hell ships" described by Charlie Rubin. But in terms of life-style and conditions, the distance traveled in a century and a half seems very slight indeed.

If there was one individual in whom the seamen's reputation for rootless, colorful, reckless, and debauched behavior came together in quintessential form, it was perhaps Showboat Quinn. According to Helen Lawrenson's rendition of the Quinn legend, Showboat was born in Australia, where his Irish great-grandfather had been sent as a convict for throwing a rent collector down a well. In spite of these inauspicious beginnings, the family prospered in its new environment, and Showboat was shipped to England at the age of fourteen to attend boarding school. Instead of enrolling in school, he bummed around the country, worked for a circus, and was shanghaied aboard a ship in Liverpool to work as a coal passer.

This was the beginning of a long and illustrious career at sea. In recounting some of the highlights, Lawrenson commented that Showboat was

what you might call accident-prone. He joined the rank-and-file rebels against the old International Seamen's Union and was almost beaten to death in Houston in 1935. . . . He was shot at by goons in Port Arthur and again in Galveston. In Newport News, during the 1936 strike, he was stabbed in the abdomen by finks, for which he was sentenced to a year in jail for trespassing. He sued the Baltimore & Ohio Railroad for false arrest. The case was thrown out and so was he. In the 1937 strike he had an ear cut half off in a knife fight, and his chin and nose bore other knife scars. He had his throat cut in Boston and, enroute to the hospital, said, "Tell the boys I died for the union." In New York, drunk, he fell out of a third-story window and broke his back. He was in a plaster cast for six months. Found to have TB, he was ordered to the marine hospital. . . . Instead, he shipped out for Africa. He was arrested for picketing in Durban and fell overboard from his ship in Lourenço Marques. Back in New York, he walked in front of a truck . . . but only an arm was broken. He got in a fight, fell over a fire hydrant and fractured a shoulder. . . . The last time I saw him, he was rushing along 8th Avenue, wearing a moth-eaten fur cape. "I'm on my way to the North Pole," he said.[20]

Of course, Showboat Quinn was by no means a typical seaman. For every Showboat there were plenty of men who led relatively quiet lives, whether at sea or ashore. And for every marine worker, life aboard ship involved a large dose of monotony. But there was in Showboat Quinn a coalescence of the qualities associated with seamen and their subculture that made him stand out as a real, if exaggerated, representative. When the seamen looked at this bizarre character, they saw at least a part of themselves.

At the same time, the Showboat Quinns, the riotous crew of the brig *Betsy,* the hell ships, the axe scars on Joe Curran's back, the degraded sailortowns, all served to reinforce the image of seamen as "semivagrant children of the sea" who were unable or unwilling to better their own conditions. Until 1915, federal law officially defined them as wards and the equivalent of orphans. As we have seen, the infamous *Arago* case reaffirmed the long-standing legal view that seamen were "deficient in that full and intelligent responsibility for their acts which is accredited to ordinary adults." Their religious benefactors called them "childlike and irresponsible." The shipowners characterized them as "of a low order of society . . . the driftwood from their native countries," the "most vicious" and "most unruly" elements of the "overplus of the European countries."[21]

The shipowners seemed determined to make their image of the seamen become a reality. In order to drive down wages and undermine conditions, they developed a conscious policy of flooding the merchant marine with workers from China and the Philippines, unemployed drifters, college boys on vacation or out to see the world, and desperate "workaways" who would sail a ship for no wages at all. It was partially in response to this human flood that the sailors' union officials began to sound very much like the shipowners in their description of the seamen. Andrew Furuseth, longtime president of the International Seamen's Union, declared that the merchant marine was becoming the "domain of the sewage of the Caucasian race" and accused the owners of treating the sea as the "cesspool of humanity." During a desperate struggle with the IWW for the allegiance of the men, he described seafarers as "thieves, smugglers, and users of narcotics, dirty and crummy in person, dirty and revolutionary in speech."[22] Historian Richard Morris asserted that in colonial America "the population of the forecastle often comprised criminal and degenerate elements, unwilling impressed hands, and men who recognized no authority other than force." Economist Elmo Hohman described the crews of nineteenth-century sailing vessels as drawn from the ranks of "misfits, ne'er-do-wells and unprincipled adventurers." Surely no representative of this stereotype could have outdone James Prendergast, who was as degenerate and defiant as Showboat Quinn was eccentric. A Nova Scotian who worked on both sailing vessels and coastal steamships, Prendergast actually spent more time in jail than at sea. According to Judith Fingard, "His rebelliousness took a number of extrovert forms. He continued to smash windows, he threw stones at passers-by, and he thieved far and wide. Not content with stabbing and frequently beating his wife [a local prostitute], he also assaulted his father-in-law, his mother, and his father, robbed them, and despoiled their property. He refused to settle his accounts at public houses, offended local morals by indecently exposing himself in the street, and in 1881 proclaimed himself an atheist to the court clerk."[23]

In the face of this stereotype the seamen of the Revolutionary generation, at least, have found a vigorous defender in historian Jesse Lemisch. Drawing on insights and methods derived from the work of Eric Hobsbawm and E. P. Thompson, Lemisch declared that the stereotype of the seafarer as a jolly, riotous rake was based more on class prejudice than on a careful examination of the seamen's conditions of life and work. He found in the practice of impressment—the kidnapping of mariners and others for service in the British navy—and in the provisions of the Stamp Act and other imperial legislation a very real and material threat to the life, liberty, and property of the seamen. In the light of this threat from the press gangs, and Jack Tar's riotous response, Lemisch contended that "what may have seemed irrational violence can now be seen as purposeful and radical." The sailor "was fighting to defend his 'liberty,' and he justified his resistance on grounds of 'right.' "[24]

The momentous and crisis-filled years between 1930 and 1945 provide us with another excellent laboratory in which to examine the seamen's reputation as "semivagrant children of the sea" and their alleged incapacity for sustained and purposeful activity to better their own conditions. Here too their conduct belies the stereotype. Without attempting to add to the mountain of false romance that has been placed on the marine workers' backs, and without obscuring the debauched and sometimes nihilistic overtones of their sub-culture, it remains a fact that in the 1930s and 1940s the seamen displayed a great capacity for courage, discipline, and adherence to principle.

In a decade noted for violence against labor, perhaps no other group of workers faced more bitter, even murderous, opposition during the thirties. On the New York waterfront, in the "outlaw" strikes of 1936 and 1937, it was all too common to find a striking sailor, who had been assigned to picket duty on some farflung pier, lying dead in an alley, his head split open by a baseball bat. In the cities on the Texas Gulf Coast, insurgent seamen experienced so much violent repression that some of them ventured the opinion that "there wasn't much difference between Port Arthur under the oil companies and Hamburg under the Nazis." Richard Boyer, a close observer of the marine workers, maintained that twenty-seven seamen died in the Fall Strike of 1936 and 1937. In any case, the violence against the seamen clearly surpassed even the bloodshed of the famous Little Steel strike of 1937.[25] But in spite of bitter obstacles, the marine workers persisted. They developed new and dynamic leaders from the ranks; they built new organizations—the Maritime Federation of the Pacific Coast and the National Maritime Union (NMU)—and remained one of the most democratic, vibrant, and volatile forces in the working-class upsurge of the 1930s.

The coming of World War II confronted the seafarers with another life-and-death struggle. While most workers were swept up in the frantic pace of war production, merchant seamen found themselves in a unique position. They were civilians, but their jobs took them into war zones where bombs and torpedoes were an integral part of their working conditions. Even before the declaration of war on the Axis, attacks on U.S. merchant shipping along the Atlantic Coast had become commonplace. So many ships were sunk off the tip of Florida that the seamen called it Torpedo Junction. When war was declared, the most treacherous passage was the famed run to the Soviet port of

Murmansk. Twelve percent of all ships attempting to run the Nazi gauntlet to Murmansk were sunk and one ill-fated convoy lost twenty-two of its fifty ships. Overall, nearly six thousand merchant seamen perished during World War II, many of them in the terrifying explosions that obliterated munitions ships or in the oil fires that erupted in the wreckage of sinking tankers.

And yet in the face of this kind of terror, the seamen made good on their pledge to "Keep 'em Sailing." In spite of many opportunities, and much provocation from the shipowners, NMU seamen in particular never struck a single ship for the duration of the war. For this they won widespread praise. Generals lauded their courage and Congress hailed them as heroes. But the seamen preferred to express their commitment in their own salty idiom. As Elliot "Constitution" Gurnee put it after twenty-four days on a life raft during which six of his mates died and he was the sole survivor: "I kept one thing straight in my mind. I was going to come through. I went through the '36 and '37 strikes. I helped build the union. I said to myself, 'I'll be God-damned if I'll let a few Nazi bastards kill me!' "[26]

Reviewing this splendid record may raise as many questions as it answers. If we have avoided the condescension with which shipowners, philanthropists, and some scholars have viewed the seaman, it won't do to swing to the opposite pole and portray him as the incorruptible stalwart of the proletarian novel. The seafarer was colorful, he was militant, and he was often imbued with a spontaneous radicalism that was a reflection of the world as he experienced it. But recent innovations in the study of labor and social history have taught us much about the complexity of working-class consciousness. We have learned that extreme deprivation is no guarantee of militancy, and that relatively stable, economically secure lives do not necessarily lead workers to quiescence and conservatism. Consciousness derives from a whole gamut of often contradictory factors. In assessing consciousness, we must recognize that there is a wide range of responses lying between the extremes of rebellion and inertia.

Some of the most revealing studies of the complexity of popular consciousness have focused not on the mature working class but on the world of chattel slavery and the early years of working-class development in England. One historian has argued that among slaves, "even reactions which seemed most irrational in terms of straightforward appearances and consequences rested upon a rational appraisal of the slave environment." Likewise, in a brilliant essay on gentry and plebs in eighteenth-century England, E. P. Thompson has pointed out that in studying social groups with alternative views of life, "everything transmitted to us through the polite culture has to be scrutinized upside-down." Otherwise, "we are in danger of becoming prisoners of the assumptions and self-images of the rulers." Thompson affirms the "immense distance between polite and plebeian cultures, and the vigour of the authentic self-activity of the latter."[27]

We cannot equate the degraded status of the seamen with chattel slavery, nor can we transpose the dynamics of eighteenth-century English society onto the interaction between shipowner and seaman in the twentieth century. But there are insights and parallels here that can be applied fruitfully to an understanding of the seafarer's consciousness and subculture. We must indeed turn the condescending view of the shipowner and his allies upside down, not to exalt the seaman but to better understand the autonomous dimension and the rationality of his behavior. Of course, he was quite capable of irrationality and a streak of nihilism. There were always some men, at the most degraded depths of seafaring culture, who were beyond the realm of rationality. But these "friendless nomads" were hardly typical. More representative by far was the man who sought—through rational calculation—to enlarge the area of his freedom within the cultural and institutional confines available to him. At a historical moment that seemed to offer the hope of substantial change, such a calculation might point toward collective and militant protest. At a less auspicious moment, the only possible path might seem to be the familiar, restless one that led from foc'sle to sailortown and back again.[28]

There is abundant evidence that the latter course was often chosen. Desertions from the British merchant marine averaged about ten thousand a year between 1850 and 1910. In 1860 and 1861, while still in his mid-teens, a British seaman named Robert Thomas deserted ships in Montevideo, Buenos Aires, Boston, and Newfoundland (having also traveled to Liverpool, Oporto, Naples, and Hamburg). As late as 1937, the United States Maritime Commission was startled by the "excessive turnover" on American ships. It declared that "many seamen report 8 and 10 years of service, of which perhaps not more than four months have been spent on one ship or even in one line."[29]

To the shipowner, the sailor's well-deserved reputation as a chronic deserter was compelling evidence of his semivagrant nature. Looked at from the seaman's perspective, however, desertion was often a means of escaping from an onerous contract in order to improve his wages and conditions. Jumping ship was especially common in ports where manpower shortages drove the price of labor upward. Even more typical were those instances where conditions aboard ship seemed unbearable and the employers' institutional and legal power appeared to be overwhelming. Here the act of flight represented a simple but rational attempt to create some breathing space in an otherwise stifling environment. However limited and individualistic, it was a way of beating the prevailing system of maritime institutional power at a time when changing it by means of organized collective action seemed to be impossible.[30]

Another legend that needs to be scrutinized "upside down" is the seaman's attraction to the waterfront gin mill and his reputation for drunkenness. If the words *drunken* and *sailor* have become welded together in the popular idiom, we should see in this phenomenon something deeper than a "childlike and irresponsible" nature. It was an expression of powerlessness, a reflection of alienation and rebellion, an act of camaraderie among men who lived beyond the pale of bourgeois civility. In the case of the gin mill, the prevailing view has been that it was a seat of degradation, immorality, and lawlessness. Middle-class reformers described Joe Beef's Canteen, Montreal's most famous waterfront bar in the late nineteenth century, as a "den of robbers and wild beasts" where "dirt, bestiality, and devilment held high carnival." Similarly, the author of a maritime history of New York declared that the sailor lived and socialized only "where the vilest men and women abided, in the black sea of drunkenness, lewdness, and sin." It was to rescue the seaman from such an environment that philanthropists and moral reformers established their waterfront missions. But these organizations inevitably bore the stamp of their benefactors' class prejudice. The seafarer could make use of the services available at the Seamen's Church Institute, but he could never feel at home there. The saloon, however, was free of the restraints imposed by preachers and police (although the latter were liable to intrude at any moment). Recalling the ambience of the waterfront bar, Herman "Dutch" Thomas declared that "a great many of us did not want life any other way, because for those few days ashore we felt free, that we could live the way we wanted to."[31]

Thomas's statement touches on an important point, for the attraction of the saloon went far beyond the liquor dispensed there. It was first and foremost a social center that provided a much-needed opportunity for self-expression and easy camaraderie. Even Herman Melville's Redburn, who was given to moralizing about the depraved condition of "poor Jack," was fascinated by the cosmopolitan excitement and conviviality he encountered on the Liverpool waterfront. Likewise, Helen Lawrenson, who married a Communist seaman in the 1930s, was struck by the earthy wit, political sophistication, and collective spirit of the men who frequented the waterfront bars in New York's Chelsea district. She recalled the seamen standing "for hours on end, buying rounds of beer, matching picket cards, swapping reminiscences of ports from Capetown to Odessa, talking union endlessly, talking ships." At the Welcome Inn, her husband's favorite haunt, there were occasional brawls and many animated political arguments. But beneath these surface phenomena, beneath even the attraction of drink, the gin mill met a vital need for the seamen. After the harsh discipline and monotony of life aboard ship, the waterfront saloon possessed an aura of warmth and sociability that was downright irresistible, especially when compared to the barrackslike conditions at the Seamen's Church Institute and the overbearing religiosity of the other waterfront missions. As Jack London put it, the saloon was a place where "men talked with great voices, laughed great laughs, and there was an atmosphere of greatness." Not until the rise of insurgent unionism in the 1930s would the majority of seamen find a more lasting and substantial means of measuring their self-worth.[32]

Because of the web of contradictory factors that shaped the seaman's world, his life was characterized by a duality that makes easy generalizations perilous. The same men who could destroy a barroom in a violent drunken brawl one day could engage in a heroic rescue at sea under death-defying circumstances the next. Understanding this duality is necessary if we are to comprehend the character of the rank-and-file insurgency that hit the waterfront with hurricane force in the 1930s.[33]

On one side of this duality is the seaman's long-standing reputation for openness to revolutionary ideas. There are several important reasons why the seafaring world has been hospitable to movements and ideas representing a challenge to the prevailing social order. First, seamen were among the most exploited and oppressed groups of workers in the United States. They knew well the meaning of deprivation and were keenly aware of the enormous distance between the lives of rich and poor. Secondly, and of even greater importance, they lived on the fringes of society and had little or no recourse to family, church, ethnic, and other institutions that served the purpose of reconciling working people to the hegemony of the employing class or of creating a stable subculture that reinforced an alternative value system. Although many seamen were literate and well-read, few had had much formal education. Likewise, the transiency inherent in their calling meant that few seamen voted or showed much interest in the activity of the major political parties. The International Seamen's Union was very active on the legislative front and sometimes supported candidates in electoral campaigns. But the average seaman probably found the antipolitical syndicalism of the Wobblies more sensible than the legislative and electoral program of the ISU.

The nature of the seafarer's calling made it difficult to maintain a normal family life, and his low wages made it nearly impossible to support himself, not to mention a wife and children. He was, in the words of *Fortune,* "homeless, rootless, and eternally unmoneyed"—free of the responsibilities of home and family and yet, in many cases, wistful for the comfort and security of a more normal life.[34]

In the realm of religion, the seaman was hardly noted for his piety or church membership. Many a sailor must have felt some kinship with the suffering of "Jerusalem Slim," but he was likely to regard clergymen as "sky pilots" who directly or indirectly served the interests of the shipowners. As for ethnic identity, seamen tended to congregate in boardinghouses on the basis of ethnic ties, and the various seafaring crafts were dominated to some extent by particular nationalities. But on the Pacific Coast the ethnic boardinghouses faded away as crimping declined and the shipowners reached a long-term accommodation on hiring with the Sailors' Union of the Pacific. In general, the transiency of marine life prevented the development of the diverse and deeply rooted ethnic organizations that were a prominent feature in many working-class communities.

In sum, the seaman's isolation from a wide range of social institutions prevented him from being integrated into the larger society or, alternatively, into a stable working-class subculture. His status was that of an outsider, even a pariah. In 1849, reflecting on his own experience at sea, Herman Melville lamented "the low estimation in which sailors are held . . . they are deemed almost the refuse and offscourings of the earth." Nearly a century later, at a time when insurgent unionism was transforming conditions on the West Coast waterfront, an obscure marine worker provided an equally compelling glimpse of the seaman's historic status. He asked his fellow workers to temper their euphoria and stiffen their resolve by recalling the way of life they were transcending. Remember, he said, the times you came off "a miserable old scow" with a payoff in your pocket, which you promptly drank up in the "joints on the front." Remember, then,

> the dirty look and growl you got from the bartender when you asked for a shot? Remember how tempting and good [the] chow looked in those joints where they fried and cooked it right before your eyes and how you stood on the sidewalk cussing to yourself and wondering where in hell you were gonna eat.
>
> Remember [how] you tried hammering on a couple of back doors and they had the biggest, meanest looking mutts you ever saw, as anxious to bite you as you were to feel some chow between your teeth.
>
> You won't ever forget that trip to the Coast in the dead of winter, flopping in houses [and] box cars and when you hit the coast how slack your jeans were around your waist.

Tommy Ray was one maritime veteran who never forgot the stigma that the seaman bore when he ventured beyond the sailortown. Nearly fifty years after the fact he recalled how he had been wandering aimlessly in uptown San Pedro one day, when a policeman recognized him and snarled, "You're a seaman. Get back to the waterfront where you belong."[35]

By themselves, however, rootlessness and isolation, extreme exploitation, and low social status would not necessarily have been enough to make the maritime workers susceptible to radical ideas. But there was an additional factor that played a vital role in shaping their consciousness. While seamen lived on the fringe of American society, the nature of their calling meant that they routinely saw a good deal more of the rest of the world than their shoreside counterparts. Oftentimes this experience opened their eyes to the breadth of injustice and suffering and rendered them somewhat cynical about conventional depictions of reality. Harry Bridges, who came from a comfortable middle-class English family that had emigrated to Australia, grew restless with a clerk's life and went to sea at the age of fifteen. He recalled in later years the profound effect that his stint as a seaman had upon his outlook: "I took a trip that gave me a look at India and another at Suez, and what I saw there didn't seem to line up with what my father had told me about the dear old British. Then I got 'home' and saw London. It was the filthiest, most unhealthy place I had ever seen. And the people in the slums were worse than the natives in India and Port Said—dirty, nasty, no good. So this, I say, is British democracy. . . . I kept traveling around, and the more I saw the more I knew that there was something wrong with the system."

Hugh Mulzac, a West Indian who was to become the first black man to win his master's license and captain an American merchant vessel, vividly remembered his initial encounters in foreign ports as a young seaman. He was shocked by the contrast between the ostentatious wealth of Constantinople and the "abject wretchedness" of its people. He recalled that "the glaring contradictions made a lasting impression on me." In his next port, the Rumanian town of Sulina on the Black Sea, he watched as "a swarm of barefooted, scantily-dressed teenage girls" descended upon the ship to sell themselves to the crew members in exchange for a tin of crackers or a bar of soap. On the docks, emaciated longshoremen whose basic diet was "black bread, onions, and enough vodka to enable them to drown their misery" loaded bulging sacks of grain aboard the ship. Said Mulzac: "I could not understand why, with so many Rumanians starving, we should come in for a shipload of grain to take back to the British Isles."

Blackie Meyers had much the same experience. A Brooklyn youth who first sailed on fishing smacks at the age of fourteen and later became a Communist and leader of the National Maritime Union, his first trip on a merchant vessel, at age sixteen, "proved to be quite an education." He saw famine in China, the brutal face of colonialism in India, where he witnessed British police firing on native demonstrators, and in Naples he caught a glimpse of fascism. Everywhere he went "he saw an abject . . . poverty that made him wonder if this was the best of all possible worlds."

For others there were memorable encounters with history in the making. Long before he became a committed Marxist, Charlie Rubin happened to attend a funeral service for Lenin in the Soviet port of Batumi, where his ship had been delayed because of bad weather. With little knowledge or opinion of the merits of Lenin and the new Soviet state, he marveled as all around him in the town square "thousands upon thousands of Batumi people and countryfolk stood there, deeply grieved, feeling a real personal loss." A Soviet commissar addressed the Italian, Dutch, British, and American seamen who stood in the square, telling them, "So long as you live you will never forget this historic day."[36]

Of course, not every seaman was radicalized by his encounters in the ports of the world. Some shipped only in the coastwise trade, along the shores of

North America, and many in the foreign trade confined themselves to the gin mills and whorehouses that were meant to ensnare the sailor in every port. But a breadth of experience, a worldliness, existed among seafaring men and it undoubtedly contributed to their relative openness to radical and revolutionary ideas.

As one indication of this openness, the Wobblies in their heyday gained a foothold among seamen and retained a real presence there long after they had become little more than a fading memory in most other industries. In 1913, the entire Atlantic Coast marine firemen's division of the International Seamen's Union seceded from the AFL and joined the IWW. Likewise, when the shipowners had effectively broken the ISU after a disastrous strike in 1921, large numbers of seamen joined the Wobs.

Like the AFL unions, the maritime Wobblies also foundered on the rocks of the employers' post–World War I open-shop offensive, but they continued to maintain an organizational structure—Marine Transport Workers Industrial Union No. 510—and a visible presence among the seamen. Many seafarers who became Communists passed through the Wobs. Harold Johnson, a Seattle-born seaman who celebrated his twenty-third birthday in jail during the San Francisco general strike, remembered that on his first voyage "there was an old-timer on the ship who had been a Wobbly in the Montana metal mines. He gave me my first sense of what it was all about." Likewise, Tommy Ray, who was to serve as secretary of the National Maritime Union's founding convention, recalled that his initial encounter with the IWW came on his first trip to sea, when he heard members of the black gang singing Wobbly songs as they worked in the engine room. Ray joined the IWW in 1924, but like many seamen he quickly became disenchanted with their lack of effective organization. Even so, individual Wobblies played an active and sometimes significant role in the maritime rank-and-file upsurge of the 1930s. As late as 1948, Len De Caux attended a Marine Transport Workers local meeting of about fifteen members in Houston and argued philosophy and politics with the anarcho-syndicalists there.[37]

In the 1930s the Communists quickly eclipsed the Wobs as the leading radical voice on the waterfront. They took over much of the IWW program and recruited a significant number of revolutionary-minded seamen (many of them ex-Wobblies) into the "Red" Marine Workers Industrial Union (MWIU). Although the MWIU never achieved a stable membership of more than five thousand it played an important role in fighting for emergency relief for destitute seamen "on the beach," improving conditions aboard ship through "job actions" and quickie strikes, and building unity between seafarers and longshoremen. When the MWIU was disbanded in 1935, most of its battle-tested militants were too obviously Red to assume leading positions in the unions that emerged in the middle and late thirties. But the Communists continued to recruit and develop new leadership on the waterfront. Nathan

Glazer has estimated that the Communist party came closer to a "mass membership" in "marine and longshore" than in any other working-class constituency. The Party recruited about six hundred seamen in New York alone during a two-year period in the mid-thirties. The Cold War created enormous pressure to drive the Communists out of the strategic maritime industry, but they were not easily dislodged from an environment where they had sunk deep roots. As one marine worker put it, "If they're Red bastards, they're *our* bastards."

The Party's Waterfront Section had its own personality and was famous for its irreverent attitude toward the Party bureaucracy. Waterfront Section legend has it that angry Communist seamen once dangled an emissary from Party headquarters out of an upper-story window until he agreed to retract some "foolish directive." Although the story is probably apocryphal, it illustrates an important truth, namely, that seamen who became Communists already had a distinctive life-style and consciousness that did much to mold the character of the Communist party on the waterfront. The seamen were not mere clay to be shaped by an external force. They received, but they also gave.[38]

The powerful ideological currents that shook the world in the 1930s had a profound impact on the seamen. In a way perhaps unique among American workers, they came face to face with fascism, and many of them were politicized by that encounter. Harry Hynes, an Australian seaman sailing out of U.S. ports, had spent six weeks "on the beach" in Hamburg in 1931, when it was a stronghold of left-wing activity. Upon his return in 1935, he walked the streets searching in vain for some sign of the Red Hamburg he had known.

Hynes was a Communist, and he had enough savvy to tread warily in the Third Reich. But William Gill, a young American seaman, was to pay a price for his own lack of caution. He was beaten, arrested, and imprisoned for whistling a few bars of the "Internationale" and making a "derogatory remark" about Hitler while returning to his ship after a drunken night on the town. Although Gill spent only ten days in jail before his expulsion from Germany, Lawrence Simpson, another American seaman, was arrested aboard the U.S. liner *Manhattan* in Hamburg harbor and imprisoned for eighteen months in a concentration camp on the charge of possessing Communist literature in his locker. Simpson's imprisonment deepened antifascist sentiments among many American seafarers, and it was to trigger a major riot in New York harbor, when Communist seamen tore the swastika from the bow of the German liner *Bremen*.

On the large American passenger ships that sailed to German ports, the stewards department, often with more than three hundred members, "was overwhelmingly German and therefore was thoroughly nazified." As one seaman recalled, pro-Hitler stewards "were smuggling Nazi literature and small arms into New York . . . we were overwhelmed by the [Nazi] element on the ship and it was dangerous to disagree with them . . . Our Nazi fellow workers told us of the glories of the Reich under Hitler and how we were to comport ourselves in Hamburg. I was told that I had to salute when someone said 'Heil Hitler' and that if I did not . . . I could get in trouble."[39]

During the rank-and-file strikes of 1936 and 1937, which led to the formation of the National Maritime Union, this nazified element comprised a large portion of the strikebreakers who continued sailing while their fellow workers walked the picket lines. When the men finally returned to the ships, there were sometimes pitched battles between strikers and scabs. Joe Stack, an orphaned youth who began shipping at the age of fifteen and eventually became a vice president of the NMU, recalled that when he and other strikers returned to a vessel on the Hamburg run, the "out and out Nazis" attacked them with baseball bats, chipping hammers, and other weapons, and nineteen men ended up in the ship's hospital.[40]

In the turbulent years of the 1930s, when massive and bitterly fought strikes erupted in industry after industry, it was this international dimension of the seamen's experience that distinguished them from their fellow workers in other occupations. It is not surprising, then, that seamen constituted a disproportionate number of the Americans who fought in the International Brigades, the volunteers from around the world who came to the aid of the Spanish Republic in its premature war against fascism. Among the several thousand Americans who fought in Spain, there were two hundred and fifty recruits from the New York waterfront and hundreds more maritime workers from other poor cities. Harry Hynes, the Aussie who had served as editor of two historic rank-and-file newspapers, the *Waterfront Worker* in San Francisco and the *ISU Pilot* in New York, left the picket lines in 1937 and went to Spain, where he was killed by a sniper's bullet. Joe Bianca, another experienced and widely respected veteran of marine labor struggles, was regarded by the men of his battalion as "the best soldier in Spain." He too was buried there, along with more than a hundred other volunteers from the ranks of the seamen.[41]

While acknowledging that seafaring men were often inclined to militant activity, and that significant numbers of them were attracted to revolutionary ideas, it will not do to portray the seamen as a consistently militant and radical force. They may have been unusually cantankerous, and more turbulent in life-style than most of their shoreside fellow workers. But an examination of the history of maritime unions shows too many periods of quiescence to grant any validity to a "social sore" theory positing an inherent radicalism in seamen based on their unusually grim conditions of life and work. The seamen, in spite of their circumstances, were by no means the first American workers to organize. While they achieved some success in building viable unions on the West Coast as early as the mid-1880s, the Atlantic and

Gulf coasts were generally without effective organization for another fifty years. During the ebb tide of trade unionism in the 1920s, the seamen's unions were as moribund as any in the AFL.[42]

The truth is that there were as many factors making for inertia and division among the seamen as there were factors leading to unity and conscious or spontaneous radicalism. For one thing, the naval tradition of hierarchy was transferred to the merchant marine. The social ladder of seafaring men consisted of four distinct rungs, with masters and mates at the top, deck sailors a considerable notch below, followed by the engine room men, or black gang, and then the stewards' department. Government licensing of marine personnel only served to further institutionalize this stratification and establish a system of minute gradations, with corresponding rates of pay and authority, from the master of the vessel on down to the lowly messboys. The deck department, for example, was divided into bosuns, bosun's mates, able-bodied seamen, and ordinary seamen. Each craft had its own delineations from top to bottom.[43]

The gulf beween the officers, or licensed personnel, and the unlicensed seafarers is hardly surprising. But the unity of the common seamen was disrupted by craft separation and by rivalry between the men on the different kinds of ships. Generally the deck and engine departments vied for top billing, with the deck sailors usually accorded the higher standing. But it was universally agreed that the stewards ranked at the bottom of this informal status hierarchy. They were by reputation the "belly robbers." Never mind that the companies were responsible for the terrible slop that the seamen generally had to consume: the men who cooked and served the food were the most accessible targets for the complaints of the crew. Dan Boano, a messboy who went on to become a member of the National Maritime Union's National Council, frequently complained that the deck and engine departments "do not consider messboys as seamen. I claim to be the world's greatest messboy. . . . But because I'm a messboy, I'm not a seaman. I'm some kind of an odd character."

Charlie Rubin recalled that "I had nothing but contempt for the guys on the passenger ships"—especially for the stewards, who worked for tips. "They had to cater to the passengers all the time. And the sailors were the same. A lot of the guys didn't act natural when passengers were around. They'd get all 'perfumed up' and worry about how they looked." But, said Rubin, it was different on the freighters. "We didn't have to worry about catering to passengers. We could act natural, dress the way we pleased, and concentrate on [the fight for] conditions."[44]

This sense of separation and rivalry was also reflected in the structure of the International Seamen's Union, a federation of sixteen relatively autonomous divisions, from the Eastern and Gulf Sailors' Association to the Alaska Fishermen's Union. Although the ISU leadership conducted legislative campaigns on behalf of all its constituent unions, and solidarity sometimes prevailed during strikes, the craft jealousies and interunion disagreements that characterized the AFL as a whole were also a divisive force throughout the entire lifetime of the ISU.

There was also antagonism based on race and nationality. The seamen of the era of sail were mainly from the British Isles and northern Europe. Traditionally, the deck sailors were Scandinavian. They formed the backbone of the Sailors' Union of the Pacific long after the demise of sailing ships. The black gang was by tradition the province of the Irish, and the cooks and stewards were of many nationalities. Gradually, on the West Coast, the shipowners began to employ Chinese and Filipino workers, first in the stewards' department and then in all of the unlicensed ratings. This led the ISU leadership to engage in increasingly strident calls for "Asiatic exclusion."

On the East Coast, the traditional domain of the northern Europeans was breached even earlier. By the first decade of the 1900s black seamen constituted a large percentage of the deck sailors in the coastwise trade. By 1915 more than half of the East Coast firemen were Spanish or Latin American. The employers skillfully played one race and nationality against another, with predictable results. Wage rates and organizational efforts lagged behind those on the more homogeneous Pacific Coast.

In 1908 the Marine Cooks and Stewards opened a branch office exclusively for blacks. The ISU newspaper claimed that in initiating this Jim Crow policy, "every right and privilege which the colored men could justly claim has been fully considered, anticipated, and most generously provided for by their white comrades." A few years later the East Coast sailors' affiliate denied black seamen the right of membership, and on most steamship lines blacks were increasingly relegated to the stewards' department. Hugh Mulzac, who had sailed as an able-bodied seaman on British ships, recalled that when he began shipping out of U.S. ports, "I could sail as messman . . . but the deck gangs were white as lilies." In the engine room, ethnic hostilities were so divisive that even the xenophobic Furuseth exclaimed that "nationality prejudice is running mad" among the firemen. He complained that "the Irish and the Liverpool Irish in Boston . . . think themselves superior to everybody else." The antagonism between the entrenched Irish minority and the Spanish-speaking majority became so intense that the latter voted to take the marine firemen's union out of the ISU and into the IWW in 1913.[45]

While the above factors often led to division and bitter conflict within the ranks of the seamen, there were in addition two factors that led directly to inertia and quiescence. The first was rooted in the seaman's fabled "independence." If independence can manifest itself in a tendency toward rebellion and militancy, it can also lead to individualism and an incapacity for effective organization. Among the seamen, this kind of independence may have derived in part from their relationship to the labor process. Deck work on the Pacific Coast lumber schooners required a high level of cooperation. But this appears to have been the exception. For the most part, according to economist Elmo Hohman, the merchant seaman remained "basically a small-scale producer in an individualistic industry."[46]

The institutional world in which the seaman found himself ensnared also seemed to invite individual solutions, especially in times of union disorganization and weakness. The standard procedure was that if you didn't like conditions aboard ship, you could get off at the end of the voyage and try another one. And, of course, many a sailor refused to wait until the end of the voyage. He would jump ship in some far-flung port and console himself in a gin mill or brothel until the arrival of a better prospect or, more likely, till his desperate financial straits drove him aboard any "rust bucket" that would sign him on.

The problem of excessive turnover on individual ships was compounded by the extraordinary rate of turnover in the merchant marine as a whole. This phenomenon had two main causes: first, the erosion of skill in the seaman's calling as a result of the transition from sail- to steam-powered vessels; and secondly, the shipowners' policy of lowering wages and conditions by seeking to displace experienced, union-conscious seamen with the cheapest labor supply they could find. The *Seamen's Journal* stated in 1921 that "the old time deep-water windjammer sailor, who was unique in his line, . . . who daily displayed his skilled seamanship in a hundred different ways, has been displaced by the more modern steamship sailor. The latter does not have the same skill required of him and is already in danger of being termed a deckhand and regarded as unskilled. . . . Seamen now face competition with any who may be willing to take a trip to see the world." Similarly, in 1926 Captain Walter Petersen, a shipowner spokesman, commented that "the allurement of the sea is gone. It is a drab, uninteresting trade at the present time," characterized mainly by "the cleaning of paint and the polishing of brass." Petersen, who administered the employer-dominated shipping hall, or Marine Service Bureau, on the West Coast in the 1920s, acknowledged that while Pacific Coast ports needed ten thousand seamen in 1926, the Marine Service Bureau certified more than twenty-three thousand men as eligible for jobs. In 1929 Andrew Furuseth estimated turnover in the industry as 300 percent or more. Of course, there was always a solid core of seamen who persevered at their calling no matter how difficult the circumstances of marine life. But the revolving-door atmosphere in the merchant marine as a whole, as well as on the individual ships, can only have contributed to the disorganization and anarchic individualism that characterized and victimized the seamen until the 1930s.[47]

The subculture of the sailortown also reinforced these characteristics and provided a series of opiates that dulled the pain but also tightened the shackles. Dan Boano, who expressed a good deal of craft pride in claiming to be "the world's greatest messboy," recalled in later years that "from the very first trip I hated life at sea." But there was some consolation: on that first trip, a tanker run from Bayonne, New Jersey, to the Texas Gulf ports, Boano "was introduced to a new world in Texas City, a waterfront whorehouse and marijuana." These and other palliatives were sufficient to remove an otherwise disgruntled Boano from the field of organized struggle until he was swept up in the rank-and-file strikes of 1936 and 1937. And so it went with many a seaman. His "independence" was too often expressed in ways that reinforced his bondage.[48]

The other factor leading directly toward quiescence was the maritime law and tradition that threatened to extract a high price for any resistance to the officers' authority, on the high seas or even in port. A celebrated example is the so-called mutiny on the S.S. *California* in 1936. Actually a sit-down strike, it occurred while the ship was docked in the port of San Pedro. But even though the charge of mutiny was only supposed to apply to acts of resistance at sea, there was a tremendous outcry from the shipowners and the Department of Commerce to arrest Joe Curran and other strikers as mutineers.

A less celebrated, but perhaps more revealing, example of the repressive force that could accompany any hint of mutiny occurred in 1927, as the steamship *Colombia* approached the Panama Canal. According to the *Nation* magazine,

> Just before the vessel reached the Canal three Filipino stewards refused to do work assigned to them because they said it was duty usually performed by seamen. They were put in irons, upon which twenty-eight other stewards knocked off work and endangered the safety and lives of the passengers to the extent that the latter had to make their own beds. The next day the three stewards had a change of heart, were released, and returned to work, but the twenty-eight were arrested at Panama, taken ashore, and held for trial, charged with mutiny on the high seas, an offense that under American law is punishable by as much as five years in prison and a fine of $1,000.[49]

Incidents such as this made a profound impression on the editors of the *Nation,* who characterized seamen as "the last serfs." They undoubtedly had an even more profound impact on any marine worker who contemplated resistance to arbitrary authority and oppressive conditions. All workers faced a legal system that time and again proved to be weighted against them and in favor of the employers, but the unique traditions of seafaring life and the harsh provisions of maritime law confronted the seamen with unusual obstacles to effective organization and militant activity. This factor undoubtedly served to strengthen the tendency to seek individual solutions, or at least consolation, in the restless, nomadic life that led from foc'sle to sailortown and back again.

In weighing the contradictory sets of factors that made for both rebelliousness and accommodation, militant solidarity and cynical disorganization among seamen, it is clear that both were always present and that certain historical events and circumstances would bring first one and then the other to the forefront. While it is true that neither set of factors can be overlooked no matter how ascendant the other at any given time, they do not necessarily add up to an evenly balanced duality. The seaman's rootlessness, his separation from integrative social institutions, the extremely oppressive conditions he faced aboard ship and ashore, the worldliness he acquired in plying his trade—all these factors taken together propelled him toward a radical and turbulent disposition and in the long run overshadowed the factors weighted toward quiescence. In practically every country with a seagoing labor force, the sailor's receptivity to revolutionary ideas and his place at or near the crest of popular insurgency are well documented: the riotous but purposeful Jack Tar at the core of the American Revolutionary crowd; the British naval mutineers of 1797 who raised the banner of Jacobinism and declared, "Long have we been endeavouring to find ourselves men. We now find ourselves so. We will be treated as such"; the crew of the battleship *Potemkin,* and the famed Kronstadt sailors who served as shock troops first of the Bolshevik Revolution and then of the popular opposition to Bolshevik rule; and, yes, the American merchant seamen of the Big Strike of 1934 and the subsequent era of insurgency who declared their willingness to "fight capitalism to a finish" if the shipowners refused to meet their demands.[50]

In John Steinbeck's *Of Mice and Men* the "harvest stiff" George gives voice to what is perhaps the universal lament of the migratory worker. "Guys like us, that work on ranches," he says, "are the loneliest guys in the world. They got no family. They don't belong no place. They come to a ranch and work up a stake and then they go inta town and blow their stake, and the first thing you know they're poundin' their tail on some other ranch. They ain't got nothing to look ahead to."

This lament could just as easily be applied to the nomadic seaman, who in his own words was a man with "no come from and no go to," a "hopeless wanderer on the face of the earth." In fact, Eugene O'Neill expressed exactly this theme of rootlessness in *Bound East for Cardiff,* where the dying Yank says, "This sailor life ain't much to cry about leavin'—just one ship after another, hard work, small pay, and bum grub; and when we git into port, just a drunk endin' up in a fight, and all your money gone, and then ship away again."

But Yank has a vision of a better world, a dream of land, home, and family. He says: "It must be great to stay on dry land all your life and have a farm with a house of your own with cows and pigs and chickens, 'way in the middle of the land where yuh'd never smell the sea or see a ship. It must be great to have a wife and kids to play with at night after supper when your work was done. It must be great to have a home of your own."[51] Of course, Yank's dream is entirely apolitical. In times of disorganization and quiescence, the dream often took on the individualistic dimensions voiced by Yank. But in periods of upsurge the vision often broadened to encompass militant maritime solidarity and, sometimes, a new social order based on the unity of the working class.

In either case, this theme of homelessness—along with the dream of home—is all-pervasive in the world of the seaman. It crisscrosses both the inert and the rebellious aspects of his subculture and provides them with a dialectical unity. On the one hand, the absence of the stability and peace of mind associated with home and family is a major factor driving him along his nomadic path and reinforcing the atomized "independence" that renders him so powerless. Tommy Ray once said that "you can go to sea with a man for twenty years and never know where he comes from. He doesn't tell you. There's no place for a sailor to go." A generation after his first trip to sea, Ray lamented that he still saw young seamen "doing what we did, all gassed up with no place to go."[52]

But on the other hand, for men with "no place to go" the dream of such a place could infuse the struggle for seemingly ordinary trade union demands with the visionary aspects of a crusade. J. Vance Thompson, an editor of the ISU *Seamen's Journal,* observed that for seafarers "the ties of organization are doubly strong." Among men deprived of their "natural rights," a union "offers fraternity and usually fills more of a void in the sailor's life than does the organization of workers ashore."

The leadership of the International Seamen's Union stated that their aim was to build "the Brotherhood of the Sea." But the top officials of the ISU were, by and large, men who had been away from the sea for many years. They operated in the higher echelons of the AFL and were among its most conservative and straitlaced representatives. What they really sought for the seaman was legal equality and respectability in the eyes of the shoreside world. For them the lofty goal of "the Brotherhood of the Sea" had none of the deeper meaning that it possessed for the true seafarer.

Among the marine workers themselves, the alienation stemming from rootlessness often created a deep hatred of injustice and sometimes led to the goal of a new social order. J. Vance Thompson offered a glimpse of this powerful impetus when he said that "the seamen have nothing to lose but their chains, they have been denied the right to live a natural life and it is always more than a question of hours and wages. . . . The ultimate goal is not only the brotherhood of the sea, but the fellowship of all workers."[53]

Both the individualistic and the more dynamically social quest for the equivalent of home and family is strikingly illustrated in the life of Charlie Rubin, a Jewish immigrant who became a pioneer organizer in the rank-and-file movement of the 1930s. Rubin was born in Poland and emigrated to America at the age of eleven. After completing elementary school, he wandered from job to job until he succeeded in enlisting in the navy at age sixteen.

There the boxing skills he had acquired as a newsboy defending his street-corner turf brought him a measure of pride and success as a bantamweight fighter. But his handy fists also led to disaster. When a surly officer grabbed him by the shoulder and barked at him, Rubin instinctively punched him in the jaw and earned a stay in the brig. He then embarked on a downward spiral that led from one breach of discipline to another and, finally, to confinement in a psychiatric ward in a government hospital. His naval home had become a nightmare, but Rubin was resourceful enough to plead his case until he received a discharge.

From there the transition to the merchant marine was a natural one, and his *Log of Rubin the Sailor* captures much of the restless, nomadic quality of seafaring life. He wandered from ship to ship and port to port, always searching for something better than the rotten conditions and the spiritual waste that so often pervaded the foc'sle and the sailortown. Unlike many seamen, Rubin had come from a fairly stable family environment, and his parents' Jewish faith had provided a certain religious and cultural identity. But upon going to sea he lost touch with both his family and his Jewish identity and was haunted by the sailor's sense of rootlessness. He recalled in later years that "a lot of seamen were very lonely, because they had no place to go when they came into port. So they'd go to gin mills and whorehouses and places like that."

But Rubin's quest was for something less readily available than drink and flesh. He recalled that after his parents' death, "I adopted a family in San Pedro, and every time my ship came in I'd go to see them. . . . I didn't have anybody. So this was a new experience, like finding a family. I was fascinated with them. I always felt at home there. It changed my life." After meeting them, he remembered, "I always looked forward to coming into San Pedro, because I had a home there. Until then, every time I got on a ship I wanted to get off it, and every time I came into a port I wanted to get out of it."[54]

However, Rubin's restless search did not end with his adopted family. Like Eugene O'Neill's Yank, he longed for a piece of "dry land where yuh'd never smell the sea or see a ship." He found such a place in Southern California, and in the idiom of every sailor's dream, he named it Snug Harbor. Often after a trip he would head for Snug Harbor and lovingly care for his land until lack of money, and the seaman's proverbial restlessness, drove him back to the sea.

In the final analysis, neither his adopted family nor his beloved piece of dry land could stem the tide of discontent within Charlie Rubin. The glaring injustice and manifold humiliations of marine life created in him a deeper vision of truth and harmony. It was in unionism and the Communist party that Rubin the Sailor found the most logical and secure sense of home. On these way stations of his journey he was to find many a comrade and fellow worker.

To identify a part of the impetus toward unionism and revolutionary commitment in a phenomenon that is not entirely rational is not to imply that the most militant and rebellious seamen were therefore irrational and some-how deviant. On the contrary, the seaman had good reason to rebel against both the shipowners and the archaic unionism of the ISU and to raise his voice in protest against the injustice he perceived throughout the world. If his outcry sometimes exceeded that of his fellow workers in other industries, if he seemed to be relatively more open to radical syndicalism and international-ism, it is because he experienced a perhaps more degrading form of exploita-tion without recourse to social institutions that could offer a sustaining or consoling influence. That a rebellious rank-and-file strike leader could see in the maritime upsurge of the 1930s the quest for "one big family" is testament to an untutored but rational vision of a better world rooted in the harsh realities of seafaring life.[55]

2

Craft Unionism and Syndicalist Unionism, 1885–1930

The history of the International Seamen's Union (ISU) and, the regional organizations from which it grew spanned more than fifty years. From its founding in 1899 until its demise in 1937, the ISU claimed to be the only legitimate organization of unlicensed seafarers in the United States. This chapter will not discuss the entire history of the ISU, but rather will examine its character as a federation of craft unions in an era when craft skills were becoming increasingly obsolete and trace the widening gap between the outlook of its leadership and that of the men who sailed the ships. The leaders of the ISU had a deep commitment to craft unionism. Andrew Furuseth's devotion to craft was legendary. Along with Furuseth, "white shirt" sailors like Paul Scharrenberg and Victor Olander were highly respected figures in the AFL, Scharrenberg as secretary of the California State Federation of Labor and Olander as secretary of the AFL's statewide affiliate in Illinois. Although they enjoyed reminiscing about their early years on sailing ships, Olander, Scharrenberg, and other white-shirt sailors were far removed from the rough-and-tumble environment of foc'sle and sailortown, whose inhabitants they criticized for "their filthy language, their beastly carousing, [and] their dirt."[1]

Furuseth and his associates in the top echelons of the ISU appealed to one side of the seamen's experience. Among men who were set apart from shoreside society by the nature of their calling and their status as pariahs, the dogma of craft separation conveyed a soothing sense of pride and place. In an industry where an oversupply of labor was common and loss of work through technological change or jurisdictional imperialism was a constant threat, the jealous safeguarding of craft prerogatives seemed to offer a measure of job security. Moreover, the ISU leaders' status as respected, even honored, members of the larger community lent credibility to their promise to deliver the seamen from bondage.

But there was another side to the marine workers' experience, a side that went very much against the grain of Furuseth's craft obsession and the white-shirt sailors' middle-class respectability. The volatile combination of raw exploitation, isolation from the American mainstream, and international transiency lent a class dimension to the seamen's feeling of separation from bourgeois society. At the very least, it impelled them toward a strong sense of identity with their fellow workers on the docks and inclined them to raise the banner of One Big Union in the maritime industry. Sometimes it led them even further—toward a syndicalist vision of society, a vague but powerful sense of working-class brotherhood. The movement that derived from this syndicalist impulse constituted a fundamental challenge to the unionism of Furuseth. He accused his opponents of representing an alien ideology, when in fact they were the bearers of an outlook and program that flowed naturally from the seamen's environment. Furuseth repulsed his challengers, but ultimately the prize was an empty shell. The ISU barely survived the barren twenties and collapsed in the turbulent thirties.

The International Seamen's Union was founded in 1899, but its history really began in the mid-1880s with the formation of the Coast Seamen's Union. At that time the shipping industry was in the throes of a nationwide depression, and seamen, like other workers, were beginning to organize. The announcement of a wage cut on the West Coast led to a meeting of several hundred angry sailors at San Francisco's Folsom Street Wharf on the evening of March 6, 1885. There in the darkness they listened to speeches by members of a socialist organization, the International Workingmen's Association (IWA). Sigismund Danielewicz, a barber turned coasting sailor and a member of the IWA, had been the decisive force in bringing his fellow seamen together on that historic night. But the most dynamic presence was Burnette Haskell, lawyer, editor, and eclectic radical who had founded the IWA in 1883 as a haven for every shade of leftist from dogmatists to dynamiters. Labor economist Ira B. Cross characterized Haskell as "one of the most erratic and brilliant geniuses in the history of the labor movement on the Pacific Coast." In any case he became the founding father of the Coast Seamen's Union, and the organization's first constitution specified that day-to-day administration of the union's affairs was to rest in the hands of an advisory committee composed of shoreside members of the IWA.

Given the subsequent conservatism of the West Coast sailors' union, and its almost pathological hostility toward landsmen, the catalytic role of Haskell and his socialist comrades is ironic. But in the union's early days the sailors proudly marched in step with the IWA and even furnished a substantial portion of its membership. In the face of Haskell's many detractors, they vigorously defended the man "under [whose] instruction the sailors have learned to assist each other and to master many of the social problems which every workingman should understand." "He has told us over and over again that he is a Socialist," they declared, "but we prefer him to any capitalist or reactionary as our representative."[2]

Whatever the ideological proclivities of the coasting sailors, it soon became apparent that socialism in one union was impossible. Haskell's erratic tendencies contributed to the demise of his dream, but so did the intransigent opposition of the shipowners and the hysterical fear of labor radicalism that gripped the nation in the wake of Chicago's Haymarket bombing. Haskell conclusively demonstrated his lack of judgment when he proposed that the Coast Seamen's entry in San Francisco's first official Labor Day parade should be a float depicting armed sailors storming the Bastille. The parade was scheduled for May 11, 1886, only a week after the Haymarket violence. His deficiencies seemed all the more apparent when the employers crushed a union-led seamen's strike in September 1886. In the wake of this defeat, Haskell was discredited, the advisory committee of IWA members was disbanded, and the sailors gravitated toward pure and simple unionism.[3]

One of the first issues around which the men organized themselves was the method of hiring. The sailortown boarding-masters not only determined who worked, but they received an advance on the seaman's wages in return for providing him with bed, board, booze, and clothing. It was the waterfront version of the company store, with all the same abuses. From the very beginning, then, the sailors demanded that their union develop a method of hiring that would free them from enslavement to the crimps. Less than a month after its founding, the Coast Seamen's Union opened its own shipping office in San Francisco. For the first time anywhere in the world, seamen appointed their own job dispatcher and attempted to take control of the hiring process.

But the shipowners and crimps also saw control of hiring as a life-and-death matter. In June 1886 they formed an employers' association that operated its own shipping office. All hiring was to be conducted through this agency, and no man was to be eligible for a job unless he surrendered his union book and obtained a grade book in return. This blacklisting or "fink book," as the seamen called it, was to be a bone of contention in maritime labor relations for more than half a century. In this instance it helped precipitate the bloody strike of September 1886 in which several men were killed and the union suffered its first major setback.[4]

Although the employers won the first round, the seamen periodically renewed their quest for control of hiring. Increasingly, however, their union officials dismissed this demand as impractical and even condemned it as a violation of the principle of freedom of choice. Andrew Furuseth stated that when the boarding-master controlled hiring, "there was no freedom, no choice, either on the part of the seaman or the officer who was to have him under his command." Likewise, he warned, when the union controlled hiring and dispatched men on a rotary basis, "there is the same want of the exercise of the free will on the part of the seaman and the officer, the same going where one is not willing to go; the same obstruction to free choice and individual effort." Furuseth's views prevailed for many years. But in the long run the ISU officials' inflexible commitment to this venerable notion of contract served to widen the gulf between themselves and their membership. In the 1930s the demand for a union-controlled hiring hall was to become one of the rallying cries of the great rank-and-file upsurge, and one of the rocks upon which the ISU leadership foundered.[5]

The next step toward the formation of the ISU was the amalgamation of the Coast Seamen's Union with an organization of steamship sailors in 1891 to create the Sailors' Union of the Pacific (SUP). The SUP was the most dynamic component of the ISU throughout the international union's existence. In fact, without the West Coast sailors' affiliate, it is unlikely that the ISU could have survived the many lean years when seamen's unionism on the other coasts was at a low ebb. The SUP prospered for several reasons. First, with its relative isolation and smaller population, the Pacific Coast did not have either the volume of shipping or the vast oversupply of labor that characterized the Atlantic Coast. Second, the character of shipping on the West Coast, especially in the coastwise trade plying the waters from San Diego to the Canadian border, required that seamen be adept at handling cargoes of lumber and hides in far-flung ports where work was too sporadic to employ longshoremen on a regular basis. Thus, the West Coast seamen acquired a greater variety of skills than most of their seafaring counterparts and were less easily replaced by unskilled hands. Finally, the vast majority of Pacific Coast sailors were northern Europeans. Their numerical preponderance in the maritime crafts gave the West Coast work force a homogeneity that was entirely lacking among the ethnically and racially diverse seamen on the Atlantic Coast.

These characteristics were most clearly evident on the steam schooners that carried lumber from the logging ports of the Northwest to expanding coastal cities such as San Francisco and Los Angeles. The steam schooners were small in size, but they numbered well over a hundred, and for many years they provided employment for the majority of West Coast seamen. Their crews were made up of highly skilled sailors who also loaded and unloaded lumber when the vessels arrived in port. One East Coast seaman who sailed with these men on occasion remembered them as "artists" when it came to handling winches and cargo. Overwhelmingly, they were Scandinavians. Among the 6,669 deck sailors on the West Coast in 1917, more than 3,100 of them were of Scandinavian origin, while only 529 had been born in the United States.

Jim Kendall, an American-born seaman, recalled shipping on one steam schooner where "I was the only 'foreigner.' " The rest of the crew was Danish. Harry Lundeberg stated that as late as 1940, 30 to 35 percent of the men on deck in the lumber schooners were aliens of Norwegian, Finnish, and Swedish citizenship. Through them the steam schooner fleet earned its tongue-in-cheek designation as the "Scandinavian navy."[6]

Because of their ethnic homogeneity and craft skill, the steam schooner sailors were the backbone of marine unionism on the West Coast. They played a leading role in virtually every maritime strike. In the early 1920s, the Wobblies made significant headway among the steam schooner men, especially in San Pedro and the Pacific Northwest, and in the mid-thirties the syndicalist militants in the SUP based themselves on the steam schooner sailors and hailed them as "the lever which the seafaring crafts have [always] used in order to raise conditions and wages on the Pacific Coast." Also, that they combined longshore and sailors' work made them the center of frequent controversy. The seamen's and longshoremen's unions engaged in a prolonged and acrimonious dispute over the division of labor on the waterfront.[7]

Although organizing efforts on the Atlantic and Gulf coasts and the Great Lakes met with minimal success, enough activity was generated to maintain at least the trappings of organization. In 1899 the various sailors' unions came together to form the International Seamen's Union of America. Their combined efforts represented only about three thousand members, the majority of them on the West Coast. The delegates created three districts: the Atlantic and Gulf coasts, the Great Lakes, and the Pacific Coast. They declared that in each district separate and autonomous unions were to be developed for the deck, engine, and cooks' and stewards' crafts. Initially all of the affiliated unions were composed entirely of deck sailors. In 1901 the Pacific Coast Marine Firemen became the first union from another maritime craft to affiliate with the ISU. Throughout its existence the International Seamen's Union was to be characterized, and plagued, by the craft and regional distinctions (and jealousies) that were reflected in its structure.

For most of the first two decades of the twentieth century the Sailors' Union prospered while the other ISU affiliates struggled to survive. The SUP secured recognition from the employers and engaged in collective bargaining for more than fifteen years with such effectiveness that the shipowners claimed they were "completely at the mercy of the Sailors' Union." By 1903, sailors' wages on the West Coast were set at forty-five to fifty dollars per month (compared to thirty dollars on the Atlantic), with fifty cents overtime pay after nine hours and overtime on Sundays and holidays. Ten minutes' coffee time was allowed, and union patrolmen were granted the right to visit ships. In return, the SUP disavowed sympathy strikes and agreed to follow a prescribed grievance procedure before striking a vessel.

Meanwhile, on the Atlantic Coast, the unions were undermined by the oversupply of labor and by racial and ethnic antagonisms among the seamen, which resulted in the setting up of a Jim Crow local for black cooks and stewards and in the defection of Spanish-speaking firemen to the IWW. On the Great Lakes, the entry of giant corporations like Ford and U.S. Steel into the shipping business meant that they brought their antilabor policies with them and further undermined the already weak seamen's organizations on the lakes.[8]

The ISU's most persistent activity occurred in the legislative realm. Over a period of years President Andrew Furuseth waged a single-minded lobbying campaign that resulted in the passage of the La Follette Seamen's Act of 1915. The first milestone in this battle was the passage in 1895 of the Maguire Act, which outlawed imprisonment for desertion in the coastwise trade. The culmination of the effort came when President Woodrow Wilson signed the La Follette Seamen's Act into law on March 4, 1915. This legislation extended the earlier ban against imprisonment to American seamen in the overseas and intercoastal trades and also decreed that foreign seamen deserting their ships in U.S. ports could not be imprisoned. It allowed American seafarers to receive half of their pay upon demand in virtually any port and specifically prohibited the payment of an advance on the seamen's wages to crimps or other "landsharks."

By far the most important accomplishment of the La Follette Act was its dramatic impact on the wages of foreign seamen. The law granted them the right to abandon ship in a U.S. port without fear of imprisonment, thus virtually compelling foreign shipowners to pay their men higher wages in order to keep them from deserting to American vessels. The foreign owners bitterly resisted this trend at first, but the seamen's response overwhelmed them. ISU attorney Silas B. Axtell commented in 1919,

> There were desertions by the hundreds; a vessel from Copenhagen or Liverpool would no sooner land at a Brooklyn pier with a low wage crew, than a demand for half wages would be made, and if the demand was refused, which it often was, the seamen left, . . . retained counsel, and sued for the balance of their wages. Many a British ship early in 1916, and other foreign ships in the fall of 1916, came into port with a crew of deckhands and firemen at twenty to twenty-five dollars per month, and departed with a crew at fifty-five to sixty dollars per month.[9]

For American seamen, however, the victory was more symbolic than immediate and practical. To be sure, the symbolism was important to seamen. Paternalistic statutes and insulting judicial language about childlike and credulous beings were now swept aside as the seafarers finally achieved the legal standing of ordinary men. Moreover, the newly won right to partial payment of wages upon demand in virtually any port made it easier to desert the ship without fear of immediate destitution. But the act's amendments that decreed improvements in the conditions of life and work aboard ship were systematically ignored by most employers. Furuseth's biographer, Hyman Weintraub, has admitted that "whenever the Department of Commerce was asked to interpret the Seamen's Act, the decision was almost always in favor of the shipowners." During the open-shop era between 1921 and 1934, the law was for the most part a dead letter.[10]

However, in 1915, the Seamen's Act and Furuseth became the objects of the most extravagant praise. Robert La Follette informed the marine workers, "I am permitted at last to hail you as free men under the Constitution of our country. The Fourth of March, 1915, is your emancipation day. The act approved by President Wilson makes America sacred soil and the Thirteenth Amendment finally becomes a covenant of refuge for the seamen of the world." Furuseth was widely hailed as the "Emancipator of the Seamen."[11]

Anyone who would understand the International Seamen's Union must also comprehend the character and philosophy of its president, Andrew Furuseth. To those who admired him, Furuseth was larger than life. In fact, some of his admirers worked long and hard to place their hero on a plane with Abraham Lincoln and even Jesus Christ. ISU attorney Silas B. Axtell declared that Furuseth's "Life and Work exemplified the Life and Work of CHRIST." Another ISU associate predicted that "the time will come when the work of this grand old man will be studied in the public schools, and he will stand enshrined in the hearts of all free people alongside of that other great and lonely leader—Abraham Lincoln." Although the prediction has not come true, the legend of "St. Andrew the Sailor" and the "Abraham Lincoln of the Sea" has endured for generations. William Denman, an admiralty lawyer and federal court judge who was a confidant of Presidents Wilson, Hoover, and Franklin Roosevelt, called Furuseth "the finest human spirit and the American of the greatest individual accomplishment for his fellow man of our lifetime." Samuel Gompers, with whom Furuseth shared much in the way of ideas and temperament, called him a "genius of extraordinary power" and said he "felt drawn to the man as . . . to few persons." George P. West, a journalist who often disagreed with Furuseth, nonetheless characterized him as a "gaunt figure of courage, of stark sincerity, of consecrated devotion, a man so truly noble that merely by being he lifts the race."[12]

Furuseth was born in Norway in 1854. At the age of nineteen he began shipping on sailing vessels. He sailed under at least six flags and, after deserting a British ship in 1880, made San Francisco his home port. He joined the Coast Seamen's Union soon after its formation and played a major role in wresting leadership from the members of the International Workingmen's Association. With the socialists out of the way, Furuseth emerged as the dominant figure in both the SUP and the ISU. Shoreside union duties took him from San Francisco to Washington, D.C., where he functioned mainly as a lobbyist for the rest of his life. From 1894 to 1901 he served as AFL legislative representative in Washington, and he soon became one of the elder statesmen on the craft federation's executive council.

Furuseth's tireless energy, Spartan life-style, and passionate, eccentric individualism were the hallmarks of his character, and they stood out as pointedly as the sharp features on his deeply furrowed face. Paul S. Taylor described his "Norse profile" as "like the prow of a viking ship." Tall and gaunt, with piercing eyes and a shock of uncombed white hair, the elderly Furuseth must have had the appearance of an avenging angel to those who felt the sting of his wrath.[13]

But even among those who despised him, few questioned his commitment or his honesty. He often worked as many as sixteen hours a day. He wore simple, wrinkled, loose-fitting clothes, which, according to legend, "he ironed by putting them under his mattress—sailor style." He showed little interest in food or items of personal comfort and lived in a room not much larger than a sailor's space in a foc'sle. Like many seamen, he never married, but unlike them he showed no interest in relations with women. Weintraub has said that "in practice, he was married to the union. It received more devotion, more loving care than any woman could expect."[14]

Devotion to craft and skill was the foundation of Furuseth's philosophy. He argued that "crafts are essential to civilization . . . civilization goes onward and onward as men develop skill, and civilization dies as men forget how to develop it." "It is skill," he said, "that puts the mechanic nearest the gods." As a craft unionist, he turned the seamen's separation from shoreside workers into a fetish. The fact that West Coast sailors loaded and unloaded cargo naturally led to jurisdictional quarrels, which Furuseth pursued on both philosophical and pragmatic grounds. He argued that "a real seaman is a longshoreman, and a rigger, as well. He is a skilled man." So there was no reason for him to defer to the experience and skill of another worker when the ship docked. Pragmatically, he recognized that work and wages were at stake. If longshoremen discharged and loaded cargo, seamen would stand idly by, without pay, while the vessel was in port. So he fought the longshoremen relentlessly and condemned bitterly those who argued in favor of unity between the two crafts.

In a setting where traditional skills were rapidly being undermined by technological innovation, and laboring people were becoming increasingly alienated from the work process, Furuseth retained an obsessive devotion to the inherent dignity of work. In a famous Labor Day speech to students at the University of California, he declared that "work is worship—to labor is to pray . . . because that is to exercise the highest, the divine faculties implanted in us as the sons of God. It matters not if the labor be the writing of a thesis or the digging of a ditch."[15]

As coal, steam, and electric power replaced sail, and the character of seafaring work was transformed accordingly, Furuseth retained a mystical belief in the importance of a seaman's traditional skills. He declared that "the sea has remained unchanged through all the ages. So also the seaman. The qualities of mind and body that were needed in the seaman of the earliest times are yet needed and there can be no real seamen where those qualities are not." In this assertion Furuseth received the support of several of his trusted ISU lieutenants whose careers at sea, like his, had ended with the passing of the era of sail. But otherwise few agreed with him. Within his own union a respected official like Walter Macarthur could acknowledge that "the operation of steam vessels has been simplified by the adoption of various devices, all making for the displacement of skill and experience." And the Wobblies and Communists heaped scorn on his "reactionary" position. He in turn blasted his critics as "traveling longshoremen" and lamented the lack of skill in the younger generation of seamen.[16]

With the employers, however, Furuseth was more patient and conciliatory. Of the shipowners he said, "They are not hard-hearted men, but they do not understand us. They do not know our hopes and aspirations." The ISU president believed that if he could get the shipowners and the government to understand the seamen's needs, they would respond favorably. Indeed, this inordinately proud individual was capable of literally begging the rich and powerful for favors if he saw no other recourse. In 1921, hoping to avoid a strike, he beseeched President Harding to arbitrate the seamen's dispute with the shipowners and promised to accept his decision as final. During the campaign for the Seamen's Act, when the bill's passage seemed in doubt, he went to the president and "personally begged Wilson to 'make him a free man.' " On another occasion he intoned, "We now raise our manacled hands in humble supplication and pray that the nations issue a decree of emancipation." It was this penchant for "humble supplication" that led a Communist opponent to accuse him of using "words that would make any self-respecting seaman vomit."[17]

One of the qualities that made Furuseth so appealing to friends and maddening to opponents was his absolute sense of rectitude. He was a peculiar combination of the pragmatist and the visionary, for he imbued his cautious and conservative unionism with an aura of otherworldly virtue. He once told an audience that "the labor movement received its charter on Mount Sinai," and he enjoined SUP members to "be saturated with the spirit of the crusader." With equal zeal he could campaign for reform legislation and do battle against those elements in the labor movement who dared to envision a transformed social order. Thus he characterized the Seamen's Act as a "miracle," while describing the IWW as "a blighting pest [that] has descended upon place after place to leave nothing but wreckage, misery, and despair behind." In the face of recurring challenges from the Left, he thundered, "We know what is impossible," and warned the seamen that "the wrongs of centuries cannot be righted in a year or two." George P. West characterized him as a "beautifully sincere pessimist."[18]

But those on the receiving end of his blasts did not find his sincerity so beautiful. After witnessing a Furuseth tirade against critics within the union, an SUP member declared, "I, for one, rebel against a father who attempts to destroy my honest brother for no other reason than a difference of opinion." Walter Macarthur, who knew Furuseth well for more than fifty years, put this complaint in larger perspective. "Throughout his career as Secretary of the Sailors' Union and President of the International Seamen's Union," said Macarthur, "Furuseth has pursued the policy of browbeating and libeling every man who has shown a disposition to think for himself and to speak his own mind. Many members so disposed have been denounced as 'tools of the shipowner.' Either that, or they were just 'plain fools.' By this means discussion was suppressed or if insisted upon, usually resulted in bad feeling all around. In some instances heads were broken in the attempt to 'persuade' Furuseth's critics to accept his leadership."[19]

There was one vital issue, however, on which Furuseth and his ISU associates—critics and supporters alike—were in full accord, namely, their unyielding commitment to white supremacy. When the Marine Cooks and Stewards Association of the Pacific Coast was founded in 1901, its members declared their determination to "relieve ourselves of the degrading necessity of competing with an alien and inferior race." "We have . . . form[ed] a Union," they said, "for the purpose of replacing the Chinese and Japanese now on the Coast by American citizens or by those who are eligible to citizenship." Furuseth himself was deeply disturbed by the shipowners' increasing use of Chinese and Filipino seamen on American vessels. He saw this policy as "a peril to Christian civilization," and he characterized his tireless campaign for the La Follette Seamen's Act as "the last great struggle of the white man to maintain himself on the seas." According to historian Jerold Auerbach, Furuseth's "cry for seamen's rights [became] indistinguishable from Nordic racism." His views on race were representative of a wide spectrum of opinion within the labor movement and the larger society. Anti-Chinese agitation had long been a defining characteristic of organized labor in California, not only among conservative craft unionists like Furuseth but among the movement's radical elements as well. Burnette Haskell, the SUP's socialist founder, had exhorted his fellow toilers to prepare for a race war between Caucasians and Chinese, whom he characterized as "savage, vicious, idol-worshipping, and barbarous." Olaf Tveitmoe, a Norwegian immigrant whose career in the labor movement was even more flamboyant than Burnette Haskell's, combined an active involvement in the building-trades unions with a strong intellectual attraction to socialism, syndicalism, and the cult of violence. "Let the workers of the world clasp hands over the oceans which divide them," he wrote in praise of international solidarity. But his epic vision of class unity excluded the "almond-eyed Mongolian" and the Japanese, whom he described as "the most dangerous spies that have ever been allowed to exist this side of HELL." Eminently respectable SUP officials like Furuseth and Macarthur opposed a "gorilla" like Tveitmoe on many trade union and political issues, but they readily joined hands with him in 1905 to form the Japanese and Korean Exclusion League. As late as 1929 *Seamen's Journal* editor Paul Scharrenberg, who took great pride in the nickname "White Hope of the West," could warn that if the laws restricting "mass migration from the Orient" were repealed, "the white workers will literally be crucified by the proletariat from Asia."[20]

As Scharrenberg's statement implies, the Sailors' Union of the Pacific served as a persistent and influential advocate of immigration restriction. Generally, its focus was on the danger of the "proletariat from Asia," but sometimes the union joined forces with those who sought to restrict "the competition of Southern Europe" as well. Moreover, the SUP consistently barred black Americans from its ranks. J. Vance Thompson, a bitter opponent of Furuseth, once editorialized in the *Seamen's Journal* that "the very anatomy of the negro is inferior to that of the whites, and . . . [he] can never attain to the average intelligence of the white man." Furuseth was more circumspect with regard to blacks, but he did state publicly on one occasion that only "the least skillful and least self-respecting among white men" would share their shipboard quarters with blacks. This attitude met with a sharp challenge from the Wobblies and the Communists, but to little avail, for it remained pervasive among West Coast sailors. One black seaman, a chief steward, testified in 1955 that he had never seen a black in the deck or engine department of any ship he sailed on over a period of forty years.[21]

Furuseth and his associates attempted to justify their discriminatory policies on at least three grounds. First, they often gave expression to the frank racism that permeated American society in the late nineteenth and early twentieth centuries. They simply took it for granted that whites, and Anglo-Saxon or Nordic whites in particular, stood at the summit of a hierarchy of races and nationalities. Weintraub has concluded that "few men, even on the West Coast, outdid Furuseth" in the blatant chauvinism he expressed toward Orientals. Sometimes, however, the sailors offered a narrower, more pragmatic rationale for discrimination, stating that blacks, Asians, and "cheap Greeks and cheap Italians" debased the labor market by their willingness to break strikes and work for low wages. Macarthur recalled that as early as 1891 "Jap scabs" became "a thorn in the side of the Sailor's Union." And in a plea to President McKinley, the San Francisco Central Labor Council warned that "the encroachment of Asiatic labor" would "displace the American workman and degrade the labor of the State to a condition of mere peonage." (Although this fear was no doubt real, much of the most virulent anti-Oriental agitation came from sectors of the labor movement—the building trades, for example—that faced little or no competition from Asian immigrants. Among the seamen, the record was more complex. Generally, Orientals were limited to the stewards' department, although they sometimes worked on deck and in the engine room aboard vessels that sailed mainly to Asian ports.)[22]

A final, and more grandiose, rationale for discrimination incorporated the Social Darwinist vision of a worldwide conflict between races, nations, and civilizations. As the *Seamen's Journal* put it in 1901, "the real struggle of to-day lies between the civilization that draws its breath from beef and barley and that which rests upon rice and dried fish." Echoing Alfred Thayer Mahan's widely read work, *The Influence of Sea Power upon History,* Furuseth argued that "sea-power has at all times meant world power. Those who controlled the sea always went where they wanted to go; stayed where they wanted to stay; took what they wanted and brought it home." In hearings upon the proposed Seamen's Act, he testified that "under this bill . . . we are trying to keep the sea for the white race. . . . Pass this law and the Japanese and Chinese will not have any advantage; then we can fight them for control of the seas" and mastery of the world. Although usually expressed in narrower—and cruder—form, this Nordic racism would leave an indelible mark on the character of the Sailors' Union of the Pacific for many years to come.[23]

One of the greatest challenges to Furuseth's unionism—his obsession with craft pride, the sanctity of contracts, and "obedience to lawful commands on shipboard"—came in the years between 1914 and 1923. This was, of course, the era of World War I, with its carnage, sacrifice, and ritual patriotism, followed by mass disillusionment. It was also the era of the Bolshevik Revolution, when millions of workers who were not revolutionaries watched with a sense of pride as the first "workers' republic" battled for survival. In both Europe and America, it was the era of the New Unionism, when "syndicalism" and "workers' control," "direct action" and the "general strike" became slogans of a decade of upheaval.

World War I dramatically altered the circumstances of maritime labor. The enormous expansion of shipping meant that the chronic oversupply of men suddenly turned into a shortage of qualified personnel. Sensing their advantage, Atlantic Coast seamen struck in 1916 and received significant pay increases. Wages on the Great Lakes and the Pacific Coast were increased without a strike. The wartime shipping boom continued into 1920, greatly increasing the leverage of the unions. War zone wages, including bonus payments, reached a rate of $112.50 a month for able seamen and firemen. But in addition, the ISU sought to institutionalize a concession that the employers and the U.S. Shipping Board viewed with increasing hostility, namely, union preference in hiring. This became the issue that precipitated the 1919 strike. Although the ISU leadership tried to avoid a walkout, marine firemen voted to strike on July 15 and they were immediately joined by hundreds of rank-and-file sailors and stewards' department personnel. Within a week, one observer reported "400 vessels tied up, 50,000 seamen out between Maine and Texas, and half a dozen Dutch and Scandinavian and one British ship tied up in sympathy." The *New York Times* reported that between five and eight hundred vessels were idled by the walkout.

The strike ended after twelve days in a partial victory for the union. The employers refused to grant union preference in hiring—although it remained in effect on the Pacific Coast—but they did concede the right of union delegates to visit ships and they granted a ten dollars a month wage increase. More important than the settlement, however, was the character of the strike. The rank and file had seized the initiative from the ISU leadership. As two labor journalists put it, "American sea labor is just as unrestful in its itch for a unionized industry as is land labor the world over." Moreover, they said, "*the itch is in the rank and file: the big strike started against the wishes of union leaders* when firemen and sailors began quitting without authorization."[24]

By 1920 the ISU was at the pinnacle of its power. The membership reached a hundred and fifteen thousand. The most spectacular advances came on the East Coast, where the number of unionists jumped from forty-five hundred in 1915 to eighty one thousand in 1920. The *Monthly Labor Review* estimated that 90 percent of the unlicensed seamen on both coasts were organized. Surveying the scene in November 1920, the ISU leadership professed to be more than satisfied with its accomplishments. The *Seamen's Journal* declared that the union's "reasonable and humane policies have earned for the seamen of America a public recognition never surpassed by any movement of the wage earners."[25]

To the perceptive observer, however, the storm warnings were clearly etched on the horizon. By the fall of 1920 a shipping slump had caused widespread unemployment on the waterfront. Admiral William Benson of the U.S. Shipping Board openly lectured the seafarers on the need for public spirit and improved efficiency, and the shipowners were clearly determined to reverse the wartime gains of the maritime unions when their agreements expired in May 1921. Meanwhile, the marine workers' growing militancy and expanding sense of class brotherhood alarmed both the shipowners and the ISU leadership. Sailors' Union members in Seattle and San Francisco rejected the counsel of their officials and voted in favor of hiring through the union hall on a rotary basis. On the East Coast, the Marine Cooks and Stewards ignored the ISU's long-standing opposition to the organization of Asian seamen and helped to build the Oriental Seafarers' Association, which recruited four thousand members in New York.[26]

But the most insistent demand for "a closer affiliation or industrial form of

Unionism" continued to come from the longshoremen, whose organizations were forced into a life-and-death struggle with antiunion employers. As early as 1914 the Riggers and Stevedores' Union in San Francisco had spearheaded the formation of a local Waterfront Workers' Federation, which the Sailors' Union joined in spite of Furuseth's opposition. In 1916 a large majority of the San Francisco stevedores voted in a membership referendum to "withdraw from the I.L.A. [International Longshoremen's Association] and spend the money it would cost us to continue our affiliation with the International in an effort to amalgamate all the unions of the Maritime Transport Industry, between the Warehouse at Shipping Point and Warehouse at Receiving Point into one big powerful organization, meeting, thinking and acting together at all times." Although this proposal was never carried out in full, the San Francisco longshoremen did withdraw from the ILA, and they continued their aggressive advocacy of broader maritime unity.[27]

In the apocalyptic atmosphere of 1919, the Riggers and Stevedores' Union and the waterfront employers engaged in one of the bitterest conflicts in the history of the West Coast maritime industry. In the negotiations preceding the strike, the union shocked the employers and conservative labor leaders alike by demanding worker participation in the ownership, direction, and profits of America's industries. Declaring that "an awakening has taken place in the minds of the workers of the world, which has caused them to realize that they are the producers of all wealth," the Riggers and Stevedores maintained that only a radically new industrial policy would prevent the United States from "running Red with revolution like the European countries and Russia." Naturally, the employers rejected this demand and accused the union of planting the "seeds of Bolshevism and anarchy."

The strike began on September 15. Ships' clerks and riverboatmen walked out with the longshoremen, and the shipowners flooded the waterfront with strikebreakers. Significant numbers of them were black and Mexican, but the majority were whites, who according to one reporter were mostly "young men of the 'gangster' type from our big cities." In the wake of the violence that ensued, some of it triggered by armed strikebreakers parading in front of the union hall, the employers charged the Riggers and Stevedores with mounting a campaign of "brutal attacks, maimings, riots and murder." They warned the citizens of San Francisco that the strike was "conceived in a revolutionary and anarchistic spirit," and that "I.W.W. agitators" were attempting to use the port as a stepping-stone toward "red revolution" and "the chaos that has resulted to industrial Russia."[28]

In spite of the sharp ideological polarization, the principal issue from the strikers' standpoint was neither worker ownership nor Red revolution. Rather, the longshoremen felt that mechanical innovations in cargo handling had made the pace of work on the docks unbearable. They told reporters that the machinery was setting "a man-killing pace," and a University of California labor economist later agreed that "work under these circumstances [would have] dissipated all of a man's energy in a few years." Thus the majority of the longshoremen demonstrated a tenacious commitment to the demand that work gangs be increased in size from six to eight men.[29]

After nearly three months of bitter, often violent, conflict, the strike was undermined by the formation of a dual organization, the Longshoremen's Association of San Francisco and the Bay District, which split off from the Riggers and Stevedores' Union in December and promptly signed a five-year, closed-shop agreement with the waterfront employers. Spearheaded by gang bosses who had organized their own "Harmony Club," the Longshoremen's Association claimed the allegiance of a thousand dockworkers, about 25 percent of the work force. Within a few months the Riggers and Stevedores' Union was essentially a dead letter, and for the next fourteen years every longshoreman was compelled to join the "Blue Book" (so named to distinguish it from the red membership book of the Riggers and Stevedores'—or "Red Book"—Union) in order to gain access to work on the waterfront.[30]

San Francisco was by no means the only center of syndicalist militancy on the West Coast in 1919. Unionists from British Columbia, Seattle, and Tacoma also fanned the flames of One Big Union sentiment up and down the coast. In fact, an organization calling itself the One Big Union (OBU) swept through the ranks of western Canadian unionists in the spring and summer of 1919 and spread south toward Seattle and other port cities. In spite of its name the One Big Union had no connection with the IWW. As the organization's principal historian has put it, "OBU advocates were not bums or bindlestiffs but skilled tradesmen, veterans of craft unionism, who attacked from within" the mainstream of organized labor. Their goal was industrial unionism and the development of a "class conscious labor movement." Significantly, some of the leading OBU adherents in British Columbia and Washington were longshoremen, including Jack Kavanagh, a socialist who was elected president of the British Columbia Federation of Labor in 1919; Joseph Taylor, of Victoria, the ILA district president; and Harry Wright, of Tacoma, the district secretary. In 1917, the ILA Pacific Coast District had already called for the amalgamation of the longshoremen's and seamen's unions and the formation of a coastwide maritime federation. Now, in May 1919, the district convention repeated its call for the merger of the two marine unions and instructed its locals to approach the ISU "with the end in view of getting in closer touch with each other along Industrial Lines." Moreover, it went on record in favor of "forming an industrial union patterned after the British Columbia 'One Big Union'" and declared its intent to submit such a proposal to all ILA locals and maritime unions on the West Coast. A referendum among dockworkers supported the OBU proposal by a five-to-one margin.[31]

Characteristically, the ISU leadership rejected—and even ridiculed—these initiatives. The *Seamen's Journal* declared, "There is something distinctly pathetic about the manner in which the Pacific Coast longshoremen have from time to time attempted, 'in the name of industrial unionism,' to assimilate the organized seamen. . . . From one end of the Pacific Coast to the other they are organized in 'locals' whereas the seamen have for decades had a real 'one big union,' embracing all the seamen along the Pacific Coast." In a move designed in part to fend off the demand for genuine industrial unionism on the waterfront, the ISU leadership organized a Seafarers' Council of licensed and unlicensed offshore unions on the Pacific Coast. The ISU affiliates resigned from the Waterfront Workers' Federation in order to join the Seafarers' Council, and the *Seamen's Journal* proudly announced that "the links of a chain are being forged which will solidify all the toilers of the sea."[32]

But the seamen demonstrated that they were not satisfied with this maneuver. In January 1921 the membership of the Sailors' Union of the Pacific elected J. Vance Thompson editor of the *Seamen's Journal*. Thompson, who was becoming increasingly well known for his outspoken advocacy of closer ties between longshoremen and seamen, ousted Furuseth's lieutenant and mouthpiece, Paul Scharrenberg, by a margin of forty-four votes. Soon after his victory, I. N. Hylen, who had served as secretary of the Alaska Fishermen's Union for more than twenty years, was defeated in his bid for reelection after he advised acceptance of a 10 percent wage cut. Both Hylen and Scharrenberg were vice presidents of the ISU. As another ISU vice president, Peter B. Gill, acknowledged, "Their defeat indicated dissatisfaction with Furuseth's policies and a demand for effective industrial unionism."[33]

In early 1921 the shipowners and the Shipping Board demanded that the unions accept a substantial wage reduction, the elimination of overtime pay, the open shop, and a retreat from the conditions that the seamen had won during the war. Admiral Benson characterized overtime pay as "graft" and declared it "foreign to the spirit and customs of the sea." Because of the depression and deflationary spiral that had accompanied the winding down of the wartime economy, Furuseth was willing to make significant concessions in the area of wages and overtime. But he balked at the shipowners' determination to do away with union preference in hiring and at the Shipping Board's new policy of refusing to allow union representatives access to their members on the ships. When the unions refused to surrender on these issues, Benson declared that new wages and conditions would take effect on Shipping Board vessels as of May 1, and he demanded that the private operators follow his lead. In what was now clearly an attempt at "complete annihilation of the unions," Benson directed the navy to man ships carrying U.S. mail and decreed that any seaman who refused to sign a statement accepting the new wages and conditions was to be ordered off the ships.[34]

The seamen fought back courageously. In New York, the *Times* reported six thousand marine engineers and forty thousand seamen on strike, with more than three hundred ships idle. There were frequent battles on the New York waterfront, and when a picket was fatally shot by a scab, nine thousand strikers marched in the funeral procession. In Baltimore, after reports of riots aboard several vessels, three naval sub chasers with guns mounted on deck were stationed in the harbor and seven hundred police patrolled the waterfront. On one occasion, hundreds of strikers stormed the U.S. Custom House, where the government was mobilizing scabs. Similar reports came from the South Atlantic and Gulf ports.[35]

But in the final analysis, the seamen were victimized by the fury of the government/employer offensive and by the depression conditions, which left thirty thousand seafarers unemployed in Atlantic ports alone. Hugh Mulzac recalled that "thousands of rootless workers, plus the young wartime recruits, made excellent 'finks.' Vessels put to sea with scab crews . . . while militant sailors marched the picket lines ashore." Moreover, on the East Coast in particular, the unions were hamstrung by one of the long-standing weaknesses of the ISU. Having refused to accept blacks in the Eastern and Gulf Sailors' affiliate, the ISU now found that large numbers of black seamen were serving as strikebreakers. There were many incidents of violence between white strikers and black strikebreakers, with a white fireman shot and killed in New York and a black sailor beaten to death in Portland, Maine. After nearly two months on strike, the East Coast unions ordered their men to go back to work, preferring to return with no agreement rather than accept the terms offered by the Shipping Board.[36]

On the Pacific Coast, with its stronger union tradition and more homogeneous work force, the strike was more solid and the shipowners were compelled to admit that San Francisco was "the tightest port in the country." Up and down the coast, more than a hundred steam schooners were idle, as employers made no effort to operate them with scabs. In fact, the steam schooner owners eventually broke away from the other shipowners and offered the ISU a compromise settlement. In contrast to the Shipping Board position, the steam schooner offer would have granted the Pacific Coast unions many of their long-standing prerogatives, but it also involved a cut of 15 percent in wages and 40 percent in overtime rates, and included a clause requiring seamen to work with scab longshoremen. Moreover, according to Thompson, the shipowners' chief spokesman poisoned the atmosphere by displaying "a dictatorial attitude right from the jump." The *Journal* editor declared that

> Outside of a certain familiarity savoring of contempt displayed towards some of the oldtimers on the seamen's committees, the chief representative . . . of the shipowners assumed an attitude at different times suggestive of a peddler beating down the price of old clothes; a master to his whining slave, or Bismarck dictating terms of peace.

When objections were offered to the infamous strikebreaking clause, that worthy emitted a roar like a baited lion, excoriating everybody connected with longshore work as reds.[37]

Furuseth was quite willing to overlook the manner in which the terms of peace were offered, because he believed that salvaging some of the union's prerogatives through the steam schooner offer was the only alternative to disaster. And, of course, he cared not a whit for the longshoremen. Thus he campaigned vigorously for the steam schooner proposal. But the Sailors' Union membership rejected it by the overwhelming vote of 1,607 to 118. Only eight sailors sided with Old Andy in Seattle; only fourteen in San Francisco, where more than a thousand voted against his recommendation. Once again, Furuseth's concept of unionism was clashing head-on with the syndicalist impulse that was sweeping across the industrial world. As West observed, "The disaffection of the Pacific Coast seamen is part of a disaffection as wide as the country." Over the next several years the conflict between craft and syndicalist unionism in the maritime industry would equal and perhaps surpass the bitterness of the struggle between workers and employers.

The seamen clearly resented the ISU leadership's suggestion that they work with scab longshoremen at a time when economic conditions and the employer offensive were decimating the stevedores' union up and down the coast. In Seattle, for example, the wartime peak of thirty-three hundred longshore jobs had fallen to five hundred by April 1921; the ILA had been broken in a recent strike; and the employers now hired through a despised "fink hall." In the midst of their own life-and-death struggle with the shipowners, the seamen recalled the longshoremen's many overtures toward closer cooperation in recent years, and they now resolved to respond in kind. At the same Sailors' Union meeting that rejected the steam schooner offer, a resolution calling for "a policy of closer cooperation between the maritime and transport workers and others" was, in Thompson's words, "adopted by a unanimous roar from nearly twelve hundred throats."[38]

At the initiative of longshoremen in San Pedro and the Puget Sound area, a Federation of Marine Transport Workers of the Pacific Coast was formed, and many maritime unionists greeted the fledgling organization with genuine enthusiasm. Under the banner headline "Transport Workers Awake," Thompson declared in the *Seamen's Journal:*

Adversity is teaching the membership of labor unions the necessity of a greater solidarity; the need for effort, sacrifice, and adherence to ideals. The meaning of the adage that "an injury to one is the concern of all" is being impressed upon the minds of the workers with telling effect.

Realizing their helplessness under the system of organization prevailing, both longshoremen and seamen have consolidated with other marine transport workers of the Pacific Coast. The formation of a powerful federation of marine transport

workers is now in full swing. Longshoremen, seamen, teamsters, warehousemen, launch and tugboatmen, and other bay, river and harbor workers are joining
in one big federation taking in every port of the Pacific Coast.[39]

From his Washington office, Furuseth blasted the "incomprehensible
stupidity" of the West Coast seamen and lamented that the "work of years and
years is going into the wast[e]-basket." But, he declared, "bad as things look
on the Pacific, there might be some hope of saving the remnants, if I could go
out there for a couple of weeks." He returned to San Francisco in late July
determined to end the strike and destroy Thompson's influence. At a dramatic
mass meeting in the civic auditorium, in preparation for which his lieutenants
scoured the city searching for sailors and ex-sailors loyal to the Old Man,
Furuseth's charisma prevailed. He succeeded in pushing through a vote to end
the strike and a resolution repudiating the Federation of Marine Transport
Workers. In the vote to terminate the strike, he was aided by the fact that after
nearly three months, the marine engineers had returned to work, scabs were
manning more and more vessels, and there was clearly no prospect of victory
for the seamen. The resolution repudiating the marine federation, however,
seems to have been the result mainly of a demagogic attack on Thompson and
other advocates of maritime unity. West described how "with arms upraised,
the gaunt old viking cried out the names of the men who had died or gone to
jail for the cause, and evoked their curse on those whom he branded as
traitors." Placing all his prestige on the line, Furuseth equated the marine
federation with the IWW and asked the membership to choose between
Thompson and himself. In this situation, the sailors were not ready to
repudiate the legendary figure whose name remained synonymous with
seafaring unionism.[40]

Furuseth was not satisfied with this victory, for several reasons. First,
Thompson was still the editor of the *Seamen's Journal,* and he displayed no
sign of fear or repentance in the face of the ISU president's ongoing campaign
of vilification. Second, among the membership of the SUP, there remained a
significant ground swell of opposition to Old Andy and his policies. The *San
Francisco Chronicle* reported that hundreds of men protested his dictatorial
methods at a headquarters meeting in early September. According to the
Chronicle, Furuseth delivered a "bitter denunciation of reds, radicals, and
I.W.W.'s" in the face of "heckling and . . . jeers which at times were almost
deafening." When he insisted on adjourning the meeting immediately after his
speech, "pandemonium broke out," and police were called to protect the
union president from the angry membership.

Finally, to head off the waterfront employers, who had announced a plan to
reestablish hiring halls and the hated fink books, Furuseth approached the
shipowners and declared: "If you will give me sixty days I'll clean out the
union. If you will agree not to establish any more shipping offices and not to

establish any grade book, or black-listing book, I will clean out the I.W.W. from the union." The employers agreed, and immediately Furuseth went to the Sailors' Union armed with a plan to muzzle Thompson. He introduced a resolution declaring that *"The Seamen's Journal* has for some considerable time advocated the ideas of the I.W.W., the Marine Transport Workers' Industrial Union No. 510, which is a section of the I.W.W., and of the One Big Union, which is only another name for the I.W.W." The resolution instructed Thompson to "cease all such propaganda in the *Journal* at once." When the editor refused to retreat from his principles, Furuseth had him and about thirty of his closest sympathizers expelled from the union.[41]

It is important to pause for a moment to take a closer look at J. Vance Thompson, whose career reveals the power of the syndicalist impulse at this historical moment and the utter lack of truth in Furuseth's accusation that Thompson was an IWW conspirator. Thompson's background is obscure. In 1921, when West described him as "a middle-aged man of English birth," he had been a member of the ISU for more than twenty years. During that time he had served a brief term as editor of the *Seamen's Journal* in 1900, and as a delegate from the Alaska Fishermen's Union, he attended six ISU conventions between 1914 and 1920. For most of these years he was employed as an investigator for California's Commission of Immigration and Housing, which was formed in the wake of the Wheatland hop fields riot of 1913. In this capacity, he associated with a number of the West Coast's leading Progressives, including the outspoken intellectual Carleton Parker, who was the commission's first director. In the summer of 1914, Parker launched a covert campaign of spying on the Wobblies, whom he regarded with sympathy as reflections of an irrational industrial system and with reluctant hostility as incorrigible foes of labor peace in California's agricultural districts. Commission investigators, including Thompson, were ordered to "jungle" with the Wobs in order to collect information on their activities. At least two years before the Justice Department's massive crackdown on the IWW in 1917, the California commission was secretly advocating federal suppression of the organization, and reports such as those submitted by Thompson were eventually used as evidence to justify the federal government's action.[42]

Thompson's letters from the field in 1916 and 1917 indicate that he viewed the Wobblies as a threat to national security and to the labor movement. His thinking was tinged with racism, an obsession with "preparedness," and a fear of sabotage. In other words, on these issues, his ideas were exactly opposite those of the IWW. One letter, in particular, argued that the Japanese and "the large Mexican population in the southern end [of the state] . . . constitute a menace which is worthy of observance." He warned that during some growing seasons "the Japanese greatly outnumber the whites" in certain areas and "are in a position to mobilize much faster than the white population."

Moreover, on some ranches where whites, Mexicans, and Japanese were employed, "the Japanese and Mexicans mingle and fraternize perfectly, and neither have any particular love or respect for the white laborers." He concluded by saying that "the present unsettled world conditions, and our own unpreparedness, gives the situation in California a serious aspect; *especially if considered in connection with I.W.W. preachments and plots.*"[43]

Other letters dealt more directly with IWW activity in the labor movement and on the waterfront in particular. Even during his tenure as an investigator for the Commission of Immigration and Housing, Thompson continued to chair the regular meetings of the Alaska Fishermen's Union in San Francisco, and he described the efforts of Wobbly "missionaries" from Puget Sound ports to "capture" this ISU affiliate for the IWW. He warned that several unions were "seriously menaced by this dual organization," and concluded: "As an organization the IWW are not growing fast but their propaganda and their ability to grasp opportunities to spread the same is having serious effect amongst our submerged element." By July 1917 he had become convinced that "the psychology of the I.W.W. is more destructive to American institutions than ever before," and he accused the "agitators and radical I.W.W.s" of "treason."[44]

This, then, was the man whom Andrew Furuseth hounded out of the Sailors' Union on the charge that he was an agent of the IWW—one who had spent several years spying on the Wobblies and aiding government efforts to destroy their organization. But clearly by 1921 he had been deeply affected by the ferment of war, upheaval, and revolution. The syndicalist excitement that had convulsed the industrial world from Turin to Seattle to Sydney had also taken hold of J. Vance Thompson. In 1917 he had warned that the Wobblies would sooner or later have to be reckoned with. However, as he watched the employers destroy the longshoremen's organization up and down the Pacific Coast, and as he witnessed the shipowners' attempt to break the seamen's unions in 1921, Thompson came to believe that there was a far more dangerous enemy afoot than the Wobblies. He warned of the "capitalistic aggressions" of the "super trusts," whose continued advance "must inevitably result in group slavery for the masses." "The attacks of these predatory combinations upon the workers are of such vicious and determined nature," he said, "that the present system of trade unions has been rendered ineffective as a protection." He deplored the "obstinate stupidity" of the AFL leaders who "stubbornly cling to the obsolete system of craft unionism," and expressed the hope that their kind would soon become "extinct."[45]

Although Thompson generally stopped short of advocating One Big Union, he was caught up in the fervor of the times, and on occasion he adopted the apocalyptic vision of the syndicalists as his own. He once wrote in the *Seamen's Journal* that "we must affiliate with the transport workers in all parts of the world. . . . With our representatives in every port of the world, and perfect solidarity among the workers, our right to a voice in industry can be asserted. Our power . . . lies in organization, which must include a consolidation of all the workers in one industry, and all the industries together in one federation." Moreover, far more than his predecessors, Thompson opened the pages of the *Journal* to the seamen, and the advocates of One Big Union took advantage of the invitation to voice their ideas. Letters poured in attacking Furuseth's sacred craft principles as antiquated and calling for the formation of *"One Big Labor Alliance the world over."* [46]

But Thompson himself never endorsed or in any way encouraged the activities of the IWW. The spirit of syndicalism reached far beyond the IWW's limited range of influence, and many who regarded the Wobblies as sectarian and destructive nonetheless reflected the syndicalist tendencies that were so widespread in the era of the New Unionism. According to West, the impetus for the Federation of Marine Transport Workers in 1921 came from "unionists in search of a middle ground between the irreconcilable craft unionism of the A.F. of L. and the industrial unionism of the I.W.W." Thompson himself told West that he viewed the marine federation as "a concession for holding the men, for keeping them out of the I.W.W., for meeting the spirit of inclusive brotherhood among them." In evaluating Furuseth's charges against Thompson, ISU Vice President Gill later acknowledged that "many [union] members have subsequently stated that they do not believe Thompson was ever a member of the I.W.W." [47]

Thompson's expulsion from the union marked the end of his long career in the ISU, but it hardly suppressed the syndicalist impulse among the seamen, which continued to erupt for several years. The IWW's Marine Transport Workers Local 510 (MTW) had never made much headway on the West Coast, but in the wake of the 1921 strike's disastrous conclusion and Furuseth's vendetta against his critics, large numbers of seamen and longshoremen left the AFL unions to join the Wobblies. Ken Austin, who first joined the MTW in 1921, recalled that in the Puget Sound lumber ports it seemed that "everybody belonged to it." Harry Bridges, who joined the IWW briefly after the failure of the 1921 strike, remembered that the Wobs were "very strong on the steam schooners" in the early twenties. On the East Coast, one observer estimated that about half of the ISU's membership just plain quit the union, and that another 25 percent joined the IWW. A year after Furuseth's pledge to "clean out the I.W.W. from the union," the Wobbly newspaper reported that the Marine Transport Workers were booming. *Industrial Solidarity* suggested that "we ought to try and get the harvest workers and the construction workers to go into the marine industry when their work is done. The M.T.W. needs more wobblies in it. The craft unionists have come to it in droves. They need to associate with some of the older members of the I.W.W. . . . . Let's try and swing the harvest stiff to the sea." [48]

The port of San Pedro emerged as the main IWW stronghold in the maritime industry. Longshoremen, seamen, and fishermen joined the MTW, and, according to Weintraub, IWW job delegates "kept San Pedro in a continuous state of turmoil" with quickie strikes and other job actions. One observer later recalled that on San Pedro's Liberty Hill a big sign that read "Join the IWW" was clearly visible to seamen as their ships entered the port.[49]

Given the obstacles to unionism of any kind in the early 1920s, the Wobbly resurgence is all the more remarkable. Nowhere was the "return to normalcy" pursued with more zeal than in California, where business worshipped with evangelical fervor at the shrine of the open shop. The Golden State had passed a criminal syndicalism law in 1919, and the Wobblies claimed that under this statute "mere membership in the Industrial Workers of the World" was sufficient grounds for a prison sentence of from one to fourteen years. By the end of 1922 the police were making mass arrests at the IWW hall in San Pedro; a steady stream of Wobs was heading for San Quentin prison; and, in the spirit of the old free-speech fights, the IWW was calling on its members to drop everything and man the battle lines in San Pedro.[50]

In April 1923 the Wobblies called a general strike that received significant support among marine, lumber, oil, and some construction workers on the Pacific Coast. The principal demand was for the "release of class-war prisoners." In addition, each industry raised its own economic demands. In San Pedro, the strike took on many of the dimensions of the IWW's great strikes of the past, with massive picket lines and marches; a festive spirit continually reinforced by songs, skits, and mass meetings; and, of course, a heavy dose of repression by local authorities. There were more than seven hundred arrests, with strikers detained in temporary stockades, or "bull-pens," along the waterfront. When Upton Sinclair attempted to read the Bill of Rights on Liberty Hill, which was private property owned by a strike sympathizer, the Los Angeles police chief told him that " 'this Constitution stuff' does not go at the Harbor" and had him arrested. A restaurant proprietor was "dragged out from behind his counter and jailed for feeding the strikers"; the charge against him: "prolonging the strike."[51]

When the conflict erupted on April 26, Furuseth predicted that the IWW wouldn't succeed in tying up a single steam schooner on the Pacific Coast. Within a few days, however, ninety ships lay idle in San Pedro harbor. Although there may have been as few as two hundred and fifty Wobblies involved, the estimated number of strikers ranged from fifteen hundred to more than three thousand. West claimed that three thousand longshoremen were on strike, with significant numbers of seamen and other harbor workers also participating. The great southern California building boom was threatened with paralysis, because virtually its entire lumber supply arrived by water. According to West, "Hundreds of millions of feet of lumber lay immobile on the decks of steam-schooners from Washington and Oregon that crowded every berth and lay anchored in the outer harbor."[52]

But in spite of this "joyous demonstration of power," the forces arrayed against the strikers gradually prevailed. After about a month on the picket lines, a mass meeting of six hundred men voted to transfer the strike back to the job. The criminal syndicalism convictions continued to deprive the IWW of its most dedicated organizers and strike leaders, and the stiff prison terms of from one to fourteen years proved a far more effective deterrent to activism than the old thirty-day misdemeanor sentences of the free-speech fights. Moreover, vigilantes from the Ku Klux Klan and the American Legion conducted a series of raids on the IWW hall. Women and children were brutalized. Organizers were kidnapped and then tarred and feathered. The name of San Pedro soon became a synonym for repression and violence—the open shop propped up by the mailed fist. Coupled with the general decline in the fortunes of the maritime industry in the early twenties, and the historic weaknesses of the IWW as an organization, repression reduced the once proud Marine Transport Workers Union to rubble. Furuseth's constant accusations that it was honeycombed with provocateurs could perhaps be marked off to his extreme bias, except for the fact that Harry Bridges suspected the same thing during his brief membership in the MTW in 1921. In any case, the organization became little more than a memory preserved by a few isolated delegates and a way station for militant seamen who would one day enter the Communist party and its Marine Workers Industrial Union. In January 1925 the IWW newspaper declared mournfully, "All the so-called active delegates left San Pedro and . . . No one is willing to take over the branch. San Pedro has to be rebuilt—that's all."[53]

The Wobblies were the most consistent and aggressive advocates of syndicalism among the maritime workers. But as we have seen in the case of J. Vance Thompson and the quest for a marine federation, the syndicalist impulse among longshoremen and seamen always exceeded the limited membership and influence of the IWW. First and foremost, it was rooted in the maritime workers' conditions of life and work. But particularly on the West Coast there were other forces that touched the marine workers' lives, strengthening both the mood and doctrine of syndicalism on the waterfront. One of these forces was the Northwest lumber industry and its work force. The ties between lumber and marine workers were very close. Ken Austin, who grew up in the Grays Harbor and Puget Sound areas, declared that "the whole area was nothing but sawmills and steam schooners. . . . A lot of guys would go from steam schooners to longshoring to the woods," and back again. Although this pattern of work was possible mainly in the Northwest, more than half of the Pacific Coast seamen were employed in the steam schooner trade whose source was the lumber industry of northern California,

Oregon, and Washington. Thus they had frequent contact with the distinctive subculture of life and work in the logging ports. The legendary transiency of the seamen certainly reinforced this contact. Herman "Dutch" Thomas, who began sailing in 1913 at the age of thirteen, recalled that a great many deserters from the foreign flag ships "wound up in the woods on the West Coast, and in the fisheries. They got to know the bindle stiffs and drifted with them all over the country and Canada." Ken Austin, who was a member of the IWW and the SUP for many years, was the son of an Alaska gold prospecter. He was first employed in sawmills and box factories in the Grays Harbor area, and after a stint in the U.S. Navy he worked alternately on the docks, in the logging camps, and aboard steam schooners and other vessels from 1921 until the late thirties. Among the longshoremen, anthropologist William Pilcher found in his study of Portland dockworkers that "many loggers and sawmill workers, tiring of their vagabond life, settled in the city. The loggers' skills were not useful in every trade, but they were certainly useful on the waterfront where much of the cargo shipped out of the port consisted of logs and lumber products. Loggers were also familiar with rigging and gear of much the same type used on ships. Thus, there have always been many ex-loggers among the Portland longshoremen."[54]

The significance of the close contact between these two groups of workers lies in the similarity of their conditions and the impulses that derived from these conditions. Like the maritime workers, the "timber beasts" and "sawmill savages" faced an isolated and oppressive existence. One reporter characterized shingle weaving in the sawmills as more a battle than a trade. "For ten hours a day the sawyer faces two teethed steel disks whirling around 200 times a minute." Eventually, "if 'cedar asthma' . . . does not get him, the steel will." As for the loggers, they lived in far-flung camps where the employers practiced a form of industrial feudalism characteristic of the extractive industries. The typical bunkhouse sheltered between twenty and fifty men. Harvey O'Connor, a former logger, recalled the "'muzzle-loading' bunks where men crept in at the foot of the bunk and inched forward." Tom Scribner, whose career as a lumberjack began in 1914, remembered that "in the winter of 1914–15 I saw 150 men living in one bunk house in Northern Minnesota. Shower baths were . . . unheard of. Can you imagine the stench of 150 pairs of socks hung up to dry around the bunk house stove[?] These bunk houses were vermin infested and the 'Jacks would boil up their clothes on Sunday, and if the weather was fit, would burn sulphur in the bunk house to kill the vermin."[55]

These conditions created a pattern of long periods of intense work coupled with short bursts of debauched social life reminiscent of the seamen's experience. The loggers' "skid road" shared many characteristics of the sailortown, and the lumber workers' rootlessness rivalled that of the seafarers. The "timber beasts" were often characterized as "homeless, womanless, and voteless." Murray Morgan described the logger as "a man apart, strange even to the millworkers," and declared that the typical logging camp had "three crews—one coming in, one on the job, one going out."[56]

Here, then, was the same raw exploitation, the same isolation from the integrative institutions of the American mainstream, the same restless transiency that gave rise to the mood of syndicalism among the maritime workers. Not surprisingly, the IWW maintained a highly visible presence among the loggers of the Northwest, and some of the industry's pioneer activists credit the Wobblies with a major contribution to the improvement of conditions in the sawmills and logging camps during the era of the New Unionism.[57]

The lumber industry and its tradition of militant unionism contributed a number of important leaders and activists to the maritime unions in the 1930s. Carl "Shingles" Tillman, a former logger and shingle weaver from Coos Bay, Oregon, was a major spokesman for the syndicalists in the Sailors' Union in the mid-thirties. Likewise, William Fischer, a former IWW organizer in the Northwest woods, was a leader of the Portland longshoremen who became president of the Maritime Federation of the Pacific in 1936 and promptly aligned himself with its syndicalist elements. Ken Austin, the itinerant worker who "never had a home port," went from the MTW to the Marine Workers Industrial Union to the SUP, where he was an active ally of Harry Bridges and the Communists. Among the Portland longshoremen, William Pilcher found that in the 1930s "the most active and influential members of the local were the men of IWW persuasion and background," and he called the ex-loggers "one of the chief sources of the left wing ideology that so permeates the union."[58]

Another factor that strengthened the doctrine and the mood of syndicalism among the marine workers on the West Coast was their relationship with the maritime workers of Australia. The Australian Seamen's Union and the Waterside Workers' Federation of Australia were both strong organizations with long-standing traditions of militancy. Both played a major role in the greatest eruption in the history of Australian labor, the general strike of 1917. Moreover, socialists, syndicalists, and Communists were a vocal—and sometimes leading—force in both unions. The Great Strike was in many ways typical of the era of the New Unionism in that it represented a sharp break with several well-established patterns of Australian labor development. For the decade and a half preceding the strike, the trade unions had relied mainly on a system of arbitration to resolve industrial disputes, and an Australian Labor party had won widespread acceptance as the electoral voice of the working class. During World War I, however, economic dislocation and a bitterly divisive referendum on the question of conscription caused a crisis of legitimacy for both of these institutions. The trade union leadership often found itself at odds with an increasingly assertive rank and file, and the Australian branch of the IWW played a spectacular role in dramatizing the major issues facing the nation's workers and in spreading the slogans of "industrial unionism" and "direct action."

In August 1917, a walkout by railroad workers quickly escalated into a general strike. The seamen, longshoremen, and coal miners were the first to come to the aid of the railwaymen, and the number of strikers eventually reached ninety-five thousand. The government loudly proclaimed that "at the back of this strike lurk the I.W.W. and the exponents of direct action." The prime minister charged that the strike was an example of "the uprearing of syndicalism, naked and unashamed." He was right, but not with regard to the Wobblies, who played a negligible role in the conflict. As in the United States, repression had thinned their ranks, their energies were mainly consumed by legal battles on behalf of the rising number of IWW "class war prisoners," and they were openly critical of the manner in which the general strike unfolded. As the Wobblies pointed out with disdain, it was from the very beginning a spontaneous uprising that defied the union leadership's efforts to control and limit its direction. As one trade union official acknowledged, "The difficulty was not in getting men to come out, but to keep them in." Another declared, "This revolt against governmental tyranny is a spontaneous manifestation of feeling. The men took matters into their own hands. The officers had nothing to do but voice the demands of the rank and file. . . . With a passion for class loyalty as grand as unparalleled they took the field and swept to battle."[59]

The strike lasted eighty-two days (one less than the great West Coast maritime strike of 1934 in the United States). It was ultimately smashed by the combined efforts of the government and the employers, who spared no effort in mobilizing scabs from among the ranks of businessmen, farmers, students, and ex-soldiers. In addition to recruiting ten thousand strikebreakers, the government assisted in the formation of loyalist unions whose members were later given priority in employment over regular trade unionists. A number of union officials, including leaders of the longshoremen and seamen, were arrested on conspiracy charges, and thousands of workers were blacklisted when the strike was over. However, even though their defeat was total, many rank and filers returned to work with a remarkable spirit of anger and defiance. One historian has noted the wave of disgust with arbitration, electoral politics, and capitalism that followed in the wake of the strike. This feeling was intensified by the news from Russia and by the constant confrontation with the loyalists on the job.[60]

Out of this combination of circumstances, a One Big Union movement gained momentum among many sections of the workers and continued into the early twenties. Although this movement was largely independent of the moribund IWW, it reflected the mood of syndicalism that was so widespread at this historical moment. Many of the self-conscious syndicalists eventually lined up with the Australian Communist party, but "a certain temper"—

militant, irreverent, "on the job"—characteristic of the era of the New Unionism remained evident in some quarters for many years, especially among the
waterfront workers.[61]

The close contact between American and Australian maritime workers
made the lessons—and the mood—of 1917 that much more accessible to
American longshoremen and seamen. Membership books in the Australian
Seamen's Union and the Sailors' Union of the Pacific were interchangeable,
and a young Australian seaman named Harry Bridges routinely transferred his
membership to the SUP when he arrived in San Francisco in April 1920. A
number of American shipping lines made regular runs to Australian ports, and
there were persistent rumors that major West Coast shippers such as the
Matson line carried union crews on these voyages during the open-shop years
from 1921 to 1934 only because the Australian longshoremen made a practice
of slowing down on the job when dealing with nonunion vessels. Australian
maritime workers enthusiastically supported their American comrades during
the 1934 strike. Likewise, Americans on the West Coast displayed a keen
interest in the affairs of their fellow marine workers down under. As late as
November 1935, a Maritime Federation of the Pacific convention witnessed a
spirited debate on whether arbitration or "dis-organized strikes" had had a
more negative impact on the development of the Australian labor
movement.[62]

Harry Bridges was the foremost Pacific Coast unionist to emerge from the
Australian crucible, and he frequently referred to the importance of that
experience in shaping his ideas about unionism and "the class struggle." As he
put it during the first of four U.S. government inquisitions on his relationship
to the Communist party, "I have been a member of a trade union since 1916.
There was no Communist Party in 1916, and a lot of my views on trade
unionism I had before there was ever a Communist Party. The labor movement in Australia is a pretty old one, and was a pretty militant and progressive
one, and I learned a few things there that maybe came in handy later."

Although overshadowed by Bridges, other Aussies also left their mark on
West Coast maritime unionism. Longshoreman Henry Schrimpf became a
leader of the rank-and-file movement in the ILA. He was a member of the
Communist party in the mid-thirties but soon left the Party and sided with the
syndicalist element in the Maritime Federation of the Pacific. H. M. Bright,
an Aussie seaman, was a spokesman for syndicalism and international solidarity within the Sailors' Union of the Pacific. Al Quittenton, another Aussie
seaman, became a leader of the resurgent SUP after the 1934 strike. Unlike
Bright, he sided with Bridges and the Communists on many of the issues
facing the maritime workers.[63]

Although the question of ideological transmission among masses of workers remains a difficult and elusive one, it seems clear that the West Coast
maritime workers' close ties with the lumber industry in the Pacific Northwest

and with the Australian labor movement helped to reinforce the syndicalist impulse in their ranks. If this impulse derived first and foremost from their own conditions, it was deepened by the influence of others who shared much in the way of experience and outlook.

Repression played a major role in quenching the fires of syndicalist unionism, but the "golden twenties" were to prove equally inhospitable to the craft unionism of Andrew Furuseth. In the bitter aftermath of the 1921 strike, the extent of the ISU's decline was phenomenal. According to Joseph Goldberg, the seamen's unions were "laid low as if by a tidal wave." Weintraub observed that "the members melted away, vanished, disappeared." Membership fell from the peak of a hundred and fifteen thousand in 1920 to sixteen thousand in 1923, and Goldberg estimated that the number declined to five thousand during the depths of the Great Depression.[64]

In part because white-shirt sailors like Macarthur, Olander, and Scharrenberg were preoccupied with responsibilities outside the ISU, leadership of the union increasingly fell to men who were timeservers or petty grafters, or both. Olander agreed to take the job of secretary-treasurer as a personal favor to Furuseth only after the previous occupant of the position had disappeared with $4,000 in union funds. Although this spectacular instance of graft was exceptional, an aura of corruption and incompetence was to pervade the union for the remainder of its existence. For example, the Marine Cooks and Stewards' affiliate on the Atlantic and Gulf coasts became the fiefdom of its flamboyant president, "Emperor" David Grange, a West Indian who sported spats on his shoes, a red rose in his lapel, and a gun in his shoulder holster. He seldom called union meetings—one rank and filer claimed that there had been only three in a five-year-period—and when he did, Grange showed little patience with the formalities of democratic procedure. The Emperor once bragged that his means of dealing with opposition from the floor was to shove a gun in the offender's guts "and beat his head in."

The lower echelon ISU officials in each port were generally appointed from among the group that Charlie Rubin has termed the "pinochle hounds" and "palace guards" who hung around the hall and attended union meetings during the years when no one else bothered to come around. For the most favored among these loyalists, the payoff was a delegate's position, with the responsibility to visit incoming ships and collect dues. In more than a few cases, these men had long-standing reputations as bullies and petty crooks. One seaman characterized them as "nothing but a bunch of small time . . . racketeers." And labor historian Philip Taft, citing "information from a former official of the I.S.U.," acknowledged that some of the delegates "were lax in their duties, spending most of their time outside the office visiting the 'bookie parlors' and other waterfront resorts."[65]

In 1929 the ISU's financial crisis reached the point where the union was forced to accept a donation from the British seamen's union in order to stay afloat. In 1930 ten delegates assembled in Washington, D.C., for what was to be the union's last convention until the fateful year of 1936. There they listened to Furuseth's sorrowful acknowledgment that "as it now stands, there can be neither collective nor individual bargaining. Collective bargaining is only possible when we have enough men in the Union, and in the right temper to become seriously effective with owners who refuse to meet us; and individual bargaining is not possible in a shipowner's shipping office, where he sets the wages and determines the condition, not only of shipping and wages, but of nearly all else, through the blacklist."[66]

Any discussion of union weakness in the 1920s must also take account of the power of the waterfront employers, who were able to exercise nearly complete dominance in maritime labor relations between 1921 and 1934. The employers' hegemony can be viewed from at least three angles. First, it was part of a broader, nationwide offensive against unionism under the banner of the "American Plan." Second, it was made possible by the shipowners' relationship to a wider network of power and influence that dwarfed the meager resources available to the marine unions. And third, it was a response to the economic circumstances of the maritime industry, which were anything but golden. Shipping's status as a "sick industry" seemed to require a major assault on marine workers' wages, working conditions, and finally, the very presence of unionism. Ironically, however, the great success of the employers was to be their undoing. For the more effective their power, and the more ruthless their dominance, the more sustained and explosive would be the maritime workers' counteroffensive when the tide of history shifted in their favor.[67]

The U.S. Maritime Commission declared in 1937 that "shipping has been . . . a sick industry for many years." Ironically, a major source of long-term decline was the extraordinary expansion of waterborne commerce during and immediately after World War I. In 1914 ships of other nations carried more than 90 percent of American cargoes destined for foreign ports. Between 1917 and 1922, however, the United States built 2,316 vessels and emerged as one of the foremost shipping powers in the world. When the worldwide increase in shipping tonnage was matched by a sharp postwar decline in the volume of world trade, a chronic problem of surplus carrying capacity developed. Shipowners around the globe responded with a surge of cutthroat competition. Because U.S. wage rates were considerably higher than those of other countries, American operators in the overseas trade found themselves at a severe disadvantage. While American vessels in the coastwise and intercoastal trade were protected by law from foreign competition, they too faced serious problems due to excess capacity and growing competition from rail and truck transportation.[68]

The difficulties confronting virtually all American operators were magnified by the character of the U.S. shipping industry, which was highly decentralized and "individualistic." It had no equivalent of U.S. Steel or General Motors to create order out of chaos by imposing stable rates. There were frequent attempts at cooperation, through conferences of shipowners engaged in each major trade route. But invariably some company or other would seek to enhance its position by lowering rates, and the fragile cooperative structure, or "conference system," would collapse. Thus, cutthroat competition remained the norm, and slashing labor costs became the principal means of achieving a competitive advantage.[69]

Surveying the chaotically diverse U.S. merchant marine in 1937, *Fortune* pronounced it "easier to malign than to define." "It operates a slow and aged fleet; it has attracted little capital and not much first-class gray matter; its total tonnage on the seas has declined annually since 1922; it cannot support itself, but it contributes to the worldwide oversupply of tonnage." However, as *Fortune* acknowledged, there was a good deal more to the shipping industry than chaos and chronic depression. It was indeed possible to prosper in the world of waterborne commerce—as an account of the evolution of the Dollar and Matson steamship companies will demonstrate—through some combination of ruthless competition and innovative management, and, above all, with the aid of government subsidies. The federal government spent almost $3.5 billion on the shipping industry between 1914 and 1937. These subsidies took a number of forms: government funding of the cost of building ships (outright grants during the war, generous loans thereafter); the sale of government vessels to private companies at bargain-basement prices; and the notorious mail subsidies, which averaged $26 million annually after 1928. Mail subsidies made it possible to carry general cargo overseas at rates that would not otherwise have been profitable; and with such incentives U.S. shipowners ventured boldly into areas of the Pacific that had long been dominated by British and other European carriers.[70]

Robert Dollar was a Scotsman whose life story is etched in the classic lines of the American rags-to-riches mythology. After his family migrated from Scotland to Canada, he worked in lumber camps by day and studied "writing and figures" at night. Eventually, Dollar moved to northern Michigan, where he used his energy and skill to accumulate twenty thousand acres of timberland. The sale of this property financed his move to California, where he prospered in lumber and shipping. After expanding from the coastwise to the overseas trade, Dollar purchased seven vessels from the U.S. Shipping Board in 1923, at a fraction of their original cost. Two years later he added five more. Again the government's terms were generous and mail subsidies made it possible for the old man (who was now past eighty) to launch round-the-world freight and passenger service. Gradually, Dollar developed "the largest fleet carrying the American flag."

The Matson Navigation Company was built upon a similar foundation of restless ambition. But unlike Robert Dollar, whose enterprise evolved from land to sea, William Matson's empire developed from the sea to the land, notably the rich Hawaiian Islands, where "Captain Bill" developed close ties with some of the most powerful business interests on the Pacific rim of the United States. Born in Sweden, Matson first went to sea at the age of ten and sailed to New York at fourteen. Four years later he arrived in San Francisco and gradually worked his way up to master of a lumber schooner. He caught the attention of sugar magnate Claus Spreckels, who enticed him into the Hawaiian sugar trade, where he made a fortune. Its basis, of course, was shipping, but he also invested heavily in California oil fields, Hawaiian sugar plantations and hotels, and a mutually beneficial relationship with Alexander and Baldwin, Castle and Cook, and other kingpins of the Hawaiian economy. By the 1930s the Hawaii carrying trade would account for only 27 percent of Matson's $44.7 million in gross assets. Meanwhile, Captain Bill's son-in-law, William P. Roth, expanded the company's freight and passenger service into the South Pacific, with generous federal assistance that included over a million dollars a year in mail subsidies.[71]

The "sick" and "depressed" shipping industry not only gave birth to profitable offspring; it also adopted some of the largest and most powerful corporations in the nation—Standard Oil and U.S. Steel, for example—which developed their own specialized fleets and became major employers of maritime labor. And yet even the healthiest of these enterprises joined with struggling and marginal companies in declaring that shipping's highly competitive rate structure made it necessary to slash seafaring wages. Andrew Furuseth's rejoinder that "the wage cost is now about the smallest item of cost in the operation of a vessel" was only a slight exaggeration. Careful estimates in 1924 and 1937 found that wages constituted 12 percent of operating costs in the former year and 14 percent in the latter. But since labor costs were the only ones that could be reduced substantially, the employers decided that they must take full control of the labor market. The unions' determination to defend their wartime gains, along with the increasing radicalism of the syndicalist militants, only served to convince the shipowners that their quest for competitive advantage had become a great battle for fundamental American principles. The very presence of bona fide unions became an intolerable obstacle to their dream of "industrial freedom."[72]

"Individualistic" employers who were unable to cooperate in the setting of cargo rates found it eminently possible to unite for the purpose of containing—and ultimately destroying—unions on the waterfront. The first formal coastwide organization of employers of seamen was the Shipowners' Association of the Pacific Coast, founded in 1904. Its ranks included most of the firms engaged in the steam schooner trade, many of which were owned by or closely associated with the West Coast lumber companies. In 1919 the

Pacific American Steamship Association was formed. It embraced virtually all West Coast operators, including the steam schooner owners, the oil companies, and major overseas carriers such as Dollar, Matson, and American-Hawaiian. But the pacesetter in the offensive against unionism was the Waterfront Employers' Union of San Francisco, which included steamship and stevedoring companies that hired longshore labor. It was this association that threw down the gauntlet to the Riggers and Stevedores' Union in 1919, declaring its refusal to deal with "any organization having an avowed or latent purpose of radicalism, Bolshevism or anarchy"—in fact, any organization that would "do or say anything against the principles of Americanism." After crushing the Riggers and Stevedores and establishing a company union in its place, the Waterfront Employers' Union joined forces with the two shipowners' associations to break the seamen's unions in 1921.[73]

This power was all the more devastating because it extended far beyond the waterfront. The shipping and stevedoring companies were part of a vast network that included multi-industry employer associations, major newspapers, police departments, the American Legion, and a host of lesser groups that could be mobilized to battle unionism and "Bolshevism" in the name of "100 percent Americanism" and civic pride. By far the greatest of these forces were two regional employer organizations, the Merchants' and Manufacturers' Association of Los Angeles and the Industrial Association of San Francisco. The former, founded in 1896, commanded the allegiance of 80 to 85 percent of the city's large firms in its relentless campaign against union power. The Industrial Association, founded in 1921, was a leading example of the so-called American Plan. Drawing effectively on the wellsprings of patriotism and the propaganda techniques unleashed during World War I, major employers directed a nationwide campaign that purported to eliminate the "un-American" closed shop but really sought to undermine unionism altogether. In Irving Bernstein's words, "Old Glory had been draped over the gun barrel." And with devastating effect. In a few years' time, the union movement lost nearly a million and a half members.[74]

The Industrial Association spearheaded the antiunion drive in San Francisco and northern California. It enrolled about a thousand member companies, including such giants as the Southern Pacific Railroad, Standard Oil of California, Pacific Gas and Electric, California and Hawaiian Sugar, Firemen's Fund Insurance, and Crocker National Bank. Members paid annual dues and contributed nearly $5 million in emergency funds between 1921 and 1934. During the great strike of 1934 the Industrial Association not only supported the shipowners; it ultimately controlled and directed their activities in accordance with its own perception of the interests of the area's business community. A U.S. Senate investigating committee characterized the organization as "an example par excellence of . . . success in denying labor its collective-bargaining rights."

The employers' campaign for the open shop succeeded not only on the waterfront but in many uptown industries as well. Labor had once held "undisputed sway" in San Francisco. It could claim two robust power centers, each with its own newspaper and separate Labor Day parade; two hundred and fifty local unions and more than thirty thousand unionists by 1904. But the Industrial Association succeeded in bringing even the powerful building-trades unions to heel. Then, to maintain the open shop in construction, it established an elaborate apparatus that included apprenticeship schools, an employment agency, and a permit system for the purchase of building materials as far away as Los Angeles and Salt Lake City. Predictably, construction wage levels in San Francisco, which had been among the highest in the country, declined until by 1930 they were among the nation's lowest for cities of comparable size. Meanwhile, the Industrial Association's monthly organ, the *American Plan,* was able to brag in 1923 that "three years ago over 90 per cent [of the city's manual laborers] worked under absolutely closed shop union conditions. To-day over 85 per cent work under open shop conditions." As Ira B. Cross put it, "the results of the efforts and sacrifices of scores of leaders and thousands of union members were swept into the discard." But for those citizens at the apex of the social pyramid, San Francisco became—once again—"a metropolis of millionaires, free spenders, and fun."[75]

Conversely, for the maritime workers, in virtually every port, the twenties were lean years indeed. Immediately after the 1921 strike the shipowners followed through on their plan to slash wages and undermine conditions. The 1920 average monthly wage of eighty-six dollars for able-bodied seamen fell to forty-nine dollars by 1923. (Joseph Goldberg found that "in some cases able seamen were being paid as little as thirty dollars per month.") The general economic recovery after 1923 brought the average wage up to sixty-one dollars in 1924, and it fluctuated between sixty-one and fifty-nine dollars for the next seven years, until the Great Depression drove it to a new low of forty-seven dollars. Thus, even in the boom period of 1924–29, seamen's wages were twenty-five to twenty-seven dollars lower than they had been during the wartime and immediate postwar upsurge of organization. And—with the union powerless and the men disorganized—the twelve-hour day, cramped, vermin-infested quarters, and "rotten grub" once again became the norm in U.S. shipping. Moreover, most shipowners showed little interest in welfare capitalism, employee representation plans, and other paternalistic schemes that many of the large corporations devised to undermine unions and maintain loyalty and stability among their employees. On the contrary, maritime employers consciously sought to flood the waterfront with an over-supply of cheap, unskilled, and transient labor in order to justify and maintain the lowest possible wages and conditions.[76]

On the crucial issue of hiring, control once more reverted to the employers, even on the West Coast, where union preference had been in effect since

1906. After the 1921 strike, Pacific Coast shipowners began hiring through a Marine Service Bureau in San Francisco and San Pedro. (The government operated a parallel Sea Service Bureau for ships under its jurisdiction.) The head of the Marine Service Bureau was Walter J. Petersen, a former Oakland police captain. As spokesman for the shipowners, Petersen declared in 1925 that the bureau had been formed in order to "bring about a better order, to endeavor to change hatred into kindly consideration; to build a new condition of mutual respect between employer and men." Employing "the new tools of Brotherly Kindness and Consideration," he said, the Marine Service Bureau "acts in *loco parentis,* and as guide, philosopher, and friend for the seafaring fraternity."[77]

At times, however, Petersen was more candid about the role of his bureau. He told one interviewer, "I was hired during the 1921 strike to break Andy Furuseth's union and I broke it." On another occasion, after declaring that "we are trying to put the spirit of Jesus Christ" in the seamen, he admitted that "of course, you've got to put the fear of God in them, too." For this task, his police background served him well. One observer noted that "all those members of the Bureau staff who come in contact with seamen are possessed of police authority." They "are constantly armed with loaded pistols and occasionally with night-sticks and tear-gas guns."[78]

The seamen charged, with considerable support from outside observers, that the bureau, or fink hall as they called it, operated on the basis of favoritism and payoffs and that it consciously discriminated against union members. The mechanism that made systematic discrimination possible was the continuous discharge book, the infamous fink book, which featured a character rating by each employer for whom a seaman had worked. One notation about "agitator," "troublemaker," or "union man" was enough to blacklist a sailor for years. The seamen's deep hatred for these instruments of employer domination was to provide the rank-and-file upsurge of the mid-1930s with much of its explosive power. As Pete Gill stated, "In proportion as seamen were treated like slaves, herded through the fink halls, made to live under revolting conditions, worked like mules, and watched, spied upon and intimidated, so did their disgust for the conditions and their hatred for those who were responsible for the conditions grow."[79]

In 1922 an ISU official lamented the "sad state of affairs" in the union. "The only thing to do," he said, "is to go along the best we know how, until times improve." But when times did improve, in 1934, the fury of the Big Strike caught the ISU leadership entirely by surprise and served for the most part to widen the gap between the officials' hidebound conservatism and the growing militancy of the rank and file. The aging Furuseth, who was by now in his eighties, tended to denounce any and all who opposed him as "Communists," just as he had flayed earlier critics as agents of "I.W.W.ism."

In his imagination, the loyal union majority was perpetually at sea and therefore unable to assert itself against the alleged manipulators who were turning the seamen on the beach against him and his principles. The conclusive act in this drama came in 1936. At a time when militant seamen were pulling job actions up and down the Pacific Coast to force a better deal from the employers, Furuseth waged a final battle to preserve his unionism, even though it meant exorcising his union. Sadly, he recommended that the ISU convention expel his beloved SUP and charter a new union in its place, on the grounds that the Sailors' Union members were refusing to abide by the ISU constitution. To uphold his own conception of the seamen's interest, Furuseth was finally willing to engage in dual unionism, a practice that he had condemned for many years. Characteristically, he expressed complete confidence that the "loyal members of the Pacific" would heed his call once again. But almost to a man they turned their backs on Old Andy. Many denounced him as a traitor.

Furuseth "crossed the bar" in January 1938. It is perhaps ironic that he outlived the union that in many ways had become a mirror image of his principles and idiosyncracies. In the face of recurring waves of rank-and-file upsurge, the inept and myopic ISU officials continued to commit one blunder after another until, finally, the AFL shelved the International Seamen's Union in late 1937. According to Walter Galenson, "The demise of the ISU marked one of the few instances in recent history in which an established AFL union was driven out of business by a rebellious group." It is to the character and leadership of this rebellion that we now turn our attention.[80]

3

Red Unionism: The Communist Party and the Marine Workers Industrial Union

The Communist party played a major role in the maritime insurgency of the 1930s. Any discussion of that role must begin by focusing on the Atlantic Coast ports, because in the early thirties the Party concentrated most of its maritime cadres there and participated in a number of struggles that had an important bearing on the overall development of marine unionism. To be sure, the Party fell far short of its objective of building a viable revolutionary industrial union on the waterfront. But one cannot comprehend the subsequent history of maritime unionism without understanding the development of the Communist-led Marine Workers Industrial Union (MWIU).

In recent years a number of students have begun to transcend old categories of good and evil and to erect a new framework for the discussion of communism in the United States. The technique of narrow institutional narrative is giving way to a focus on the relationship between communism and particular communities and subcultures. The telescopic examination of the Soviet Union's hegemony in the Communist movement is yielding to a microscopic concern with the activity and consciousness of individual Party members. It is becoming clear that Communist activists at the grass roots brought their own aspirations and cultural baggage with them into the CP. As bearers of the Party line and program, they sometimes adjusted and reshaped that line to fit their own needs and circumstances. Of course, it would be wrong to underestimate the larger, unifying faith at the root of the Communist vision: the sense of participation in a worldwide army of the proletariat, with the Soviet Union as headquarters, beacon light, and guarantor of the embattled army's ultimate triumph. This certitude fueled the Party member's determination to persist in the teeth of overwhelming hardship; it also allowed the Soviet Union, the Communist International, and the national Party leadership to impose rigid constraints on the thought and behavior of individual Communists. However, in the real world beyond Communist theoretical journals and FBI reports, the Party was not a monolith. Its inner life was characterized by sharp disagreements at every level, especially in relation to the immediate issues that generally preoccupied its membership; and the independent initiative of Party cadres sometimes led to activity that was sharply at odds with the prevailing Communist line.

The Party's claim to revolutionary legitimacy and leadership was flawed by its slavish loyalty to the Soviet Union, the lack of genuine democracy in its internal life, and the arrogance and sectarianism that beset any self-appointed vanguard. But for better or worse, the Party inherited the mantle of American radicalism and increasingly it attracted members because of its vigorous pursuit of legitimate political goals and rational social objectives. Those who persist in viewing the organization only in terms of conspiracy and deviancy do a real injustice to the thousands of individuals who joined the Party because they saw it as the only viable instrument for the achievement of a humane and just social order.[1]

A significant number of seamen found a home in the Communist party. To some degree, the Party transformed their lives and reshaped them in its own image. But these men were also an active force and the bearers of a distinctive tradition. They gave the Party's Waterfront Section an inner dynamic that sometimes placed it in sharp contrast with the Communist apparatus uptown.

In spite of the widespread militancy among seamen and longshoremen in the early 1920s, and the long-standing reputation of maritime workers as a source of radical consciousness, the Communist party paid little attention to the waterfront until 1926. Late in that year the Party opened branches of the International Seamen's Club (ISC) in several American ports, in conjunction with the establishment of such organizations in port cities around the world. The *Seamen's Journal* characterized the ISC as "an international propaganda agency" whose purpose was "to make use of the world's seamen as the shock troops for communism." But in practice its goals seem to have been a good deal more modest. In New York, for instance, it opened quarters a few doors away from the Seamen's Church Institute and offered a place where seamen and "all marine workers" could come together and enjoy a library and reading room and an inexpensive lunch counter "without being looked upon as bums and . . . kept under the ever watchful eye of a cop." In addition to this social and educational role, the ISC declared that its chief principle was "organization," and its leadership encouraged seamen to agitate for a "class struggle program" within the ISU and the IWW.[2]

This approach was in accord with the policy that prevailed in the international Communist movement for most of the 1920s. But in the initial afterglow of the Bolshevik Revolution, Communists had expressed disdain for the long, slow road of "boring from within" the existing unions. In 1919 Lenin had declared: "The victory of the proletarian revolution on a world scale is assured"; and the Comintern had predicted that "the great International Soviet Republic will be born in the year 1920." The American Communist movement was born during this moment of limitless euphoria, and its initial policies sounded the same strident notes. It greeted the great strike wave of 1919, and the steelworkers' historic battle for union recognition, with the declaration that "every strike must be a small revolution, organizing, educating and disciplining the workers for the final revolutionary struggle." As for the existing unions, they were "the arch enemy of the militant proletariat." One of the announced tasks of the Communist party was "the destruction of the existing trades union organizations."

Since the membership of the fledgling Communist movement came largely from adherents of the IWW's policy of revolutionary industrial unionism (which in practice meant dual unionism), it is not surprising that the Party press initially expressed contempt for the AFL and a brash disdain for the economic demands of striking workers. (In New York City, subway trainmen on strike for a wage increase were lectured on the need for "armed insurrection, soviets, and the proletarian dictatorship.") But when the world revolution failed to materialize and Communist-led insurgencies suffered bloody defeat in several European countries, Lenin began to develop the outlines of a more cautious Communist strategy predicated on the postponement of revolutionary upheavals in the capitalist West. With particular force he condemned the "infantile disorder" of refusing to participate in "bourgeois parliaments" or to work in "reactionary trade unions." In 1921 American Communists reluctantly abandoned their "ultra-Left" enthusiasm for dual unionism and joined in condemning both "the policy of the revolutionary elements leaving the existing unions" and the IWW's long-standing practice of "artificially creating new industrial unions."[3]

However, in the late twenties events in the Soviet Union foreshadowed another radical change of direction. Stalin's relentless consolidation of his power, and his determination to steal the thunder of left-wing critics in the Soviet Communist party, set the stage for a new period in which the international Communist movement would once again embark upon a path of revolutionary posturing and dual unionism. The outlines of a new policy began to emerge in February 1928, when the Comintern called upon the American Communist party to organize trade unions "in those branches of industry where workers are not organized at all or [are] very inadequately organized," including the "water-transport" industry. A meeting of the Red International of Labor Unions a month later made this declaration more explicit, and the *Communist International* ridiculed the American Party for "dancing a quadrille" around the American Federation of Labor and overestimating "the importance of the Fascist A.F.L." William Z. Foster, whose name had long been synonymous with a policy of boring from within the established trade unions, was one of several American Party leaders who waged a bitter struggle against the emerging new line. But to no avail. Once he capitulated, Foster acknowledged what few others were prepared to admit, namely that "we are now entering upon a prolonged period of dual unionism." This policy was solidified and given its ideological grounding at the Sixth Congress of the Communist International in the summer of 1928. The Comintern announced the coming of the so-called Third Period, based upon the predicted end of "capitalist stabilization" and the beginning of "a new revolutionary upsurge."[4]

In the fall of 1928 the Party's maritime cadres launched the Marine Workers Progressive League and a monthly newspaper, the *Marine Workers Voice*. The *Voice* called upon "all seamen, longshoremen, and harbor boatmen to . . . build a fighting Marine Workers Union," an industrial organization that would compete openly with the existing unions for the maritime workers' allegiance. According to the *Voice,* "The seamen have about as much use for the I.S.U. as for an old water-logged hulk." Dismissing the idea of boring from within such a hulk as laughable, the *Voice* declared: "No militant seamen are going to waste their time capturing the Labor-fakers Snug Harbor." In the lumber ports of Washington's Olympic Peninsula, league organizers exhorted longshoremen to "smash the corrupt I.L.A.!" and boasted that they had successfully thwarted an organizing drive by the AFL union. As for the IWW, William Z. Foster characterized it as isolated and sectarian. (The *Voice* would soon dismiss the remnants of the IWW as "a few degenerate, spittoon philosophers.") Foster called upon marine workers to build a union "based upon the daily needs of the masses of workers, fighting on issues that the workers understand." However, his Third Period conception of issues that the workers understood was very broad indeed, for he told a meeting of the International Seamen's Club in New York that "the workers must rally to the defense of Soviet Russia, and when war comes they must turn their weapons against the war-makers, as the Russian workers did in 1917."[5]

Within a few months, the Marine Workers Progressive League shortened its name to the Marine Workers League (MWL), opened branches in every major port city, and aspired to become "a class struggle organization conducted as a Union." However, as the Wobblies had already discovered, the shipowners and their allies were not about to allow a revolutionary organization to function freely on the waterfront. The *New York Times* acknowledged that the opening of each MWL branch was "attended by disorder, rioting, and arrests"; and league officials complained that halls were frequently raided and organizers arrested. In San Pedro, "raids were an almost daily occurrence and a call for a meeting was the sign for a large mobilization of police in front of the hall." San Pedro MWL organizer Tommy Ray was arrested on several occasions and he had his left arm twisted out of the socket by the Los Angeles Police "Red Squad." Looking back on this experience, it seemed to him that "Hitler was alive in San Pedro before he was in Germany."

In spite of the repression, the *Marine Workers Voice* published a battery of glowing accounts from league branches. Houston reported on the necessity of establishing a "larger headquarters . . . in this port to accommodate our membership." Baltimore delegates visited 123 ships in a month's time. Even the besieged San Pedro branch commented on "the great number of men taking out [MWL] cards." A former member estimated in later years that the league achieved a membership of several thousand, and the members allegedly demanded "the formation of an Industrial Union."[6]

However, these reports cannot be taken at face value. The late 1920s were years of extreme quiescence among the maritime workers, and even the coming of the Great Depression did not trigger a significant wave of protest activity on the waterfront. The initiative for the formation of a new union came not from rank-and-file seamen but from the Communist party, in accordance with the new political line of the Third Period. Given the moribund status of the International Seamen's Union, and the absolute determination of its officials to exclude dissidents from their ranks, it may have seemed impossible for Communists to bore from within the ISU. Thus the creation of an independent union made sense, and it's entirely possible that hundreds—perhaps even thousands—of seamen and longshoremen were receptive to the formation of such an organization. But there is no evidence that strategic considerations of this kind played a major role in the decision to form a new union. The impetus came from outside the maritime industry.[7]

On April 26, 1930, about 180 delegates from port cities around the nation gathered in New York City to form the Marine Workers Industrial Union (MWIU). There were thirty-five delegates from New York and an equal number from Philadelphia; twenty-seven of the Philly delegates were rank-and-file longshoremen, many of them black. San Pedro sent ten delegates, and there were five seamen and five black longshoremen from Houston. Many of the delegates arrived by riding the freights, and one of them was detained for five days on a South Carolina chain gang. If this congregation of rebel workers evoked images of the Wobblies, it was no coincidence. According to the *Daily Worker,* more than half of the delegates had once been members of the IWW. Roy Hudson, a future leader of the MWIU, stated that "the largest single section of the delegates was overwhelmingly the IWW, and I include myself in this tendency." Most of the ex-Wobblies had left the Marine Transport Workers not because of any disagreement with the IWW program, but because the organization had proven ineffective. Thus, it is natural that they would have greeted any Communist initiative toward independent industrial unionism with real interest, especially when the new union adopted much of the IWW program. The MWIU proclaimed itself an industrial organization, embracing seamen, longshoremen, and other harbor workers. Its basis of operation was to be the old Wobbly system of ship and dock committees, although characteristically one MWIU leader now claimed that "the model for this system was to be found in the Soviet Union." The MWIU also followed the IWW policy of keeping dues as low as possible, calling for a one-dollar initiation fee and dues of fifty cents a month. Finally, it was frankly dual unionist, announcing its intention to "open a membership drive at once," and to recruit from the ranks of the ISU and the International Longshoremen's Association.[8]

Hudson maintained that there were only a handful of Communists among the nearly two hundred delegates at the MWIU's founding convention. If this is so, it is also true that this handful played the leading role in shaping the MWIU's statement of purpose in accordance with the political imperatives of the Third Period. The MWIU preamble declared:

> While striving constantly for the immediate betterment of all living and working conditions of the maritime workers, the M.W.I.U. does not limit itself to immediate economic demands alone, but declares that the liberation of the marine workers from exploitation is only one part of the revolutionary struggle of the whole working class against the capitalist system. The M.W.I.U. urges upon all its members the most active participation in the general struggles of the working class, economic and political, directed toward the goal of the establishment of a revolutionary workers' government.

Moreover, the convention resolved that "the Marine Transport Workers of America will not handle ammunition for, or take part in, any imperialist wars," and that "they will defend the Soviet Union, the only workers' government in the world." The meeting was characterized throughout by a spirit of optimism and revolutionary fervor. As a banner on the wall of the convention hall put it, "Here we come, the New Red Union of Marine Workers."[9]

On the surface, it would seem that the stage was set for the "New Red Union" to achieve a significant following on the waterfront. Conditions had been bad enough in the twenties, but the Great Depression imposed unprecedented suffering on the maritime workers. One seamen's publication recalled that "wages sank in many instances to $22.50 a month. Quarters were cramped and filthy. Food served the crews on many ships was barely fit to eat. . . . The 12-hour day prevailed on many lines. Manning scales went down—in some instances as much as 50 per cent." Many veteran seamen found themselves in the ranks of the unemployed, while inexperienced "workaways"—who agreed to ship out in exchange for a bunk, substandard food, and a wage payment of one dollar a month—received an alarming proportion of the available jobs.[10]

As in any period of economic crisis, unemployment and hunger stalked the waterfront with a vengeance. Tens of thousands of bona fide longshoremen and seamen were out of work, or worked only occasionally. Bribery, or "piecing off," became a more important commodity than experience and skill in finding a job, and the general problem was compounded by the hordes of unemployed drifters who swelled the waterfront work force. Moreover, the transiency of the seamen made them ineligible for the small amounts of government relief that were available to other citizens. As the *Marine Workers Voice* put it, many of them were driven to "beg at the sacred portals of the Missions and holy rollers that are springing up on the skidroad and doing a thriving depression business."

By itself, however, misery has seldom if ever been a sufficient incentive to drive masses of people to rebellion. To be sure, across the nation the unemployed sometimes mobilized in impressive numbers, often under Communist leadership, and there were many spontaneous battles to ward off evictions, feed hungry families, and eke out a living with a measure of dignity. But on the waterfront and elsewhere it was difficult to breach the wall of hopelessness that enveloped many workers. As Studs Terkel recalled, "The millions experienced a private kind of shame when the pink slip came." Moreover, the pattern of maritime employment and relief implied that the only solution to problems was an individual one: there are only a few jobs on the docks or the ships, so have your "piece-off" ready; there are only a few beds in the seamen's mission, so get there early and don't raise a ruckus. Even veteran seamen were willing to swallow their pride and ship out as workaways when all else failed. Joe Curran recalled that "starving people get to a point . . . where they don't care any more. A guy would know me as an old friend and he'd say, 'Brother, I like you but I'm starvin'.'"[11]

In the face of this complex reality, the MWIU aspired to unite all marine crafts on the basis of a militant economic program leavened by the call for political struggle toward "the establishment of a revolutionary workers' government." The union demanded full longshore gangs, full crews on all ships, decent working and living conditions, no wage cuts, and no workaways. These demands were sensible enough, but for the most part the MWIU never functioned as an industrial union, for it was unable to shake the stevedores' allegiance to the International Longshoremen's Association. By the 1930s the ILA had achieved at least some recognition as the legitimate representative of dockworkers in cities from Boston to the Texas Gulf ports. In New York, where more than half of the nation's longshore labor force was concentrated, the ILA and the waterfront employers had signed a portwide agreement in 1916 providing for union preference in hiring, and the agreement had been in effect ever since. However, as of 1930 the ILA's jurisdiction in most ports extended only to regular longshoremen in the foreign and intercoastal trades. Men who worked on the coastwise docks and in the banana trade were not included, nor were the many casuals who periodically walked the waterfront in search of a day's work. This pattern would be challenged by the upsurge of unionism that accompanied the passage of the National Industrial Recovery Act in 1933 and by the powerful example of the West Coast longshoremen a year later. By the mid-thirties, unorganized longshoremen on the Atlantic coastwise docks were clamoring to join the ILA, and rank-and-file pressure sometimes compelled their absorption into the union. But in many ports, even under the most favorable circumstances, 40 to 50 percent of the longshore work force remained outside the ILA. And in the South Atlantic and Gulf District of the union, stretching from Cape Hatteras to the Mexican border, the ILA's presence was more than a shadow only in the Texas ports of Corpus Christi, Galveston, Houston, and Texas City.

Overall, in comparison to the ISU, this was a major presence. But it seemed to leave a significant opening for the MWIU among unorganized longshoremen. However, other factors—namely, the ethnic complexion of the labor force, the organization of work on the docks, and the ILA's heavy-handed methods of operation—created obstacles that the most patient and skilled MWIU cadres were unlikely to overcome. Longshoremen in the major Atlantic Coast ports were organized, and divided, along lines of race and nationality. In New York the Irish and Italians predominated, although there were significant numbers of Scandinavians and blacks. In Boston the union membership was largely Irish or Irish-American of the second generation. In Philadelphia, about half of the workers were black, and the majority of the whites were either Polish or from other Slavic nationalities. In Baltimore and the South Atlantic ports blacks made up a clear and sometimes overwhelming majority of the labor force.[12]

The organization of work tended to harden the lines that separated one race and nationality from another. In the great majority of U.S. ports the infamous "shape-up" served as the principal method of hiring dock labor. As the men "shaped" in a circle around him, the hiring foreman had complete freedom of choice in selecting a gang, and often nationality would serve as the principal criterion. In New York, where there was a shape-up at every pier, each dock would be the bailiwick of one racial or ethnic group and was sometimes regarded as off-limits to all others. Joe Curran recalled the relationship between nationality and the "pier by pier operation . . . in New York. Where longshoremen are working on Pier 84, if their pier goes out of business, they can't work on Pier 85. Their seniority applies to only one pier. You've got the Irish up on the West Side. You've got Croats on one part of the West Side. You've got the Spanish down on the East Side. You've got the Italians in Brooklyn. You've got the Negroes in one area. They murder each other if they move from one [area] to another. That was one of the principles—keep them divided, keep them fighting and keep them disorganized."[13]

On the Atlantic Coast, unlike the Pacific, relatively few longshoremen were ex-seamen. Most of them came from ethnic and working-class neighborhoods along the waterfront. The Chelsea section of Manhattan, which supplied more work for longshoremen than any port city outside New York, was heavily Irish. Red Hook, in Brooklyn, was mainly Italian. Pennsport, in Philadelphia, was a Polish neighborhood. Aspiring dockworkers from these communities used family and ethnic ties as a means of gaining entrance to the industry. One woman who lived her entire life in Pennsport recalled, "It seemed like you had to have relatives on the docks to become a stevedore. It was always fathers passing jobs on or getting jobs for younger generations."[14]

The structure and operating methods of the ILA reinforced this pattern of family and ethnic enclaves on the Atlantic Coast waterfront. In New York, for example, one observer commented: "There are so-called Irish locals, Italian locals, Hungarian locals, in fact locals of almost every national and racial group that plays an important role in the longshore work of the port." ILA President Joseph P. Ryan brazenly supported this policy of particularism, encouraging each local to build "strong walls" around itself. Although some locals occasionally demonstrated a rebellious sense of autonomy in their relations with the international union, for the most part they were tied together and kept subordinate by Ryan's infamous network of pluguglies. Since longshoremen were, by reputation, "huge of limb and tough of muscle, hard-swearing, quick-fisted, big of heart," intimidating them was no easy task. It required men of a certain disposition and training to keep order on the docks. Ryan maintained his long tenure by employing some of the nation's most notorious gangsters as officials of the union; and he was shrewd enough to utilize his hoods with careful attention to ethnicity. Anthony "Bang Bang" Anastasia and his brother Albert patrolled the Italian sections of the Brooklyn waterfront, while Owney Madden's Irish underworld "serviced" the ILA locals in the Chelsea.[15]

Ryan was also determined to preserve the carefully nurtured craft separation between longshoremen and seamen, especially when MWIU seamen threatened to bring "alien" ideas to his semi-feudal principalities on the docks. He was aided by the fact that most of the MWIU activists were indeed seamen, many of whom elevated transiency to a badge of working-class honor. Thus they were ill equipped to understand workers whom they derisively called the "home guard"—men whose working lives were confined to a single pier and whose culture was bounded by family, ethnicity, and neighborhood.

On one occasion in the early thirties, when unorganized longshoremen struck a coastwise dock in New York, MWIU organizers rushed to the scene to spread the gospel of revolutionary industrial unionism. There they met up with Ryan, who declared with contempt that "if I handed you these guys on a silver tray, you'd lose 'em all tomorrow. You don't know what it's all about." In this instance, at least, Ryan's observation may have been correct. The MWIU succeeded in leading a few struggles among black stevedores, particularly in the South Atlantic and Mississippi River ports. But in essence the union was to remain an organization of seamen throughout its existence. And Ryan's longshoremen on the Atlantic and Gulf coasts were to remain relatively isolated from the waves of militant unionism and ideological ferment that swept through the ranks of the maritime workers in the 1930s.[16]

In addition to agitating for industrial unionism, the MWIU also made a sustained effort to build unity among black and white maritime workers. But here too the union's principled stand was not enough to overcome an intractable reality. Communists generally were outspoken opponents of the special oppression that black people have faced in the United States. Recalling his shop-floor experience in the 1950s, historian David Montgomery has stated that "every place where I ever worked, there were a number of older Black workers who . . . had considerable respect for [the Communist party], and would for the most part think of the Third Period . . . as the one in which these guys proved themselves, in the unemployed movement, and in the Scottsboro campaign." Even some left-wing critics of the Communists have echoed the same theme. Frank Marquart, a Socialist autoworker in Detroit, credits Communist shop papers in the late 1920s "for making me conscious of the fact that Negroes have special problems as a minority group, apart from the general conditions of wage earners. . . . the CP opened my eyes to things about which I had been stone blind!" Likewise, Martin Glaberman, a Trotskyist opponent of the Communists in the auto industry during World War II, has acknowledged that "on a personal level and on the shop floor, CP members were the most consistent and principled element in the labor movement in fighting for the rights of black workers."[17]

Glaberman's observation applies with special force to the maritime industry, where the Communists were by far the most outspoken advocates of racial equality. But although the MWIU led a number of strikes among black longshoremen and attracted a few outstanding individuals to its ranks, black workers seldom joined the Red union. Again the pattern of unionism in the industry provided an obstacle that the MWIU found difficult to surmount. Sterling Spero and Abram Harris concluded in 1931 that the black worker "probably plays a more important role in [the ILA] than he does in any other labor union. The International Longshoremen's Association has three Negro vice-presidents and regularly seats several score of Negro delegates at its national conventions." However, Spero and Harris were quick to point out that black workers had not achieved a position of equality in the union and the industry. Rather, the long history of racial conflict on the docks had finally convinced whites and blacks that an accommodation had to be reached—an accommodation whereby black longshoremen were welcome in the ILA so long as they accepted a limited and subordinate role. As a black ILA official in Brooklyn put it, "We are in the union today because the white man had to take us in for his own protection. Outside the organization the Negro could scab on the white man. Inside he can't." (Actually, the official's statement is a bit misleading. In the early history of longshore unionism, blacks had more often been the victims of white strikebreaking. Black longshoremen organized for self-protection against white attempts to take over their jobs as early as 1868.)[18]

The MWIU called on blacks—and all maritime workers—to challenge this ongoing pattern of inequality by striking at the hiring methods that were at the root of the racial and ethnic particularism on the waterfront. A unity conference called by the MWIU in September 1934 demanded that "there shall be no discrimination against race, creed, or color in giving out jobs. There shall be no checkerboard gangs. Negro workers [are] to be entitled to any job on any dock." To implement such a demand would have revolutionized ethnic and race relations on the waterfront. Any attempt to achieve such a breakthrough would not only have elicited the wrath of Ryan's goons; it would also have ripped apart the informal consensus that had provided blacks with their secure but subordinate position in the waterfront labor force. This was especially true in the South, where, as one Gulf Coast longshoreman has recalled, the black stevedore "was the aristocrat of southern black labor, and was quite conscious of it." It is hardly surprising, then, that in general black longshoremen refused to rally to the MWIU banner.[19]

Among the seamen black workers suffered from a more pervasive discrimination. They were virtually excluded from the deck and engine gangs on most ships, and were thus relegated to the stewards' department. But even this discriminatory practice created an enclave that allowed black seamen to organize and strengthen their position in the industry. During the early thirties, when the ISU's fortunes had reached their lowest point, the Marine Cooks and Stewards' Union (MCS) was perhaps its most functional affiliate on the East Coast. Headed by "Emperor" David Grange, himself a black West Indian, the MCS was hardly a democratic union. Grange was an absolute dictator. But he won the support of black seamen not only because he was the lone symbol of black authority in the ISU, but also because he secured a contractual agreement from the Eastern Steamship company that provided significantly better conditions for its overwhelmingly black crews than prevailed on other shipping lines.

Thus, on the ships as well as on the docks, black workers found that the existing AFL unions provided them with a modicum of leadership and security. In the short run, this often made the MWIU's vigorous appeals to blacks relatively ineffective; but in the longer term, the Communists' championing of the rights of black workers did not fall on deaf ears. In the CIO era, blacks became steadfast members of a number of unions in which Communists played a prominent role, even when these unions came under sustained attack during the Cold War. Once black workers discovered that the Left-led unions had both the will and the power to provide them with genuine equality in the union and at the workplace, they generally turned their backs on appeals to forsake the Reds and affiliate themselves with "American" unions.[20]

   In addition to stumbling on historic craft and racial barriers, the MWIU was also hampered by the ultrarevolutionary dimensions of the Third Period line and program. For example, a typical article in the *Marine Workers Voice* declared that "the struggle to better our conditions" must also become "an active struggle against imperialist war." The paper not only called upon the maritime workers to "defend the Soviet Union," but looked forward to the day when "the American workers will own the ships, and the other industries, and operate them as the workers do in the Soviet Union." On occasion, the *Voice* even allowed itself the prediction that the "strength" and "prosperity" of the USSR would "show such an example to the parasite ridden workers of the capitalist world that they will rise in their might and set up THE WORLD SOCIALIST REPUBLIC."

The Communist party often criticized the MWIU and other Red unions for their failure to lead mass economic struggles. A *Daily Worker* article entitled "Face to the Water Front!" complained that the MWIU "is still a propaganda center instead of a center of action." "Instead of developing broad mass struggles," it said, "the union is still carrying on work within its own shell." However, the article also insisted that these economic struggles be conducted within the larger framework of defending the Soviet Union and opposing the "intensive military preparations" of the "imperialist united front"; and it concluded with the Leninist exhortation to "turn the imperialist war into a class war—civil war—a war of millions of toiling masses against those who make wars." If such rhetoric did not attract large numbers of maritime workers to the MWIU, it was not because an internationalist outlook was foreign to the experiences of the marine labor force. But the MWIU's mechanical effort to define emancipation in terms of the Soviet experience had a limited appeal at best among men who had seen enough of the world to be skeptical about the claims of its self-appointed saviors.[21]

   In spite of the MWIU's close adherence to the political line and slogans of the Third Period, it would be wrong to regard the organization as a pure and simple creature of the Communist party. Most of its leading activists were seamen, and their politics had roots that were independent of the Party. They had concluded that revolutionary industrial unionism was the appropriate vehicle for changing the marine workers' degraded conditions, but they had come to this conclusion on the basis of their own life experience and not mainly as a result of intellectual reflection or obedience to external political directives. Roy Hudson recalled that the ultraleft tone of the MWIU founding convention reflected not only the sectarianism of the Communist party, but the mood of many non-Communist seamen who were present. There was a widespread feeling that "we're gonna be under attack anyway, so we might as well go as far as we want to go." Most of the ex-Wobs were even willing to swallow the Communist emphasis on political action when they saw that the MWIU was indeed organized along industrial lines. However, the ex-IWWs did not fully digest the new fare. A strong undercurrent of syndicalism coexisted with the more prevalent Communist frame of reference throughout the MWIU's existence. Hudson himself wrote in 1934 that "if we have strong organization *on the job,* no power in the capitalist world can smash our union." Although he went on to include the proper political references to fighting against "imperialist war," the foundation of his statement was the old syndicalist principle of waging the battle at the point of production.[22]

Throughout the MWIU's existence, these revolutionary seamen would maintain a relatively consistent stance. In the early days of ultraleftism, their roots in the day-to-day realities of working-class life made them more pragmatic than the Party as a whole. But in the waning years of the union's existence, as the Communist party groped toward the more flexible politics of the Popular Front, many of these seamen resisted the strategic shift to working within the established trade unions. They continued to believe in revolutionary industrial unionism, and some of them fought bitterly against the decision to liquidate the MWIU. Hudson recalled that there was some "just plain sectarian" opposition to the dissolution of the union among "a few very good men." He recalled with genuine respect, however, that these Communist seamen had "minds of their own."[23]

If these men were sectarian, it is also true that their roots in the maritime industry gave them an orientation that did not come easily to the Party functionary. Steve Nelson, a Croatian immigrant and a Communist, has commented on the recurring contradiction between the imperatives of the Party's political line and the realities of workers' lives. Speaking of Communist activity in the unemployed movement of the early thirties, he said that involvement in the daily struggles of the unemployed helped Party cadres move away from "a narrow, dogmatic approach" and to become more responsive to people's immediate needs. In regard to political priorities, he recalled that "those inclined to argue for general socialist propaganda and publicizing the accomplishments of the Soviet Union were more likely to be full-time staffers for the Party with fewer day-to-day connections in the factories. When you work in a Party office all day and never talk to anybody but other highly politicized people, it distorts your view of reality." The Communist seamen in the MWIU had no such disability. Their involvement in the daily struggles of their fellow maritime workers came naturally. Apart from their politics, they were otherwise indistinguishable from the mass of men who lived and worked on the waterfront. Joe Curran recalled that the local representatives of the MWIU in New York "were all guys we knew from the ships." George Cullinan, who first encountered the union in the port of Tacoma, remembered the MWIUers as "honest guys" who "talked about the issues, about things that affected us" as seamen. And more than a few marine workers responded positively to the Red image that these familiar and persistent organizers projected. As one seaman put it, "If these people were Communists, that's what I wanted to be, and I'd never read a bit of literature."[24]

If the sectarianism of the MWIU was an obstacle to the organization of the waterfront, it can hardly be argued that other approaches were more successful. The IWW, which damned the Soviet Union with as much ritual fervor as AFL President William Green, lost much of its membership to the MWIU. Likewise, the AFL craft unions reaped no benefit from the catastrophic conditions of the early thirties. If anything, their membership continued to decline. The most generous contemporary estimates gave the MWIU about fifteen thousand members during this period, far more than the moribund ISU. But the actual number of MWIU members was probably much closer to that of its rival, and the MWIU membership may have been a good deal more transient than the ISU's. Roy Hudson, who served as national secretary of the Marine Workers Union for most of its existence, stated that by the time of the West Coast maritime strike of 1934 "the membership of the MWIU had become equal to if it did not exceed that of the . . . ISU." Since the ISU's membership probably numbered about five thousand, that would be a reasonable estimate for the MWIU as well.[25]

But Hudson also put his finger on a crucial difference between the two unions. He added that "the MWIU was an action organization," while "the ISU was a shell, stagnating and passive." While the MWIU fought for emergency relief for destitute seamen on the beach, Victor Olander declared disdainfully that the ISU "is not organizing flophouse unions," and another ISU official characterized a large part of the marine labor force as "tramps, ne'er-do-wells, drug addicts, [and] drunks." Whenever the MWIU succeeded in tying up a ship in the fight for better conditions, the ISU leadership offered to provide the vessel with replacements. Joe Curran, who claimed in later years that his education in unionism began when he joined the MWIU briefly in 1934, recalled that "sometimes we were able to hold a ship and get a lot of conditions changed." But meanwhile, "the ISU would be working to get the scabs aboard. They were scab herding at the time."[26]

We can learn a good deal about the MWIU—as reality and as legend—by examining the lives and personalities of the union's leading activists. These men projected an aura of optimism, tireless energy, and unswerving commitment that elicited widespread respect, even among seamen who were wary of the Reds. Mike Pell said of MWIU organizer Joe Bianca that he "worked himself to a frazzle, never thinking about his health. I'll bet he hadn't had a square meal for a month before I met him and you could have lit up a room with the shine on his pants." Pell's observation about Bianca's empty stomach was no exaggeration. Bill Bailey recalled that "in the tough days—winter time when nobody had any money," a number of union activists would meet in a cafeteria run by the Communist party in New York. "We'd go in there with a nickel and get a cup of [hot water] and a tea bag, and we'd maybe go back ten or fifteen times with the one tea bag, and put it in the hot water. And of course they'd never refuse. You could get all the hot water you wanted. And that tea bag was just squeezed to death. . . . When things got real bad we'd get the hot water and put ketchup in it . . . and have tomato soup!"

Al Lannon, who joined the MWIU while visiting an International Seamen's Club in a Soviet port, remembered with pride how he went on to become a volunteer organizer for the union in New York. His assignment was to distribute literature among the barge crews that docked at the Ninety-sixth Street piers. "I slept in the union hall," he wrote, and

each morning I would be given a bundle of literature & I would walk to 96th St.[,] about 5 miles. I would spend about 3 hours on the Barges & the crews were good guys who would give me something to eat & then I would walk back to the hall. . . . In the evening I would go out, with others, & distribute leaflets in the flop houses & help clean & mop the Union Hall.

I did this for 3 months . . . My shoes wore out & I got blood poisoning in my legs. This got so bad that I had to be taken to the Marine Hospital on Ellis Is[land]. I spent 3 weeks in the Hospital & when I was cured I went back to the union hall.

As a reward for his tenacity, the MWIU made him an "official" member of the port organizing committee at a salary of twenty-five cents a day.

The extraordinary commitment Lannon exemplified made an impression on a significant number of seamen. Remembering his first encounter with the MWIU and its active members at a dingy hall in Baltimore, Charlie Rubin stated that "the place strongly reminded me of the pictures I had seen of the early Christian disciples sleeping in caves—people who considered no personal sacrifice too great to spread their message." At first, Rubin resisted the magnetic attraction of these deeply committed activists, but before long he too had become an MWIU organizer.[27]

The imagery of early Christian disciples can be carried to extremes, but the aura of courage, honesty, and selflessness that surrounded some of the MWIU's leading members easily translates into religious terms. Among those who knew them in the early and mid-thirties, men such as Joe Bianca, Harry Hynes, and Al Kaufman became legendary heroes of almost saintly proportions. Hynes, an Australian, was the MWIU's first national secretary, until the Communist party decided that his temperament was ill suited for the responsibilities associated with such a position. He then went to the West Coast, where he met fellow Aussie Harry Bridges and played an important role in launching the historic *Waterfront Worker* on the San Francisco docks. Bianca served for a time as MWIU port organizer in New Orleans, and Kaufman held the same post in Philadelphia. But all three of these men were deeply imbued with the "rank-and-file" temper that was often regarded as a hallmark of the Wobblies. (This was no accident. Bianca and Hynes had both been members of the IWW; Kaufman may have been as well.)

Kaufman, a Jewish upholsterer from Philadelphia, had been in the Communist party for years and was serving as head of the Communist apparatus in Baltimore when Al Richmond first met him in March 1932. Richmond recalled that "when he talked to the [Party] brass, he wasn't obsequious. He was a difficult character for them to deal with. Profane, but a very intelligent man." The Party soon replaced him in the Baltimore leadership with "a guy fresh out of the Lenin school," and Kaufman began shipping out. He was, he said, a "roughneck organizer" who found that he was happiest away from the trappings of power. Likewise, Bianca was more comfortable and effective as an agitator than as a leader in the conventional sense. Richmond described Bianca's role as an active militant in the Sailors' Union of the Pacific (after the dissolution of the MWIU). Although a man of "absolute dedication," he was "inconspicuous, the agitator in the rear of the meeting hall, fanning the flames of discontent in his bass whisper." Even the mild-mannered, soft-spoken Hynes could be harsh in his criticism of "bureaucrats," including Communist party functionaries. Bill Bailey recalled Hynes saying to him one day, "You're the guy that's out there in contact with the enemy every day, while they are snug and safe behind a desk. Don't let [them] browbeat you when you think you're right."

Bianca, Hynes, and Kaufman were all dedicated Communists; all three died fighting with the International Brigades in Spain. Of Hynes in particular it was said, "He took sheep and turned them into men, he gave them a reason for living." In a memorable portrait, Richmond characterized him as "the best man I ever met . . . he came closest to being a pure revolutionary." In less heroic times, other left-wing seamen would invoke the names of Hynes and his fellow martyrs to condemn their Communist successors in the marine unions. In 1947 Charlie Keith, himself a Spanish vet and a member of the National Maritime Union, would declare: "What comparison is there between a Harry H[y]nes, a Joe Bianc[a], an Al Kaufman, who worked day and night to build our Union, and [the current generation of Communist union officials] who cannot even come to work on time? These people are dragging in the mud the high honor of the name Communist."[28]

Another legendary figure in the MWIU was George Mink, the organization's first national chairman. Few seamen knew Mink as well as they knew the more accessible Bianca, Hynes, and Kaufman. His name has survived and achieved a certain notoriety mainly because of his reputation as a conspirator. A veteran of the IWW and the Communist party, he was not a seaman. Apparently he had once been a taxi driver in Philadelphia. According to those who knew him well, or claimed to, he was "brash, tough, shrewd"—"an arrogant sort of a guy." Even his physical appearance suggested the conspirator, and the predator. Richard Krebs, who loathed him, said that "his mouth was small and cruel, his teeth irregular, and his eyes had a faint wild-animal glint." Al Richmond, who did not dislike him, remembered Mink as "short, stocky, with small eyes, gleaming and quick; the configuration of his nostrils and mouth suggested . . . a predatory quality." Richmond was repelled by what he regarded as Mink's "utter cynicism." He recalled one occasion when an MWIU delegation from San Pedro visited the national chairman in New York, "armed with a long list of demands and proposals." Mink received the delegation and did not wait for it to leave before throwing its proposals in the wastebasket.

William McCuistion, an MWIUer who became a professional anti-Communist, testified that Mink was "the direct representative of the Soviet Government in the United States." Krebs, who under the pseudonym of Jan Valtin became a favorite of the Dies Committee,* declared that Mink "was more often in Berlin, Hamburg and Moscow than in New York. Officially, he was engaged in revolutionary trade union work; secretly, he had become part and parcel of the Counter-Espionage *Apparat* of the G.P.U." Krebs dubbed him "Mink, the harbor pirate" and claimed that even the head of the Red International of Seamen and Harbor Workers referred to him as the "cut-throat from the Bowery."

Mink obliged his rabid critics only once, by getting arrested in Denmark on the charge of attempting to smuggle anti-Nazi literature into Germany. There was speculation that he was involved in a plot to assassinate Hitler. In any

---

*In 1938 the House of Representatives created a Special Committee on Un-American Activities, with Congressman Martin Dies of Texas as chairman. Although some of the committee's original proponents had seen it primarily as an instrument for exposing fascist organizations in the United States, Dies turned it into a forum for attacks on communism, the New Deal, and the CIO, all of which he regarded as more or less synonymous. In its first few days the committee heard witnesses who branded 640 organizations, 483 newspapers, and 280 labor unions as communistic.[29]

case, he disappeared from sight thereafter, and his absence only fed the fires of the Mink legend. During the height of the Cold War his reputation reached such fantastic proportions that a popular monthly magazine could speculate that he was the head of a Communist spy ring on the New York waterfront. According to *Bluebook,* "Of all the fanatic characters turned out by the Lenin School of Sabotage and Espionage in Moscow, George Mink is perhaps the most dreaded and the most deadly." The magazine declared that during the late thirties the Soviet secret police had sent Mink to Spain, where his assignment was "to eliminate any Loyalist not believed to be loyal enough. Within a year he is credited with having murdered over two thousand persons. He got the name, 'The Bloody Butcher.' Wherever he went men died."[30]

These stories tell us less about Mink than they do about the compulsion of professional anti-Communists to manufacture myths, half-truths, and outright lies about Communist plots to infiltrate, disrupt, and ultimately sabotage the merchant marine. A number of ritual statements that appeared in Communist publications during the ultraleft Third Period gave a certain credibility to this myth, but for the most part it represented a crass distortion of Communist objectives.[31]

From the standpoint of the MWIU, the Mink legend is fascinating not because of its conspiratorial dimension, but because it reinforces the argument that Communists on the waterfront were somewhat autonomous from and sometimes antagonistic to the Party apparatus in the United States. According to McCuistion, Joe Bianca once punched Party leader William Weinstone in the jaw at a meeting, and when Weinstone threatened Bianca with expulsion, Mink retorted, "You will be expelled before any of these seamen will." McCuistion testified before the Dies Committee that Mink

> could bawl out 40 organizers, and he could tell [Party General Secretary Earl] Browder where to get off. Mink would come and go as he pleased, and could break into political bureau meetings, and if anybody raised any question about his authority, he could tell them to go to the devil. . . .
>
> I have heard Mink tell Browder that he will have to change his line . . . and I heard him dictate actually to Browder various things that Browder would have to do, and I have heard Browder, in a veiled way, threaten that—well, Mink could be pulled off his high horse yet. There was always quite a bit of sparring between the two, when they got together. Each one of them resented the other one's being quite a big shot, and having a little too much authority.

McCuistion's lurid tales about an independent kingdom of sabotage and subversion on the waterfront were welcome grist for the Dies Committee's propaganda mill. But in fact Mink's power was nowhere near as great as McCuistion's comments would suggest. This became abundantly clear when the Party leadership removed Mink from his position in the MWIU in late 1933 and assigned him to the Comintern. He and several of his comrades reacted to this decision with shock and anger. Richmond remembered him pouring out his bitterness about it at great length one evening. But Mink acquiesced in the decision and disappeared from the scene. Although at strategic moments professional anti-Communists continued to conjure up his presence like some evil genie from a bottle, he was never a factor on the waterfront again.[32]

However, if McCuistion's congressional testimony was at best wildly exaggerated, there is a definite ring of truth in his contention that Mink and the MWIUers were frequently at loggerheads with the national Party leadership. But in tailoring his stories to fit the self-serving dogmas of his audience, McCuistion misrepresented the nature of the antagonism. It was rooted neither in international intrigue nor in rivalry for power, but in a clash of cultures. Although Mink himself was not a seaman, his Wobbly background and tough, irreverent style were very much at home on the waterfront. Whatever became of him after his disappearance from the United States, his legend has been created and used to reinforce the essentially false notion that Communist trade unionism was an instrument of conspiracy.

Roy Hudson was far less flamboyant—and mysterious—than George Mink, but his career illuminates another aspect of the relationship between the Communist party and the MWIU. Tall, sandy-haired, and ruggedly handsome (in spite of the nickname Horseface), Hudson had been a seaman for more than a decade when he first heard about the MWIU. He joined the U.S. Navy at the end of World War I and sailed for four years on coal burners, oil burners, even some windjammers. After leaving the navy, he shipped on merchant vessels for the remainder of the twenties. He joined the IWW and tried to line up his shipmates in the Marine Transport Workers, but it did not take him long to realize that the Wobblies' best days were behind them. Even after leaving the IWW, he retained a strong commitment to revolutionary industrial unionism, and initially he distrusted the Communists because of their boring-from-within policy. In Baltimore he encountered the Marine Workers League and listened with growing enthusiasm as league members spoke about their intention to form a new Red industrial union on the waterfront. Along with many other ex-Wobblies, he attended the MWIU founding convention to see if the Communists were serious about their new trade union line.

Hudson's reservations about the Communists were quickly laid to rest by his experience in the MWIU. He joined the Party and won widespread recognition as both a dedicated revolutionary and an able trade union leader. Replacing Harry Hynes as national secretary of the union, he became the MWIU's most visible spokesman. There were those who regarded him as a mere henchman of the Party leadership. One outspoken and unusually independent Communist remembered him as "Browder's maritime union man," and more than any other individual, he did personify the close ties between the Communist party and the MWIU. Eventually he left the maritime industry and became a national Communist leader, serving as the Party's main liaison with the trade union movement for nearly a decade.

Given his increasingly important role in the Communist hierarchy, Hudson was bound to uphold the policies imposed by the Party at the national and international levels. However, given his long experience at the point of production and his capacity for patient and protracted work, he also recognized the necessity of moving beyond mechanical answers and "looking into the particulars of a situation." He was sensitive to the immediate needs of workers and wary of what he viewed as the Party's "tendency to fall back on formulas and generalities." In fact, to a degree that was unusual if not unique in the MWIU, he questioned the right of Communist party members to use the union as an automatic platform for campaigns that had no direct relationship to the waterfront. Above all, he wanted to root the MWIU in day-to-day reality as the men themselves experienced it, and he played a vital role in steering the union toward the united front approach that eventually led to important advances in Baltimore and San Francisco.[33]

Hudson recalled that in late 1932 the demoralization of the early depression years began giving way to a "rising mood of struggle" on the waterfront. Clearly, the MWIU was the only force with the program and the human resources to respond effectively to this development. The upsurge began not on the ships but among the unemployed seamen on the beach. In 1932 somewhere between a fourth and a third of the seagoing labor force was unemployed, perhaps as many as forty or fifty thousand men. The magnitude of the suffering on the waterfront eventually compelled the federal government to make some relief available for its seafaring wards. This money was administered by charitable organizations such as the Seamen's Church Institute (SCI)—the widely despised "Dog House"—and the Seamen's Friends Society. Since nearly half of the unemployed seamen were concentrated in the port of New York, several millionaire shipping magnates there launched a special fund-raising campaign to save "*hundreds* from hunger and want." While thousands slept in Battery Park or huddled in doorways in the Bowery, the emergency committee of seamen's agencies announced that it would provide 270 free beds for destitute seafarers at the Jane Street Mission.[34]

This combination of widespread suffering and inept philanthropy provided the MWIU with the opportunity to crystallize the latent anger of the seamen into a significant force for change. In the summer of 1932 the union concentrated its fire on the SCI. The institute had just announced that the shortage of relief funds was forcing it to cut back on the use of its facilities as of July 31. But the MWIU and its allies claimed that more than a third of the institute's beds were already empty every night because most unemployed seamen couldn't afford the thirty-five-cent fee. Moreover, while pleading poverty, the SCI was raising money to pay for new stained-glass memorial windows in the chapel at a cost of $5,000 and new chapel chairs at fifty dollars each. "For the price of one chapel chair," said the *Daily Worker,* "a jobless seaman could spend 143 nights in one of those empty beds." Even men with access to the beds had ample cause for complaint. One of the most frequent gripes was that the institute functioned as a crimp joint. Curran recalled that at "about 5 o'clock in the morning they'd come around and shake you out because they had a job on some old bucket, and I mean bucket. And if you didn't take that, they'd . . . throw you out in the street."

Thousands demonstrated in front of the "Dog House" in mid-July, and MWIU agitators sparked several turbulent demonstrations inside the building. The union also held a well-attended outdoor mock trial of the institute, with George Mink serving as judge and hundreds of unemployed seamen on the jury. In August verbal protest and street theater gave way to what Al Richmond remembered as "a splendid riot" inside the institute. "One seaman took an emergency fire hose from the wall and played its spray into the chapel," Richmond recalled. "Some overturned tables, chairs, and other pieces of furniture. There was bedlam and shambles."[35]

This campaign failed to accomplish any of its stated objectives, although the *Daily Worker* did announce that after the mock trail "the Institute suddenly served ice cream with the next 10-cent meal!" However, a later offensive at the Jane Street Mission was more successful. There an MWIU-led sit-in succeeded in filling the 270 free beds far more quickly than the mission staff had intended, packing seventy-five additional seamen into the facility, and winning an extra meal a day. It was here that Chairman Mink offered his maximalist advice: "The first thing you do is fight for two meals and when you get two meals you fight for three meals and when you get three meals you fight about the menu." The MWIU organized a house committee to direct the activity of the mission's increasingly assertive occupants, and pretty soon word of the "Jane Street Soviet" was spreading to other ports.[36]

Inevitably some of this combative spirit was transferred to the ships as men succeeded in finding jobs. The year 1933 saw a tremendous increase in the number of strikes, although most of them were quickies, many over small demands that the shipowners could meet with relative ease. In spite of the MWIU's efforts to organize ongoing ships' committees that could direct the fight to improve conditions and consolidate gains, the seamen's habitual transiency meant that they seldom stayed aboard ship to savor their victories. Thus concessions could be withdrawn in the interim between the departure of one crew and the arrival of another.

Even so, the union threw itself into the fray with characteristic energy. Bill Bailey recalled boarding one Munson Line ship, the *Mundixie,* in New York with instructions to have the crew ready to strike the vessel by the time it arrived in Baltimore. Bailey and his few comrades found it difficult to get much of a response from their fellow workers, who persisted in reading "pulp junk"—romances, mysteries, etc.—during their watch below, ignoring the calls to action that the MWIUers had secretly been distributing all over the ship. After some initial confusion, the organizers hit upon a scheme to compel the crew's attention: they gathered up all the pulp junk they could find and threw it over the side! In later years, when the Communist party was concerned with projecting a more responsible image, the Waterfront Section would warn its members, "Don't throw the 'pulp' junk overboard! This is sectarian and plays into the hands of the red-baiters." But these were less cautious times, and in this particular instance the tactic worked. In spite of much grumbling about the mysterious disappearance of their customary reading material, the crew members were soon absorbed in the MWIU literature. Bailey called a well-attended meeting to discuss conditions aboard ship, and after an intense, two-hour debate, the crew voted to strike the ship when it reached Baltimore. By December 1933, the *Marine Workers Voice* was declaring, *"There were more ship strikes during the past month than there have been during the entire past 10 years!"* On some ships, said the *Voice*, the "mere threat of action" was enough to force the companies to meet the men's demands.[37]

It was no accident that Bailey was instructed to strike the *Mundixie* in Baltimore, because, increasingly, that city was becoming the focal point of the MWIU's greatest achievements. Why Baltimore? Unlike the vast and complex port of New York, it was a medium-sized city with an unusually compact waterfront district, allowing for regular interaction among the men who worked in the maritime industry. Also, over a period of several years, some of the MWIU's most able and energetic organizers, including Joe Bianca and Al Lannon, were assigned there. The city's close proximity to Washington, D.C., was another factor, because the nation's capital provided a natural target for protest activities. Seamen marching the forty-five miles from Baltimore to Washington in order to make demands upon the federal government became a recurring theme of the maritime union movement throughout the 1930s. Charlie Rubin and others celebrated one such pilgrimage as the "midnight march of the Baltimore Brigade."[38]

The first major victory in Baltimore came in January 1934, when the MWIU led a successful battle to take control of the waterfront relief program away from the Seamen's YMCA (the Anchorage), which had been administering it for the federal government. Elizabeth Wickenden of the Federal Emergency Relief Administration (FERA) recalled that in early January a small delegation of seamen from Baltimore came to her Washington office and "described a situation of rebellion and unrest verging on mutiny." She noted that while the spokesmen's "terminology and temper was obviously radical," they were "extremely intelligent men." They complained that the federal relief set-up in Baltimore was being administered by former Anchorage officials whom the seamen regarded as "grafters" and "hypocritical tyrants" and who were failing to provide decent food and accommodations. The essence of the men's demands, said Wickenden, was that the Anchorage officials be dismissed and that the seamen be permitted "through an elected committee of their own" to see that decent care was provided for any among their ranks who were in need.[39]

After protracted negotiations and numerous demonstrations, the seamen won an unprecedented victory. The MWIU declared it "the first time in the history of the United States that any group of workers administered their own relief." The victory also demonstrated that the union was becoming increasingly skillful at building its campaigns on a broad basis. Nearly a thousand seamen participated actively in the relief struggle, supported at times by strikes aboard ship and by longshore gangs on the docks. Moreover, the union succeeded in mobilizing significant numbers of small businessmen in the campaign. Because the Seamen's YMCA administered all waterfront relief on its own premises, these hotel and restaurant owners were losing a substantial amount of their normal business. The MWIU promised them that in return for their support, and decent food and lodging, the new relief administration would steer recipients in their direction. The businessmen were eager to oblige, and the union made good on its promise.[40]

It was a great psychological victory for the seamen to be free of the bureaucratic red tape and the stringent rules and regulations imposed by the Seamen's YMCA. The new relief administration was much more generous than the old in providing food, lodging, and a hospitable environment for the men, who responded with a good deal of pride and self-discipline. One seaman reported that the MWIU "promised me 'a good clean flop' and three good meals a day, [plus] tobacco twice a week while I waited for a job." A federal official who inspected the Anchorage acknowledged that this was no empty promise. "My impression was favorable," he wrote. "The rooms were well lighted and the floors and walls fairly clean, the bed linen fresh and all beds made up properly, there not being more than two beds to any one room." Given these conditions, and the generous attitude of the seamen's elected leadership, it is hardly surprising that in a two-month period the number of men on relief increased from less than a hundred to approximately five hundred.[41]

One daring and effective innovation of the new regime was the offer of relief to seamen on strike. As a result, men were more willing to strike a ship in Baltimore than in other ports because they knew that when they "hit the bricks" they could—in Hudson's words—"get support, [and] get something to eat." One MWIU leader claimed that there were more than fifty strikes in Baltimore in two months. At the same time, however, because they had no interest in establishing a permanent bureaucracy, the seamen claimed that they were able to administer the relief more cheaply than their predecessors. Even William McCuistion, in his testimony before the Dies Committee, maintained that "we did administer the relief . . . for far less than the Government was able to administer it, and the records will bear that out."[42]

As morale on the waterfront soared, the MWIU came forward with a proposal for the next major advance. On February 10, 1934, at a mass meeting of approximately seven hundred seamen, Roy Hudson suggested the formation of a centralized shipping bureau to take control of hiring away from the shipowners and the crimps. As soon as he had outlined his proposal, someone shouted, "Well, what are we waiting for?" The response was virtually unanimous. The next day the marine workers established their own Centralized Shipping Bureau (CSB), controlled by a united front committee of seamen, where men hired out on a rotary basis. The MWIU claimed that "ninety-five percent of the unemployed seamen voted to boycott every shipping shark. Negro and white, American and foreign-born, union and non-union men, they stood solidly behind their decision." The result was that for over three months every shipping company in Baltimore, with the exception of Standard Oil, which refused to cooperate, had to come to the CSB in order to get crews and had to take the men assigned by the bureau. Harry Alexander, a Communist seaman and MWIU member, served as chairman of the United Front Shipping Committee, which administered the rotary system of hiring. He estimated that in three months more than a thousand men shipped out of the Centralized Shipping Bureau. Challenging the usual pattern of transiency head-on, the CSB slogan was, "Get on the ships and make them better." Alexander maintained that "when a ship called for a crew there was no trouble getting men, because if the ship was rotten the men would go on strike and demand better conditions and about three hours later the demands would be granted. Conditions grew better on every ship sailing out of Baltimore."[43]

The unity of black and white, in both relief and hiring, was also a remarkable achievement. Undoubtedly, it was the MWIU's Communists, with their outspoken commitment to black-white unity, who played the main role in alleviating the long legacy of racial hostility in the marine industry. One conservative white seaman complained that the Centralized Shipping Bureau was "completely filled with Communist propaganda. . . . There were signs about the 'Scottsburo martyrs' and pleas for racial equality and the 'Daily Worker' was there." When a black "fellow worker" referred to President Roosevelt as "Rosie" and threatened to "tie up shipping in Baltimore and den every port," the white seaman declared that the "darky . . . should have been flogged." But in the euphoric atmosphere pervading the waterfront such racist sentiments were quickly put to rout. The result was that the shipowners could no longer play one race off against the other, and the Jim Crow policies of the AFL unions were swept aside. As the *Marine Workers Voice* triumphantly declared, "You can't find a scab in Baltimore."

Indeed, for a few months at least, the whole face of the waterfront was changed. Hudson recalled that in many ports the first thing an incoming crew would encounter was "hungry guys on the pier trying to bum a feed." But "they didn't find that in Baltimore any more." As Harry Alexander summed it up, "For the first time in years the seamen in Baltimore began to live like men."[44]

Although the entire operation was conceived and led by MWIU activists, both the relief project and the hiring hall were formally independent of the union and were run by committees elected at the mass meetings ashore. But this was small consolation to the ISU officials, who recognized that their already tenuous relationship with the seamen was eroding even further. In the fall of 1933, ISU spokesmen had noted a "certain amount of restlessness" among seamen, and one official had expressed the belief that "the opportunity to organize is great." However, reports from the ISU's Eastern and Gulf Sailors' affiliate in the early months of 1934 repeated the same lament over and over: "No meeting held in this branch during the week. We have not had enough members around at meeting time for ever so long to hold a quorum." In Baltimore, where the AFL sailors' local had enrolled only two new members in the last quarter of 1933, ISU officials frantically collaborated with the employers' efforts to undermine the Centralized Shipping Bureau, supplying strikebreakers from their own hall and recruiting scabs from as far away as New York. But nonetheless, many ISU members continued to ship through the bureau with the same rights—and apparently the same enthusiasm—as everyone else.

Thus, one ISU official took it upon himself to communicate directly with President Roosevelt to warn him about the dire consequences of the federal government's relief policies. Frank Stockl, agent of the ISU's Marine Cooks and Stewards' affiliate in Baltimore, reported that seamen's relief

has been placed, I do not know by whos orders, in the hands of the so-called Marine Workers Industrial Union, which Union is affiliated with the Trades Union Unity League & the 3rd or Red International (of Moscau) and now since they have been entrusted with the Federal Relief for Seamen, they branched out & established a so-called Central Shipping Bureau, dictating to all that the Crews must be shipped thru theyr facilitys and of course men, even [though] they would not otherwise belong to such an outfitt, have to submitt to them & theyr tactics & even joinup with them in the communist Party. . . . They invarably tell the men that the N.R.A. does not mean anything & that if they want better conditions they will have to fight (strike) with & under the leadership of the Marine Workers Industrial Union.

The shipowners echoed many of Stockl's charges. They claimed that on the Baltimore waterfront "federal relief was actually encouraging communism, mutiny through intimidation, voluntary idleness, and even violence." A steady drumbeat of such complaints—and the increasingly volatile situation in the port—was bound to compel a reassessment by relief officials already sensitive about criticism of unprecedented government assistance to the unemployed. One federal official lamented that "the tie-up of relief with industrial warfare cannot be too strongly emphasized in this case," and another warned that "the Administration [must be] kept out of a class struggle." Although an FERA representative allegedly admitted that "he and everybody else knew that the seamen ran the relief more efficiently than any other agency," the government finally closed the seamen's shelter, scattering the men and forcing them to work two days a week at a rate that the MWIU characterized as "pauper wages."[45]

Meanwhile, the employers concentrated their fire on the Centralized Shipping Bureau. The MWIU claimed that the waterfront suddenly experienced several familiar variations on the carrot and stick theme. A number of militant seamen were "dumped" by roving goons, while other men were offered an abundance of "whisky and marijuana cigarettes." According to Harry Alexander, "Even the fairer sex was drawn into the dirty business. A couple of shady ladies were stopping fellows on the street, offering to buy a few beers, and then giving them a proposition very different from what the seamen thought was coming—a proposition to ship out." When these enticements failed, the shipowners began boycotting the port, or bringing crews from other ports in buses under the cover of night.

In the face of great odds the seamen fought valiantly to hold on to their gains, but to no avail. Although word of the Baltimore victory sparked great excitement up and down the Atlantic Coast, the MWIU was unable to duplicate this achievement elsewhere. On May 2, the Maryland state relief administrator exulted that "the seamen have capitulated completely." But in an important sense, the "Baltimore Soviet" did live on—as an inspiring legend, a fighting program, and a crucible from which men went forward to leaven other struggles.[46]

In spite of its failure to achieve lasting gains in Baltimore, the MWIU's experience there seemed to hold the promise of continued growth. The Centralized Shipping Bureau, the struggle for control of waterfront relief, and the increasing commitment to a united front with other elements in maritime appeared to represent a sound strategic foundation for future gains. In fact, just as the East Coast campaign was winding down, the MWIU found itself in the middle of another struggle, of much greater magnitude, where the lessons of Baltimore seemed to be of immediate relevance.

The great West Coast maritime strike of 1934 erupted on May 9, as longshoremen walked off the job from San Diego in the south to the port of Bellingham near the Canadian border. One of the longshoremen's major demands was for union control of hiring, and the MWIU pointed with pride to the precedent of the Centralized Shipping Bureau. Moreover, while the ISU affiliates vacillated on the sidelines, the MWIU's membership played an important role in bringing seamen off the ships and transforming the stevedores' walkout into a broader maritime strike. Some of the first ships' crews that struck in support of the longshoremen were composed of men who had been through the Centralized Shipping Bureau in Baltimore. Overall, the MWIU was to be an aggressive and highly visible force throughout the eighty-three-day conflict.[47]

However, the MWIU was unable to capitalize on the upsurge of unionism that accompanied the West Coast strike. Ironically, it was the conservative AFL seamen's unions that prospered. They finally won recognition from the employers again, after thirteen lean years, and their membership increased dramatically. Clearly, while many seamen respected the MWIU's fighting stance, they looked upon the ISU as a more permanent and realistic trade union organization. This assessment was no doubt influenced by the long campaign of police harassment against the MWIU and its members. During the reign of terror that accompanied the San Francisco general strike, police and national guardsmen raided the MWIU hall, made numerous arrests, and systematically vandalized the premises. Thereafter, authorities forcibly closed the hall every time the MWIU attempted to reopen it. Before long, a left-wing paper was complaining about the police practice of "arresting workers who had M.W.I.U. books in their possession" and reluctantly admitting that to join the MWIU meant "the blacklist" and "police intimidation." By December of 1934 an official of the independent radio telegraphers' union acknowledged that "the M.W.I.U. is virtually dead on this Coast." The Marine Workers' leadership liquidated the organization in February 1935, calling on the membership to join the ISU and turn it into a fighting union.[48]

The demise of the MWIU and the revitalization of the AFL maritime unions were major steps in a complex pattern of development characterized by spectacular growth and continuing fragmentation. On the West Coast the exhilarating example of the 1934 strike initially created a powerful impetus toward solidarity. The AFL's conservative policies were cast aside and for a time it seemed that long-standing craft divisions would become obsolete. The Maritime Federation of the Pacific was hailed as the precursor of One Big Union. But such hopes were eventually shattered by ideological differences and personal enmities that sharpened the historic tensions between the longshoremen's and sailors' unions.

Meanwhile, on the East Coast, Joe Ryan employed an army of goons and gangsters to keep the longshoremen isolated from the surge toward united action on the waterfront. Among the seafarers, MWIU members, including some of the Communist seamen who had piloted the union, were able to join the ISU and develop an oppositional center called the Rank-and-File Committee. Their dedication, experience, and sensible program, when combined with the utter ineptitude of the ISU officialdom, laid the basis for a new organization, the National Maritime Union, which emerged in 1937 proudly proclaiming itself the legitimate heir of the MWIU. Eventually a situation developed in which the West Coast longshoremen and the East Coast seamen became stalwarts of the CIO and leaders of its Communist wing, while the East Coast longshoremen and West Coast sailors remained with the AFL and fought against Communists (real and imagined) with as much zeal as any of the federation's rock-ribbed traditionalists. It was a pattern that reflected a peculiar convergence of historical, ideological, and personal factors, but to the outsider it was just plain baffling. As one wag put it, in contemplating the maritime scene, "Nobody can make heads or tails of it. Everybody is at sea except the seamen."[49]

Among the MWIU's leading cadres, relatively few went on to become important figures in the maritime unions that mushroomed in the middle and late 1930s. Some of them, like Hudson and Al Lannon, were absorbed into the Communist party apparatus. Others, like Bianca, Hynes, and Kaufman, died fighting fascism in Spain. A few succumbed to alcohol or just drifted out of sight. But a substantial number remained on the waterfront, only to find that the unionism of the Popular Front era required a different set of skills and a less obviously Red image; new men came forward and quickly made their way to the top of the maritime union hierarchy.

Thus the MWIU and some of its leading activists passed away, and to some degree this must be judged a bittersweet irony. For the era of insurgency in the middle and late thirties owed much to the example of the Marine Workers Industrial Union. But the new era's most dynamic inspiration came from the West Coast (the MWIU's weakest link), from longshoremen rather than seamen, and as a result of policies that represented a sharp break with some of the accustomed practice of the MWIU. Insofar as there was continuity, it came from the Communist party. The Marine Workers Union was created by a CP decision, and it was liquidated in the same way. In the meantime, Communists gained valuable experience and became in the eyes of many a legitimate presence on the waterfront. More than that, they served as a vital link between the embattled militant unionism of the early thirties and the vastly more powerful era of insurgent unionism that commenced with the West Coast maritime strike of 1934.

4

Prelude to the Pentecostal Era: Communists and Longshoremen in San Francisco

On the West Coast the early years of the 1930s saw a bitter and prolonged debate within the Communist party over the correct approach to organizing on the docks. A number of Party members made a determined effort to shed the sectarian trappings of the Third Period and to develop a practical basis for unity with the natural leaders of the San Francisco longshoremen. Out of this groping and turmoil there emerged a quiet, sometimes reluctant, but nonetheless decisive reorientation of Communist policy on the West Coast waterfront. Party members committed themselves to the reconstruction of the AFL longshoremen's union at the same time that the Party nationally was denouncing the AFL as a bastion of reaction and even fascism. Although this change foreshadowed a much wider and more fundamental shift in Communist policy, it had little to do with the twists and turns of the international Communist movement. Rather, it reflected the fact that individual Party members were prepared to take the initiative and develop a program based on their own experience and ideas.

But the initiative did not come entirely from Communists. Since 1919 longshoremen on the West Coast had been suffering the consequences of unchecked employer domination. For years they seemed to be the helpless victims of a variety of human predators who together tightened the screws of the shipowners' rule. Beneath the surface, however, a great wave of discontent was smoldering, and the coming of the Great Depression only fed the subterranean flames. Gradually, men began to realize that it was necessary—and possible—to build a real union that would serve as an instrument for the improvement of their conditions and the restoration of their dignity. Here too the shape and complexion of this instrument became the subject of intense debate. Out of the longshoremen's own reckoning, there emerged a dedicated and resourceful leadership group on the strategic San Francisco waterfront. The consolidation of this group, and its close working relationship with the Communist party, would have enormous consequences for the revitalization of maritime unionism up and down the coast.

Depression conditions on the Pacific Coast were nearly as bad as those on the Atlantic. By 1926 there had already been more than twice as many seamen registered through the Marine Service Bureau as there were jobs available, and in a time of massive unemployment the hiring picture became even more grim. By the summer of 1932, in the port of San Pedro, it took approximately nine months of waiting in the "fink hall" before a job turned up. In the meantime those who were unable or unwilling to find a "flop" at a waterfront charity were forced to sleep under viaducts, in lumberyards, or in some other spot that provided a measure of protection from the elements and the San Pedro police. It was not uncommon for unemployed seamen to be arrested for vagrancy, or even suspicion of criminal syndicalism, and then released with a warning to get out of town. For those who did manage to ship out, wages were gradually reduced to the starvation point. One seaman recalled that "it couldn't get any worse, and [yet] it was getting worse. Some of the companies were paying as little as seventeen dollars a month." And the increasingly omnipresent workaways "were just waiting for you to drop dead so they could get your job."[1]

Among the longshoremen, there was less transiency, and thus relief was more readily available, but otherwise their conditions were little better than those of the seamen. By 1933 the average weekly wage for dockworkers in San Pedro was $10.45, and an investigator for the federal government wrote that "a very conservative estimate would probably place more than 50 per cent of all the longshoremen on the relief rolls."[2]

In San Francisco, the terms *shape-up, speed-up, kick-back,* and *Blue Book* became the principal watchwords of a long litany of misery. The Blue Book, officially known as the Longshoremen's Association of San Francisco and the Bay District, was in essence a company union, organized by gang bosses and used by the employers to break the 1919 dock strike and undermine the venerable Riggers and Stevedores' Union. Although the Blue Book's constitution and bylaws solemnly proclaimed "the duty of each member to be true to the Union and the labor cause generally," it was widely regarded as "a scab organization, formed . . . to keep the Longshoremen of the port in a state of bondage approaching slavery." Harry Bridges recalled that after attending one meeting of the organization, "it became obvious to me . . . that it was a company controlled union and a racket." A study by University of California labor economist Robert Francis concluded that "there never has been any union spirit within the organization." In fact, throughout its existence, "the foremen have been most interested in keeping the organization alive." Even a leading employer spokesman acknowledged in retrospect that the Blue Book made no effort to protect its members against the "atrocious system of hiring" that prevailed on the docks, nor did it "afford protection to the men against working conditions which were little short of barbarous."[3]

However, the Blue Book had its defenders, not only among the shipowners but in the upper echelons of the labor movement as well. John A. O'Connell, secretary of the San Francisco Labor Council, and Paul Scharrenberg, editor of the *Seamen's Journal* and secretary of the California Federation of Labor, were instrumental in arranging for the affiliation of the Blue Book with the San Francisco Labor Council. To pave the way for the Blue Book's entrance, the Riggers and Stevedores' Union, which had maintained a continuous existence on the waterfront since 1853, was expelled from the Labor Council in 1929. O'Connell stated that bona fide trade unionists had taken control of the Longshoremen's Association and had signed an agreement with the shipowners that "corrected a number of the prevailing evils" on the docks. He praised the Blue Book as an "organization [that] keeps good faith and order within itself and in the conduct of its business," and predicted it would earn "an honorable place within our movement." (The longshoremen themselves never concurred in this judgment. Many of them made a practice of dodging the union's delegates in order to avoid paying dues. After the passage of the National Industrial Recovery Act (NIRA) in June 1933, they deserted the company union en masse and rejoined the ILA, whereupon the president of the Blue Book abandoned further pretense of upholding the labor cause and went directly onto the payroll of the Waterfront Employers' Union.)[4]

Until 1933 the Blue Book had a closed-shop agreement with the employers. Every dockworker was supposed to pay dues to this company union in order to gain access to employment on the front. But any attempt to use the Blue Book's grievance procedure was an invitation to the blacklist. John Olsen, chairman of the ILA picketing committee during the 1934 strike, recalled the case of a star winch driver named Foghorn Charlie. Winch drivers were the aristocrats of the docks, but Foghorn Charlie made the mistake of demanding that the American-Hawaiian Steamship Company live up to its rules and pay him an hour of penalty time for working through his dinner hour. The Blue Book handled the grievance, and Charlie received his pay. But, said Olsen,

> the next ship, when they were hiring . . . in front of the dock, nobody saw Charlie. They saw the fella behind him, and the fella on the right of him, and the fella on the left of him, but they didn't see him. They all went to work, and he was left standing there, and he was a regular star winch driver. He went back to the union and said, "I got fired. . . . What can you do?" The union agent told him, "I can't do anything. . . ."

So he learned his lesson and had to take what they gave him. . . . That was an example of the way it was. The old Blue Book had good rules, but nobody lived up to them. And if you complained, then you weren't one of the ones picked the next morning, no matter how long you'd been working there. Very simple.[5]

If the Blue Book had a rival as the most despised symbol of the longshoremen's oppression, it was the shape-up—the infamous system of hiring on the docks. As far back as 1861, Henry Mayhew had stood on the London pierheads and watched as "masses of men of all grades, looks, and kinds" gathered around the foremen in the hope of finding a day's work. As the foreman came forward, "some men jump on the backs of the others, so as to lift themselves high above the rest, and attract the notice of him who hires them. Some cry aloud his surname, some his Christian name, others call out their own names, to remind him that they are there. Now the appeal is made in Irish blarney—now in broken English. Indeed, it is a sight to sadden the most callous, to see thousands of men struggling for only one day's hire."[6]

In San Francisco, the Embarcadero was known as the "slave market," but to many who witnessed it the shape-up bespoke an even lower form of existence. Bridges testified that the men were "hired off the streets like a bunch of sheep," and an observer in Boston commented that the stevedores who gathered around the hiring bosses were "like starving dogs at the sound of the dinner gong, each knowing that there were enough scraps left to reach just a few of them." The ILA rightly declared that "a more cruel, graft-ridden and senseless system of hiring could not be devised. . . . Thousands of men seeking employment were forced to hang around the piers at all hours, exposed to every kind of weather. Often, hundreds would report at a single pier at dawn, stand around for hours, only to be told, 'No work today,' long after there was any chance of obtaining work elsewhere." One longshoreman recalled that "for thirty five days, rain or shine, I was out there on the waterfront from five in the morning till all the crews were filled; but I never got a job."[7]

Depression conditions aggravated the problem of an already swollen work force. According to the ILA, many experienced longshoremen were forced to seek government relief while others "worked like slaves in shifts from 24 to 36 hours without sleep." As the favored few worked themselves into a state of exhaustion, crowds of hungry men would hover like vultures by the pierheads, on the chance that someone would get hurt on the job or fail to keep pace with the speed-up.[8]

Of course, the shape-up hiring system invited abuse, ranging from petty corruption to systematic extortion. Typical examples included the gang boss who "sold moonshine from his thermos bottle at two bits a shot to all of his gang that did not want to be fired"; a boss who for fourteen years "had the boys packing him booze and doing odd jobs around his house, etc. in order to get a job"; and the practice on the Dollar line docks, where the men regularly kicked back 10 percent of their wages to the gang bosses.[9]

The MWIU set out to change these conditions among both seamen and longshoremen. But for the most part its efforts on the Pacific Coast were sporadic and relatively ineffective. Sam Darcy, who directed the work of the Communist party in California, expressed the opinion in later years that the Marine Workers Union was "more a name than a substance. . . . You never knew who had books and who didn't and who paid dues and who didn't. It was all very vague." Contemporary estimates tend to bear out his recollection. In 1932, more than two years after the union's founding, the Party's *Western Worker* admitted: "Except for the scattered A. F. of L. and company unions, it can be said that the marine workers were unorganized." At that time, the MWIU had only one branch headquarters on the Pacific Coast, in San Francisco, and scattered delegates in several other ports. In July 1933, while acknowledging that the marine industry was the "most strategic" in California, the *Western Worker* declared that the union still faced the "first step" of establishing effective ship and dock committees "before we can expect to form any real mass organization of the M.W.I.U." The Communist party concluded: "Essentially the [Red unions remain] isolated from the most basic sections of the workers on the coast, in marine, railroad, agriculture, oil, and those in the large plants."[10]

In early 1934, however, the pace and effectiveness of the union's activity increased somewhat. It led a few strikes aboard ship, including one on the *Andrea Luckenbach* where the MWIU mobilized five hundred pickets on the Seattle docks to support the crew's demands for higher wages and better conditions. But inspired by the example of the "Baltimore Soviet," most of the MWIU's efforts during this period seemed to focus on the question of seamen's relief. In San Francisco a *Western Worker* headline declared, "Longshoremen, Seamen Fight for Rights Won in Baltimore." In San Pedro, only a week before the beginning of the Big Strike, the MWIU spearheaded the formation of a Seamen's Unemployed Council, which demanded that "the seamen shall be permitted to administer their own relief through their elected committees."[11]

Within a matter of days, these struggles were cast into the background by the epic coastwide strike that the longshoremen initiated on May 9. And in this instance the Communist party was well prepared. For insofar as the Party on the West Coast made any significant headway in the maritime industry from 1930 to 1934, it was among the stevedores. The advances came by applying policies whose emphasis varied sharply from the main thrust of the Third Period line and program. While the Communist-led industrial union on the Pacific Coast languished, or moved ahead only in fits and starts, the Party gradually applied itself to the task of rebuilding the AFL craft union on the docks. How this happened is a complex, even tangled, story, highlighted by several strong-willed, independent personalities whose roles shed significant light on the inner workings of the Communist party and the rebirth of maritime unionism during these years.

One of these personalities was Sam Darcy, who became Communist party district organizer for California, Nevada, and Arizona at the beginning of 1931. Historian Cletus Daniel has asserted that in Darcy "Communists in California gained a district organizer as resourceful and effective as any who served the American party during the 1930s." Born Samuel Dardeck in the Ukraine, he came to the United States at the age of two and grew up in the hothouse world of socialist politics and needle-trades unionism in New York City. One of his most vivid early recollections was of a garment workers' picket line where his father, an ardent union member, was beaten by police billy clubs and carried away on a stretcher. "From then on," he said, "I was a Communist." In the late twenties he went to the Soviet Union for sixteen months and served as an American representative to the Young Communist International. Upon his return to the United States, he was the main organizer of the Communist-led demonstration of the unemployed in New York City on March 6, 1930. The demonstration, one of many across the country and around the world, drew a huge crowd and resulted in a bloody confrontation with heavily armed police.

Soon after this event Darcy ran afoul of the newly appointed Communist leader Earl Browder, who apparently found his keen intelligence disquieting and his prickly manner annoying. The Party's failure to reap a sufficiently rich harvest from the massive gathering of the unemployed was drawing criticism from the Comintern, and Darcy may have been a convenient scapegoat. In any case, Browder had him exiled to California, where the Party district was in a shambles and the opportunities for failure seemed abundant. Obviously, Browder did not anticipate that this backwater would become a storm center of some of the greatest upheavals of the 1930s and that Darcy's stature would be greatly enhanced by his role in the massive strikes in agriculture and maritime.

Over the years the two men were to develop a long history of mutual antagonism. In 1944 Browder had Darcy expelled from the Communist party; and after his own expulsion, he characterized William Z. Foster and Darcy as "my permanent (but usually secret) opposition in America." For his part, Darcy stated with pride that "Browder and I never had good relations." In fact, his disdain for a number of national Communist functionaries, whom he described as "middle-class rejects who couldn't make it in the bourgeois world," earned him much enmity at the top levels of the Party. Among lower-level cadres and Party sympathizers, his reputation as a martinet was legendary. Union organizer Caroline Decker characterized him as a "very strict disciplinarian [who] blows up at the slightest inefficiency. I have big fights with him." However, another California cadre remembered him as "a slave driver, but a convincing one" who was "beloved by the rank and file." Only twenty-five years old when he took command of the Party apparatus in California, this precocious, ambitious, and abrasive district organizer was ideally situated to develop policies that suited his own perceptions and ideological predisposition.[12]

The question of dual unionism had caused sharp disagreement within the Communist party for many years. In 1930 Darcy wrote an article in a Communist publication that declared that the "senility" of the AFL was providing "a glorious opportunity for revolutionary trade unionism." This, of course, was the line of the Third Period, and publicly Darcy was willing to condemn those who deviated from it. But his own father had long been a member of an AFL union, and the son had apparently grown up "very firm in the conviction that dual unionism was out." In California, far from the "cave of winds" in New York City, he launched an increasingly open campaign against the excesses of the Third Period. His forceful intervention helped to dramatically strengthen the leadership role of the Communist-led Cannery and Agricultural Workers Industrial Union (CAWIU) by shifting its focus from revolutionary propaganda to agitation around the workers' immediate economic demands. In agriculture, however, there was virtually no AFL presence, and therefore dual unionism was not a real issue.

But in maritime the situation was very different, for although the AFL unions were nearly defunct, they had a long-standing and widely recognized claim to represent the marine workers. If indeed Darcy had again become convinced that "dual unionism was out," the MWIU presented a difficult problem. He later recalled that he had always regarded the MWIU as sectarian and more extreme than the other Red unions. In 1934 he publicly criticized the MWIU's "serious sectarian errors" and the tendency of many Communists to engage in "mere name-calling" and to become "professional critics and 'line-givers.' "[13]

For a time, the MWIU was very much overshadowed by the volatile situation in agriculture. But in late 1932 several Communist cadres and a number of rank-and-file stevedores launched a campaign to break the shackles of the Blue Book and build a bona fide union. The question was, which union?—the MWIU, which actively sought to rally the "steves" under the banner of revolutionary industrial unionism, or the ILA, which had been defunct on the docks since 1919.

For most MWIU activists the answer was simple. By experience, outlook, and temperament, these men felt a strong affinity with the political line and program of the Third Period. Not only did they share the seamen's historic experience of stark deprivation and isolation from mainstream America, but many of them had come out of the IWW's Marine Transport Workers' Union. They had rejected the MTW because it was isolated, ineffective, and increasingly eccentric. However, in many cases they had not repudiated the IWW's dual unionism and aggressively revolutionary style. On the contrary, it was precisely the recreation of these traits in the MWIU that made the transition from anarcho-syndicalist unionism to Communist unionism an easy one.

Harry Jackson, who became the leading MWIU spokesman on the West Coast, was in many ways the living embodiment of the ultrarevolutionary aspects of the Third Period line and style. A former Wobbly, he was reputedly a founding member of the Communist party. Using his real name, Henry Gliksohn, he ran for San Francisco supervisor on the Communist ticket in 1929; his program called for the seven-hour day, five-day week, unemployment insurance, and turning the "coming imperialist war . . . into a civil war against the capitalists." Al Richmond remembered him as a "phenomenal soapboxer," but his role was more that of organizer than agitator. The Party assigned him to some of its most dangerous concentration points. For a time he served as a district organizer in the deep South and was involved in the Scottsboro campaign and the bitter class warfare between coal miners and agents of the employers in Harlan County, Kentucky.

According to Darcy, Jackson was a restless type who, although born and raised in San Francisco, "talked like a Brooklyn tough guy and took great pride in that posture." When Jackson testified before the National Longshoremen's Board in July 1934, a time when public attention was riveted on the maritime situation, Darcy was appalled because he felt Jackson was putting on his "Brooklyn gangster act." He recalled saying, "Harry, why don't you cut out that Brownsville Brooklynese crap and talk like an American?"—to which Jackson responded, "What's the matter? *You* goin' college on me, too?" Earlier, speaking on a platform with Malcolm Cowley, Waldo Frank, Sidney Hook, and other luminaries of the world of arts and letters who were supporting William Z. Foster for president, Jackson had declared that "capitalism is a great big dung heap. And the role of the intellectual is to sprinkle it with perfume."

To William McCuistion, who claimed to have known him since 1929, Jackson's role in the Communist movement was akin to that of George Mink. McCuistion testified that Jackson had a "direct connection" with the Comintern, and that "he is a guy who can jump on the Communist Party's policies . . . where other people would get expelled for the same thing." Earl Browder, while acknowledging him as "a very militant, courageous comrade, whom we all value very much," was nonetheless taken aback when Jackson told the Communist party central committee to mind its own business during the 1934 strike. A part of the Jackson legend is that he once responded to a particularly inappropriate order from Browder with a telegram that read, "Dear Comrade Secretary Browder: Kiss my ass!"[14]

Tough, abrasive, outspoken, independent—these qualities exemplified not only Jackson but the MWIU and most of its veteran cadres. Moreover, these men were deeply committed to the industrial unionism and the revolutionary stance upon which the MWIU was founded. Thus, it is only natural that they would clash bitterly with anyone in the Communist party who proposed that the MWIU should take a back seat to the ILA on the docks, especially in San Francisco, where the ILA had not been heard from in years.

But even within the MWIU there was the basis for a more flexible policy. For one thing, Harry Hynes was based in San Francisco, and he was an uncommonly sensitive and thoughtful man. For another, Roy Hudson, the union's national secretary, was developing into a tactician and strategist of unusual skill. While his growing Party responsibilities imposed significant constraints, Hudson, like Hynes, was to prove himself able to adapt to new circumstances. Very early in his MWIU experience, in the port of Philadelphia, he had seen the longshoremen's discontent with the retrograde policies of the ILA, and he had also witnessed how MWIU agitation on the docks had met with "all kinds of applause, encouragement, discussion." But when the ILA contract expired, and the MWIU encouraged the men to go on strike under the leadership of the newly formed industrial union, they hesitated and finally opted to remain in the ILA. The MWIU program and fighting style had aroused the enthusiasm of the Philadelphia longshoremen, but dual unionism had confused and ultimately repelled them. Hudson remembered that "there was tremendous dissatisfaction, but these men were organized. I learned from this experience that when you were dealing with organized workers who had a contract, you had to work *within* their situation."[15]

Gradually, out of the crucible of experience, a multifaceted approach toward the longshoremen and the ILA began to emerge. Sometimes, as in Philadelphia, there was direct competition with the ILA. On other occasions, the MWIU concentrated its main efforts among unorganized longshoremen and called on ILA members to unite with the Marine Workers Union membership around a common program that would strengthen both unions. In late 1933 the *Marine Workers Voice* reported that "work among the longshoremen in the new Boston [MWIU] local is pr[o]gressing very speedily, especially on the unorganized coastwise docks." At the same time, the *Voice* acknowledged that "the Boston ILA men are of exceptionally high organizational quality and militancy" and foresaw the "immediate possibility of organizing an effective opposition group" within the ILA. At its best, this multifaceted approach seemed admirably flexible; at its worst, it appeared contradictory and confused. To some degree, it probably reflected uncertainty and disagreement among the Communists who played the main role in hammering out MWIU policy.[16]

But the question of a correct approach to organizing on the docks was by no means confined to the internal deliberations of the Communist party. As the depression ran its course, more and more longshoremen began to debate this issue and to play an active role in determining their own destinies. Out of this growing wellspring of discontent Harry Bridges was to emerge as a quintessential rank-and-file leader who was eventually to become one of the most prominent—and controversial—trade union officials in the history of the United States. A portrait of Bridges in his role as spokesman for the dockworkers must await the moment of his meteoric rise from obscurity during the 1934 maritime strike. But even in obscurity, he was an important figure on the San Francisco waterfront in the early thirties and his background is well worth examining.

Bridges was born in a middle-class suburb of Melbourne, Australia. His father was a realtor and his mother a devout Irish Catholic who insisted that he attend parochial schools. After leaving school at age fourteen, Bridges collected rents for his father and worked as a clerk in a stationery store. He found the first job distasteful and the second one dull. But the adventure stories of Jack London fired his imagination and he took to hanging around the Melbourne docks. His father allowed him to sail on a ketch that ran the stormy seas between Melbourne and Tasmania, in the hope that the trip would dispel his romantic illusions. The ship was blown a hundred miles off course in a raging storm, and the elder Bridges recalled that his son was delighted by the experience. "After that," he said, "there was no stopping the boy from going to sea."

Bridges was shipwrecked twice, but his most vivid memories were of unionism and strikes. In 1917 he got caught up in the general strike movement that swept across Australia. "We piled off the ships for a stop-work meeting on the front," he recalled forty years later. "There were two or three thousand men gathered there and the meeting was lit up by torches. The whole country was shut down and even the electricity had been turned off."

In April 1920 Bridges got off a ship in San Francisco, joined the Sailors' Union of the Pacific, and began shipping out of U.S. ports. He was a participant in the 1921 seamen's strike, serving as a picket captain in New Orleans. Disgusted with the policies of the Furuseth leadership, he joined the IWW soon after the strike was broken. But Bridges quickly found himself in disagreement with the stridently antipolitical stance of the IWW. Moreover, some of the top people in the organization behaved so bizarrely that he began to suspect they were paid agents of the shipowners. "That's what finished me with the IWW," he recalled in 1981, although he acknowledged that Wobbly policies continued to play an important role on the waterfront long after the organization had faded.[17]

Bridges began working on the San Francisco docks in October 1922. Frances Perkins later recalled that his reputation was that of "a steady, competent workman." In his own words, he was "a damned good longshore-man"—an able winch driver who worked with star gangs for months, and sometimes years, at a time. But his hatred of the Blue Book also gained him a certain notoriety, and his refusal to keep his dues paid up often cost him his job. He recalled: "I became so well known to the delegate of the Blue Book Union that soon it was impossible for me to get employment for more than a day or so on a job before the Blue Book delegate would catch up with me and have me fired." In early 1932 he had been working on a new job for no more than two hours "when Red Edgerton, the delegate of the Blue Book Union, came to the dock and had me fired. I was at this time sixteen months behind in my dues. Many other men in the gang who were much further behind than I were not bothered by the delegate of the Blue Book. I asked Red how he knew so quickly I was working at Pier 26 and he replied that he knew where I was all the time."[18]

When the first Blue Book contract with the shipowners expired in 1924, Bridges and a number of other dockworkers attempted to rebuild a bona fide union on the waterfront. In the Labor Day parade that year, four hundred longshoremen marched up Market Street under the banner of the Riggers and Stevedores' Union. But these were the Golden Twenties, labor's leanest years. Most of the longshore marchers were blacklisted, and there were to be no more Labor Day parades in San Francisco until the triumphal march of 1934, in the afterglow of the Big Strike.[19]

Gradually the lean, hawk-nosed "Limo" with the cockney twang became a fixture on the waterfront. At the shape-up, on the job, and in the gin mills, he listened to the men's gripes with the air of someone who had seen and heard it all before. He greeted their complaints with a cocksure "of course," and then went on to talk about the necessity of organizing to combat the employers. When asked how he had met Bridges, veteran longshoremen Henry Schmidt remembered that "all of a sudden the man was there talking," and "he knew what he was talking about." Even a Communist longshoreman recalled how the few Party members on the docks would defer to Bridges: "We had a pretty good theoretical grasp of what it was all about, but when it came to practical knowledge and what to do from one day to the next, we just naturally turned to Harry. He always had an answer."[20]

One thing Bridges knew for sure: "The class struggle is here." He knew it not because he had read about it in books, but because he had experienced it—aboard ship, in the Australian general strike of 1917 and the 1921 seamen's strike, and on the San Francisco docks every day. However, in spite of his cocksure air, he was an intensely practical man who knew instinctively that any effort to organize the maritime workers would have to take full account of their limited aspirations and consciousness. He saw the Communists soapboxing on the waterfront in the early thirties. He met fellow Aussie Harry Hynes and later acknowledged that Hynes "knew a damn sight

more than I did about unionism at the time." He watched with keen interest as
the MWIU preached the gospel of revolutionary industrial unionism. In an
interview with Theodore Dreiser in 1940, he recalled: "The Communist Party
was making a drive on the waterfront. . . . the stuff they put out fell on
sympathetic ears, because they were telling the truth about conditions." But
they didn't get anywhere at first, because they had "a very left and revolutionary line. . . . it went right over [the longshoremen's] heads. They were
sympathetic to trade unionism but not to revolutionary trade unionism. I used
to argue with these people—the Communists—and point that out. We sym-
pathized with them, but they would always go so far, and then could go no
farther. . . . At that time I refused to join the Marine Workers Industrial
Union. I talked to them frankly. They were trying to make me a member. I
refused to join, because I told them it wouldn't work." Independently, Harry
Bridges and Sam Darcy were arriving at the conclusion that the MWIU could
not be the vehicle for organizing longshoremen on the West Coast. A strategic
shift and a vitally important alliance were in the making.[21]

The first visible step toward effective organization on the docks
came with the appearance of the *Waterfront Worker* in December 1932. This
small mimeographed bulletin achieved a remarkable degree of popularity
because it provided a uniquely authentic voice for expressing the deep grievances and vague aspirations of the men on the docks. In the words of one
maritime worker, "it spoke in terms that the guys couldn't help but respect. It
was their own language."[22]

Historians have generally agreed that the *Waterfront Worker* was initially
published by the MWIU and later taken over by a group of longshoremen that
included Bridges, Harry Schmidt, and several others who became rank-and-
file leaders of the 1934 strike. The root of this view rests in part with Bridges
himself, who testified at both his 1939 and 1941 deportation hearings that he
and some of his fellow dockworkers inherited the paper from the MWIU
during the summer of 1933. In his biography of Bridges, Charles Larrowe
states: "The point that the *Waterfront Worker* was trying to make was an
obvious one: the right union for the longshoremen was the MWIU. But while
the paper helped whet the longshoremen's appetite for a union of their own in
place of the Blue Book, it failed to persuade them that the MWIU was the
answer." According to this view, the MWIU was shunted aside following the
passage of the NIRA, when the stevedores rushed to join the International
Longshoremen's Association, and Bridges transformed the *Waterfront Worker* into an instrument for promoting a militant program within the AFL
union.[23]

It is certainly true that the dramatic resurgence of the ILA in June and July
1933 marked a vital turning point in the development of maritime unionism,
and that it imposed a new focus on the *Waterfront Worker*'s activity. But a

careful examination of the available evidence, including the six issues of the paper that appeared before July 1933, makes it clear that it was not published by the MWIU, and that it never called on the longshoremen to join the Marine Workers Union. Moreover, although the Communist party nationally seems to have regarded the *Waterfront Worker* as "one of our shop papers," it was a genuine united front effort from the very beginning. As Darcy pointed out in 1934, "In the group which published the *Waterfront Worker,* were included a minority of Communists, and other militant elements." Their common purpose was to develop a core of workers who would take the lead in destroying the Blue Book and establishing a "real union." Until July 1933, the paper's editors took an increasingly open stand in favor of an industrial union of longshoremen and seamen, but they did not endorse the MWIU, and they were careful to declare that "such a union . . . cannot be built from the outside. It must be built by US, the stevedores, right here on the docks."[24]

It is difficult to reconstruct the emergence of the group that issued the *Waterfront Worker,* because the evidence is meager and contradictory. Some of the MWIUers, notably Harry Hynes and Tommy Ray, seem at first to have regarded the Communist party district leadership, and Darcy in particular, as an obstacle to organizing on the waterfront, because of Darcy's apparent contempt for seamen as "unruly people," his strong (in their judgment, obsessive) commitment to building the Cannery and Agricultural Workers Union, and his consequent neglect of the more strategic maritime industry. However, in the spring of 1932, according to his own recollection, Darcy began to direct increasing attention toward the waterfront, and the San Francisco longshoremen in particular. After a period of intense discussion, he and a handful of Communist cadres began attending the shape-up on the Embarcadero, mingling with the longshoremen assembled there and, sometimes, mounting the soapbox to call for the rebirth of unionism on the docks. It is significant that the MWIU was not directly involved in this effort, and Darcy and his comrades were content to advocate militant unionism without specifying a particular organization. Orrick Johns, who often attended these early morning events, recalled that the longshoremen were generally "sullen and indifferent" when the Communists addressed them, perhaps because Party agitation brought the "Red scare," and an enlarged police presence, to the Embarcadero.

But gradually barriers were broken down and ties were developed with a number of longshoremen. One of the first men to come forward was John Larsen, a colorful Dane who was nicknamed Pirate because he wore a patch over one eye. A former seaman, Larsen had apparently been a member of the IWW in the Northwest before coming to San Francisco. He had worked on the docks for many years when he attracted the attention of the Communists by his courageous advocacy of their right to speak during a confrontation with the police at the shape-up. It was Larsen who first introduced Darcy and his associates to Bridges, Schmidt, Henry Schrimpf, Dutch Detrich, and other longshoremen who became the heart of the rank-and-file movement. Most of these longshore militants remained organizationally independent of the Communist party, and they were to play an important role in orienting the *Waterfront Worker* toward the day-to-day realities on the docks.[25]

Among the Communists, as the launching of the *Waterfront Worker* approached, there was an intense struggle between those who emphasized organizing on the basis of the longshoremen's immediate grievances and those who upheld the political line of the Third Period and argued for a campaign to develop the MWIU as an industrial union among dockworkers as well as seamen. Although Darcy was the leading proponent of the former position, it was, ironically, Harry Hynes of the MWIU who initially played the key role in getting out the paper and giving it the strategic orientation that Darcy advocated. Most other MWIUers, especially the outspoken and influential Harry Jackson (who was not in San Francisco when the paper was initiated), bitterly opposed this course. Hynes clearly participated in the *Waterfront Worker* as a Communist, not as a formal representative of the Marine Workers Union. In fact, it would be months before the paper publicly acknowledged the cooperation of the MWIU, and the *Marine Workers Voice* characterized the appearance of the paper as "a surprise."[26]

The first issue of the *Waterfront Worker* announced only that it was published "by a group of longshoremen for longshoremen." The MWIU was nowhere mentioned, and the tone of the paper was very much in keeping with a recommendation from Tom Mooney, labor's most famous "class war prisoner," that it should "stick to the task of interesting the workers in their day to day problems." The paper offered a full page of biting anecdotes about the corrupt and overbearing behavior of unpopular gang bosses. There was also a bitter criticism of the Blue Book for agreeing to a ten-cent wage cut, and a brief call to organize "small undercover groups of those whom we know on each dock" as "the only way we can lay the basis for a real union."

The second issue, published in February 1933, devoted more space to the question of organization, but remained vague and narrow in focus. The March issue stated that "our main purpose is to prepare the whole waterfront between now and next December" to combat any attempt to impose another wage cut. Again the tone was cautious, emphasizing slow, painstaking work toward the formation of a new union and the protection of activists' jobs. "We, too, have jobs to lose," said the editors. " 'Safety first. Take no chances' is our slogan."[27]

The *Party Organizer,* a national CP publication intended for the internal use of its members, welcomed the appearance of the *Waterfront Worker* while criticizing its failure to speak "clearly and decisively" about the course that the longshoremen should follow. It also criticized the omission of any reference to the MWIU. But, significantly, the Communist journal did not indicate that it was the task of the MWIU to recruit longshoremen. Rather, it emphasized the MWIU's role in developing a united front among the rank and file of the various waterfront unions and declared that it was crucial to "carry the struggle for the demands of the longshoremen *into the ILA locals.*" A month later the *Party Organizer* repeated that the task on the San Francisco docks was to "work inside" the Blue Book and the ILA, "build up the oppos[i]tion movement, and at the same time unite all longshoremen, organized and unorganized, in a common struggle on the waterfront despite the resistance of the leadership of these unions."

Meanwhile, the Party's *Western Worker* had its own idea about the proper course on the San Francisco waterfront. At a time when the *Party Organizer* was calling for work inside the Blue Book and the ILA, and the *Waterfront Worker* was advocating the formation of unaffiliated activist groups on each dock, the *Western Worker* declared: "Longshoremen have a reputation as fighting men. Join the Marine Workers Industrial Union."[28]

A statement by the MWIU's West Coast executive committee in the March 1933 issue of the *Marine Workers Voice* provides further indication that the *Waterfront Worker* was independent of the MWIU and also implies a certain ambivalence on the part of the union's leadership. The MWIU declared:

> The issuing of a mimeographed bulletin, the "Waterfront Worker" by a group of longshoremen comes as a surprise on the "Frisco" waterfront. . . .
>
> The first issue of their paper . . . brings out a number of interesting points. It has a number of minor shortcomings . . . but the general line of the bulletin is correct. It is a good start.
>
> The Marine Workers Industrial Union endorses this beginning of organization by some of the "Frisco" longshoremen and pledges the support of its members and will give every assistance possible as long as the group follows a correct working class policy.

In April a "Letter of Greetings" from the national leadership of the MWIU was printed in the *Waterfront Worker,* which for the first time acknowledged that the union "here on the West Coast has helped us." The MWIU letter again welcomed the beginnings of organization and offered a number of comradely criticisms aimed chiefly at what it regarded as the paper's overly cautious approach to organizing. "We must NOW fight against the smallest daily gr[iev]ances," said the MWIU letter, "instead of the 'ultimate' solution of waiting to next December." The letter concluded, however, with a proposal that ranged far beyond the frame of reference that had so far characterized the *Waterfront Worker.* The form of any new organization on the docks, it declared, "must be industrial and international in character, linked up with the seamen and other waterfront workers, not only in other U.S. ports but all over the world."

The April issue of the paper seemed to mark a turning point in its development. The editors expressed their agreement with the points raised by the

MWIU, and there was suddenly a flurry of news and commentary that highlighted the activity of the Marine Workers Union and the (Red) International of Seamen and Harbor Workers. Also, the paper featured a strongly worded article that called on the stevedores to "take a stand against war" and pointed with pride to the example of the Seattle longshoremen who had refused to load munitions designed to aid the fight against the Russian Bolsheviks in 1919. This change in the tone of the paper was no doubt occasioned to some extent by the criticisms expressed in the *Party Organizer* and the MWIU communications, and perhaps also by the surge of activity that the MWIU had been spearheading among seamen on the Atlantic and Gulf coasts in recent months. Moreover, the growing popularity of the *Waterfront Worker* probably emboldened its editors and made them feel more comfortable about combining a focus on immediate grievances with a sharper statement of their political views.[29]

The key question remained—which union? Here, too, the paper's direction became more bold. Several articles on the history of craft unions on the waterfront appeared, and the paper clearly expressed the opinion that craft unionism and "craft scabbing" had long been synonymous. An invitation to send fraternal delegates to the forthcoming national convention of the MWIU was highlighted and accepted, although the letter of invitation was careful to acknowledge that any delegates from the San Francisco waterfront "would be bound and guided by the instructions of the rank and file longshoremen."

The crest of this new wave came with the June 1933 issue. The *Waterfront Worker* openly applauded the fact that a recent effort to revive the ILA in San Francisco had failed, and expressed the opinion that this failure represented the longshoremen's rejection of craft unionism and the ILA. "The lesson is clear," it said. "Unless the longshoremen and seamen are organized in ONE UNION with one united leadership the prospects of success in any big struggle with the shipowners are slim indeed."[30]

These bold words seemed to imply an endorsement of the MWIU as the right union for the longshoremen. In any case, they echoed a sentiment that had been expressed on the waterfront for generations and that would find a measure of fulfillment with the birth of the Maritime Federation of the Pacific in 1935. But in June 1933 they were quickly overshadowed by the excitement that greeted the passage of the National Industrial Recovery Act and its celebrated section 7(a), granting workers "the right to organize and bargain collectively through representatives of their own choosing." The government would often prove unable or unwilling to deliver on this promise, but millions of workers took it seriously and began to implement it on their own. In the famous unionization drive that revitalized the United Mine Workers in the coalfields, John Brophy said that "the miners moved into the union *en masse*. . . . They organized themselves for all practical purposes." In the steel industry, labor reporter Harvey O'Connor recalled that "all over the steel country union locals sprang up spontaneously. . . . You name the mill town and there was a local there, carrying a name like the 'Blue Eagle' or the 'New Deal' local." Likewise, on the San Francisco waterfront, the passage of the NIRA was followed almost immediately by the reestablishment of an ILA local that the stevedores joined in droves. As Henry Schmidt recalled, "We didn't have to be pushed to get into that union. We knocked down the god darned doors."[31]

Ten days after the recovery act became law, a man named Lee J. Holman appeared on the docks with a new ILA charter from President Ryan and began "selling organized labor for 50¢ apiece," as one longshoreman put it (referring to the special ILA initiation fee). Holman was something of a mystery. The *San Francisco Call-Bulletin* asserted in 1934 that he "has been prominent in San Francisco labor circles for the last twenty years"; and Holman himself declared that "for 14 long years I was the only semblance of any organization in this Port." The scanty record, however, does not bear out such claims. Apparently he began longshoring in 1911. The Blue Book expelled him in 1924 for his persistent advocacy of the old Red Book union, and he recalled later that "on many occasions I was forced out in the sticks to work for a few months and save the money to carry on the battle—on many occasions my family starved!" In August 1931, alarmed by growing Communist agitation, he tried to enlist Ryan's aid in rebuilding the ILA in San Francisco. Although Ryan's initial response was cautious, nine "oldtime" longshoremen met in late September to establish the nucleus of an organization. After electing Holman temporary president and business manager, they decided that "for the time being we will continue with same small membership until further orders from International." In the absence of such orders, the group apparently became inactive until the early months of 1932, when several communications from the ILA Pacific District rekindled Holman's enthusiasm and led him to declare: "I know that the ILA can organize this Port if it wants to." But he recognized that the union faced a formidable task: "to show these men that it is not run or dominated by a bunch of grafting Politicians [whose aims] are nothing other than to collect dues for their fat Salerys."[32]

Eventually, with some support from the union's Pacific District, Holman and his associates formed an ILA organizing committee and issued an appeal for "the approval and support of all Longshoremen who are tired of Communistic Rot, tired of silly and senseless Soap Box Ravings, and sick of Blue Book Misrepresentation." Initially, however, these appeals met with little response. In fact, it is almost certain that Holman's semiclandestine efforts before the NIRA were very much overshadowed by the more dynamic presence of the *Waterfront Worker*. Thus, at the moment when he surfaced and began openly selling the ILA, Holman must have remained unknown to the vast majority of men on the docks. But he quickly overcame this disability, because he had the support of the international union and because the longshoremen's "elementary sense of self-preservation" led them—in the short run—to choose the safer and more conventional alternative.[33]

Holman not only looked to Ryan for support; he also imitated his methods of leadership. He installed a complete set of officers without an election and used San Francisco policemen to enforce his rule at the first membership meeting. When a member suggested that a chairman for the meeting should be elected from the floor, Holman had the police remove him from the room. Although he concentrated most of his fire on the Blue Book, Holman also attacked the *Waterfront Worker* and warned the longshoremen to stay away from the Reds. From the standpoint of the Left, this was hardly an auspicious beginning, but the workers continued to flock to the ILA.[34]

A week after Holman's appearance on the docks, the *Waterfront Worker* held its first public meeting, with about a hundred stevedores in attendance. The editors announced that they had joined the ILA, and they called upon the longshoremen to "make the new union a real fighting weapon" by developing a program for rank-and-file control. Apparently, however, they were still somewhat reluctant to endorse the ILA as the only viable union on the docks. The August issue of the *Waterfront Worker* published an outline history of the ILA that concluded that its record had meant "a harvest for a few officials and slave conditions for thousands of stevedores." Such an article could hardly have been construed as a call to embrace the ILA, even for the purpose of rebuilding it along militant lines. But given the editors' determination to develop organization from within the ranks of the dockworkers, their revulsion at the prospect of bucking Ryan and Holman was soon cast aside. By mid-August, in response to growing anger and anxiety about the ILA's failure to deliver on its promises, the *Waterfront Worker* was declaring: "Why has the ILA not become the fighting organization we want on the front? Because we have never taken affairs into our own hands. We have from the first le[f]t everything in the hands of a few individuals we know little about. Tonight [at the second ILA membership meeting] we must make the break. We must take the organization into our own hands. The rank and file must run and control the ILA."[35]

Again, however, the Communist party was speaking with more than one voice. The group around the *Waterfront Worker,* which included a few Communists, wasted no time in joining the ILA and, in spite of some reservations, developing a program for revitalizing the union on a militant and democratic basis. But some Communists continued to hold out for the MWIU. An article signed "A. Girard" in the *Western Worker* accused Holman and the ILA of exploiting the militant sentiment created by the *Waterfront Worker,* for the purpose of "build[ing] up another Blue Book Union under a different name." After reviewing the shabby record of "Ryan's Racket," the author asked why the longshoremen had joined "the union of

Ryan." He answered: "In some measure the *fault* can be found in the *failure* of the Marine Workers Industrial Union to follow up, with concrete organization of M.W.I.U. groups on docks, the sentiment aroused by the *Waterfront Worker*." After a further attack on the record and on the policies of the ILA, the author concluded that MWIU members should "form militant groups . . . within the I.L.A. to fight for the election of honest officials and compel a policy of militant struggle against the shipowners. Further, and even more important," he argued, was joining the MWIU and building "organized grievance committees" on the docks and ships to carry on this struggle.[36]

The MWIU had been developing a policy of uniting militant elements from different maritime unions and rank-and-file groups around a common program of struggle, and had publicly approached the *Waterfront Worker* in that spirit. But this was hardly the tone of the Girard article, which placed the question of affiliation above that of program and essentially called on the MWIU to compete with the ILA for the allegiance of the longshoremen. That such a sentiment went beyond one isolated individual is clear not only from the fact that the Girard article was published in the *Western Worker,* but also from Sam Darcy's acknowledgment a year later that there had been "some tendency among the Communists at that time to organize competitive M.W.I.U. recruiting."* However, as Darcy concluded, "The I.L.A. movement was so overwhelming among the men . . . that it would have been suicide to take the handful of militants away from the general stream of the movement."[38]

Thus the question of which union was finally resolved. The stevedores flocked into the ILA, the *Waterfront Worker* began its campaign to transform the AFL union, and the MWIU limited its focus to the seamen and the task of building an effective alliance between the men who sailed the ships and those who worked along the shore. There were some Communists who continued to

---

*Harry Bridges did not recall any of this infighting when I interviewed him in 1981. He said that "right from the start the Party supported the organization of the ILA," and that the MWIU also "cooperated wholeheartedly." How, then, does one account for the contrast between Bridges's and Darcy's recollections? In answering this question, it is necessary to depend more on reasonable inference than hard evidence. First, Bridges was not a member of the Communist party and therefore he was unaware of the controversy raging within the Party's ranks. For the most part, Communists did not air their internal disagreements in public, although, as we have seen, their line was not always as unified as the popular stereotype would have us believe. By the time Bridges became a part of the organizing effort, the principal combatants within the Party had apparently achieved at least a fragile unity. Moreover, Bridges seems to have related mainly to Harry Hynes, who was capable of handling difficult matters with great sensitivity. Hynes was one of the leading representatives of the MWIU on the West Coast, and he was instrumental in getting out the first few issues of the *Waterfront Worker*. This could account for Bridges's recollection that the paper was initially published by the MWIU and also for his statement that the MWIU cooperated wholeheartedly with the longshore militants' organizing activities.[37]

balk at this division of labor, but overwhelmingly the Party committed itself to this policy and applied it with flexibility and skill. Certainly the further development of the *Waterfront Worker* as the voice of the longshore rank and file, and the growing unity of stevedores and seamen, would have an important bearing on the success of the Big Strike.

After the passage of the recovery act, the struggle on the San Francisco waterfront assumed three important dimensions. The first, as always, saw the longshoremen pitted against the shipowners. The employers, while paying lip service to the National Recovery Administration's call for reform, remained completely unwilling to relinquish their control of hiring or to recognize the ILA. The second struggle, between the ILA and the Blue Book, was really an extension of the first, for the Blue Book had always functioned as an instrument of the employers. Although they would later claim that the recovery act had outlawed the closed shop, the shipowners clung tenaciously to their long-standing closed-shop agreement with the Blue Book as a means of staving off the development of legitimate unionism. The third struggle, between the militants and the old guard in the ILA, remained in the background until the fate of the Blue Book was decided.

With the appearance of a bona fide union on the docks, the employers and the Blue Book launched what one ILA official called "a counterdrive to get [the men] whipped back into line." On July 18 Holman notified the National Recovery Administration that a San Francisco stevedoring company had discharged four men for refusing to belong to the company union. The next day a longshoreman named Martin "Whitey" Winblad was fired at the insistence of a Blue Book delegate. After working at the Matson Navigation Company for almost two years, he was suddenly informed by the paymaster: "You can't work here. You haven't paid your dues."

It had long been commonplace for Blue Book delegates to blacklist young militants like Bridges and old-time Red Book partisans like Holman. But the firing of Whitey Winblad, who had avoided paying dues to the Blue Book for almost ten years, was a new development that immediately affected the livelihoods of hundreds of men on the waterfront. The offensive was concentrated at the Matson company, the largest employer in the port and the center of company union strength. At the shape-up on July 20 Matson representatives told the assembled stevedores, "Everybody has to have a Blue Book from now on," thus initiating a lockout not only of ILA men but of anyone who wouldn't—or couldn't—pay his Blue Book dues. (Some delegates demanded payment of several years' back dues in one lump sum.) Three weeks later an old-timer reported: "The Matson Lockout on non-Blue Bookers is still ironclad. . . . They [would] rather go short-handed and rawhide those inside . . . than hire men who haven't got the Blue Book."

Was this campaign of intimidation effective? The response of a longshoreman named Arnold Hessler provides the answer. On July 23 he was hired at the Matson shape-up and from there reported to the timekeeper, who asked him for his blue book. When he replied that he had none, the timekeeper shouted "Get out!" Hessler recalled: "I had been hired and thus was immediately discharged because of this company union and my refusal to comply with it. . . . I had worked for Matson's for about 3 ½ years straight, and without a blue book either, . . . and I have been at Matson's every day since, but have not been picked again. I didn't belong to the ILA at that time but I am signing up now."[39]

In early September the employers and the Blue Book got an apparent boost from a special NRA Board of Adjustment in San Francisco. The three-man board, which included San Francisco Labor Council Secretary John O'Connell, ruled that "the Longshoremen's Association of San Francisco is not a company union and is not under the control and domination of the Waterfront Employers Union." The men on the docks knew better, however, and the ruling only strengthened their willingness to take matters into their own hands and defy legally sanctioned authority. In mid-September a group of stevedores on the Matson dock tore up their blue books and dumped them in a pile on the sidewalk. In early October, when Matson fired four men for wearing ILA buttons, the *Waterfront Worker* called for a show of solidarity and four hundred longshoremen wildcatted for five days. This action forced the NRA's hand, and this time the board ordered Matson to reinstate the fired men and to refrain from discriminating against ILA members. "That was the end of the fear and the intimidation," Bridges recalled. "From that time on the [ILA] was established, it was recognized, it was in business."[40]

With the Blue Book reduced to an empty shell, the struggle within the ILA escalated rapidly. Initially the conservatives seemed solidly in control. Ryan appointed William Lewis, a veteran of the 1919 strike, as head of the ILA Pacific Coast District, and Lee Holman was elected president of the San Francisco local. Both Holman and Lewis favored a policy of accommodation with the employers, but the shipowners continually undermined their position by—in George Creel's words—"absolutely refusing to acknowledge the existence of the ILA." Holman in particular jeopardized his standing with the union membership by opposing every burst of militancy from the ranks.[41]

At the other end of the spectrum stood Bridges and the militants grouped around the *Waterfront Worker*. Soon after the reestablishment of the ILA in San Francisco, they formed a caucus within the union to work for the implementation of their views. The caucus met in a hall on Albion Street in San Francisco and was often referred to as the Albion Hall group. (They also called themselves the Committee of 500, an audacious name for an outfit that never exceeded, and perhaps never even approached, one-tenth of that number.) The caucus met in the Albion Hall because one of its members, Henry Schmidt, belonged to two German fraternal organizations that rented space in the building. Schmidt was a German immigrant who had come to San Francisco by way of a Manitoba farm and the flour mills of Minneapolis. He began working regularly on the waterfront in 1928 and went on to become a major force in the longshore union and a close ally of Bridges for many years. His friends described him as a man of "absolute integrity," and even his enemies regarded him as "quiet, forceful and competent."[42]

Darcy has stated that the Albion Hall group had its origins in a Sunday morning class that he organized "to teach elementary trade unionism to people we were training to become leaders of the union." As it evolved, the caucus included ILA members ranging from Communists to pure and simple militants. Although it did indeed facilitate the development of an able and relatively cohesive leadership group in the union, politically the mix was unstable. Schmidt recalled that on occasion someone would interrupt the discussion to complain that "some of the people sitting around in this gathering [are] IWW's or maybe even Communists."[43]

The key to the Albion Hall group's growing success was not only the quality of its leadership, but also the fact that its program expressed the needs of the stevedores and was based on an accurate assessment of the waterfront's harsh realities. The main thrust of its program aimed at establishing a democratic union structure and an active, militant union presence on the job. The caucus insisted that the ILA's officials should be "men from the Waterfront, whom we know well," and that the local should elect a large executive board, with representation from the various docks, "so that the organization will remain in our hands and be kept from the control of a few officials." The caucus also called for the building of dock committees at each workplace so that the union could assist the men in defending their interests on the job.[44]

To some degree, this program reflected the influence of the Communists and the MWIU on the longshore militants. In fact, one of the significant characteristics of the *Waterfront Worker,* and later of the Albion Hall group, was that they adopted much of the program of the MWIU while avoiding its sectarian trappings. The development of dock and ship committees had always been central to the program of the Marine Workers Union, and the militants around the *Waterfront Worker* had begun their own organizing campaign by advocating the formation of activist core groups, essentially informal dock committees, at every workplace. During the summer of 1933 the militants began initiating slowdowns and other job actions on the San Francisco waterfront. Bridges recalled that "other men on the docks . . . saw that we were getting away with it and began to imitate us." Gradually these tactics became more open and aggressive. By early May 1934, on the eve of the strike, the *Western Worker* was reporting instances of job action where the men were winning their demands "right on the spot."[45]

As for the Communists, they used their own instruments of communication to press for an even wider democracy than that advocated by the Albion Hall

group. An article in the *Western Worker,* written by a "Communist Stevedore" in September 1933, echoed Albion Hall's advocacy of a large executive
board but also called for a system of "immediate referendum and recall" and
declared, "Let no official hold office for more than a year. There are plenty of
good men on the docks so that we can rotate our officials." Eventually, the
program and structure of the San Francisco longshore union came to reflect
many of the points listed in this article.[46]

While the conservatives succeeded in maintaining their control of the ILA's
district leadership, the momentum was on the side of the militants. This
became especially clear at a historic coastwide union convention that met in
San Francisco in late February and early March 1934. At this meeting, the
conservatives elected a district executive board composed overwhelmingly of
their own candidates, but rank-and-file delegates from twenty-four ports were
able to push through a militant program calling for a coastwide agreement, a
union-controlled hiring hall, and the formation of an industrywide waterfront
federation that could develop a unified response to the shipowners in the event
of a strike. Essentially it was the program of the San Francisco local, which
meant that it bore the mark of Albion Hall, the *Waterfront Worker,* and the
Communists. The militants were also able to win acceptance of resolutions in
support of Tom Mooney and the Scottsboro Boys and against the loading or
unloading of any ship flying the Nazi flag.[47]

In mid-March the union conducted a coastwide referendum in which 6,616
longshoremen voted in favor of a strike, with only 699 opposed. In spite of
this overwhelming sentiment, Lee Holman informed Ryan that he was against
a strike and that such a course was being forced upon the membership by a
radical minority. He urged Ryan to step into the San Francisco situation and
cancel all union meetings, and he told the press that unless Ryan intervened
on the side of "the solid conservative element in the I.L.A. here . . ., there is
every indication that this majority will leave the I.L.A. and start an independent longshoremen's organization able to settle its differences with the
employers." To the union membership this must have sounded like a threat to
reestablish the Blue Book. They suspended Holman from the presidency and
ruled him ineligible to hold office for a year. He then left the ILA, virtually
alone. (In the middle of the strike he announced the formation of an independent union and claimed that "approximately 1,000 men, mostly family
men who want to get back to work, were ready to join." But Darcy reported
that "he has not even succeeded in getting the signatures of ten bona fide
longshoremen." However, Holman was persistent, even in pursuit of a lost
cause. Calling for a "common sense movement" of "good old-time
Longshoremen," he eventually formed the Maritime and Transportation Ser-
vicemen's Union of the Pacific Coast. "This is an American union," he
declared, "not a Moscow dues collection agency! This is a Workingman's
Union—not a revolutionary political party! This is a union of Americans, by

Americans and for Americans—not a pie card for Australians and Russians!" These peals of thunder fell on deaf ears. It is doubtful that over a period of several years Holman attracted even a handful of defectors from the ILA. The safer and more conventional alternative had been exposed as hopelessly inept and reactionary.)[48]

District President Lewis also came under fire for bowing to pressure from the Roosevelt administration and reaching a compromise agreement with the shipowners. When he presented the terms of this "gentlemen's agreement" to the membership in San Francisco, Bridges subjected the proposal to a scathing critique and the men repudiated it. At a subsequent meeting, another district official was howled down when he attempted to defend the deliberations of a Roosevelt-appointed mediation board. Again, Bridges rose to attack the district leadership's temporizing, and again the membership greeted his remarks with warm applause. In desperation, Lewis leaped to his feet, raged at Bridges, and declared, "The activities of the Communists on the waterfront must stop." But there was no stopping the aroused ILA membership. They voted to inform the waterfront employers that "unless something definite shall have been arrived at . . . by Monday Evening Eight P.M. May 7, 1934, negotiations shall be discontinued."[49]

Thus the stage was set for the Big Strike. The employers continued to believe, or at least to profess, that the longshoremen had worked under "satisfactory and harmonious conditions for the last fourteen years," and they warned the men that "you have nothing but wrong on your side." George Creel wrote that "the shippers were confident of victory and gave me to understand confidentially that even if they lost two or three million, it would be worth that to destroy the union."[50]

On the workers' side, there was every bit as much determination. The program of the militants had been endorsed by the rank and file, and in the port of San Francisco the militants had won organizational control of the union as well, with the election of a strike committee chaired by Bridges. Both of these factors would have an important bearing on the strike's outcome, and both were a tribute to the efforts of a small group of longshore militants and Communist cadres who had come together around the *Waterfront Worker* in December 1932. But in spite of all the ominous talk about Reds and radicals, it was the insurgent spirit of the mass of longshoremen that would be the foundation for the historic advances of the Pentecostal era that was about to unfold. A generation of humiliation and degradation fed the men's anger, while the hope inspired by the NIRA and the lessons learned in the course of their own struggles kindled a sense of joyous anticipation. Perhaps Henry Schmidt best summed up the force of these combined impulses when he recalled that "I wasn't the least bit religious, but I *prayed* for the coming of that strike."[51]

Crew of the American bark *Hesper* in a Puget Sound port, probably in the mid-1890s. (Credit: Wilhelm Hester, Special Collections Division, University of Washington Libraries).

Harry Bridges (rear, second from left), as a teenage crew member of the Australian sailing vessel *Southern Cross*, 1917. (Credit: *Friday Magazine,* International Longshoremen's and Warehousemen's Union.)

Tranquility before tragedy: Al Quittenton (seated, left) got off the *Manurewa* in an Australian port shortly after this photo was taken. On the next voyage the ship went down, with all hands lost. (Credit: Al Quittenton.).

Crew of the intercoastal passenger liner S.S. *Pennsylvania* in San Francisco harbor, 1936. (Credit: Barney Lynch.).

Longshoremen in San Francisco on the eve of the Big Strike. (Credit: Bancroft Library.).

ILA members picketing on San Francisco's Embarcadero during the first week of the strike. (Credit: Bancroft Library.)

The AFL "Old Guard": ILA President Joseph P. Ryan (seated, center) and Andrew Furuseth, in San Francisco, June 1934. (Credit: Bancroft Library.)

Rank-and-file leader Harry Bridges ("The Nose"), at National Longshoremen's Board hearings, San Francisco, June 1934. (Credit: Bancroft Library.)

Strikers battle police in San Francisco, July 1934. (Credit: San Francisco Archives, San Francisco Public Library.)

Bloody Thursday, San Francisco, July 5, 1934: Longshoreman Howard Sperry (right) was killed by police gunfire; Gene Olson (left) survived. Strike supporter Nick Bordoise was also killed by police, as battles raged along the waterfront throughout the day. (Credit: Bancroft Library.)

Mourners preparing to march up San Francisco's Market Street on July 9, 1934, in a massive funeral procession for the martyrs of Bloody Thursday. (Credit: Bancroft Library.)

Seamen burning their fink books before returning to work at the end of the Big Strike. (Andrew Furuseth is standing in foreground, fourth from right.) (Credit: International Longshoremen's and Warehousemen's Union.)

Harry Lundeberg, secretary of the Sailors' Union of the Pacific, "may well have been the toughest man in the American labor movement." (Credit: Wide World Photos.)

Joe Curran (foreground, second from right) and his fellow "mutineers" on the S.S. *California*, San Pedro, March 1936. (Credit: National Maritime Union.)

Harry Hynes (1937 passport photo), shortly before he journeyed to Spain to join the International Brigades. (Credit: Ruby Hynes.)

Bill Bailey (standing, right), still wearing the overcoat and beret of the International Brigades, returning from Spain in December 1938. (Credit: Bill Bailey.)

5

The Big Strike

Every year, in early March, Andrew Furuseth sent an anniversary message to the Sailors' Union of the Pacific to commemorate its founding in 1885. In 1929, when the union's fortunes were at an all-time low, Furuseth's letter to the few diehard members and their guests burned with a zeal that was peculiarly out of character with the times. *"I wish we could all of us be saturated with the spirit of the crusader,"* he said. "Let us make this meeting a Pentecostal one, and go away from it with the determination to achieve, to live up to the highest and best that is in us."[1]

Five years and two months later, maritime workers erupted with the "spirit of the crusader" and waged one of the great battles in the history of the American working class. Even by the standards of 1934, one of the most extraordinary years in the annals of labor, the Big Strike fully merited the adjective its partisans assigned it.[2] This eighty-three-day drama transformed labor relations in the Pacific Coast maritime industry and ushered in an era of militant unionism that caught Andrew Furuseth and the leadership of the International Seamen's Union completely by surprise. In fact, the character of this upheaval was such that it alarmed Furuseth as much as it did the employers. Although the Big Strike ended on an ambiguous note, and in its immediate aftermath was sometimes characterized as a defeat for labor by friend and foe alike, the insurgent maritime workers armed themselves with the lessons of the strike and applied these lessons to their workaday world with stunning results.

Before discussing the contours of this Pentecostal era, we must examine the major characteristics and lessons of the Big Strike, because they became a major part of the foundation on which the new order was constructed. One of the problems in presenting these lessons is that even a sober and restrained portrayal may appear as one-sided and romanticized as a crude proletarian novel. But in this case the real world is more dramatic than fiction. To be sure, there was complexity and unevenness. For example, the vital port of Los Angeles remained open throughout the strike; and a substantial number of seamen never joined the ranks of the strikers, in some cases because their ships anchored in the outer harbors and refused to let the men debark, in other cases because they consciously decided to stay aboard the vessels. But in the final analysis, these and other examples of weakness failed to overshadow or undermine the strike's central characteristics.

Among the many threads that were a part of the Big Strike's dynamism, four stand out as crucial: first, the strikers' militancy, steadfastness, and discipline in the face of an adversary who wielded an arsenal of weapons ranging from private security forces and vigilantes to the bayonets and machine guns of the National Guard; second, a solidarity that swept aside old craft antagonisms and culminated in a general strike; third, a rank-and-file independence and initiative that came to mean frequent defiance of AFL norms and officials; and finally, in the face of an increasingly hysterical and violent wave of anti-Communist propaganda, a willingness to assess the Red presence in the strike independently, from the workers' own standpoint, and a growing tendency to view Red-baiting as an instrument of the employers.

The strike began on May 9 with the longshoremen's coastwide walkout. Within days seamen and other maritime workers swelled the picket lines, and teamsters refused to handle scab cargo. As the magnitude of the conflict became apparent, Assistant Secretary of Labor Edward McGrady rushed to San Francisco and presided over several efforts to reach a compromise. Two such agreements were concluded, one on May 28 and another on June 16. But both were negotiated by top AFL officials who had no authority to represent the strikers, and they were emphatically repudiated by the rank and file. The strikers' rejection of the mid-June agreement convinced the shipowners that reason was of no avail, and they developed a plan to open the port of San Francisco by force. On July 3 the waterfront became "a vast tangle of fighting men" as seven hundred police tried to move scab cargo through the picket lines. Two days later, on what became known as Bloody Thursday, all hell broke loose. The *Chronicle* called it "War in San Francisco!" as "blood ran red in the streets." At the end of the day, two workers—longshoreman Howard Sperry and strike sympathizer Nick Bordoise, a Communist—lay dead; National Guard troops were erecting barbed-wire fortifications on the waterfront, and armored personnel carriers replaced the pickets.[3]

It appeared that labor was defeated, but on July 9 a massive funeral procession for Sperry and Bordoise paraded up Market Street, and the uncanny power of this event crystallized sentiment for a general strike. With a renewed surge of confidence, the general strike began in both San Francisco and Oakland on July 16. However, the strike apparatus was in the hands of

AFL conservatives, and they were able to terminate the general walkout after four days. Shorn of their most vital allies, the maritime workers had little choice but to agree to place their demands before the presidentially appointed National Longshoremen's Board. After eighty-three days, the men returned to work on July 31.

From the beginning of the walkout, the strikers displayed awesome courage and militancy. In the first few days there were violent outbursts up and down the coast, as employers hired large numbers of strikebreakers and tried to maintain business as usual behind a protective shield of police. In Oakland, according to newspaper reports, four hundred strikers stormed the gates of the municipal pier, "drove police before them and staged a hand to hand battle with 72 strike breakers." In Portland, "a mob of 400 striking longshoremen threw one policeman into the water and severely beat several others" in an attack on a ship housing scabs.

The most dramatic confrontation occurred in Seattle, where a timid and conservative ILA leadership stood by as employers put strikebreakers to work on every pier. In response on May 12 a flying squad of six hundred Tacoma longshoremen, along with several hundred strikers from Everett and "all of the militant men we could find in Seattle," stormed the docks. The army of two thousand men battered down pier doors, swept police aside, and halted work on eleven ships where strikebreakers had been handling cargo. The flying squad also paid visits to other cities, with so much success that a shipowner spokesman complained: "Within a few days all work at Pacific Northwest ports had to cease owing to violence by strikers and to lack of police protection. The strikers took over entire control of the waterfront."[4]

The high point of this militancy came on Bloody Thursday in San Francisco, when an army of police tried to reopen the port by terrorizing the maritime strikers into submission. According to the eyewitness account of a "small investor" named Donald Mackenzie Brown,

> Struggling knots of longshoremen, closely pressed by officers mounted and on foot, swarmed everywhere. The air was filled with blinding gas. The howl of the sirens. The low boom of the gas guns. The crack of pistol-fire. The whine of the bullets. The shouts and curses of sweating men. Everywhere was a rhythmical waving of arms—like trees in the wind—swinging clubs, swinging fists, hurling rocks, hurling bombs. As the police moved from one group to the next, men lay bloody, unconscious, or in convulsions—in the gutters, on the sidewalks, in the streets. Around on Madison Street, a plain-clothes-man dismounted from a radio car, waved his shotgun nervously at the shouting pickets who scattered. I saw nothing thrown at him. Suddenly he fired up and down the street and two men fell in a pool of gore—one evidently dead, the other, half attempting to rise, but weakening fast. A gas bomb struck another standing on the curb—struck the side of his head, leaving him in blinded agony. The night sticks were the worst. The long hardwood clubs lay onto skulls with sickening force, again and again and again till a face was hardly recognizable.

Late in the afternoon, when "the police were mopping up the remaining combatants," Brown walked by the ILA headquarters. There "two men were helping a staggering picket away from the fray. He was stripped to the waist showing a gaping bullet hole in his back." Henry Schmidt later recalled a grim moment that may have involved the same striker. During a lull in the battle, near the ILA hall, "I noticed a man in front of me, and I figured that's a cop and he's got a shooting iron ready for action. Then I noticed another man in front of him. There was absolutely no reason for this policeman to do anything, but he raised his rifle, or whatever it was, and he shot this striker in the back. He went down like a load of lead."

For most of the day, even the sadistic violence and superior technical equipment of the police could not deter the strikers. Brown, the businessman, was overawed by the workers' "insane courage." "In the face of bullets, gas, clubs, horses' hoofs, death; against fast patrol cars and the radio, they fought back with rocks and bolts till the street was a mass of debris. . . . They were fighting desperately for something that seemed to be life for them."[5]

Bloody Thursday was an epic moment, but it was by no means unique. Class warfare has punctuated the American industrial landscape for more than a century. What may be even more noteworthy than the militancy of the strikers and the violence of their adversaries is the staying power and growing discipline that the maritime workers demonstrated over a period of nearly three months. Perhaps the most remarkable example of this steadfastness occurred in Los Angeles and its adjacent port city of San Pedro, where the strikers persevered and increased their numbers in spite of the weakness of their unions and the blatantly obvious role of the police as instruments of capital. The passage of the NIRA had forced the Los Angeles employers to temper their long-standing crusade for the open shop, but the coming of the strike rekindled their zeal for the methods that had earned Los Angeles its reputation as "scab city." When 97 percent of the longshoremen who voted in a representation election chose the ILA, waterfront employers signed a contract with the company union that had received the votes of only thirty-two men. Representatives of the Merchants' and Manufacturers' Association helped to enlist thousands of strikebreakers, many of whom were housed in stockades along the waterfront. The Los Angeles Police Department assigned some seven hundred officers to the harbor area, and they were aided by hundreds of special deputies and private security guards. The $145,000 required to maintain this police army came not from the city but from the employers themselves. In fact, these ties between the police and the large employers in Los Angeles became so lucrative for the former that after a subsequent maritime strike, a police official recommended that "each executive from each oil company in the harbor district should be invited and entertained at our police range for lunch . . . and there presented with a police badge in recognition of their splendid cooperation and in furtherance of their friendly relationship [with] our department."[6]

Between the police and the maritime strikers, however, there was anything but a friendly relationship. One observer characterized the Los Angeles Intelligence Bureau, or "Red squad," as "unbelievably sadistic," and even the *Los Angeles Daily News* belatedly acknowledged the "definite campaign of brutality and terrorism indulged in by the police red squad in the confines of the harbor department jail." The *Nation* reported that approximately five hundred arrests were made in the port of San Pedro during the course of the strike. The fate of Thomas Sharpe, a member of the International Seamen's Union, was by no means exceptional. His statement about his ordeal is worth quoting at some length because Sharpe's case symbolizes not only the method and rationale of the authorities, but also the extraordinary staying power of the workers in the face of a sustained campaign of terror. Sharpe reported:

> On Monday the 16th of July, I went on picket duty on Terminal Island. We were not out to do violence. . . . We had no clubs or weapons of any kind. . . . I went across the street, where I saw a man dressed as an unemployed seam[a]n, standing against the wall with a police riot club hanging besides his right leg. . . . He grabbed me by the arm and walked me across the street to the police car. . . . This man I learned from the description I have from other seamen at the hospital who were beat and tortured by him was Strand of the 'red squad.'

Strand took the young seaman to the police station and pushed him into a dark hallway where, Sharpe reported,

> he hit me on the right shin bone with his riot club, which was a solid wooden club about two feet long and 1½ inches thru. I fell to the floor and every muscle in my body went limp. While I was on the floor he beat me unmercifully. The only thing that was said was, I'm going to run all the reds out of San Pedro if I have to break their damn necks. I answered that I ain't no red. He then grabbed my right foot and hit me eight or nine times, again and again on the same shin bone with his club. Then he twisted the right foot until the bones he had splintered with his club cracked and came thru the flesh, severing an artery. It started [to] hemorrhage and the blood simply poured out of me.

Sharpe remained either in the hospital or in jail, with a cast on his leg and another on his shoulder (also broken in the beating), until August 14, nearly one full month after his incarceration, when he was taken into court and the charges against him were dismissed.[7]

As grim as the Sharpe incident was, and there were innumerable examples of lone strikers being arrested, or kidnapped, and beaten, a far more massive and deadly confrontation had occurred on May 14 at a stockade that housed a large number of strikebreakers. A twenty-year-old longshoreman named Dick Parker died that night of a gunshot wound in the heart. The *Los Angeles Times* claimed that a mob of strikers rushed the stockade, set it on fire, and jeopardized the lives of police and private security guards who were protecting the facility. Parker was shot, said the *Times,* while "leading some 300 strikers in their attack." (Tom Knudson, a forty-five-year-old ILA member, died later of injuries sustained in the incident.)[8]

The newspaper of the marine workers maintained, however, that "the police opened fire on a large crowd of pickets . . . before any of the men could take a step toward the armed fortress." One participant, striking seaman Bob McElroy, who was standing no more than ten feet from Parker when he was shot, recalled in later years that the demonstration had begun as "an impromptu thing. . . . There was no provocation, no commotion, no threats, no nothing—just a gun going off and Parker going down." At a special coroner's inquest, McElroy and others identified a former Los Angeles police officer who was serving as a private security guard at the scab stockade as the man who shot Parker. But there was no indictment and trial. Dick Parker, who had joined the ILA only a few hours before his death, became the first martyr of the Big Strike.[9]

In spite of the beatings, the arrests, and the two killings, in spite of the fact that they were never able to shut down the vast Los Angeles harbor, the ranks of the strikers remained solid and the scale of their activity increased. Whereas there had been only about three hundred pickets on the docks in the early days of the strike, their numbers increased to about eighteen hundred as seamen and teamsters joined the picket lines. One striking seaman reported in early July that "open meetings are held daily and the crowds are so large that loud speakers are necessary." This growing combativeness and unity led a Sailors' Union activist to declare soon afterward that "the 1934 strike did more to solidify the longshoremen and the seafaring men of San Pedro than anything that was ever done before."[10]

The most dramatic examples of the strike's increasingly disciplined militancy occurred in San Francisco. On Bloody Thursday, in the "Battle of Rincon Hill," the strikers conducted themselves with remarkable precision and imagination in the face of three successive assaults by policemen, who according to Henry Schmidt were "using their firearms freely and laying down a barrage of tear gas bombs." And in the famed funeral procession in which labor honored Sperry and Bordoise, tens of thousands of marchers demonstrated a unity of purpose and a solemn dignity that left friend and foe alike awestruck. The *Chronicle* reported that in life Sperry and Bordoise "wouldn't have commanded a second glance on the streets of San Francisco, but in death they were borne the length of Market Street in a stupendous and reverent procession that astounded the city." Other eyewitnesses spoke of "an oncoming sea" and "a river of men flowing . . . like cooling lava." One participant noted "an ominous silence among spectators and marchers alike. . . . The sound of thousands of feet echoed up that hollow canyon—nothing else. . . . It was a magnificent sight—those careworn, weary faces determined in their fight for justice thrilled me. I have never seen anything so impressive in all my life." As he marched up Market Street, Roy Hudson was also struck by "the *silence*—you could hear it—not a placard, not a slogan, complete and utter silence. You could *hear* what was in the atmosphere." Even an employer spokesman sensed it, acknowledging the event as "the high tide of united labor action in San Francisco."[11]

This high tide was the culmination of many waves of solidarity that had broken down the traditional barriers of craft and nationality. It began in the ranks of the longshoremen themselves. They had cast aside the Blue Book and Lee Holman; they had built an aggressive rank-and-file movement—so aggressive that one conservative union official characterized it as "mob rule." Their pent-up fury had exploded on May 9 and in succeeding days, driving strikebreakers from the docks or forcing them to take refuge behind massive police lines. Now, particularly in San Francisco, they faced an issue that had contributed to their defeat in previous strikes. Would the union offer the hand of solidarity to black longshoremen? And would black workers honor the picket lines?[12]

Unlike the Eastern and Gulf ILA locals, which provided black longshoremen with a secure but subordinate place within the union, Pacific Coast longshore unions had always excluded blacks. In San Francisco, facing the unremitting hostility of the Riggers and Stevedores, black workers had found that strikebreaking was the only way they could gain employment on the waterfront. In the 1916 and 1919 strikes they had been "an important factor in defeating the unions." Of course, the shipowners had eagerly recruited them then, but by 1926 black longshoremen were employed on only a few docks. Labor economist Robert Francis noted in early 1934 that "today there are not more than fifty black men working on the San Francisco waterfront."

In late 1933 the Local 38-79 executive board had expressed a mild interest in "working with the colored boys of San Francisco and the bay District." But as Sam Darcy acknowledged, for the most part the ILA displayed a "passive attitude towards the question of Negro workers, and in some cases, actual antagonism towards including them in the Union." Although "the rank and file militants of the I.L.A. made a sincere effort to unite black and white workers," only a handful of black longshoremen joined the union before May 9.[13]

In the first few days of the strike employers recruited nearly a thousand scabs in San Francisco. The majority, according to one participant, were white-collar workers and college students, including a sizable contingent from the University of California football team. The ranks of the strikebreakers also included several hundred black men, and the violent flare-ups along the Embarcadero sometimes had racial overtones.[14]

However, as Henry Schmidt recalled, there was a vitally important break-through early in the strike that was to set the tone for the future of race relations on the San Francisco docks. Schmidt had gone down to the Lucken-bach pier where most of the regular black longshoremen were employed; along with a black union member he had called on them to join the strike. "On the same afternoon or the next day," he remembered, "these Negro brothers came to the then union headquarters at 113 Steuart Street. I can still see them coming up the stairs and entering the premises. . . . Somebody raised the question, 'Why didn't you come earlier to join up?' " And they replied, "We didn't know that you wanted us."[15]

An even greater wave of solidarity began to gather momentum on the very first day of the strike, as seamen walked off the ships and joined the longshore picket lines. The seamen's involvement, however, was complicated by the condition and outlook of their unions. Veteran ISU official Walter Macarthur acknowledged that the Sailors' Union officials were helpless and that "the seamen found themselves entirely at a loss for leadership or advice." Harry Bridges claimed in retrospect that the ISU affiliates "were forced to strike because of the pressure of the MWIU." Bridges' recollection was supported by Bill Caves, an outspoken deck sailor who played an important—and controversial—role in the Big Strike. Caves maintained that "the whole attitude of the SUP officials during the 1934 strike was to stay aboard the ships," and that "it was only the militant action of the MWIU that forced the issue."[16]

Although not entirely accurate, these charges have considerable merit. The ISU affiliates on the Pacific Coast were in a sorry state before the Big Strike engulfed them. The Sailors' Union had weathered the long drought better than the marine cooks' and firemen's unions, but the news from the SUP was hardly encouraging. The Seattle branch seldom attracted more than a dozen members to its weekly meetings, and Portland was able to muster one quorum in the six months that preceded the 1934 strike. As for San Pedro, it "seem[ed] to be going to hell altogether." When a local official took sick, the union was unable to find anyone to replace him. Even the San Francisco headquarters usually acknowledged that "things here are slow," and some-times "exceedingly slow."

In explaining the union's moribund condition, the SUP leadership pointed the finger at the seamen themselves. George Larsen, the Sailors' Union secretary and chief spokesman, lamented that the majority "don't seem interested in any kind of organization." When the Portland SUP agent re-ported a growing sentiment among the men that "the union should do some-thing," Larsen pointed to the international officials' long-standing effort to bring about change through the NRA shipping code hearings in Washington and blamed the lack of results on "the majority . . . who sail outside of the union." "Let the men understand that it is because of lack of organization among us that we are faced . . .[with] low wages, miserable working conditions, and intolerable employment conditions. Let them be reminded that in vessels where men are doing the hardest kind of physical labor, namely in many steamschooners, no raise has taken place since they were reduced to the starvation point some two years ago. . . . the answer is, come into the union." When the Portland official reported again that "the men would like to se[e] the Union take some action," Larsen exploded: "The trouble is not with the union, it rests with [the men]. . . . The only way to wake them up is with a big stick."[17]

Begrudgingly, the Sailors' Union spokesman acknowledged that the longshoremen had demonstrated "sense enough to get into one organization" and prepare for "concerted action." But whenever the dockworkers moved beyond mere preparation, Larsen reacted with fear and pessimism. "I can see a bunch of trouble ahead," he declared during the San Francisco stevedores' wildcat against Matson and the Blue Book. "I think the men have been ill advised." Increasingly, he was convinced that the source of these disturbances was the "considerable number of Communists" in the San Francisco ILA. "Should it come to a strike and a finish fight," he wrote in late March, "I am afraid the longshoremen will be the losers." As for the seamen, he recognized that some of them would join the walkout, but "there is little that we can do about it."[18]

When the longshoremen struck on May 9, the ISU Pacific District leadership took an ambiguous position, advising union members to stay aboard ship in those few cases where "the unions have recognition or an understanding with the owners." On all other ships, the ISU stressed the question of "liberty." Larsen wrote to Portland on May 11: "Let the men be told that none of the steamschooners recognize any of our unions, and that therefore, they are at liberty to quit. . . . But the unions are not demanding it, that is to say it is not mandatory."[19]

The Portland steam schooner men acted unanimously two days before Larsen offered them the option. They deserted the ships on May 9 and joined the longshore picket lines, thus serving as the advance guard of a spontaneous walkout that caught the ISU leadership by surprise. Larsen had blasted the nonunion seamen for losing faith in themselves. But apparently many of them had lost faith only in the capacity of the ISU affiliates to take decisive action. When the longshoremen showed the way, they followed.

The Marine Workers Industrial Union took immediate steps to give the seafarers' walkout a more organized character. The MWIU's membership on the West Coast was probably smaller than that of the SUP. But the Marine Workers had one major advantage, namely, a core of activists who were eager to strike and to build closer ties between the men on the ships and those along the shore. In fact, MWIU members began supporting the longshore strike even before the stevedores walked off the job. On May 8 the S.S. *Oakmar* pulled into San Francisco Bay and her entire crew struck in anticipation of the longshoremen's action. One seaman recalled that "every man aboard of her was a member of the M.W.I.U." On May 12, the union held a well-attended conference; the assembled delegates called a formal strike for eight o'clock that evening and put forward their own set of demands. The crews of seventeen ships responded to the MWIU's strike call and within a few days the men on practically every vessel coming into San Francisco joined the longshoremen on the picket lines.[20]

It is probable, however, that the seamen's spontaneous determination to strike was more important than the MWIU's leadership in triggering many of the actions that occurred. The deck department of the S.S. *President Hoover*, for example, walked off the ship in San Francisco and immediately pressured the SUP officials to call a strike. There had been a self-appointed organizer aboard this Dollar line vessel. But as it turned out, his role was secondary at best. Harold Johnson, a Communist seaman, recalled that "my duty was to recruit people into the MWIU, the young Communist League, and the Communist Party. I didn't succeed." In fact, he acknowledged, "I was a constant pain in the ass." Indeed, when the ship pulled into San Francisco on the first day of the strike and a number of crew members looked to Johnson for leadership, instead of taking the time to help spearhead an organized walkout, the young zealot simply packed his seabag and walked off the ship, alone.

The next day the *President Hoover* sailed to San Pedro, returning to San Francisco a few days later. This time the entire deck crew walked off together, led by able-bodied seaman Bill Caves. A stereotypical sailor, Caves had joined the navy at age seventeen and had been sailing ever since. Now in his forties, he was muscular, literate, and outspoken to the point of belligerence. He took great pride in the fact that he had broken every one of his knuckles in various brawls. (He was also a homosexual who along with half a dozen other crew members on the *Hoover* was being treated for syphilis.) Although somewhat erratic, Caves "radiated excitement." By virtue of his charisma and experience, he was far better able than the politically zealous but unseasoned Harold Johnson to help crystallize the anger and determination of his fellow seamen.[21]

The MWIU's initiative, the catalytic role of natural leaders like Bill Caves, and the massive—often spontaneous—upsurge of rank-and-file seamen hastened the inevitable. The Sailors' Union took a formal strike vote on May 15. Coastwide only 146 men cast ballots, with 131 of them voting to "hit the bricks." (The vast majority of seamen were not union members when they walked off the ships and were thus ineligible to participate in the strike vote.) Within a week all seafaring unions on the Pacific Coast, including those representing licensed officers, were on strike, and George Larsen could declare: "Most of the men going to sea have faith in the union, let's show them their faith is not misplaced. We must stick and win."[22]

With the seamen on the picket lines, the teamsters quickly became crucial to the strike's continued momentum. If they had been willing to haul scab-unloaded cargo, the maritime workers' position would have been undermined. But in spite of repeated warnings from their leadership about the sanctity of contracts, the rank-and-file truck drivers refused to handle goods that were bound to or from the docks.[23]

The high point of the strike's extraordinary solidarity was the San Francisco general strike. Although it is impossible to identify the exact number of workers who participated, it probably exceeded a hundred thousand, encompassing not only San Francisco but Oakland and Alameda County as well. Sam Darcy commented that initially "the General Strike was effective beyond all expectations. Not only had the overwhelming bulk of organized workers joined the strike, but many thousands of unorganized workers" also walked out. Of perhaps greater significance than the numbers was the attitude of the rank-and-file participants. Longshoreman Germain Bulcke lived several miles from the San Francisco waterfront, and with no streetcars running, he had a long walk to his picket duty at Pier 35. "But it was a very happy feeling," he recalled. "I felt like I was walking on air." Mike Quin claimed that in the city's working-class neighborhoods, "an almost carnival spirit" prevailed. "Laboring men appeared on the streets in their Sunday clothes, shiny celluloid union buttons glistening on every coat lapel. Common social barriers were swept away in the spirit of the occasion. Strangers addressed each other warmly as old friends."[24]

Meanwhile, across the bay, as employer representative Paul St. Sure recalled, momentum was building, until "with dramatic suddenness everything was down in Oakland." The Amalgamated Streetcar Workers met in the early hours of the morning, after the trolley system's daily shutdown at 2 A.M., to consider what action to take. Employers were confident that this vital artery would remain in operation, because the company had recently granted a voluntary wage increase and its work force included many "old-timers . . . loyal to the company." Imagine the employers' shock, then, when the Streetcar Workers passed a resolution that committed the union to walk out in sympathy with the waterfront and general strikes "and called upon the employees of the Key System and workers of the community to take over the transit company as a mass transportation system for working people." At that moment, St. Sure remembered, the East Bay business community became convinced that "there was a revolution in progress. . . . frankly we were frightened . . . [because] the streetcar workers, who had no direct connection with the strike, . . . were actually proposing taking over the property; . . . we felt this was the first step in [a] class conflict that might lead to anything."[25]

Where did such resolutions come from? In spite of all the hysteria about imminent revolution and Communists on the march, George Larsen of

the Sailors' Union readily admitted that the strike was not led by Communists—they "are loudmouthed but not in control"—nor even by trade union
officials like himself, "for they are swept along by [the workers'] deep
resentment against the shipowners." Instead Larsen pointed to the centrality
of rank-and-file anger and initiative. Perhaps no other dimension of the Big
Strike was more vital than the energy and determination radiating from
thousands of anonymous workers. The case of Ed Darling, an oiler on the
S.S. *Washington,* may not be entirely representative, but the strike could not
have succeeded without the spirit of militant activism that he exemplified. Ed
Darling was in many ways a typical seaman. He had been sailing in the navy
or the merchant marine for twenty-three years by 1934. Although he was a
high-school dropout who admitted to spending most of his money on "women
and whiskey," he was also an avid music enthusiast who never missed an
opera or a symphony when he had the opportunity in port. *Fortune* chronicled
the story of his involvement in the Big Strike:

> When he heard about the strike, he jumped the ship in Marshfield, Oregon, and
> beat it up to Portland in a boxcar. In Portland he promptly got a thirty-day
> suspended sentence for attacking a scab, which made it necessary for him to
> leave the city. Thereupon he went to Seattle, where he picketed fourteen to
> sixteen hours a day, tossed rocks at the engineers and firemen who tried to move
> freight along the waterfront, and greased the railroad tracks so that the engines
> couldn't move. From a woodworking factory he helped to steal 300 clubs that
> had just been turned out for the police and vigilantes. He was gassed and clubbed
> frequently and lost all his upper teeth in a fight with a scab. Then one day . . . he
> met the man who had knocked out his teeth, and in an attempt to break a bone for
> every tooth he had lost, he battered the scab so fearfully that he was afraid to stay
> in Seattle. The remaining month of the strike he spent on veteran's relief in
> Portland, doing nothing to excite the attention of the police.[26]

Ed Darling was one of those men who, like Henry Schmidt, had been
praying for a showdown with the shipowners. But there were many others
who discovered only during the course of the strike that they had the will and
the confidence to combat the employers. One stevedore admitted, "I have
always been afraid of strikes," but declared that his experience on the picket
lines "proves to me what power the workers have if they will only use it." The
shipowners "have treated us as if we were not human," he said, "and now that
the strike is [on] I can't see how in hell they got away with it for so long. We
must have been asleep; we should have given it to them long ago. Well, we
have the power now; if they don't behave themselves we will take the ships
and run them to suit ourselves."[27]

Such a statement may reflect a touch of picket line bravado or, if taken
literally, may have represented only a small minority of the strikers. But like
the Streetcar Workers' resolution, it is also indicative of the festive, irrever-

ent, and spontaneously radical sentiments that come to the fore in a crisis of this magnitude. In this situation it was inevitable that the conflict between the insurgent strikers and their conservative officials would often reach a fever pitch. Secretary of Labor Frances Perkins declared that "the officers of the unions have been swept off their feet by the rank and file movement." Likewise, Paul Eliel, a spokesman for the Industrial Association, commented with alarm on the declining authority of San Francisco Teamster President Mike Casey. Once known as Bloody Mike, Casey was by now a solidly entrenched member of the AFL hierarchy, and he was on friendly, even intimate, terms with the employers. Because the forces of capital relied heavily on AFL representatives like Casey to settle the strike in a way that would minimize the damage to the employers' interests, it was painful for Eliel to admit that "as strong a man as Michael Casey has absolutely lost control of the Teamsters' Union and he is unable to lead it any more. He used to be able to drive it."[28]

Appropriately, however, it was the longshoremen who provided the most vivid example of the conflict between rank-and-file insurgency and AFL conservativism. The pivotal figures in this conflict were Harry Bridges and ILA President Joseph P. Ryan. Whereas Ryan's was a familiar name in the councils of business, government, and the American Federation of Labor, Bridges was so obscure at the beginning of the strike that one veteran MWIU leader who had spent considerable time on the San Francisco waterfront in 1931 and 1932 couldn't even remember who he was. "You know him," Harry Hynes reminded Tommy Ray as they followed the strike news in a New York gin mill. "Australian Harry! He works on the Matson dock and plays the horses."

At first glance, Bridges was hardly an appealing candidate for the leadership of an insurgent movement. He lacked the surface charm of Walter Reuther, the impressive bulk and prophetic aura of John L. Lewis, the rough-edged proletarian hue of Joe Curran. To some observers, the only thing that seemed to distinguish him was his long nose. *Fortune* spoke of his "hawk eyes and nose and long spidery arms." Journalist George West found him "physically unimpressive" and said he had "no 'personality,' no charm, no radiation." Frances Perkins remembered him as "a small, thin, somewhat haggard man in a much-worn overcoat." Richard Neuberger spoke of his "monastic simplicity," but unlike Perkins he also perceived the cocksure personality who "swaggers like a racetrack bookie."[29]

As for the longshoremen, although they good-naturedly called him the Nose, they did not judge Bridges by his looks. Author Charles Madison correctly noted that he became the stevedores' spokesman through his unique "ability to verbalize their yearnings and concretize their goal." In fact, it is remarkable how often longshoremen and outsiders alike referred to the effectiveness of his use of language. His style was simple and direct. His speeches were "cold," "clean," "clear," "rapid-fire," "precise," with every word "like the blow of a hammer," building an orderly and readily comprehensible edifice for his listeners. One observer described how he captivated a meeting of two thousand maritime workers in Portland "with a few masterful words." In spite of strong opposition from the Portland ILA officials, "he presented his case with such brilliance that the audience rose to give him a unanimous vote of confidence."[30]

Fellow longshoreman John Olsen remarked that "he had a certain charisma that nobody else seemed to have. There are certain men . . . who have the ability to present something so that you understand it, and you feel a part of it." Olsen recalled one particular case in San Francisco "when we had a big meeting, and . . . all the officials of the old ILA were there opposing Harry. They all spoke first. Harry finally got up and said . . . , 'It's me against all of them.' [Then] he took something out of his pocket, and he read it. When he got through talking, he had the whole meeting on his side. He had that ability to draw you to him that very few men have."

Even men who were far removed from the stevedores' rough-and-tumble environment were struck by this quality in Bridges. Paul Eliel marveled at his "extraordinary presentation" before the National Longshoremen's Board in July 1934. He said that "speaking without notes and extemporaneously," Bridges "showed not only an unusual command of the subject matter but of the English language as well." After his testimony, said Eliel, "employers were able for the first time to understand something of the hold which he had been able to establish over the strikers both in his own union and in the other maritime crafts." Likewise, Harvard Dean James M. Landis concluded that Bridges's testimony at his first deportation hearing "was given not only without reserve, but vigorously as dogma and faiths of which the man was proud. . . . It was a fighting apologia that refused to temper itself to the winds of caution."[31]

The same qualities that inspired admiration in Eliel and Landis were infuriating to many on the employers' side. For men who were used to the friendly, even deferential posture of a Ryan or a Scharrenberg, Bridges's self-assurance appeared arrogant, his faint smile seemed a sneer, his scorn for bourgeois amenities and his refusal to shy away from controversy became the mark of treason. Admiral Emory Land of the War Shipping Board recalled that Bridges never came to Washington "without insisting on having an appointment with me. And it was always one of the most unhappy appointments I ever had. Naturally, we never agreed on any single thing. . . . He always had a snarl on his upper lip. I've always said he had a crooked brain. He was an out-and-out Commie."

Louis Adamic rightly observed that the shipowners were "mentally and emotionally paralyzed" by their hatred of Bridges. In an editorial that represented the employers' view as much as Hearst's, the *San Francisco Examiner* once characterized "the line-up in the waterfront labor situation" as

Harry Bridges vs. responsible union labor
Harry Bridges vs. the shipping industry
Harry Bridges vs. San Francisco, the Pacific Coast, the entire American seaboard.
Put in one phrase—the issue is:
COMMUNISM VS. AMERICAN LABOR.

The shipowners convinced themselves that they loathed Bridges because he was a Communist. But, in part, at least, their hatred derived from the fact that this upstart dockworker often proved a superior foe. George West described him as a "lightning thinker" and a "master of repartee." "Facing the shrewdest of corporation lawyers," he said, Bridges "makes them seem soft and a little helpless by comparison."[32]

Of course, in the eyes of the longshoremen and the other maritime workers, these very same qualities made "Limo" an effective leader and, ultimately, a folk hero. As one "Stevie" put it, "Harry Bridges is a 100% union man. . . . He's a man in a million. A union man at heart, not a faker. Maybe I admire him because they call him a radical. If Harry Bridges is a radical, I am a radical too." Even a self-proclaimed "Conservative Longshoreman" expressed similar sentiments, declaring, "Anybody can see . . . that Bridges knows what he is talking about. He stands ready to offer leadership to our local, something we have always lacked, and what's more, he is ready to fight for what he believes to be right. I have changed my mind about that man. He is not too radical for me now. He is a good trade unionist."[33]

It is important to emphasize that Bridges as leader was very much a product of the rank-and-file movement. He did not create the burst of energy that drove the maritime workers forward during the 1934 strike. Nor was he solely responsible for the continuing upsurge that would transform conditions on the waterfront and give the Pentecostal era its special dynamism. Without the determination of the Ed Darlings and thousands of anonymous rank and filers, even the most skillful and dedicated leaders would have been helpless. As one longshore activist declared, "It was collective action that won the strike, not a few individuals."[34]

It is also true that Bridges was neither as malevolent as the shipowners imagined him nor as perfect as many of the longshoremen portrayed him. Like any human being, he had faults. He was notoriously irascible, and his warmest admirers agreed that he had trouble delegating authority. These traits may have contributed to his inordinate capacity to make enemies, even among those who had once been his close allies in the union movement. According to Richard Neuberger, "Bridges demands tolerance for himself but is inclined to be intolerant of others." Darcy recalled that he was "very jealous of anyone he thought might excel him in leadership," and that he often "tried to belittle the role of other people." Herbert Resner, a left-wing attorney who knew Bridges well up until 1950, found him "notoriously lacking in . . . human kindness." My purpose, however, is not to provide an all-sided portrait of Bridges' personality and career, but rather to analyze the qualities that enabled him to become the leading spokesman for his fellow maritime workers during the thirties. Among these men, whether they were radical or conservative, Bridges was widely regarded as the embodiment of the best in themselves and their movement. As a marine fireman put it, "We like Bridges because he is rank and file."[35]

No one could accuse Joe Ryan of being rank and file, although *Fortune* did concede that he "still goes down to the waterfront to visit with his boys—after a pleasant dinner" at a New York restaurant. Whereas Bridges wore in- expensive clothes and was obviously indifferent about his appearance, Ryan dressed "with splendor," wearing painted neckties and pinstriped, elegantly tailored double-breasted suits on his massive, 200-pound frame. "Next to myself," he used to say, "I like silk underwear best." Another of his favorite sayings was "What does I.L.A. stand for? Why it means 'I Love America!' " Irving Bernstein has aptly characterized him as "an old-style Tammany politician who . . . strayed into the labor business."

Ryan began stevedoring around 1910. Several years later an injury and his gift for blarney combined to end his career as a working longshoreman. Elected to local union office in 1913, he made his way up the ILA hierarchy until he achieved the rank of international president in 1927. During his long reign, there were no authorized strikes on the New York waterfront, even though conditions for the majority of dockworkers were abominable. He fortified his regime by courting politicians and hiring criminals. Under the aegis of the Joseph P. Ryan Association, his friends sponsored annual tes- timonial dinners that raised large sums of money for his personal and political use. Among the honorary chairmen of the 1931 dinner, which raised $8,000 to send the Ryan family on a vacation trip to Europe, were New York Governor Franklin D. Roosevelt, former Governor Alfred E. Smith, and New York City Mayor James J. Walker.

Ryan also had many friends at the other end of the social spectrum. Matthew Josephson characterized the Brooklyn waterfront in particular as "a racketeers' jungle run wild." A congressional subcommittee concluded that Ryan had used his position as head of the New York State Parole Board to make ILA headquarters "the court of last resort for all shady aspirants and claimants along the waterfront, as well as the fountainhead of protection . . . for vicious criminals in key waterfront posts." Refuting Ryan's claim that his motive was the rehabilitation of ex-convicts, the committee declared that "the waterfront is not where a man can 'go straight'—it is where he can keep crooked." Finally, the ILA president was forced to fall back on the hackneyed ruse of fighting communism on the docks, telling the committee that "some of those fellows with the bad criminal records were pretty handy out there when we had to do it the tough way."[36]

With the employers, however, Ryan always preferred to do it the easy way. Although he had no authority to negotiate any binding agreements on behalf of the Pacific District union membership, the ILA president came to the West Coast and made several highly publicized efforts to settle the strike on terms that fell far short of the men's demands. In mid-June he participated in a series of carefully orchestrated maneuvers that resulted in an alleged settlement of the strike. The so-called Saturday Agreement met some of the stevedores' demands and compromised on others, but it was negotiated by ILA and Teamsters union officials who had no authorization to represent the longshoremen. In fact, their elected representatives were excluded from the proceedings. When the agreement was signed, the press immediately declared the strike over, before the men had had a chance to examine the terms of the settlement or vote on the matter. The Sunday *Chronicle* ran the banner headline "S.F. Strike Ends; Port Open Monday" and featured a picture of a smiling Ryan on the telephone, saying, "Hello Seattle! It's All Over Boys."

But the longshoremen overwhelmingly rejected the pact. In the ports of San Francisco, Portland, and Tacoma, they refused even to vote on it. The *Chronicle* was forced to admit that "the proposal [was] shouted down by a thunder of 'noes.' " Why this emphatic rejection of an agreement where the employers compromised significantly on the longshoremen's demands? Because the pact made no provision for resolution of the seamen's grievances. This was fine with diehard craft unionists like Ryan and Furuseth, but to the aroused rank and file it was a betrayal of the solidarity that had become one of the strike's most powerful weapons.[37]

The climactic moment in this escalating confrontation between the strikers and their conservative officials came when Ryan attended the San Francisco ILA meeting and attempted to explain his actions to the three thousand longshoremen who were packed into the hall. The growing clamor from the audience made it clear that he was in deep trouble. Suddenly, Pirate Larsen leaped onto the stage, pointed an accusing finger at the ILA president, and shouted, "This guy's a fink and he's trying to make finks out of us. Let's throw him out!" As Henry Schmidt recalled, "Pirate brought the house down."

From that moment on, Joseph P. Ryan—international president of the ILA, former president of the New York City Central Labor Council, crony of governors, mayors, and millionaire employers—was a dead letter on the West Coast. Before returning to the more hospitable confines of the East, however, Ryan took a parting shot at the rank-and-file stevedore who had replaced him as principal spokesman for the men. "Bridges does not want this strike settled," he declared. "My firm belief is that he is acting for the communists."[38]

It had quickly become standard procedure in many quarters to attribute the strike and the grim determination of the strikers to the machinations of the Reds. Only ten days into the conflict, Assistant Secretary of Labor Edward McGrady, his efforts at mediation rebuffed, had declared in frustration: "San Francisco ought to be informed of the hold of the Red element on the situation. A strong radical element within the ranks of the longshoremen's union seems to want no settlement of this strike." Two days later, the president of the San Francisco Chamber of Commerce eagerly followed McGrady's lead, stating matters in far more apocalyptic terms. "The San Francisco waterfront strike," he declared, "is out of hand. It is not a conflict between employer and employee—between capital and labor—it is a conflict which is rapidly spreading between American principles and un-American radicalism. . . . There can be no hope for industrial peace until communistic agitators are removed as the official spokesmen of labor and American leaders are chosen to settle their differences along American lines."[39]

Even as sanguine an employer spokesman as Paul Eliel tended to view the strike in these terms. Although he avoided the apocalyptic frame of reference, he was frankly alarmed about the broad practical implications of the waterfront strike. In a letter to the National Labor Board, he said:

> The I.L.A. in San Francisco at the present time, is absolutely and unequivocally in the hands of a group of Communists. You know I am not a Red-baiter and I more or less laugh at these Communist scares. In the present instance, however, I am convinced that the I.L.A. has definitely been taken over by a Communist group.
>
> Now the difficulty of the employers accepting a closed shop with the I.L.A. in view of this existing leadership of the I.L.A. here is that *such a crowning of the achievements of the strike committee would, it is believed, affect the entire crop-harvesting situation most adversely.* In addition, it would constitute a definite threat to the leadership of the more conservative labor men in San Francisco whose control of their unions is tottering.[40]

The control of the "conservative labor men" was indeed tottering, and in the maritime unions it was about to collapse. But Eliel was wrong in reducing the motive force in this drama to communism. To be sure, the Communist party played an active and important role in the strike, placing its newspaper, legal apparatus, and other elements of its institutional network at the disposal of the strikers. There were influential Communist cadres in several of the AFL unions, and the Communist party recruited many new members during the strike, especially among the maritime workers. Darcy estimated that there were perhaps six or eight Communists among the members of the ILA strike committee in San Francisco. The extent of the Party's influence on Harry Bridges was a matter of controversy and litigation for many years. One Communist later remarked that he "enjoyed intimate ties with the Party, usually on his own terms." And even as devout an anti-Communist as John Brophy acknowledged that Bridges "was not one to be captured or used, but had his own ideas and ambitions." Bridges himself readily acknowledged his substantial agreement with the program and political line of the Party, but denied being a member. In any case, it is symbolic of the significant and open relationship of the Communist party to the strike that during the funeral procession for the martyrs of Bloody Thursday, Darcy and Mrs. Bordoise, wife of slain Communist Nick Bordoise, rode in one car at the head of the line of march, while Bridges and Mother Mooney, whose son Tom was the nation's most famous "class war prisoner," rode in another.[41]

It is clear, if only by inference at times, that the Communist presence in the strike gave it a more disciplined and organized character and a more effective leadership, especially among the longshoremen. But the scope and dynamism of the upheaval far exceeded the ability of the rather insignificant number of Communists to control or direct it. The fact is that the Big Strike was an authentic rank-and-file rebellion that had long been waiting to happen. It drew upon deep wellsprings of discontent that required leadership and direction but did not submit easily to manipulation. There was a spontaneous impulse toward solidarity and discipline that was quite evident in the Battle of Rincon Hill, in the stirring funeral march for Sperry and Bordoise, and in other events where masses of workers flowed together "like cooling lava" in uncanny demonstrations of self-direction and self-discipline that left even their own leadership amazed. This was perhaps clearest in the funeral procession, which Paul Eliel wrongly characterized as "a brilliant and theatric piece of pro-paganda." For what stands out about this event is the self-discipline and determination that characterized the spontaneous participation of thousands of workers. They, and not its planners, made the event into a living piece of propaganda. Indeed, they made it the general strike in embryo. And they made good on their promise that if no police were present on the streets that day, the workers would maintain a dignified order that the police could only have disrupted. As Sam Darcy recalled in later years, "What was amazing was the organizational job those workers did that day. Every spot was organized along the [route of march], and it all came from the ranks. They worked out the details themselves."[42]

What is more significant than the degree of Communist involvement in the Big Strike is the fact that the constant barrage of Red-baiting made communism an issue among the strikers, or at least it forced them to take an increasingly clear stand on the question of Communist participation in the strike. While several unions responded to the anti-Red campaign by issuing statements condemning communism, the growing trend in the ranks was to view Red-baiting as another in the arsenal of weapons that the employers used to divide and conquer the workers.[43]

The issue of communism caused particularly bitter conflict within the AFL seamen's unions, largely because of the presence of the MWIU. From the day they voted to join the strike, the ISU leadership resisted every move to build a united front with the Marine Workers Union. In fact, they suspected that anyone who advocated such unity must be a Red himself. But to the rank-and-file seamen, the issue was not ISU versus MWIU or Americanism versus communism. To them the issue was the maritime strikers versus the shipowners, and the MWIU was, in the eyes of many seamen, a legitimate marine workers' organization that was making a solid contribution to the winning of the strike. As one MWIU picket put it: "Up to this very minute no one has crammed a communist license down my throat nor have I been forced to change my religion or politics. The main issue is the strike; the main point is solidarity and a continuous picket line."[44]

The issue of the united front came to a head in mid-June. On the fourteenth, the ISU walked out of the daily conference of striking maritime unions because the MWIU, with the support of the longshoremen, had been seated at the meeting. The following evening the ISU joint strike committee issued a press statement condemning communism in general and the MWIU in particular. But the stevedores' rejection of the Saturday Agreement sparked a wave of insurgency among the rank and file of the ISU. On the evening of the seventeenth, right after the tumultuous longshore meeting—the "thunder of 'noes' "—in San Francisco, a thousand seamen held a gathering where ISU strike committee chairman Bill Caves delivered a ringing speech condemning the ISU officials for refusing to unite with the MWIU. Sam Telford, a leader of the Marine Workers Union, spoke at the meeting, to a loud welcome, and the evening concluded with cheers for the united front. The next day George Larsen suspended Caves from the strike committee, whereupon his office "was stormed by an angry mob." That evening, in a close vote, the Sailors' Union membership repudiated Larsen's action and restored Caves to his position of leadership. Meanwhile, the Seattle ISU voted unanimously that "there should be no distinction made between MWIU and ISU men" on the picket lines; and a striker from San Pedro reported on the growing fraternization between MWIU members and the rank and file of the ISU on the Southern California waterfront.[45]

In addition to its triumphant moments, the Big Strike had other dimensions and was shaped by other events that threatened to undermine its splendid achievements. Toward the end of the upheaval, two factors in particular began to corrode the morale that had sustained the strikers through more than two months of bitter conflict. One was the manner in which the general strike ended, leaving the question of whether this massive outpouring of solidarity constituted a triumph for labor, an inconclusive stalemate, or a victory for the employers. The other was the systematic campaign of terrorism by police and vigilantes that accompanied the general strike. To what extent did this campaign represent a division in the ranks of the workers themselves? To what extent did it place militant labor on the defensive and signify a period of repression and retreat? These questions haunted the waterfront as the strike entered its final days.

The campaign of vigilante and police terror began with the general strike, but was preceded by a mounting wave of provocation by the media, the employers, and government officials. For example, on June 21 the *Chronicle* began an article on American Legion Week with the declaration that "San Francisco trains its guns on communism today!" A few days later the *Foc'sle Head* reported that "American Legion gangsters are cruising around the streets beating up lone pickets." On the eve of the terror campaign, California Governor Frank Merriam insisted that "a more active and intensified drive to rid this State and nation of alien and radical agitators should be undertaken *by the workers themselves* if they are to enjoy the confidence of the people." General Hugh Johnson, the mercurial chief of the National Recovery Administration, was even more direct. In a speech at the University of California, he demanded that the "subversive element" in the ranks of labor "must be wiped out. They must be run out like rats."[46]

On July 17, the same day that Johnson placed the imprimatur of the federal government on vigilante terror, there was a massive raid on the Marine Workers Industrial Union hall, the most visible symbol of the Red presence on the waterfront. National Guardsmen with machine guns mounted on trucks cordoned off an entire block. Police then entered the hall, arrested eighty-five people, and systematically destroyed everything in sight. The reign of terror continued for nearly a week and spread to many of the smaller cities and agricultural communities in northern and central California. Newspapers openly applauded the actions of vigilantes who smashed up target after target and left bleeding victims whom the police then arrested for vagrancy. In one instance, a Finnish workers' hall was "reduced to kindling, while the helpless workers watched their thousand-dollar library, their theater with its two grand pianos, all their equipment that spelled years of sacrifice, reduced to rubble." In another instance an eyewitness reported that "the Workers' Center in Oakland . . . was blood-spattered from wall to wall; the stairway that led to the street was actually slippery with coagulated blood." In San Jose a group of vigilantes—approvingly described by a local newspaper as "armed with bright new pick-handles, their faces grim, eyes shining with steady purpose"— terrorized thirteen suspected Communists and ran them out of the county. The *San Jose Evening News* exulted that "the mongoose of Americanism dragged the cobra of communism through the good Santa Clara Valley orchard dirt last night."[47]

The *San Francisco Chronicle* claimed that the activity of these "citizen vigilantes" represented a move by "conservative union labor . . . to purge its ranks of Communists." The *San Francisco Examiner* reported that "police started the raids . . . but were superseded by an infuriated band of men, reported to be union strikers." Most unions, however, vehemently denied any involvement in the terror, and there were carefully documented charges that the police and their anonymous accomplices acted under the direction of the Industrial Association. Mike Quin, a contemporary who in 1936 wrote what remains the best full-length account of the strike, declared that many of the vigilantes were "strikebreakers brought in from Los Angeles by the Industrial Association to run the scab trucks on the waterfront. A lesser number were businessmen, bank managers, and adventurous members of the industrialists' white-collar staffs." Lorena Hickok, a representative of the Roosevelt administration who was in California at the time, was told that most of the vigilantes were American Legionnaires. But it is probable that the vast majority of the raiders were policemen. Robert Cantwell of the *New Republic* reported that the raids were badly stage-managed, since the so-called "workers looked very much like police dressed like workers"; and Communist leader Sam Darcy, who had good reason to inquire, recalled, "We establish beyond question that policemen were being dressed as longshoremen to carry through the vigilante raids."[48]

Significantly, the "vigilant citizens" generally steered clear of the waterfront. With the exception of the raid on the MWIU hall and a brief episode at the ILA soup kitchen, the police and their accomplices avoided frontal assaults on the maritime strikers, their leaders, and their various headquarters. Sam Darcy maintained that in spite of the arrest of many Communist party members (more than three hundred alleged Communists were arrested in one day), "those of our comrades who were on the front line trenches of the maritime and general strikes hardly suffered at all as a result of the terror, because they were, so to speak, 'hidden' among the masses and [had] the confidence and support of large numbers of workers."[49]

The police-vigilante campaign was, nonetheless, ominous. But it is possible that the manner in which the general strike ended was even more destructive of morale on the waterfront. For more than a month before it began, the maritime workers had regarded this consummate act of labor solidarity as their ultimate weapon and had believed that it would force the employers to meet their basic demands. Hence, when it ended inconclusively, accompanied by banner headlines that shouted "General Strike Crushed by Determined Citizens" and "Bridges Admits Failure of Plot to Starve City into Defeat," the strikers inevitably fell prey to a certain amount of confusion and demoralization.[50]

The general strike was not a Red plot to starve the city into submission. Rather, it was the culmination of a massive outpouring of solidarity from within the ranks of labor. It had gained its initial momentum from the growing united front of longshoremen, seafarers, and teamsters, and had been fed by the intransigence of the employers and the violence of the police. In the wake of Bloody Thursday, and the military occupation of the waterfront, the solemn, massive funeral march in which labor paid tribute to its fallen comrades made the general strike a virtual certainty.[51]

Contrary to the *Chronicle*'s exultant headline, the "determined citizens" of San Francisco did not "crush" the general strike. Even the widespread and officially condoned vigilante activity did not bring about its demise. When the strike ended, many businessmen and public officials regarded Hearst general counsel John Francis Neylan as man of the hour. Neylan was chief guardian of William Randolph Hearst's interests on the West Coast, and he orchestrated the newspaper campaign that drowned the general strike in a sea of hostile—and largely false—propaganda. In a private letter, Neyland expressed the opinion that "I have been given entirely too much credit. . . . The plain truth is, the whole community is deeply indebted to the reputable labor leaders." Without their "courageous and intelligent action," he wrote, "we would have been faced with an extremely complicated situation, leading to bloodshed and the spread of the general strike idea to other communities."[52]

When the longshoremen and their allies first raised the idea of a general strike, most of San Francisco's established labor leaders regarded it as a "radical menace." They continued their opposition until the momentum of events threatened to overwhelm them. As Secretary of Labor Perkins informed President Roosevelt, "The conservative leaders of all of the San Francisco unions urged against the general strike. They were overwhelmingly outvoted by the rank and file members who were emotionally very much stirred by the situation." In the case of the teamsters, Mike Casey acknowledged that "nothing on earth could have prevented that vote. In my thirty years of leading these men, I have never seen them so worked up, so determined to walk out."

At the crucial moment, however, the labor leaders showed enough political sense to change direction and seize control of a movement they could no longer thwart. As one union official confided to a friend, "It was an avalanche. I saw it coming so I ran ahead before it crushed me." The top AFL officials simply designated themselves leaders of the Labor Council's strike strategy committee and then used all of their institutional power to maneuver the strike movement to serve their own purposes. The key figure in this regard was George Kidwell of the Teamsters, a man with a reputation for liberalism, pragmatism, and keen intelligence. Once he recognized the inevitability of a general walkout, Kidwell concluded that it could be the instrument for taking the entire strike situation in San Francisco out of the volatile and stubborn hands of the maritime workers. He developed a twofold agenda: first, to force both the employers and the marine unions to accept arbitration; and second, to turn an avalanche of class feeling into an orderly and limited expression of sympathy. Thus, from the beginning of the general strike, Kidwell and the other members of the strategy committee sought to defuse the potential for open class warfare and to bring the drama to a rapid, orderly conclusion. On the third day, a Sailors' Union spokesman complained that "our General Strike seems to be dissolving under our feet. . . . The strike is now being run by other Unions, and the conservatives, having all the voting power, seem to be attempting to force us back to work immediately." After four days, by a surprisingly close vote of 191 to 174, the Labor Council delegates terminated the general strike.[53]

San Francisco Mayor Angelo Rossi danced around his office for joy at the news and declared, "I congratulate the real leaders of organized labor on their decision." ILA President Ryan in turn congratulated Rossi "as one good pal to another." In Sacramento, Governor Merriam gave thanks that "the sane, intelligent, right-thinking leadership in the labor organizations has prevailed over the rash counsel of communistic and radical agitators." But the maritime workers were in no mood to celebrate. For them all that remained was the uneasy feeling that their ultimate weapon had never been fully tested and the gratuitous recommendation of the Central Labor Council that they accept the arbitration they had been rejecting all along.[54]

The premature and inconclusive termination of the general strike left the maritime workers in a difficult position. After nearly two and a half months on strike, literally thousands of arrests, at least six deaths, and hundreds of serious injuries, the men and their families were still holding the line. But their allies were gradually cutting the ties of solidarity that had been the strike's lifeblood. When the teamsters voted to return to work unconditionally, the maritime strikers were once again on their own. Paul Taylor, a scholar whose work combined objectivity with strong sympathy for agricultural and marine workers in California, sat in the ILA hall with a number of longshore strike leaders as they anxiously awaited the outcome of the teamsters' vote. "The big shabby room was depressing," Taylor reported, "and the three [or] four men sitting around were depressed. Ralph Mallen the head of the Publicity committee sat by the phone. He looked tired and beaten. In the three months he had aged years. . . . There was no confidence now, only silence and painful waiting." Although they stated that they felt "more strengthened . . . today than at any time during the entire maritime strike," their strategic alternatives were now severely limited and their morale was being tested as never before.[55]

In these circumstances, the employers' long-standing offer of arbitration to the longshoremen began to appear more palatable. The men had maintained that they would never arbitrate the hiring hall issue, and that they would not return to work until the seamen's grievances were resolved. But when in the immediate aftermath of the general strike the National Longshoremen's Board conducted a coastwide ballot on the question of submitting the stevedores' dispute to arbitration, 6,504 longshoremen voted yes and only 1,515 voted no. Even in the storm center of San Francisco, the yes ballots carried by a three to one margin. Only the lumber port of Everett, Washington, rejected arbitration, by the margin of a single vote.

The longshoremen's decision to accept arbitration left the seamen in the lurch and jeopardized the magnificent unity that the marine workers had forged during the strike. Following the stevedores' vote, there was a growing rumble of bitterness among the seamen. Long-standing craft antagonisms that had been swept aside in a matter of days now threatened to reappear and to engulf the maritime strikers in "all the muck of ages" once again.[56]

Matters seemed ready to come to a head on July 29, the eighty-second day of the strike, at a packed meeting in the Sailors' Union hall in San Francisco. A parade of officials came before the angry seamen and tried to explain why the vanguard body of the strikers seemed to be abandoning their more vulnerable comrades to an uncertain fate. In this procession two men stood out as vivid symbols of the different realities, programs, and outlooks that had been part of the seamen's experience and that confronted them with alternative choices now. One of these men was Harry Bridges; the other, Andrew Furuseth. Bridges had emerged as the strike's leading spokesman; he was a powerful force among longshoremen and seamen. But on this day, in these circumstances of reemerging craft jealousies, it appeared that Old Andy might well have the last word.

Furuseth, the grizzled eminence of the seafaring world, appeared almost ghostlike with his gaunt countenance and shock of white hair. In spite of numerous eccentricities, he remained a quintessential representative of traditional AFL unionism. The seamen of this generation knew him more as a legend than as a real person. But some of them were no doubt aware that he had favored arbitration and opposed the general strike movement, along with his friends in the top echelon of the San Francisco Labor Council. Although these conservative officials were widely regarded as sell-outs and fakers, many sailors retained a large measure of respect for "the Old Man of the Sea." Only a few days earlier, in San Pedro, he had addressed a mass meeting of eight to nine hundred seamen, and one official reported that "when Andrew got through you could hear the cheers from here to Los Angeles. . . . man after man came forward and shook Andrew by the hand."[57]

At this moment, perhaps the crucial contrast between Bridges and Furuseth lay in their differing attitudes toward craft unionism. Furuseth had staked his entire career on keeping the seamen free of entangling alliances, and his bitterest battles had been with the longshoremen. Bridges, on the other hand, had been a leading adherent of broad maritime unity throughout the strike, and along with the *Waterfront Worker* he had strongly opposed the longshoremen's decision to accept arbitration. He remained one of the most forceful spokesmen in favor of a Pacific Coast marine federation that would embrace not only the maritime crafts, but teamsters, machinists, scalers, and all other workers whose labor brought them into contact with ships and cargo.

After more than three decades of craft separation, the militants' dream of maritime unity had emerged as a powerful reality during the strike. But now that the longshoremen had in effect voted to abandon the seamen, the specter of long-standing craft antagonisms reappeared. The stevedores, the largest and strongest of the maritime crafts, had firm assurances that they would receive a serious hearing before the presidentially appointed arbitration board. What was more important, they had displayed the kind of muscle that would compel significant concessions from the arbitrators. But the seafarers were divided into more than half a dozen organizations; they had only recently received the promise that their demands would be arbitrated; and the terms of their dispute with the shipowners lacked the clear and sharp visibility that had characterized the conflict between longshoremen and employers from the very beginning. In short, the seamen were widely regarded as a mere auxiliary to the main event. As one of their numbers put it, with bitter frustration, "We had nothing to say before because it was well known all over that the longshoremen's strike was going on, but who ever heard of a seamen's strike!"[58]

This was the scenario as Bridges faced the sailors' union meeting. Characteristically, he came right to the point. "I think the longshoreman is ready to break tomorrow," he told the seamen. "They have had enough of it. They have their families to support. They are discouraged by the teamsters' going back to work. They didn't get enough support from the [central labor] council. Up to this minute, as far as I know, there may have been about twelve desertions. But . . . it doesn't take many men. A hundred or two would do the trick. . . . In this case unless you stick 100% the majority doesn't count."

Would the seamen stand their increasingly isolated ground and then accuse the longshoremen of scabbing because a hundred or two stevedores were about to break ranks and compel a retreat? "It will be terrible," said Bridges, "if we go back tomorrow and the sailors stay out." The only answer? "We must go back together and on good terms. If the longshoremen go back and the sailors stay out that will break the unity of the whole thing. That is the best thing we have in our hands. Unity!"

Bridges recognized that recent events had put the maritime workers on the defensive. "The shipowners have got us backed up," he said, "and we are trying to back up step by step . . . instead of turning around and running." Without apologizing or pandering, he acknowledged that the seamen had good reason to be angry about the stevedores' unilateral decision. "I don't know how you fellows are going to take this," he said. "It's going to be a tough pill to swallow." After a final plea for unity, even in retreat, Bridges yielded the floor to Andrew Furuseth.[59]

Old Andy, a veteran of nearly fifty years of maritime unionism, undoubtedly had never heard of Harry Bridges prior to the 1934 strike. But in spite of Bridges's courage and forthrightness, the ISU president could hardly have held him in high regard. For Bridges represented two things that Furuseth despised: longshoremen and radicalism. Now that the dockworkers had voted to go their own way, Furuseth saw an opportunity to pursue the course he had been following for decades. In a rambling speech that was vintage Furuseth, he quoted scripture—"How often shall we forgive an erring brother?"—and forgave the "erring" seamen for quitting the ISU after the collapse of the 1921 strike. He exclaimed that the moment had arrived to restore the integrity and power of the legislation for which he had compaigned endlessly. How? By embracing the ISU and its leadership, by refusing to cooperate with the fink halls that had been the most vivid symbols of the ISU's impotence, and by trusting in the goodwill of the government. "This is a federal question," he said. "The government is for us. The government feeds the men in San Pedro. They will feed them here if it becomes necessary." He passed along the personal assurances of NRA chief Johnson that "as soon as the general strike was out of the way and . . . the soldiers were out of San Francisco, . . . he himself would fight like a tiger for the seamen."

Furuseth then referred briefly to the long series of jurisdictional and tactical disputes that had characterized relations between seamen and dockworkers. He implied that the longshoremen's vote to return to work was an act of "damned cowardice," but emphasized that "they have acted as a trade union has got a right to act." Their decision "leaves the longshoremen free to act for themselves and us to act for ourselves. It leaves us to our own affairs."[60]

Here was the nub of the matter. The ILA's action had created exactly the opening that Furuseth wanted, namely, to disengage the seamen from the longshoremen and to break up the intercraft unity that he viewed with such alarm and distrust. Soon after the longshoremen's courageous rejection of the Saturday Agreement because it failed to resolve the seamen's grievances, Furuseth had arrived in San Francisco and stated to the press: "Something's got to be done quickly to get [the seamen] back on their ships. While they're in port right now they must vote on submitting their differences to arbitration." He made this plea at a time when maritime unity had reached unprecedented heights. Now, however, in the wake of Bloody Thursday, the military occupation of the waterfront, and the conservatives' successful move to end the general strike, the longshoremen were somehow guilty of "damned cowardice" when they voted to follow the same course that Old Andy had recommended for the seamen a month earlier.[61]

On any other day the seamen might well have alternated between shouts of outrage and chuckles of irreverent amusement at much of Furuseth's speech.

He asked them to trust a government whose support of the shipowners and disregard of their own most basic needs was one of the most obvious, and painful, facts of seafaring life. His reference to General Johnson's concern for the seamen must have sounded hollow at best at a time when the NRA administrators' bitter denunciation of the general strike as "bloody insurrection" and "a menace to government" was still ringing in their ears. Moreover, Old Andy's gesture of forgiving the seamen for abandoning the ISU could hardly have invoked a sentiment of gratitude among men who had left the union because they had long regarded it as impotent or worse. The maritime strike had created the opportunity, and the necessity, to reshape the moribund ISU into a real weapon in the hands of the seamen. But they had spontaneously walked off the ships, or had followed the MWIU's lead, and the ISU had belatedly joined them on the picket lines. Finally, Furuseth's denunciation of the longshoremen for their "damned cowardice" would ordinarily have been regarded as a vile slander upon courageous comrades who had paid a high price, including the death of at least four ILA members, for their determination to bring a new era to the waterfront.[62]

But on this day there was widespread confusion and a growing sense of betrayal. Old craft jealousies and antagonisms were plainly evident in remarks that the stevedores were about to "crawl back" to work, and that "we will win where the longshoremen couldn't." Moreover, Furuseth carried the hour not only by feeding the fires of negativism but also by concluding with a masterful appeal to the seamen's militancy and anger. The old man who only a few days ago had seemed to merit the mantle of ridicule implicit in the nicknames Andy the Weeping Willow, Andy Feroshus, and Andy Forsake-us now came forward with a proposal for what was to be the strike's final moment of symbolism. He suggested an act of defiance that "will go like fire" and "wake up everybody." "What do you think my proposition is? It is horrible and yet it is the most beautiful you can ever think of. . . . We are going to build a fire. Alongside of that fire we will have a can of petroleum and each man who has got a fink hall book will come along there and he will dip it into that petroleum and throw it on the fire. . . . The newspapers will know about it. The associated press will know all about it. The pictures will be shown on screens all across the country."[63]

With one stroke, Furuseth captured the seamen's imaginations, rescued them from their apparent obscurity, and seized the initiative from the longshoremen and Bridges. The meeting adjourned after a unanimous yes to the question "Are you willing to stay as you are absolutely until the International Seamen's Union orders you back to work?" Furuseth, who during the height of the strike had sought to persuade the seamen to go back to work alone, now seemed in no hurry to return to the ships. The unifying thread in the old man's apparently puzzling course was his obsessive determination to separate the seamen from entangling alliances with other crafts in general and longshoremen in particular. For the moment, Old Andy had indeed had the last word.[64]

The next day seamen in San Francisco gathered in a vacant lot near the Sailors' Union hall, built a huge bonfire, and joyously burned the hated fink books. The press reported that Furuseth "insisted on attending the ceremony, but his frail condition, due to a recent illness," kept him from taking an active part. While he watched the ritual from a nearby embankment, "solicitous [union] members brought him glasses of water."[65]

On July 31, however, the necessity imposed by the stevedores' decision caught up with the seamen. Fortified by the ritual of consigning the fink hall to a fiery grave, and by several conciliatory gestures from the shipowners, the seafarers joined the longshoremen in returning to work. After eighty-three days, the Big Strike was over.

6

The Syndicalist Renaissance

As they headed back to their jobs on the waterfront, the maritime workers stood poised between two worlds. Many a seaman and longshoreman must have wondered which one awaited him—the old order of the 1920s and the early depression years, or the new world that the strikers had begun to forge during their eighty-three-day upheaval. A host of factors—including the premature and inconclusive termination of the general strike, the police and vigilante reign of terror, the fears and questions associated with arbitration, and the apparent reemergence of old antagonisms among the maritime crafts—all seemed to surround the workers' return to their jobs on the front with an aura of ambiguity. Among their friends, there were gloomy, questioning voices. The *Nation* expressed the fear that "the maritime unions have now been abandoned to their fate" and the "general drive to crush militant unionism in San Francisco has only just . . . begun." Even Harry Bridges admitted that the forces arrayed against the marine workers "were a bit too strong for us."[1]

In the camp of their enemies there was a mood not only of relief but of jubilation. William H. Crocker, a prominent San Francisco banker, provided one of the most extravagant statements of this mood when in the midst of the general strike he declared:

> This strike is the best thing that ever happened to San Francisco. It's costing us money, certainly. We have lost millions on the waterfront in the last few months. But it's a good investment, a marvelous investment. It's solving the labor problem for years to come, perhaps forever.
>
> Mark my words. When this nonsense is out of the way and the men have been driven back to their jobs, we won't have to worry about them any more. They'll have learned their lesson. Not only do I believe we'll never have another general

strike but I don't think we'll have a strike of any kind in San Francisco during this generation. Labor is licked.[2]

Crocker's fond dream was soon to become an employer's nightmare. The Big Strike had provided a compelling glimpse of a new world. It had been a "festival of the oppressed," where long years of humiliation had given way to a new dignity and a reawakening of hope. In spite of all the uncertainty attendant upon arbitration, in spite of the fact that no issues had yet been resolved, the lessons of the strike were still fresh, and so was its spirit. When he told the troubled Sailors' Union meeting that the unity forged in the heat of battle "is the best thing that we have in our hands," Harry Bridges clearly understood the power of the strike's example. Although it is unlikely that he was consciously paraphrasing the *Communist Manifesto,* he was correct in anticipating that the "real fruit" of the marine workers' struggle would lie not in the winning of this or that particular demand, but in their "ever-expanding union."[3]

For an immensely powerful moment on the West Coast waterfront, there was indeed an expanding union and an expanding class consciousness that combined to sweep away the old order and usher in a genuinely Pentecostal era up and down the coast. The maritime workers created a virtual revolution in work relations and practices on the docks and ships and their syndicalist impulse encompassed more than the world of work; a broad range of strikes and demonstrations reflected an increasingly conscious integration of the realms of pork chops and politics. Moreover, their vibrant activity demonstrated the growing coherence and distinctiveness of their mental universe. This chapter will trace these developments to their high-water mark, consider the elusive realm of consciousness, and examine the meaning of the symbolic language that the longshoremen and seamen used to explain their present struggle and future goal.

The Big Strike had involved particular demands that now faced the prospect of arbitration. The National Longshoremen's Board would soon make important concessions to the stevedores on the questions of wages, hours, overtime, and control of hiring. But meanwhile, longshoremen and seamen demonstrated that they had an additional agenda requiring immediate attention. They were determined to rid the docks and ships of men who had scabbed during the strike, to make every work unit 100 percent union, to extend unionism into the ranks of unorganized waterfront workers. And they united to tame the gang bosses and ships' officers who had driven the marine workers with relative impunity during the long nonunion era.

Any confusion, fear, and tendencies toward recrimination generated in the aftermath of the general strike seem to have been swept aside as soon as the men returned to work. Henry Schmidt recalled that "somehow or another the men discovered . . . when they went back to work that morning that they had terrific power; they also had some courage, and they changed the working conditions immediately." Longshoreman Bill Rutter remembered that "some very good [working] rules . . . were made up, on the pierhead before we went into work that morning." Rutter was a member of a gang scheduled to load sacks of barley, and the men informed their bosses that they would work only fifteen sacks, rather than the customary twenty, per load. After about an hour, a load with twenty sacks came down, and then another. "The guys all went and got their coats and were standing there waiting to pull out," when the bosses relented and agreed to the gang's demand.[4]

Moreover, there was widespread agreement with the opinion of a rank-and-file stevedore that "we must have a good housecleaning on the waterfront" because "it is filthy with rats, finks, [and] scabs." The housecleaning also began immediately. On the American-Hawaiian docks in San Francisco, for example, more than a dozen longshore gangs shut the piers down for a few days until the company agreed to fire several notorious strikebreakers. Employer spokesman Gregory Harrison stated that from July 31, the day the men returned to work, until the day the presidential mediation board rendered its decision on the longshore dispute, "there were repeated strikes and stoppages of work along all of the waterfronts of the Pacific Coast." According to Harrison, twenty-nine were recorded during this seventy-four-day period. And when the longshore arbitration award was handed down on October 12, "far from diminishing, the strikes and stoppages of work increased in frequency and intensity."

The same pattern occurred among seamen, beginning (in Harrison's words) "the day after the return to work." Marine fireman Ernest "Red" Ramsay recalled that he shipped out on a vessel

called the *Katherine B. Sutton* and was very fortunate that everybody, right from the captain on down, had been on strike. It wasn't a matter of going back with any finks because these guys had all been on the picket line. . . . We were ready to get a load of lumber, it was on a steam schooner, and we figured, "The heck with it. We'll tie her up right here."

So we just went on strike, and from the captain on down, we refused to take her out. We got what we wanted, I mean, it was a little bit. And this is what we kept doing, a little bit at a time.[5]

The first major confrontation came on September 20, when eight-hundred longshoremen and seamen struck in support of the latter's demand that the Dollar line fire seventeen nonunion workers who had sailed on the *President Taft* during the maritime strike. When the company balked at this demand, two hundred seamen walked off the ship, and four hundred longshoremen working the Dollar line docks immediately joined them. Ship scalers and teamsters soon rallied to the walkout, and union taxi drivers refused to bring passengers to the pier. According to one report, a crowd of over a thousand men picketed the docks. After several hours of stalemate, the Dollar line capitulated and provided the nonunion men with a police escort from the ship. The *President Taft* then sailed with a crew that was 100 percent union.[6]

A similar battle occurred on the Western Sugar docks, where the ILA was in the process of organizing the warehousemen. In the face of stubborn resistance from the employers, warehouse workers began wearing union buttons and preparing for a test of strength. When the company fired one of the most active union members, the warehousemen walked off the job and were joined immediately by the longshoremen. Soon the deck gangs of the two ships discharging cargo in the area joined the walkout, and when police prevented the engine room gangs from leaving the vessels, the men returned to their quarters and relaxed in their bunks for the rest of the day. Teamsters hauling refined sugar from the docks also quit work for an hour. In the face of this kind of pressure, a mediation board quickly ordered the man returned to his job.[7]

In this atmosphere of insurgency and growing self-confidence, even a one-man strike could succeed. In the port of Longview, Washington, the radio operator walked off a Weyerhaeuser lumber schooner and began picketing the vessel to dramatize his demand for higher wages and a shorter workweek. In the old days of craft separation and sacred contracts (or, more likely, no contract at all), such an action would have been ludicrous. But in this instance the longshoremen honored the one-man picket line and refused to load the vessel until the company met the radio operator's demands.[8]

One of the main focal points of rank-and-file combativeness concerned the pace of work, the weight of sling loads, and relations between gang bosses and men on the docks. In the aftermath of the Big Strike, many of the gang bosses assumed that conditions on the docks would quickly return to normal and that they would be free once again to drive the men at the old relentless pace. But the longshoremen quickly introduced them to a new reality. In one instance, a boss demanded that his gang increase the weight of their sling loads or go home. No longer intimidated by such threats, the gang started to walk off the job; and when the outraged boss took a swing at the gang steward, the union representative "grabbed the big fink around the neck and put him to the floor."[9]

This confrontation and its outcome provide an apt symbol of the enormous change that was taking place on the West Coast waterfront. The shipowners were soon complaining about widespread "soldiering." Seattle spokesman Frank Foisie warned the National Longshoremen's Board of "a slowing down on the job to the point where . . . some of the employers are in grave danger . . . of losing their shirts . . . the evidence is overwhelming that production has gone off a full quarter." In San Francisco Thomas G. Plant charged that "without exception every terminal on the waterfront has reported a considerable drop in efficiency and unquestionably, it is deliberate." By 1936 the employers were claiming that the cost of handling cargo in San Francisco had become "probably the highest in the world." Almon Roth, the president of two shipowners' associations, declared that "a gang of longshoremen used to handle as high as 3,000 sacks of sugar per hour in the unloading operations at Crockett," but that a recent checkup showed "we were getting only 950 sacks per hour per gang. . . . Observations of this operation proved that the men in the hold were resting 60 percent of their time." Roth acknowledged that "there was a day when employees complained of speedups." Now, however, "the pendulum has swung the other way. Today employers suffer from deliberate slow-downs."[10]

The transformation lamented by Roth and other employer spokesmen was not the result of spontaneous upsurge alone. The unions established rules designed to spread the work evenly and to prevent chiselers from spearheading a return to the old order. Among the longshoremen there were numerous examples of entire gangs walking off the job early in order to abide by the regulation limiting hours of work to 120 per month. The membership of the ILA voted a twenty-five dollar fine for anyone who worked more than the 120-hour limit without the union's permission, and there were also penalties for other infractions. While most of these rules were job-related, some were considerably broader in focus. The San Francisco ILA local placed a gang boss on trial for "slandering colored brothers." Among the sailors, there was a regulation fining any union member who set foot in the Seamen's Church Institute; and the Marine Firemen's union placed a severe penalty on any of its members caught buying a Hearst newspaper.[11]

In the job-related struggles, the longshoremen in particular displayed a sense of tactics that transcended pure and simple militancy. Soon after the longshore arbitration award of October 1934, the ILA leadership in San Francisco became convinced that the shipowners were trying to precipitate another major confrontation. The *Waterfront Worker* warned against being "goaded by acts of the employers into a series of continual small strikes." In the face of demands and provocations that seemed designed to "isolate the Frisco longshoremen from the rest of the Coast and to smash the I.L.A. in this Port," a "Pineapple Man" from the Matson docks came up with an appropriate response. When the gangs working pineapple were placed under the supervision of a scab boss, "the fellows didn't want to walk off the job and put the union on the spot," he said, "so they just took it easy . . . sometimes the hook hung as long as five minutes." "Pineapple Man" concluded that "it would be wrong policy at this time to strike, so stay on the job, boys, and slow down. . . . We can force the shipowners to be good dogs in damn short order."[12]

The key link between the leadership group around Bridges and the militant rank and file was the tightly organized system of gang and dock stewards who coordinated the activity of the men. According to the employers, this brought about a virtual revolution in the locus of effective power on the waterfront. Gregory Harrison complained that because of the steward system, "authority to direct work upon the docks passed from the hands of the foremen into the hands of dock and gang stewards. The dock and gang stewards are appointed by the Union. They have an organization of their own. They meet regularly; they adopt rules; they establish the manner in which, and the speed at which, work is to be performed on the waterfronts of the Pacific Coast."[13]

Although Harrison may have exaggerated the extent of the longshoremen's control of the work process, he was certainly correct in indicating that a dramatic transformation had taken place. Even the *Waterfront Worker* expressed amazement at "the great change that has come over the workers on the waterfront." Writing only two and a half months after the men had returned to work, the popular rank-and-file newspaper commented: "Whereas before the strike [the longshoremen] were beaten, docile, and meek, they are now in a very opposite frame of mind. To state that the men are militant and aggressive would be putting it mildly; in fact, it is hard to realize that the same body of men could produce such a change of attitude in their own ranks."[14]

The most eloquent testimony about the depth of this change came from the workers themselves. A longshoreman's wife stated:

> Before the strike my husband was always complaining about conditions on the waterfront, how hard he was working and how much the bosses were hollering and so forth.
>
> Since returning to work after the strike he is a changed man entirely. He seems different and happier, and even finds time to pay a little attention to his wife. . . .
> Thanks to the strike, a change for the better has come for the men on the front and a change has taken place in our home life.

Another stevedore's wife expanded on the same theme. She looked back on the years before the strike—"the recollection of insecurity, my children in made-over clothes, thin and pale, my husband weary and beaten after sweating the docks day after day with maybe a day's work now and then, myself in a constant state of worry and nervous tension"—and declared that since the "great strike" their lives had been transformed. "[W]e have been living as human beings, my husband has lost that haggard, beaten look, my spirits are high, my children properly fed and clothed, merry-eyed and round-cheeked."[15]

A rank-and-file longshoreman recalled that "not so very long ago, when we first organized, I was fired and discriminated [against] for being a union man and wearing an I.L.A. button. I have seen my wife and two daughters go hungry." But, he proclaimed, "the old order of things shall never come back to us. . . . We are all brothers now—one for all, and all for one. The spirit of comradeship and Unionism prevails amongst us and we have learned a bitter lesson."[16]

This determination to put the misery of the past behind them forever was strengthened in the longshoremen and their families by an almost lyrical sense of the glories of the emerging new era. As in the 1934 strike, life on the front was again taking on some of the dimensions of a "festival of the oppressed," only this time in the day-to-day struggle to transform the world of work. An "Admiral Line Stevie" was convinced that "at this time on the waterfront we have the finest conditions in the world." An "Oldtimer" who had first joined the ILA in 1915 declared that "we are the most militant and organized body of men the world has ever seen." In a letter to the *Waterfront Worker,* a group of "stevies" proclaimed that the longshoremen had truly become the "Lords of the Docks."[17]

This was no small affirmation for men whose status had generally been held in such low esteem that many of them had preferred to call themselves laborers rather than longshoremen. Now, one of their numbers was moved to express this newfound sense of pride in poetic terms:

> I'm called dock-walloper and wharf rat
> With many laughs and many knocks.
> In spite of that, I glory in my element
> I'm one of the Lords of the Docks.[18]

In the face of increasingly hysterical diatribes from the employers and the press, the San Francisco ILA local issued an appeal to the public that clearly and succinctly identified not only the issues at stake in the waterfront controversy but the dramatic change in the self-image and spirit of the maritime workers. The ILA proclaimed:

> Let any San Francisco citizen walk along the waterfront today. . . . No longer will he encounter those crowds of shabby men hanging around the piers with desperation written on their faces. Today these men report to the central hiring hall and are dispatched in a prompt and business-like manner to the place where they are needed. They do not have to hang around the waterfront saloons waiting for a chance to "treat" the hiring bosses. They do not have to fawn or lick anyone's boots to get a job. . . . In short, they can afford the luxury of being MEN.

An expert witness readily agreed with this assessment. Corpus Christi longshoreman Gilbert Mers took a walking tour of the San Francisco waterfront in 1937 and later recalled: "These San Francisco guys worked the way that men ought to work. There was none of the shouting and cursing, the driving so prevalent on the Gulf Coast. I found myself thinking: In that cool San Francisco temperature and at that sensible work pace, a man ought to last until age 80."[19]

To the employers, however, this emerging new order was scandalous and even subversive. A group of "public-spirited citizens" took out a full-page ad in the *San Francisco Examiner* to warn that "radical leaders of the I.L.A." intended to "Sovietize" the waterfront. Gregory Harrison charged that "on American ships and American docks there generally prevails a condition of insubordination and refusal to work as ordered." The efficiency of labor, he declared, has been "scandalously affected."[20]

The San Francisco ILA was quick to retort that the conflict on the waterfront was rooted in inherent and antagonistic differences in the priorities of labor and capital. The employers demanded efficiency. The maritime workers insisted that the recently attained "luxury of being men" should become a basic right. The arena where these opposite priorities clashed most directly was the work process. The problem, said the ILA, derived from "one word—CONTROL." After fourteen years of complete domination of the waterfront, the shipowners still "want to deal with 'dependents,' grateful for handouts—not with MEN. They cannot—or will not—adjust themselves to the New Era that has come to the waterfront. Still in their eyes, they are the MASTERS; we are the SLAVES."[21]

For longshoremen and seamen alike, the foundation of the emerging new order was indeed control—especially control of hiring. The dockworkers had established the union hiring hall as their number-one demand during the strike. Although the arbitration award of October 1934 provided for the establishment of hiring halls operated in each port by labor relations committees of employer and union representatives, the ILA won the sole right to select the job dispatchers. With the union in charge of dispatching, and the men on the docks ready to "hang the hook" on any employer who refused to accept candidates sent from the hall, full control of hiring quickly passed into the hands of the ILA. The shipowners were soon complaining that "the award provisions for [joint] operation of the longshore hiring halls, and the rights of employees thereunder, have been entirely defeated, . . . although the employers have always contributed one-half of the expense of their maintenance."[22]

In the case of the seamen, the obstacles to union control of hiring were more formidable and their eventual victory was all the more dramatic. The first obstacle, of course, was the shipowners' complete opposition to relinquishing any of their long-standing prerogatives. Even though they had often been willing to hire the least qualified men at the lowest possible wages, the employers were always ready to oppose any encroachments on their authority by pointing to their legally mandated responsibility to man vessels in the safest possible manner. Backing up the shipowners' claims were the age-old traditions of the sea, which endowed the master of a vessel with virtually unlimited authority and made it appear unthinkable that seamen would be able to extend their jurisdiction as effectively as their longshore counterparts.

On the union side, Furuseth and other officials of the ISU had long been opposed to a union-controlled hiring hall, which they regarded as an unworkable nuisance and a violation of the freedom of both employer and employee. Carl Lynch, a seaman who proclaimed himself "absolutely independent" but ended up as a paid spokesman for the old-guard officials, gave eloquent expression to the quaint individualism of the ISU leadership when he declared: "The hiring hall violates the very first principle of justice in the relations between seaman and shipowner, namely, freedom of the seaman to seek employment without interference by any middleman." Moreover, said Lynch, "it lowers the standard of competency among seamen by encouraging, and in fact compelling the employment of incompetent and ill-disposed persons." He warned that the hiring hall would become the rallying place of the "riff-raff of the port." Its general tone "is determined by the lowest elements in it. Radicals and left-wingers of the most extreme type find in the hiring hall a congenial meeting ground in which to sow the seeds of their various isms."[23]

Virtually any seaman could have told Furuseth and Lynch that the freedom they celebrated was a one-way street that the employers had exploited in every conceivable way, and that the standard of competency they upheld was an expression of craft exclusiveness reflecting the realities of a bygone era. A historic tendency of the men themselves, expressed more or less consistently by dockers the world over, and by seamen during periods of upsurge, was to seek protection and equal treatment for the broadest number of workers plying their trade, in opposition to the craft unionist's obsession with defending the job opportunity of the "competent" minority.[24]

But the seamen's arbitration awards did not reflect this historic tendency. Rather, the decisions were much more compatible with the views of the shipowners and the conservative ISU officials. The steam schooner award of February 1935 stated clearly and concisely: "No seafaring employee shall be required as a condition of receiving employment to register with any private hiring hall or any similar employment institution. All employment shall be direct from the offices of the union or from the docks. The rotation or tag system of employment shall not be used." The award covering foreign and intercoastal shipping, issued in April 1935, was even more concerned to clarify and defend the prerogatives of the shipowners. The award reaffirmed that "employment shall be at the docks or at the Union offices *at the option of the employers. The employer shall have entire freedom of selection from those eligible.*"[25]

Clearly these awards outlawed union control of hiring. But like the longshoremen, seamen refused to wait for arbitrators or to be bound by decisions that violated their vital interests. Initially, the militants were thwarted by the conservative ISU officials, but the activity of rank-and-file seamen on the ships soon turned the tide. Carl "Shingles" Tillman, a former shingle weaver in Northwest lumber mills, recalled that in October 1934, when he and a few friends placed this issue on the agenda of a Sailors' Union meeting, only seventeen men supported his motion while seventy-nine voted against it. He persisted, however, and within a month 200 members at a San Francisco SUP meeting unanimously demanded that all shipping go through the union hall. The key to the changed attitude was that men on the ships insisted on union control of hiring and backed up their resolution with the threat of job action. Individual steamship lines soon began capitulating to the seamen's demands, and by February 1935 a rank-and-file newspaper declared that "the steamschooners are 100 percent Union and hiring is done exclusively from the Union hall." In Seattle, according to another enthusiastic report, 95 percent of all hiring was through the union hall, and this breakthrough was accomplished by the militant action of rank-and-file seamen in a series of strikes on individual ships.[26]

Thus, at the very moment when the arbitrators were issuing awards that reaffirmed the employers' "entire freedom of selection from those eligible," the seamen had established virtually full union control of hiring. And they refused to give an inch in the face of the arbitrators' decrees. Harry Lundeberg, a Seattle militant who was emerging as the sailors' leading spokesman, declared that any man caught shipping off the dock would be "classed as a fink and treated as such." By July 1935 Shingles Tillman could report that in San Francisco, "from 350 to 500 men have shipped out of the hall each week. The few individuals who chiselled have been caught and given from 30 to 60 days on the beach to cool off."[27]

Having breached one of the venerable traditions of the sea, the seamen were prepared to carry their audacity to even loftier heights. A significant proportion of the shipping along the Pacific Coast was intercoastal; that is, it originated in Atlantic or Gulf ports, and the men on these vessels were under the jurisdiction of eastern ISU affiliates. To complicate matters further, the eastern and Gulf Coast unions of the ISU remained under the control of old-guard officials who showed no sympathy with the demand for union control of hiring, and who routinely issued union books to men who had sailed on intercoastal vessels throughout the Big Strike. Technically the union affiliation of these seamen and the manner in which they were hired—usually through crimps, company offices, or government fink halls—was no concern of the West Coast men. But the ISU militants on the Pacific were not about to let the odious remnants of the old order pass through their midst unchallenged, especially when many of the seafarers in question had scabbed during the 1934 strike. Thus, as intercoastal ships docked at West Coast ports, ISU patrolmen would board the vessels and check the union books of all unlicensed personnel. Anyone who did not carry a book, or who was recognized as a fink, was removed from the ship and replaced by a bona fide union man dispatched from an ISU hall in the port. In some cases entire crews were "pulled off in true West Coast style" when it was determined that the men had passed through picket lines of striking maritime workers in other ports.[28]

That a union representative could board a ship and remove seamen who had been hired via the legal mechanism of government and steamship company, that the authority of the master of the vessel could be breached with such impunity, was indeed a bold new development. But the maritime workers did not stop at the boundary of work relations and practices. The struggle between labor and capital invaded the realms of culture and politics and provoked a vigorous debate on the meaning of Americanism and the place of workers in the social order. Clearly there was a good deal more at stake here than "the hope of driving a new Buick."[29]

This larger field of vision is evident in the distinctive tradition of maritime workers on the march that developed in the aftermath of the Big Strike. As they marched in Labor Day parades, Bloody Thursday memorials, and other events that galvanized the ranks of labor, as they strode forward with heads held high, clad in their work uniforms of jeans, hickory-striped shirts, and white caps, the longshoremen and seamen became a vivid representation of working-class pride. In these same events, they also displayed the expanding focus of their symbolic universe and demonstrated their increasing integration of job-related concerns with broader, more overtly political issues.

The tradition had its beginning in the funeral procession for the martyrs of Bloody Thursday, on July 9, 1934, in San Francisco. Little more than a month after their strike had ended, maritime workers were again on the march. On Labor Day 1934, more than fifty thousand representatives of organized labor paraded up Market Street in an event that was much more than a normal Labor Day celebration. Rather, it was an attempt on the part of both the established AFL leadership and the insurgents to sum up the lessons of the eighty-three-day maritime strike and to unify the trade union movement around competing ideologies. The *San Francisco Chronicle* spoke for one side in characterizing the day as "dedicated to the stalwart Americanism for which the American Federation of Labor has always stood." The longshoremen, however, showed no interest in allowing the face of militant labor to be buried under a wet blanket of conservatism masquerading as patriotism. More than three thousand ILA men turned out and put on a forceful display of the spirit that was transforming the waterfront and sending shock waves through the rest of the labor movement. The police, the governor, and the "scabby" Hearst *Examiner* "received a tremendous razzing," according to the *Waterfront Worker,* while all along the line of march "the workers on the sidelines cheered and clapped for the fighting longshoremen."[30]

A year later the marine workers, now marching as a unified body under the banner of the Maritime Federation of the Pacific, had an even larger impact on

San Francisco's Labor Day celebration. The birth of the Maritime Federation in April 1935 had united all the marine crafts in an organization that many hoped would be the precursor of One Big Union on the waterfront. Parading together twelve-thousand strong, the Maritime Federation contingent made up 20 percent of the total of sixty thousand marchers in San Francisco. Moreover, several of their major adversaries became the focal point of symbolic gestures of contempt involving significant numbers of workers. William Randolph Hearst had earned the bitter enmity of insurgent unionists, intellectuals, and political progressives for his "cesspool" journalism and constant Red-baiting of those who did not share his version of Americanism. Remembering Hearst's vilification of the general strike, the marine workers and other marching unionists no doubt warmed to the words of the anonymous poet whose verse topped the masthead of a University of California student publication:

> Hearst in war, Hearst in peace,
> Hearst in every news release,
> Spreads his filth and desolation
> To increase his circulation.

According to the *Voice of the Federation,* as the head of the Labor Day procession approached the Hearst *Examiner* building, "a thunder of boo's surged up and reverberated around the local headquarters of 'Labor's Enemy Number One' " and continued for a full three hours as the marchers paraded by. (Many years later, Warehouse Union organizer Louis Goldblatt still recalled vividly that "in all the Labor Day parades, the one thing you'd hear down the whole length of Market Street was . . . that 'boo' echoing through the hills of San Francisco" as unionists passed the *Examiner* building.)[31]

The *Voice* had already announced the "determination of 35,000 organized Maritime Workers to provide Labor on the Pacific Coast with its own newspaper." On this occasion, a Maritime Federation float proclaimed: "The Voice of the Federation Tells the Truth about the Waterfront. Read Labor's Own Newspaper." *Voice* newsboys sold three hundred copies of the paper in the front of the *Examiner* building and enjoyed a brisk business all along the line of march. In fact, that evening the ejection of a *Voice* salesman from the hall where Central Labor Council President Edward Vandeleur was about to deliver a Labor Day address sparked a walkout of more than a thousand people from the proceedings. For a growing number of workers, the *Voice of the Federation* was becoming as vivid a symbol of working-class insurgency as Hearst was of capitalist intransigence.

The other major symbolic event of the day involved what the *Voice* characterized as "the greatest gesture of contempt ever accorded a Frisco Mayor." In this case the mayor was Angelo "Little Fink" Rossi. The marine unionists believed he had sided with capital throughout the 1934 strike and was responsible for much of the police violence against the strikers. According to the *Voice,* the entire Maritime Federation contingent and thousands of other workers turned their backs on Rossi and looked the other way as they passed by the reviewing stand where he was presiding.[32]

The most powerful symbol of maritime workers on the march was the annual memorial for the martyrs of the Big Strike. Beginning on the first anniversary of Bloody Thursday, maritime labor stopped work up and down the Pacific Coast, initiating a tradition that the longshoremen have continued ever since. It was, and is, a one-day strike in honor of those who sacrificed their lives in the cause of waterfront unionism. Ironically, in 1935 a coastwide ILA ballot resulted in a vote not to observe a twenty-four-hour memorial holiday, but in many ports units of the Maritime Federation engaged in such action anyway. In San Francisco, where the ILA local had voted overwhelmingly in favor of a memorial strike, all maritime labor stopped work until 1:00 P.M., while stores and bars on the front cooperated by closing their doors for part of the day. The *Voice* claimed that twenty-five thousand people marched up Market Street while "tens of thousands of quiet, awed San Franciscans" watched. Even the conservative *American Seaman* praised the event as a "Monster Parade" whose size "astounded" the city of San Francisco.[33]

In Portland, there were picket lines on the waterfront from 7:00 A.M. to midnight, and seventeen vessels in the Columbia River were tied up for the entire day. The crews of three English ships also joined the strike and participated in the day's activities. In Seattle, "5,000 tanned, windswept, grim, and silent men," including striking lumber workers, teamsters, and the unemployed, marched to the strains of the "Marseillaise." Even in the small port of Raymond, Washington, where the ILA membership numbered only 107, more than a thousand people participated in the Bloody Thursday memorial, suggesting, in this case as in others, the ability of the maritime workers to galvanize significant numbers of shoreside workers around their activity.[34]

Meanwhile, at the "point of production," in addition to the job actions aimed at transforming work relations, there was growing insurgency around broader, more overtly political issues. There were, for example, brief work stoppages to protest the killing of a San Pedro stevedore and the frameup of maritime workers charged with murder and conspiracy in a bitter intraunion dispute in San Francisco. After a policeman killed longshoreman Norman Gregg on a San Pedro street, a wave of anger swept the waterfront and spilled over into other sections of the community. The next day maritime workers and other unionists shut down the entire port—"every dock, every store, and every street car in San Pedro," claimed the *Voice of the Federation.* The *Los Angeles Times* acknowledged that thirty-five hundred demonstrators "blocked traffic for several blocks around the scene of the shooting, erected banners of fifteen unions, and compelled all passers by" in the vicinity to remove their hats. A *Voice* editorial sought to draw the appropriate political lesson: "It is time that we take control of government out of the hands of the employers, who use government to increase profits and laugh at justice. It is time that union labor elects ITS OWN MEN to public office. . . . Murders like that will end when we ELECT OUR OWN MEN."[35]

In the case of four ILA members who were accused of killing a man during a brawl at the Ship Scalers' hall in San Francisco, there was much evidence that the fight had been instigated by antiunion employers. To support their fellow workers, approximately twenty-thousand men—members of the Maritime Federation and rank-and-file teamsters—walked off the docks for half an hour during the trial. Three days later a San Francisco jury acquitted the accused ILA members after deliberating for a mere seven minutes.[36]

In spite of the obvious seriousness of the marine workers' cause, it was not unusual for their actions to take on a note of levity and even unashamed irresponsibility. On one occasion the sailing of the S.S. *President Coolidge* was held up for several days because the ship's crew didn't like the way their eggs were cooked. (This incident has survived in waterfront lore as the "ham and eggs" beef.) In another instance a rambunctious steam schooner crew "borrowed" a cow and coaxed it aboard the vessel after the skipper had balked at their demand for more fresh milk. In a more serious—but still festive— vein, dockers, seamen, and licensed officers united to disrupt a *bon voyage* party for University of California football coach "Navy Bill" Ingram and his team. Ingram had played a leading role in recruiting students as scabs during the 1934 strike and, as an exercise in conditioning and character building, had virtually ordered his football players to serve as strikebreakers. (The University of Southern California football team had played a similar role in San Pedro.) The maritime workers harbored a bitter grudge against these "Phi Beta Kappa finks" and against Ingram in particular. Longshoremen and seamen rejoiced over the difficulties that both Cal and USC were having on the gridiron in the fall of 1934, especially when little St. Mary's College "ran Bill Ingram's scabs all over the lot." But the sweetest revenge came at the hands of the marine workers themselves. When Ingram and his football team appeared on the docks again, this time to board the S.S. *President Taft* to travel to Hawaii for two games, the entire crew, from the captain to the mess boys, staged a brief walkout and the longshoremen refused to carry the team's luggage aboard the ship. This was a different kind of education for the chagrined university students, and the *Waterfront Worker* was only too happy to drive the lesson home: "The college scabs . . . couldn't seem to grasp the significance of it all. To be a football player in an American college is to be a hero and yet here were these maritime workers refusing to man a ship they were to sail on. But lugging their baggage aboard amid cries of fink, scab, and rat, the boys had something to think about."[37]

Given the international dimensions of the seamen's experience, and the cosmopolitanism that pervaded the waterfront, the issues of war and fascism proved to be especially volatile in the mid-thirties. The 1936 convention of the Maritime Federation of the Pacific voted to call a coastwide strike if the United States became involved in a war on foreign soil, and the Puget Sound Division of the Ferryboatmen's Union exhorted the American Federation of Labor to "declare a General Strike of all A.F. of L. affiliates" in the event that the United States participated in such a conflict.[38]

The maritime workers were especially active in their opposition to fascism. The immediate spark was twofold: first, Germany's policy of arresting seamen from many countries, including the United States, for smuggling anti-Nazi literature into the Third Reich; and second, Italy's war of aggression against Ethiopia. Already, many seamen had witnessed the destruction of the trade unions and any semblance of democratic rights in Germany and Italy. As early as July 1933 the *Waterfront Worker* reported from Washington State that sailors from a U.S. Navy ship, along with crew members from American and Danish merchant ships, had joined together to pull the swastika from a German vessel in Olympia harbor. When the swastika entered San Francisco Bay in March 1935 on the bow of the German cruiser *Karlsruhe,* seven thousand longshoremen, machinists, and ship scalers struck for half an hour, dampening the official welcome that city officials had prepared for the crew of the German naval vessel. When the *Karlsruhe* entered the harbor at Vancouver, British Columbia, the angry response of workers there forced the ship to drop anchor in the stream and forego any plans to visit the city. In Seattle, longshoremen held a protest strike against the arrest of American seaman Lawrence Simpson—who was seized by Nazi police for alleged possession of Communist literature in his shipboard locker—while seafaring unions picketed the German ship *Schwaben*. The SUP branch in Seattle voted to picket every German ship that came into the harbor.[39]

A major outburst of antifascist activity erupted among maritime workers in Europe and America in response to Mussolini's invasion of Ethiopia. The *Voice* reported that in Paris the Federation of Dock and Port Workers ordered its members to refuse to work any Italian ships; in Antwerp a meeting of eight hundred longshoremen pledged themselves to prevent Italian munitions from being transported; in the British port of Cardiff seamen boarded an Italian steamer and "plastered her bulkhead with posters denouncing the fascist aggression." On the East Coast of the United States a Norwegian crew walked off the freighter *Spero* because it was being loaded with scrap iron destined for Mussolini's war against Ethiopia. In Seattle the Marine Firemen passed a resolution to boycott war materials, and their action was backed by the city's Central Labor Council. In San Francisco the Maritime Federation voted to boycott any cargo that could aid Mussolini's war effort. The longshoremen demonstrated that the resolution was no paper tiger by refusing to load the

Italian ship *Cellina* when it appeared that her cargo might violate the boycott of war materials. In San Pedro longshoremen and seamen went a step further. They refused to load or man the S.S. *Oregon,* even though it was bound for Singapore, because of the possibility that the aviation fuel it was carrying could be transshipped to the war zone.[40]

The largest single display of antifascist internationalism came in August 1937, when the Maritime Federation called a coastwide work stoppage, mainly to protest the growing intervention of Germany and Italy in the Spanish civil war. The Federation explained that

the action is to be taken for the following reasons: One—as a demonstration of our solidarity with our fellow workers in Spain, and as a protest against the intervention of Germany and Italy on behalf of the Fascists.

Two—condemning the dictatorships of Italy and Germany for smashing the trade union movements in those countries, and pledging our support to aid the workers in re-establishing their unions.

Three—to demand the release of all labor and class war prisoners.

The work stoppage was scheduled for half an hour, and the *Voice* claimed that it involved thirty thousand maritime workers up and down the coast.[41]

During the Italo-Ethiopian crisis, in particular, there was a tendency in some quarters to justify the marine workers' bold actions by claiming the support of the Roosevelt administration. Roosevelt had just declared an embargo on the shipment of war materials designed to aid Italian aggression, but the maritime workers went beyond the President's position by boycotting strategic raw materials as well as weapons. Moreover, a radical stance was not only implicit in their actions but quite explicit in the words of some of their leading spokesmen. Al Quittenton, who was soon to be elected to the second highest office in the SUP, declared: "Only when the workers in every land [stop the manufacture and transport of military materials] will these hideous wholesale murders called wars be prevented." From his prison cell in San Quentin, one of the widely celebrated Modesto Boys* penned an essay on "Ethiopia and Us" for his fellow seamen. After reviewing the background of the conflict, he concluded: "Whether the Movement of Mussolini in Ethiopia

---

*The Modesto Boys were seamen who were arrested and charged with possession of dynamite, conspiracy to assault with deadly weapons, and several other crimes in an alleged attempt to blow up Standard Oil gas stations and a hotel housing strikebreakers during the West Coast tanker strike in the spring of 1935. The maritime unions charged that the entire case was a frame-up engineered by the Standard Oil Company, and several of the original defendants did turn out to be "stool-pigeons"—one an undercover agent of the San Francisco Police Department, and another a private detective employed by Standard Oil. The defendants were acquitted of three charges but were convicted of possession of dynamite. The marine unions poured a tremendous amount of energy into the campaign to free the Modesto Boys (so named because they were arrested in a small town near Modesto and tried there), who became the first major "class war prisoners" from within maritime labor's own ranks.[42]

is a gigantic bluff to retain Fascist power in Italy, or a torch to set off another
War for Profit like that of 1914, let's be ready to stand by and show the world
that we approve neither Fascism nor company unions." Reporting on a
fraternal visit with Japanese seamen in San Francisco, a popular SUP patrolman named Lloyd E. (Sam) Usinger echoed the language and themes of the
IWW:

> We must eventually own the vessels as well as operate them. Then only will we
> be able to claim our rightful share of the products of our labor.
> But before we are able to do this we must lay a solid foundation of friendship
> and international solidarity and form a one-big-union where poverty and unem-
> ployment shall be unknown.
> Fellow Workers it is up to you to cooperate with all your brothers in the world
> regardless of . . . nationality, and the seamen will never have to go to war with
> any country to protect the Capitalist system which has been forced upon us.[43]

Although relatively few marine workers may have shared Usinger's explicit
commitment to a radically transformed world order, their activities clearly
reflected a growing integration of job-related concerns with politics. That
many of these actions were based at the point of production was entirely
natural, because historically the marine workers had been isolated from the
conventional channels of political expression. Thus, when they became increasingly radicalized, and saw the class and political dimensions of world
events and of the actions of the shipowners and their allies, they instinctively
asserted themselves at the point where they felt their own strength was
concentrated. As Usinger put it, "We realize that we have never got anything
by asking—only by fighting—and we must do that right where [the boss]
makes his money."[44]

The shipowners and other representatives of the employing class were
appalled by these bold initiatives. It was bad enough when the maritime
workers violated arbitration awards on the issue of hiring and other job-related
matters, but intervention in the realm of jury trials and international di-
plomacy seemed to have insurrectionary overtones. A *San Francisco Chronicle* editorial reminded the workers that "foreign relations are exclusively a
matter for the President and the State Department. . . . Unions are far out of
their jurisdiction when they assume to take a hand in the delicate relations of
international affairs."[45]

One of the leading employer spokesmen, in a speech to a convention of
Rotarians from around the world, demonstrated an acute awareness of the
political and international dimensions of the maritime labor movement.
Almon Roth discussed what he termed the "similarity of our problems in all
nations." Having received a bulletin from Australia that recited "difficulties"
on the Sydney docks, he was struck by the fact that it appeared to be an exact

summary of what had been happening on the San Francisco waterfront during the same time period. "There was a time," he said wistfully,

> when labor disputes were confined to the matter of wages, hours, and working conditions. Unfortunately, this is no longer true. Within the past two years the longshoremen on this Coast have refused to handle cargoes in a number of instances, not because of any dispute with their employers, but rather because of their political interest in the war in Spain, or the Japanese-Chinese international struggle. Exactly the same thing has happened in other countries. . . . the grounds for labor disputes in the shipping industry throughout the world have now been broadened to include social and economic objectives which are entirely outside the immediate relationship of employer and employee, and over which the employer has absolutely no control.

In spite of the dispassionate and analytical tone of his remarks, Roth was no detached observer of the world's waterfronts. He was first and foremost a shipowner spokesman, and he regarded the constant round of maritime strikes and job actions as disastrous. He quoted with obvious approval the statement of a New Zealand government official who was equally appalled by the frequent work stoppages on the part of longshoremen and seamen in his own country. "If the Union cannot control its men on the waterfront," said the official, "we will find another organization to do it. No government can tolerate this sort of thing any longer."[46]

In response to this kind of threat, and specifically to the *Chronicle*'s editorial admonition about the marine workers overstepping their jurisdiction, the *Voice of the Federation* echoed the ILA's rejoinder to the waterfront employers on the opposite priorities of labor and capital. "There isn't any question," said the *Voice*,

> but where it saves a lot of wear and tear on the nerves and conscience to take a priggishly indifferent attitude toward the unwarranted slaughter of thousands of human beings.
>
> However, the Maritime Federation, unlike the Chronicle, is not an organization set up for the sole purpose of garnering profit.
>
> We labor under the unique conception that exclusive of the acts or omissions of officialdom elsewhere, we are obliged to not permit ourselves, as sailors and dockworkers to be used to the disinterest of any innocent group of people.

Clearly, the officialdom referred to by the *Voice* was not limited to the Furuseths, Scharrenbergs, Ryans, and other AFL conservatives who had earned the contempt of the union membership on the West Coast. The arena of rank-and-file rights and responsibilities had broadened to include the entire world. In the eyes of many marine workers, Mussolini was almost as real and immediate a fink as Paul Scharrenberg or Joe Ryan, and the campaign against fascist aggression in Ethiopia was the same as the fight against company unions in the United States. As the *Voice* concluded, "We believe the Ethiopians are innocent of any activity that would require this criminal onslaught on the part of the Italians. We are *acting* accordingly."[47]

Although the maritime workers demonstrated a strong sense of internationalism, they often justified their activity in the language of Americanism. While this may seem paradoxical, it is in fact symbolic of a broader theme of the 1930s, namely, the search for heroes and values in the American past to legitimize the concerns of the present. Apart from a large and colorful stock of colloquialisms reflecting the particularities of their environment, the marine workers expressed themselves in conventional terms derived from the American mainstream. They claimed the mantle of patriotism as adamantly as their employers; and their unifying theme was unionism far more than class. In other words, they did not speak the language of Marxism, because for the most part that vocabulary had never taken root in American soil. But the common frame of reference should not obscure the reality of class distinctions in the meaning of language and the interpretation of historical events. Beneath the surface of common language the marine workers often conveyed a distinctive meaning that was profoundly different if not fundamentally opposite from that attributed to the same terms by their employers.

This was certainly true in relation to the vital and contentious theme of Americanism. William Randolph Hearst epitomized the employers' ritual patriotism when he featured the following vacuous declaration from Calvin Coolidge's inaugural address on the front page of the *San Francisco Examiner* more than a decade after its original delivery: *"We have been, and propose to be,"* said President Coolidge, *"more and more American. We believe that we can best serve our own country and most successfully discharge our obligations to humanity by continuing to be openly and candidly, intensely and scrupulously American."*[48]

By itself, this statement was harmless enough. But what alarmed and disgusted the maritime workers was the fact that the shipowners and their allies were determined to go beyond vacuity and use patriotism as an instrument of oppression. On the one hand, they constantly denounced every insurgent action of the longshoremen and seamen as alien and subversive, while, on the other, they wrapped themselves in the flag as they endeavored to thwart the most elementary demands of labor. Even acts of criminal violence and the denial of basic human rights were justified in terms of the defense of American principles. In an editorial entitled "Are All the Vigilantes Dead?" the *Shipping Register* called for the return of the old order on the waterfront: "There are thousands of red-blooded Americans here in San Francisco. What say we take a day off from our regular business and attend to the matter in a

proper manner." Or as the governor of Oregon put it, "The men on the docks
. . . must be guided back to their old-time standards." "The people of eastern
Oregon have assured me," he said, that "they would like to march on the City
of Portland and put an end" to the militant leaders of the marine unions.[49]

These flag-waving appeals to vigilante terrorism led one reader of the *Voice
of the Federation* to exclaim that if the Hearst press and like-minded publications were to be believed, "the only true Americans are scabs, vigilantes,
hoodlums, hop heads and ex-army officers," along with "a few ex-
bootleggers, gangsters, poolroom bums and stool pigeons." "Don't get me
wrong," his letter said, "I'm not one of those Communists. . . . But it sort of
gags me that the only Americans left now are those who own a bank, have a
job in city hall, or are engaged in some other form of legalized racketeering."[50]

In spite of the way their opponents degraded the term, the maritime workers
were by no means ready to concede the mantle of Americanism to the
shipowners. On the contrary, the workers saw themselves as true patriots,
defenders of democracy, and inheritors of the nation's progressive and revolutionary traditions. In the eyes of the marine workers, it was the capitalists and
their allies who were un-American, because they were trying to deny broad
sections of the people their fundamental democratic rights and to rob the
workers of an "American standard of living." A resolution passed unanimously by the San Francisco Bay Area District Council of the Maritime Federation
stated: "The growth of fascist tendencies and organizations in the State of
California . . .[is] in direct opposition to the Democratic principles upon
which our government was formed, which guarantee the right of free speech,
assembly, the right to organize and fight for better conditions." The *Voice of
the Federation* declared that "American citizens are now faced with the choice
of fighting for their Liberties or being crushed under the iron heel of a ruthless
mob despotism, organized and led by 'unAmerican' employers."[51]

It is vitally important to understand the context in which this heated
discussion of Americanism took place. If the employers were unable or
unwilling to distinguish between unionism and communism, the maritime
workers saw overtones of fascism in the politics of capital. The *Waterfront
Worker* warned that "not prosperity, but insane, bloody fascism is just around
the corner." Although the benefit of hindsight may tempt us to dismiss such a
prediction as inflammatory and even paranoid, the marine workers had good
reason to fear that what they saw and experienced was more than a passing
phenomenon. Having in many cases witnessed the true meaning of fascism in
the port cities of Germany and Italy, they saw parallel developments in the
United States, particularly in California, where it seemed that every effort to
assert labor's most elementary rights met with a wave of legal and vigilante
repression.[52]

Nowhere was this truer than in the vast realm of farm factories that dominated the Golden State's landscape. On July 20, 1934, the day after the San Francisco general strike ended, police in Sacramento had arrested seventeen leaders of the Cannery and Agricultural Workers Industrial Union (CAWIU) on the sweeping and conveniently vague charge of criminal syndicalism. Eventually eight of them were found guilty and sentenced to prison terms. But this legal persecution was only a small part of what developed into a major offensive in which the state's leading industrial interests, acting through the Associated Farmers of California, mobilized growers, law enforcement authorities, the American Legion, and other zealots in a frenzied effort to destroy unionism in agriculture and weaken it in the cities.[53]

One of the ugliest incidents of this campaign was described at length by crusading journalist Carey McWilliams in his exposé of "The Rise of Farm Fascism." The incident occurred in Santa Rosa, in August 1935, when growers and their allies moved quickly to head off a threatened strike by apple pickers. According to McWilliams, a mob of vigilantes seized CAWIU organizers Solomon Nitzburg and Jack Green,

> together with three other men, dragged them through the streets . . . and, after the three men had kissed the American flag on the courthouse steps and promised to leave the community, released them. Nitzburg and Green, refusing to comply with the demand, were kicked, beaten, tarred and feathered, and paraded around the courthouse in Santa Rosa, and driven out of the county. In seizing Nitzburg, the mob fired volley after volley of rifle fire through his home, and followed up this attack with the use of tear-gas bombs.

The *San Francisco Examiner* exulted that "the tar and feather party was hailed in Sonoma County as a direct American answer to the red strike fomentors." Moreover, the maritime workers were well aware that the Santa Rosa mob had threatened to come to San Francisco and "clean up the waterfront." After describing the orgy of violence that McWilliams later characterized as a "Fascist insurrection," the *Voice* exclaimed, "All this in the name of 'Americanism'!"[54]

On the waterfront itself, the violence which had peaked during the general strike continued to take its toll. Although the insurgent, optimistic aspect of maritime unionism remained predominant, frequent outbursts of vigilante violence contributed to a sometimes powerful undercurrent, which author Louis Adamic characterized as one of "great mental and nervous strain." Immediately after the Big Strike, a nineteen-year-old Sailors' Union activist had his throat slashed by a scab, and a year and a half after the eruption of 1934 it still remained commonplace for individuals wearing marine union buttons to be attacked and beaten at night by roving bands of thugs. In October 1935 Harry Bridges reported that "at least one ILA man is beaten up every night on the Waterfront and . . . a longshoreman was killed by vigilantes last week." Adamic recalled that as he was interviewing Bridges in April 1936, a man interrupted their conversation to "inform him that a worker had just been found slugged unconscious on a dock."[55]

The maritime workers were appalled by the polite, even friendly reception that the crew of the German naval vessel *Karlsruhe* received from government officials in San Francisco. The City Hall rotunda was decorated with swastikas for the occasion, and a newspaper representing independent merchants in the city's Mission District declared, "If that's the type of young men the new Germany is raising, the rest of the world owes her a lot of thanks and should wish her the most far-reaching success." Meanwhile, in the California legislature, more than a score of bills calling for restrictions on civil liberties were introduced in one session of the assembly. Speaking of California, the *Nation* said: "Nowhere else has there been such a flagrant denial of the personal liberties guaranteed by the Bill of Rights; nowhere else has authority been so lawless and brazen; nowhere else has the brute force of capitalism been so openly used and displayed." Although criticizing what she regarded as excessive use of the term *fascism* to describe the reactionary offensive in California, journalist Lillian Symes acknowledged: "It was like this, I imagine, in Rome in 1922, in Berlin in 1932."[56]

The maritime workers shared none of Symes's skepticism about how their tormentors should be characterized. Turning the tables on their accusers, they argued that any talk of alien and subversive activity should be directed at the employers, the Hearst press, the reactionary ISU officials, and the vigilante groups whose watchword was "intimidation and terror carried out in the dark of night." Ole Olsen, a popular official of the Sailors' Union, characterized William Randolph Hearst as "a madman . . . trying to rule us with his unamerican principles" and "Hitler's American prototype." Whereas Hearst was an aggressor against democracy, said Olsen, "We are defending our rights as American Workers. . . . Ours is the strength and the vitality of America!" Similarly, a resolution passed by the West Coast Marine Firemen on behalf of the beleaguered Atlantic Coast rank-and-file movement condemned the behavior of the eastern ISU officials, who were busy terrorizing and expelling militant seamen, as "Fascist tactics" and "anti-American policies, which resemble Hitler." The resolution called on the old-guard leadership to "operate the East and Gulf Coast Unions with Democratic American Principles as contained in the Constitution of the United States and . . . the 'Bill of Rights.' "[57]

In this epic battle, the marine workers did not hesitate to invoke the lessons of American history and the pantheon of American heroes on their behalf. In response to the frequent charge that the maritime unions were radical organizations, marine fireman Martin Garnier asked:

Why use the word "radical" at all?

Why not call us "Revolutionists"[?] Or would this ally us too closely with the principles of the early founders of America, such as Washington, Paine, Franklin, and other militant Americans who drafted and signed our glorious Declaration of Independence[?]

Or do you think we possess the spirit of Lincoln who advocated the abolishment of slavery and the emancipation of the working class[?]

When nine maritime workers were arrested on felony charges during the 1935 tanker strike against Standard Oil, the *Voice* declared: "Were law abiding citizens such as Jefferson and Lincoln alive today they would no doubt be rotting in some filthy jail much the same as our brothers at Modesto, victims of the notorious Standard Oil frame-up." Not surprisingly, the Boston Tea Party also became an example of militant Americanism that served as a precedent for the struggles of the workers.[58]

In the face of a particularly virulent attack on the maritime unions by publisher Henry Sanborn and his right-wing weekly, the *American Citizen,* the publicity committee of the San Francisco ILA local countered with a lengthy statement outlining "the kind of Americanism which the Maritime Unions subscribe to." The statement began with a long quotation that taken at face value appears to have revolutionary overtones:

Labor is prior to and independent of capital. . . . inasmuch as most good things have been produced by labor it follows that all such things belong of right to those whose labor has produced them. But it has so happened, in all ages of the world, that some have labored and others have, without labor, enjoyed a large portion of the fruits. This is wrong and should not continue. To secure to each laborer the whole produce of his labor as nearly as possible, is a worthy object of any government.

"For your information," the ILA said to Sanborn, "this is not instruction from Moscow. This is a quotation from an American, an American President to be exact, Abe Lincoln."[59]

In invoking the name of Lincoln and searching for precedents, the maritime workers were reflecting a much broader intellectual tendency of the 1930s. Alfred Haworth Jones has noted a growing preoccupation with American history during the thirties, a concern with the common man but also with heroes who could embody "the lessons of the past which the Depression generation sought to recall." In this endeavor, no figure received more attention or was endowed with more significance than Lincoln. Literary critic Alfred Kazin characterized the "passionate addiction to Lincoln" as "among the most moving aspects of the decade." Jones argues that this preoccupation with the past was profoundly conservative in that it sought reassurance from what John Dos Passos called "the kind of firm ground other men, belonging to other generations before us, have found to stand on." He also sees the widespread fascination with the American heartland, and its preeminent representatives Jackson and Lincoln, as indicative of an "insular nationalism." If his assessment is accurate, then the maritime workers' concern with history was quite different in tone and intent from that of the mainstream. For their use of history did not reflect this conservatism. While they identified with heroes and lessons from the past, they could not find much firm ground in the long record of oppression and suffering that had been their lot. They invoked the past not to demonstrate the greatness and durability of an America beset by crisis and doubt, but in order to transform the present and shape the future. Moreover, as we have seen, many of them did not view American developments in isolation from the rest of the world. Rather, their lively concern with wars of aggression on at least three continents was a reflection of a perhaps uniquely internationalist dimension of their subculture. For them, the lessons of the past were relevant to a present in which historic forces clashed not only in one country but throughout the world.[60]

It is also important to note that the maritime workers did not limit their frame of reference to the commonly accepted historical symbols exemplified by Jefferson, Jackson, and Lincoln. They also drew on a specifically working-class tradition that was, implicitly at least, antagonistic to the American mainstream. George Woolf, president of the Ship Scalers' local in San Francisco, compared the four members of his union who were arrested on murder charges during an organizing drive to the celebrated California labor martyrs and "class war prisoners" J. B. McNamara and Tom Mooney. "An active Unionist is dangerous to capital," said Woolf, "so he is arrested and framed." Ole Olsen of the SUP called on his fellow workers to learn from the "school of oppression." Every time the employers "send one of our numbers to prison," said Olsen, "every time they have one of us shot in the name of LAW AND ORDER, every time they send their vigilantes to assault one of us they are adding to our education."[61]

That there was a tension between this school of oppression—with its long litany of the victims of capitalist injustice—and the broader symbolism of American history became apparent in the controversy surrounding the observance of a Maritime Memorial Day in honor of the martyrs of the 1934 strike. There was general agreement that there should be some form of observance on behalf of the men who died during the Big Strike, but a sizable minority of the Maritime Federation delegates were opposed to a work stoppage. Moreover, many spokesmen for the maritime unions wanted the observance to be on national Memorial Day, May 30, an already established holiday honoring Americans who had died in the country's wars, rather than on July 5, Bloody Thursday, a vivid symbol of class warfare. It would appear that the division was between those who viewed the martyrs of 1934 primarily in terms of the nation's history and those who regarded them as heroes of the historic struggle of the working class. Maritime Federation President Harry Lundeberg put the case for a class observance on July 5 most clearly and forcefully when he stated that it must be "more than a Holiday. . . . July 5th will be a mighty show of the strength of our unions and of our Federation." Moreover, said Lundeberg, the entire labor movement and all friends of labor should be invited to participate, because the "cause of the maritime workers is the cause of all labor . . . the martyrs of the strike [will] take their place in history with the martyrs of labor, with the victims of Ludlow, Haymarket, Everett, Centralia, Imperial Valley, San Francisco Preparedness Day and Modesto." Lundeberg's views were echoed at SUP meetings up and down the Pacific Coast, and the seamen carried the day on behalf of a class-conscious observance for the martyrs of 1934.[62]

For the most part, however, the maritime workers did not see a sharp distinction between allegiance to their class and loyalty to their country. In fact, they were anxious to present themselves and their movement in harmony with what they perceived as the mainstream of American history and values. When the shipowners and the press waged a sustained propaganda campaign to isolate the marine unions in San Francisco from the rest of the community, the ILA, in particular, fought back with the argument that by removing unemployed men from the relief rolls and providing them with decent wages, maritime labor was "an asset to the community." The ILA contended that small businessmen would hardly lend an ear to the shipowner's "distorted arguments" because these merchants had also "reaped benefits from the increased wages of the workers." Comparing the situation on the waterfront before and after the 1934 strike, the ILA exulted that "the Embarcadero has become Americanized." Why? Because "today, . . . there are *no longshoremen on relief.* Through the collective efforts of the men themselves, the burden of their support has been removed from the backs of the tax-payers and is placed squarely where it belongs—upon the shipping industry. The men do not want charity from either the tax-payers or the shipowners. They want a decent return from that industry whose profits they help to swell and they intend to get it." Moreover, said the ILA, until we succeed in helping to bring the wages and conditions of the seamen up to those of the longshoremen, "we feel we have not done our duty as union men or true Americans."[63]

The marine workers' quest to occupy the high ground of patriotism is reminiscent of a recurring theme in American history. Periods of crisis have often featured sharp conflicts in which the very meaning of America has been a prominent part of the terrain of battle.[64] It is ironic, though, that Communists played the leading role in helping the maritime workers explore and articulate their rightful place in American history. The Communist party was a latecomer to the depression decade's preoccupation with finding a usable American past. As late as January 1935 a poem in the *New Masses* had characterized Americanism only in terms of lynch mobs and strikebreaking:

God Flag Constitution
holy trinity of exploitation
signifying American Legion
D.A.R.
Ku Klux Klan
with Declaration of Independence
in one hand
and tar and rope in the other.

But especially after the Seventh Congress of the Comintern, where the Third Period was laid to rest and replaced by the Popular Front, Communists in the United States began taking steps to rectify their neglect of the American Revolutionary tradition. This new orientation gained such rapid momentum that by July 1936 Earl Browder was declaring, "We Communists claim the revolutionary traditions of Americanism. We are the only ones who consciously continue those traditions and apply them to the problems of today. *We are the Americans and Communism is the Americanism of the twentieth century."*

The Communist party also shared in the decade's veneration of Abraham Lincoln. In a significant symbolic gesture, Browder delivered a Lincoln's Birthday address on "Lincoln and the Communists" in Springfield, Illinois, on February 12, 1936. With characteristic modesty, he claimed that "it is left to the Communist Party to revive the words of Lincoln," and he noted that Karl Marx had called Lincoln "the single-minded son of the working class." The Americans who fought in the Spanish civil war under Communist leadership did so as members of the Lincoln Battalion, and a pamphlet entitled *True Americans,* which hailed the contribution of maritime workers to the antifascist cause in Spain, declared that they "proved themselves worthy citizens of our country—an honor to a nation founded in 1776 by similar men, a credit to the great Lincoln for whom they named their battalion."[65]

On the waterfront, some of the individuals who frequently quoted American precedents were either members or close sympathizers of the Communist party, including Martin Garnier, the outspoken marine fireman who for a time published a regular column in the *Voice,* and the staff of the *Waterfront Worker.* But it would be a bit too facile to give the Communists all the credit for the marine workers' expression of militant Americanism. Some activists who spoke the language of militant Americanism were clearly independent of the Communists; and its characteristic themes were sometimes expressed in a way that was contrary to the Party's position. Thus, at a time when the marine workers vigorously upheld the Constitution of the United States as a bulwark against fascism, it remained the public stance of the Communists that *"we fight for a Soviet— a Workers' and Farmers'— Constitution as against the Existing Capitalist Constitution."*[66]

Even so, it is undeniable that the Communists played by far the leading role in popularizing the language of Americanism on the waterfront. Their success in this regard suggests a convergence of the goals of the Communist party with the aims of insurgent workers—not only in maritime but in other industries as well—at an auspicious historical moment. As the Party made the transition from the ultraleft sloganeering of the Third Period to the democratic and nationalist themes of the Popular Front, those who were more comfortable with the purer class-against-class orientation of the earlier period tended to fade into the background. In their place a new, American-born corps of cadres came to the fore. Communist functionary George Charney recalled that "this radical change in composition not only altered the 'face' of the party, it influenced policy, the choice of personnel, and methods of work. . . . It was an internal revolution." For this new generation of Communists, the Popular Front signified an escape from industrial, ethnic, and racial ghettos, a widening of horizons and opportunities, a heady engagement with mainstream America. "We rejoiced," said Charney, "because the party had achieved status as a recognized political force in the country."[67]

At the same time, the ferment of unionism and the democratic thrust of the New Deal meant that East European workers in the major cities and company towns of the industrial heartland were also becoming a recognized political force. They too were seizing the mantle of Americanism to legitimize their heritage, their present struggles, and their future aspirations. Novelist Thomas Bell, the son and nephew of Slovak steelworkers, poignantly conveyed this moment of cultural and psychological emancipation through the person of Dobie Dobrejcak in *Out of This Furnace*. A third-generation steelworker captivated by the magnetic power of the CIO, Dobie suddenly realized that even though he and his fellow CIO organizers were not Protestant, middle-class, and Anglo-Saxon, they were "thinking and talking like Americans." "Maybe not the kind of American that came over on the *Mayflower*," he reflected, but *"Made in U.S.A."* nonetheless.

"Made in the U.S.A.," he thought, "made in the First Ward [of Braddock, Pennsylvania]. I'm almost as much a product of that mill down there as any rail or ingot they ever turned out. And maybe that's been part of the trouble. If I'm anything at all, I'm an American, only not the kind you read about in history books or that they make speeches about on the Fourth of July; anyway, not yet."[68]

Likewise, for the denizens of dock and sailortown, the language of militant Americanism became an expression of class pride, an instrument of cultural integration, a way of transcending the demeaning stereotypes of dock walloper and drunken sailor. Like Dobie, they embraced the American mainstream, but on their own terms—ridiculing the demands of the nativist "Americanizers" and infusing the language and themes of Americanism with a clear class dimension. Thus, in response to a diatribe from "A Loyal American," who concluded with the familiar suggestion—"You always have the privilege of going back to Russia if you do not like it in the United States"—the *Waterfront Worker* stated that "this country of ours [is one] whose wealth we have built with our own sweat and blood. . . . *WE are the loyal Americans,* Mister, not you! We are struggling to better the conditions of the workers on the waterfront. *Our struggles are the same as the overwhelming majority of Americans.*" In the same vein, "A 100% stevedore's wife" vividly expressed the passion, and the blending of Americanism and class consciousness, that so characterized the maritime workers during the Pentecostal era. Writing in response to an anti-Communist letter that appeared in the *Waterfront Worker,* she declared:

> First of all, I was not born in Russia. I have never been out of the U.S.A. and speak no foreign language. My father was a Baptist Deacon and I was born on a farm in southern Missouri. My grandfathers both fought in the Civil War.
>
> In San Francisco I worked for 16 years in the various laundries as a press operator, and shirt finisher and it was this line of slavery that began to open my eyes to the fact that something was rotten somewhere . . . as for me I will fight with the ones that are fighting for me whether they are Methodist, Baptist, Presbyterian or Communist. My religion is in my heart, no one can take it out, and being Christian and honest, loving this great country as I do, for it is mine, I long to see the day when IT IS A FREE COUNTRY, when every man and woman is equal and hunger is abolished forever and all political rats and grafters are removed.[69]

As they thought about the present struggle and the future goal there was a general, if often unconscious, tendency for the maritime workers to resort to a syndicalist frame of reference. Even the Communists on the waterfront sometimes spoke of the object of their struggle in a manner that seemed to envision a syndicalist—more than a Soviet—America. This may seem contradictory for members of an organization that declared itself the enemy, indeed the liquidator, of syndicalism. But Communists themselves were forced to acknowledge that the soil in which syndicalism flourished was more resilient than the organizations that had been its bearers. As late as November 1935, William Z. Foster complained that traces of syndicalist ideology remained within the Communist party, in spite of long-standing efforts to eradicate them. Nowhere would this have been more true than on the waterfront, where the close affinity between work and life, and the absence of integrative institutions, made syndicalism—less as doctrine than as mood and tendency—a natural component of the maritime workers' worldview. Tommy Ray, a seaman who served as a Communist party cadre on the waterfront for more than fifteen years, recalled with bitterness that "bon[a]fide seamen"— including Communist seamen—"were considered syndicalists or anarchists by most of the officials of the C.P."[70]

In any case, syndicalist themes cropped up again and again among Communists and non-Communists alike. Harry Lundeberg once said that the maritime workers were willing to "fight capitalism to a finish," but neither he nor any of his colleagues were very specific about the kind of new beginning that would follow capitalism's finish. Certainly the few efforts of the Communists and their sympathizers to hold up the Soviet Union as the alternative to capitalism met with indifference or defeat.[71] For the most part the workers, including the Communist workers, fell back on broad formulations that reflect their own experience on the job and in the unions. An old-timer on the docks declared that "our mission will not be completed until the unionization of all who toil for a living becomes a reality. . . . Our slogan should be: Long Live Unionism, Forever and Forever." SUP activist Sam Usinger called on his fellow workers to "form a one-big-union where poverty and unemployment shall be unknown." Communist longshoreman Henry Schrimpf characterized the maritime workers as "pioneers into a new era" whose goal was "to lead the workers in the right direction, to feed the little hungry children; make happy homes and elevate the standard of living and generally advance the human cause."[72]

Another longshoreman spoke of the shape of the future as a "Universal Federation," meaning a world bearing the mark of the Maritime Federation of the Pacific. This theme was developed more explicitly in a poem that appeared in the *Waterfront Worker,* whose editors were widely regarded as Communists. An anonymous poet saw a "mighty army" marching

> Toward a great goal, workers paradise
> A government of the workers is their fight
> And now in sight that goal we can see
> For we are joined in solidarity.

What instrument would bring about this great goal, this workers' paradise? The author called on his fellow workers to "form a Pacific Coast Federation," whose example would spread to the eastern and Gulf ports.

> And when that is complete we're on our way,
> We'll be over the top a new day,
> And a worker's dream we'll realize
> The slaves will live in a paradise.

How similar this conception is to the statement of a French syndicalist that "the workers' trade union is . . . the living germ of future society" and the declaration in the IWW preamble that "by organizing industrially we are forming the structure of the new society within the shell of the old."[73]

We should reflect further on the meaning of these statements in the context of their waterfront environment. All of them share a sense of antagonism toward capital, a belief that the workers' movement was ushering in a brighter future, and implicitly at least, a belief that the living germ of that future lay in the organization and patterns of activity that they were developing in and around the world of work. If many maritime workers were determined to transform the world, they began with a model that was full of contradictions. On the one hand, it was a narrow, insular world, circumscribed by the dock, the foc'sle, and the sailortown. On the other hand, it encompassed the entire globe, or at least its port cities, which gave the seamen in particular a direct insight into some of the most momentous and ominous clashes of the 1930s. The net result was that they often showed a greater interest in the Australian seafarers who were "fighting a life and death battle for their rights as free men" than in the shadowy deliberations of the government of the United States in Washington, D.C.; a more intimate knowledge of the nature of Hitler's regime than of the mechanics of government in the various state capitals.

Their most persistent concern was with transforming the world of work, and they knew instinctively that their power was concentrated in the familiar realm of production. In this sense, they did indeed display a strong measure of job consciousness, but in times of upheaval at least, their consciousness had a radical dimension that was qualitatively different from the narrow, defensive phenomenon that Selig Perlman deemed normative for the world's workers. What Theodore Draper described as the "weight of the Left Wing Tradition"—that "trade union struggles were exhilarating and electoral activity was anemic"—was in reality the experience of vast numbers of workers. Whether at the conscious level or in the realm of bedrock assumption, a syndicalist orientation made sense to significant numbers of American workers, especially to those whose conditions of life and work—in lumber, maritime, and metal mining—placed them on the distance fringes of society's mainstream.[74]

In the case of the maritime workers in the 1930s, we have seen a powerful determination to transform the world of work, along with a strong tendency to engage in more broadly focused activity at the point of production. But we must also take note of the fact that they were by no means immune to the currents that pushed millions of American workers into electoral politics during the New Deal era. For several years much of this activity demonstrated a strong tendency to dismiss the established political parties as instruments of capital and to develop new electoral formations based upon the insurgency of workers at the grass roots. Historians Eric Leif Davin and Staughton Lynd have noted that "a remarkable number of independent labor and farmer-labor parties sprang up between the years 1932 and 1936." This movement peaked soon after the great strike wave of 1934, in which the forces of the state often sided openly with the employers. In the aftermath of the violent repression of workers who participated in the massive textile strike of September 1934, the Massachusetts Committee for a Labor Party declared: "The New Deal was supposed to give us the right to organize. Yet when the textile workers went out on strike in 1934 for recognition of their union and to stop the speed-up, Democratic governors in 12 states called out the militia to drive the workers back to work and to break the strike. In fact 14 textile workers were killed by a militia called out by Democratic governors." Likewise, the founding convention of the Labor party of Chicago and Cook County, in a statement representing the consensus of 139 official delegates from sixty Chicago-area unions, branded the two major parties as "political company unions." At the historic AFL convention of 1935, where John L. Lewis struck his famous blow for industrial unionism, no fewer than thirteen national unions submitted proposals for the endorsement of a labor party.[75]

In San Francisco, the United Labor party movement won the strong support of the maritime unions. In fact, according to one observer, they were its backbone. After Mayor Angelo Rossi announced his campaign for reelection in 1935, a conference of delegates who allegedly represented "11,000 members of the City's Labor and Liberal organizations" met in mid-July to form an independent electoral slate. The United Labor party's nominee for mayor was Redfern Mason, a veteran newspaper man who had been fired by the Hearst *Examiner* soon after he became chairman of the San Francisco Newspaper Guild. Other candidates included Anita Whitney for supervisor and George Anderson for municipal judge. Whitney was both a *Mayflower* descendant and a founding member of the Communist party. Anderson, a left-wing attorney, had represented many of the people arrested during the Red raids accompanying the general strike. Among the highlights of the party platform were the demands for 100 percent unionization of San Francisco workers and vigorous opposition to company unions; a six-hour day for all workers, with no cut in pay; representation of workers on all relief distribution agencies; repeal of the criminal syndicalism law; elimination of one-man streetcars; and freedom for Tom Mooney, the Modesto Boys, and all other labor prisoners.[76]

From the very beginning, the marine unions played a central role in supporting the campaign. The Sailors' Union of the Pacific announced its support for a labor party before the San Francisco party had been formed. The Bay Area District Council of the Maritime Federation instructed all of its delegates to attend Labor party meetings. In order to strengthen the working-class composition of the United Labor slate, three maritime union leaders were nominated for municipal office: Herb Mills, SUP dispatcher, for sheriff; Henry Schmidt, of the Longshoremen, for supervisor; and George Woolf, president of the Ship Scalers, for supervisor. The enormous pressure of maritime labor activity in the turbulent fall of 1935 eventually forced all three to withdraw from the slate. They were replaced by longshoreman John Shaw, who campaigned actively with the other United Labor candidates.[77]

Characterizing Mayor Rossi as the shipowners' candidate, Bridges stated that the marine workers "still have fresh in their minds the deaths of two of their own in last year's strike, killed by Rossi's police." The *Voice* dubbed Rossi the Butcher of Rincon Hill. In the wake of the tarring and feathering of agricultural union organizers in nearby Santa Rosa, a *Voice* editorial entitled "Crush Fascist Terror" declared: " 'Law and Order' and the rights of the American Working Class will only be restored when Organized Labor has built its own UNITED LABOR PARTY and ELECTED HONEST MEN FROM ITS OWN RANKS TO ADMINISTER THE LAW FOR THE INTERESTS OF THE MAJORITY OF THE PEOPLE AND NOT FOR THE SELFISH INTERESTS OF A SMALL GROUP OF EMPLOYERS!"[78]

Even Teamster official George Kidwell, a powerful figure in the San Francisco Central Labor Council, endorsed the United Labor ticket and denounced the incumbents as "subservient tools of Big Business." But for the most part, United Labor was united in name only. On the eve of San Francisco's Labor Day parade, Edward Vandeleur, president of the State Federation of Labor and the local Central Labor Council, proclaimed that organized labor was "1000% behind Mayor Rossi in his bid for re-election." In order to head off the United Labor party, Vandeleur and other AFL officials placed Rossi's name at the head of a nominal Union Labor party ticket. Nine days before the election Vandeleur reminded the voters that "the Union Labor party is the only bona fide Labor party . . . Union labor is not indorsing any Communists for office."[79]

When the votes were tallied, Rossi had won an overwhelming victory. The mayor received 96,655 votes to 59,129 for San Francisco Supervisor Adolph Uhl and 14,267 for United Labor party candidate Redfern Mason. United Labor's highest vote getter was George Anderson, the attorney running for municipal judge, who polled 37,673 votes to almost 103,000 for his victorious opponent. The vote reflected the relative political isolation of the radically inclined maritime unions. During strikes and job actions, and in mass events such as the annual Labor Day parades and Bloody Thursday memorials, they were able to galvanize large numbers of their fellow workers around their insurgent stance. However, in the atomized environment of the polling booth, individual workers were not yet ready to break with Union Labor in its call to stand by the traditional forms of electoral activity. William Schneiderman of the Communist party said that the "militant maritime unions were the backbone of the trade union support for the United Labor Ticket." But he acknowledged that the campaign was "very weak in the other trade unions" and in other working-class organizations throughout the city.[80]

The United Labor party campaign may have been a rocky beginning, but it was to represent the high point of unity among the maritime workers on the issue of electoral politics. Other factors, related more directly to the water-front, intervened very quickly to create increasingly serious divisions in the ranks of the marine unions. The Sailors, led by Lundeberg, and the Longshoremen, led by Bridges, were to become the opposite poles of a host of disagreements. This became as true in the political arena as in any other. While Bridges and his many allies moved toward support of the farmer-labor party movement and eventual absorption into the Democratic party, the Sailors were driven to repudiate politics altogether and to uphold economic job action as the only legitimate form of working-class struggle. In the heyday of maritime unity, however, the "syndicalist" Sailors were every bit as vigorous as the "Communist"-led Longshoremen in their support of the United Labor party. The tragic breach derived from other, more immediate factors than politics, and to the development of that breach we must now turn.

7

The Rise and Fall of the Maritime Federation

The Maritime Federation of the Pacific Coast (MFPC) began as the institutional embodiment of the extraordinary solidarity that the marine workers had achieved during the Big Strike and had continued to express in the many job actions that followed their return to work. Its emergence and early successes were a vivid testament to the Pentecostal era's radical aspirations. Its failures and eventual disintegration were emblematic of the era's ambiguity and limitations. What is most compelling about the Maritime Federation is not its institutional history but rather the development of a split between "Communists" and "syndicalists" that ultimately doomed the organization to extinction.* As we have seen, there was a good deal of ideological common ground among Communists and syndicalists on the West Coast waterfront during the mid-thirties because a syndicalist orientation was to some degree inherent in the marine workers' way of life. However, gradually, among some Maritime Federation activists, a more self-conscious commitment to syndicalism was to emerge as an alternative to the policies of Harry Bridges and the Communist party. In the evolution of a quasi-syndicalist group in the Sailors' Union of the Pacific from close ally to bitter enemy of Bridges and his associates lies the tragedy of the Pentecostal era's unfulfilled promise.

---

*Neither of these terms is entirely satisfactory, since some of the so-called Communists were not members of the Communist party, and some of the syndicalists did not have a thoroughgoing commitment to syndicalism. But in a very general sense they indicate the poles around which conflict in the federation developed.

The Wobbly dream of One Big Union, and more limited proposals for organizational unity, had long struck a resonant note among many marine workers. The 1934 strike seemed to suggest that this dream could come true. Even before the strike, in February, the historic longshore convention in which Bridges and his allies made their opening bid for coastwide leadership had included a proposal for the formation of a waterfront federation. Bridges, the ex-sailor, recalled that "he had been thinking about the need for a marine federation since the badly divided seagoing unions had been routed on all coasts in the 1921 American Seamen's strike." Likewise, Sam Darcy stated in later years that he and Bill Dunne, another veteran Communist, proposed a maritime federation, drew up a draft constitution, and discussed the matter with Bridges and other insurgent leaders soon after the Big Strike.[1]

In any case, the idea was clearly one whose time had come. By the fall of 1934 there was widespread agitation for the formation of a federation. Even the conservatives in the Pacific District leadership of the ILA advocated such an organization, mainly because they wanted to head off the Bridges group and their increasingly assertive allies in the other maritime unions. The *Waterfront Worker* warned that it was necessary to form a rank-and-file-controlled organization before the old-guard ILA men had a chance to put together a "Marine Federation of Fakers," modeled after the building and metal trades councils of the AFL. In a local development, a Marine Federation of Seattle encompassing both militants and conservatives held its first meeting in January 1935.[2]

The coastwide federation was born in April of 1935 at a convention in Seattle. Although radicals had provided the impetus for the organization, it initially represented a compromise between the various elements in maritime. Bridges, who chaired the committee that drew up a draft constitution, had fervently hoped the Teamsters would affiliate, but their leadership adamantly refused. A number of shoreside organizations did join, however, including Machinists, other shipyard craft unions, and the scalers and warehousemen who had signed up with the ILA. Bridges proposed a proportional method of representation based on the number of workers in each union, as well as control by the entire federation over the right to strike. But fearing domination by the numerically superior longshoremen, the smaller crafts insisted on equal representation for each affiliate and autonomy on the right to strike.[3]

The election of the federation's leadership also indicated the existence of divergent, and even hostile, currents within the organization. For president, Bridges and his allies supported Harry Lundeberg, who was then a relatively obscure SUP patrolman from Seattle, but one who had been spectacularly successful in leading the fight of rank-and-file seamen to better their conditions.[4] Lundeberg defeated two conservative candidates. Fred Kelley, of the Marine Engineers, was elected secretary-treasurer, and Fred Friedl, a rabidly anti-Communist Marine Firemen's official from San Pedro, won the vice presidency in a close vote over a militant ILA man from Everett, Washington. Soon after his election Friedl was killed in a violent, and perhaps accidental, confrontation with the San Pedro police. After some bitter exchanges over whether his death marked the demise of a "labor faker" or the murder of a legitimate trade unionist, the Maritime Federation replaced him as vice president with William Fischer, a Portland longshoreman who had been an IWW organizer among Oregon lumber workers before migrating to the waterfront.[5]

Harry Lundeberg was to become not only a dynamic figure in the Maritime Federation but one of the most powerful—and volatile—forces in the marine industry. A son of Norway, he was born Harald Olaf Lundeberg in 1901. His mother, an ardent socialist and feminist, played an important role in the Norwegian Labor party and served on school committees in Oslo for some thirty years. His father, a small businessman with a trade-union background, was a committed syndicalist. His eldest brother died at sea. Two other brothers sailed briefly in their youth but settled down to shore jobs at their parents' request. Harry, however, would not be deterred from the Norseman's historic calling. After graduating from high school at age seventeen, he signed on as a coal-passer on a Norwegian freighter and sailed to Africa, Australia, Java, and India. Thereafter, for fifteen years, he shipped all over the world, under nine different flags, in sailing vessels and steamships.[6]

He joined unions in many countries and seems to have been influenced by the anarcho-syndicalist orientation of labor organizations in Norway, Australia, and, perhaps, Argentina. Part of the Lundeberg legend is that he was once a member of the IWW. Journalist Benjamin Stolberg called him "an I.W.W. in his entire outlook"; noted labor historian Philip Taft spoke of his "I.W.W. background." Sam Darcy, who knew Lundeberg in 1934 and 1935, recalled that "he talked like a Wobbly and very much reflected their style." However, when he debarked at Seattle in 1923, he joined the Sailors' Union of the Pacific rather than the IWW's marine affiliate, even though the Wobs were offering a stern challenge to the declining SUP at the time and the Wobbly presence was more real and durable in the Northwest than anywhere else in the country. Although Lundeberg often voiced respect and affection for the IWW and its principles, he denied ever having been a member of the organization.[7]

After spending several years in Australia, he rejoined the SUP in 1927 and became a naturalized U.S. citizen in 1933. Ed Coester, a seaman who became one of his close associates, stated that he knew Lundeberg to be a militant fighter in the Sailors' Union during the days of the old-guard leadership, "when it was not popular to be a militant. As a result of Brother Lundeberg's activity before the [1934] strike, he was blackballed on every ship out of Seattle, with the exception of one, and had to leave San Francisco because he refused to pack a fink book." During the strike, according to Coester, Lundeberg walked off his ship in Frisco two days after the longshoremen hit the bricks; thereafter he served as the unofficial leader of the Seattle strike committee.[8]

Lundeberg's anticommunism would soon assume legendary proportions. But Darcy recalled that when he met the Seattle sailor after the 1934 strike, he seemed "more or less apathetic" toward the Communist party. He was, however, attracted to the movement that Bridges and his left-wing allies were building in San Francisco. Bridges responded in kind by promoting the SUP militant for president of the Maritime Federation and calling him "a fine trade unionist." After his election, the *Voice of Action,* a Communist-controlled newspaper in the Northwest, hailed him as a "fighting progressive."[9]

Lundeberg may have been relatively unknown when he assumed the presidency of the MFPC, but he wasted little time in demonstrating that he was a capable and energetic force in his own right. Eventually he became the virtual czar of the Sailors' Union, a deadly enemy of Bridges and, overall, one of the most flamboyant and controversial representatives of the new breed of union leaders who emerged from the turmoil of the 1930s. He was famous for his pugnacity. Biographers in the 1950s characterized him as a "Norwegian-born slugger" and "the SUP's fighting viking" who "mixes it up personally for his beliefs." According to Irving Bernstein, he "may well have been the toughest man in the American labor movement." Moreover, "[h]is capacity for suspicion and hatred knew no bounds." In the strident chorus of anticommunism, his became one of the loudest—and crudest—voices. He characterized Communists as *"psychos,"* "idealists who can't get on in the world," "opportunists," and, finally, *"phoney intellectuals* plus a bunch of just plain lazy *bastards."* "I wouldn't just knock one down," he declared proudly. "I'd kick him twice." In the early fifties, he resurrected the name of George Mink, who had disappeared from the MWIU and allegedly gone on to become a finger man for the Communist International. The *West Coast Sailors,* newspaper of the SUP, carried wanted posters of "Mink the Fink," and Lundeberg vowed, in his thick Norwegian accent, "Ve get 'Mink the Fink' yust like ve got Britches."[10]

Given the record outlined above, it is all too easy to judge the Harry Lundeberg of 1934 and 1935 by his career in later years. Irving Bernstein has described him as the "classic business agent" (hence his nickname, Lunchbox) who, despite being president of the Maritime Federation, was preoccupied only with the affairs of the Sailors' Union. However, an examination of the minutes of early Maritime Federation meetings and of Lundeberg's correspondence while he served as president reveals a different picture. The fact is that many of Lundeberg's eventual tendencies—his anticommunism, his craft particularism, his alleged antipolitical syndicalism—were overshadowed during this period by a genuine devotion to the federation, a more than passing advocacy of industrial unionism, openness toward Communists, outspoken criticism of Red-baiting, and a willingness to subordinate the activity of any one union, including the SUP, to the broader interests of the Maritime Federation.[11]

   At its birth the Maritime Federation was both a testament to growing unity and a precarious venture beset by the legacy of a long past. In spite of the herculean advances that had followed the Big Strike, it was impossible to eliminate craft jealousies overnight. Differences rooted in the separate and sometimes competing interests of the various crafts continued to affect the federation's development. Moreover, there were other contradictions, especially those rooted in politics and regional particularism. Initially, the leaders of the San Francisco Longshoremen, the Sailors' Union of the Pacific, and the small radio operators' union (ARTA) were the most articulate and consistent radicals, while the Longshoremen in San Pedro and several of the Northwest ports, along with the two major officers' unions, the Marine Engineers and the Masters, Mates and Pilots, formed the core of the conservative group. The Marine Firemen and the Marine Cooks and Stewards generally vacillated between these two poles. The magnetic role of Bridges and his allies in the San Francisco district council of the federation only increased the determination of the district councils centered in San Pedro, Portland, and Seattle to maintain their independence. William Fischer, who succeeded Harry Lundeberg as federation president in early 1936, acknowledged: "There is a feeling that [San Francisco] District Council #2 is taking too much of a lead and assuming too much say in things that affect the entire coast."[12]

The Maritime Federation did not have long to wait before its slogan "An Injury to One Is an Injury to All" was put to a severe test. Almost immediately, it inherited an unsuccessful tanker strike that had been called by the old-guard leadership of the ISU on the West Coast, before the federation's founding convention. The tankers had always been maritime unionism's weakest link, in part because of the domination of the industry by the Standard Oil colossus, and also because conditions of employment on the tankers had been more regular, and often less abominable, than on freighters and passenger ships. Unlike the transients who plied their trade on other vessels, tanker men had a reputation as company stiffs. Thus, the Maritime Federation was faced with a strike that it had not called, on behalf of a constituency whose allegiance was lukewarm at best, against an employer group that demonstrated the will and the resources for a prolonged confrontation. After threatening a general maritime strike, and unsuccessfully trying to resolve the conflict through federal mediation, the federation quietly ended the tanker strike and turned to the task of consolidating its ranks.

But no sooner had one storm subsided than another appeared on the horizon. In the early summer of 1935 the Swayne and Hoyt freighter *Point Clear,* carrying lumber from Powell River, British Columbia, docked in San Francisco. Immediately the seamen set up a picket line and the longshoremen refused to cross it. The issue was "hot" cargo, loaded by scab dockworkers in British Columbia, and a ship manned by scab engineers. Hot cargo was to become the most volatile symbol of a major controversy that swirled up and down the Pacific Coast and across the nation to Washington, D.C., bringing the marine workers into conflict with the shipowners of the United States and Canada, the U.S. government, and the international executive boards of the ILA and the ISU. In spite of the weight of the opposition, however, the Maritime Federation was to emerge from this crisis with its reputation for boldness and unity greatly enhanced.

In June 1935 Canadian shipowners in the port cities of British Columbia locked out the union stevedores, hired strikebreakers, and enrolled the new employees in a company union. In response, more than twenty-eight hundred members of the Longshore and Water Transport Workers of Canada declared a strike and called on marine workers in other countries to aid their cause. This appeal carried special weight among the maritime workers on the Pacific Coast of the United States, who were well aware that their Canadian counterparts had refused to handle scab cargo during the 1934 strike. So when the *Point Clear* docked in San Francisco with a cargo that included scab-loaded lumber, pickets were there to greet the ship. The ensuing contest of wills was so intense that the picket lines lasted for three and a half months.

Although the longshoremen did not initiate the picketing, they became the focal point of the employers' counteroffensive. The shipowners claimed that the ILA was violating its arbitration award, and that further defiance would result in cancellation of the award. When gangs were dispatched to the *Point Clear,* the men refused to work the ship, arguing that nothing in their collective bargaining agreement required them to cross picket lines. The gangs were then blacklisted, and the crisis escalated. Some of the principal waterfront employers were actually itching for a showdown with Harry Bridges and the San Francisco ILA. To forestall any attempt by the shipowners to isolate and crush them, the San Francisco Longshoremen called for a coastwide ballot on the question of working hot cargo from British Columbia. An overwhelming majority of the marine workers voted to endorse the stand taken by the Frisco insurgents, and the Waterfront Employers' Association was forced to admit, reluctantly, that "if we go ahead and precipitate trouble the whole coast would show a united front."[13]

Soon seamen broadened the controversy by tying up three ships that were scheduled to work hot cargo in Vancouver, B.C. Since these ships were carrying U.S. mail, and refusal to move the mail was a federal crime, Assistant Secretary of Labor McGrady warned that continued defiance would force the government to intervene. As the impasse continued, Louis Stark, veteran labor reporter of the *New York Times,* predicted the coming of "guerrilla warfare" and "a war of desperation" on the West Coast, with the shipowners and the AFL leadership aligned against the marine workers and their "left wing officers." In September the crisis reached even greater proportions, especially in San Francisco. A lockout of ILA warehousemen by the Santa Cruz Packing Company quickly spread to the docks, where with the obvious collaboration of the shipowners, boxcars full of scab-loaded freight began appearing on virtually every pier. When longshoremen refused to work this cargo, the employers blacklisted them and declared that they would "never work on the S.F. Waterfront again." Bridges now projected a scenario that sounded very much like Louis Stark's "war of desperation." "The employers have publicly announced," he said, "that they will keep on calling longshore gangs to work hot freight and, if they refuse, will blacklist them until the supply of ILA gangs is exhausted. When all ILA members have refused to work hot cargo the announced intention of the employers is to call non-union men to perform this work." Bridges acknowledged that the longshoremen were showing remarkable tenacity, and that "no official or member of ILA 38-79 can exert enough influence to compel [them] to handle hot cargo."[14]

Clearly the San Francisco longshoremen had learned the lessons of the Big Strike well, and a full year of struggle on the job had steeled them for this sort of guerrilla warfare with the employers. But beneath the seemingly solid surface of the Maritime Federation's united front, there were dangerous cracks. From the very beginning of the hot cargo crisis, there had been vacillation in some quarters. In late June the Marine Firemen withdrew their pickets from the *Point Clear* and were followed soon thereafter by the major officers' unions. In a second referendum, most of the longshore locals in the Northwest voted in favor of working B.C. cargo, and by late September the San Pedro ILA local was announcing that it would not support a strike triggered by this issue. Almost alone, Lundeberg and a few other Sailors' Union officials continued to argue that unrelenting solidarity with the B.C. strikers was the only proper course for the federation. Even Harry Bridges was becoming convinced that the stalemate that had engulfed San Francisco should not serve as the pretext for a "war of desperation." By October 1, responding to requests from ISU spokesmen, the Canadian longshore union agreed to withdraw its picket lines from American ships, and the crisis soon eased considerably.[15]

In the course of these events, a number of Sailors' Union activists grouped around Maritime Federation President Harry Lundeberg began to develop a sense of common commitment and identity. Eventually they would coalesce into a leadership force characterized by rabid anticommunism, a syndicalist contempt for politics, and an obsessive but militant concern with the interests of the sailors. At this moment, however, they expressed a genuine enthusiasm for the broadest maritime unity. In fact, during the summer of 1935, Lundeberg himself was one of the strongest advocates of strengthening the federation's authority over its constituent unions. Moreover, on several controversial issues, including the expulsion of Paul Scharrenberg from the Sailors' Union, the admission of ex-MWIU members to the SUP, and the proposal to develop a United Labor party in San Francisco, Lundeberg and his associates demonstrated a clear willingness to unite with Communists. The Scharrenberg case provides a vivid example of the dynamics of this alliance.[16]

In the upper echelons of California business, labor, and politics, any talk of expelling Paul Scharrenberg from the Sailors' Union of the Pacific had the ring of treason, even patricide. This white-shirt sailor had been a member of the SUP since 1899 and editor of the *Seamen's Journal* since 1913. Moreover, as secretary of the California State Federation of Labor for twenty-six years, he had earned wide recognition as one of organized labor's principal spokesmen in the Golden State, and had served on advisory commissions appointed by mayors, governors, and even by Presidents Woodrow Wilson and Franklin Roosevelt. Whereas he had once distinguished himself as a liberal who refused to be cowed by employer-initiated political offensives, by the 1930s he was as conservative as most of the AFL leaders he served. In a period of sharpening class antagonisms, Scharrenberg counseled a patient and conciliatory approach to relations with capital. At a time when "solidarity" was the rallying cry of insurgent labor, he offered the full cooperation of the AFL to the powerful employer interests who were ruthlessly suppressing agricultural unionism in California. In 1935 he stated publicly that "only fanatics are willing to live in shacks or tents and get their heads broken in the interest of migratory labor." And at a time when the American Legion had reached the peak of its notoriety as an instrument of strikebreaking and vigilante terror, he declared it an "honor and privilege" to go before the Legionnaires' California convention and announce that "the American Legion and the American Federation of Labor have very much the same ideals and the same objectives."

On the waterfront Scharrenberg was an outspoken and unrepentant advocate of policies that were now held in contempt by the majority of Pacific Coast marine workers. Although he was at first cautious in his public criticism of the Maritime Federation, he could not long abide what he regarded as a dangerous deviation from the venerable traditions of the ISU. He was soon accusing the federation of "functioning in a dual capacity to the AFL" and declaring it a "brazen attempt to discredit, disrupt and destroy legitimate unionism." Moreover, as the West Coast seamen moved cautiously toward a reversal of the ISU's membership ban against Communists, Scharrenberg devoted more and more space in the *Seamen's Journal* to anti-Communist diatribes. When left-wing publications responded in kind, it only increased his appetite for invective. "The *Seamen's Journal* is proud indeed," he wrote, "of the mendacious denunciations which it regularly receives in the various communist gutter sheets."[17]

To the majority of the seamen, however, Scharrenberg's words only proved him a reactionary and a Red-baiter. At worst, he seemed an agent of the shipowners; at best, a "swivel chair acrobat" who hadn't been to sea in thirty-five years. Declaring that Scharrenberg "is no longer an active seaman," one rank and filer argued: "There are jails . . . you cannot get into unless you are crooked and there are . . . insane asylums that you cannot get into unless you are insane, so why the HELL can we not have a union that you cannot get into unless you are a sailor." With very little urging the men were inclined to heed the recommendation of the left-wing *Seamen's Lookout* that "Paul should be sent back to the soogey bucket!" Predictably, Scharrenberg's response to the Sailors' Union trial committee was that they could "go to hell before he would ever appear before them." He was tried and expelled in absentia.[18]

Lundeberg was one of five members of the trial committee. He was to claim in later years that as early as 1932 he had introduced a resolution calling for Scharrenberg's expulsion from the SUP. Now, however, the *Journal* editor called him a mere henchman of Harry Bridges. But these accusations were wide of the mark. Harry Lundeberg was nobody's henchman. While his relationship with Bridges and the Communist party at this time appears to have been friendly, he no doubt shared the strong belief expressed by waterfront syndicalists that "the Party should keep its nose out of union affairs." Moreover, Lundeberg had his own reasons for wanting to get rid of Scharrenberg. For he surely recognized that the *Journal* editor would do everything in his power to obstruct the process of amalgamating the marine unions into a unified and militant federation.[19]

Quite apart from Lundeberg's motivation, there was strong pressure from the rank and file to settle accounts with a number of obnoxious symbols of the old order. In early April, two months before Scharrenberg's removal, the Marine Firemen in San Francisco unanimously demanded that he resign from the ISU executive board, and the SUP passed a censure resolution. Sailors' Union meetings in San Pedro and Portland called for Scharrenberg's expulsion even before the headquarters branch in San Francisco decided to move against him, and afterward a coastwide SUP referendum ratified the trial committee's verdict by an eleven-to-one margin. Although the principal charge against Scharrenberg of illegally calling the tanker strike may have been of dubious validity, it is clear that in the eyes of the militant seamen technicalities were not the main consideration. His expulsion was an important symbolic act not only of revenge but of affirmation and catharsis. In fact, it was probably the most vivid celebration of the passing of the old order since the burning of the fink books at the end of the 1934 strike.

Nor was Scharrenberg the only target. Selim Silver, another long-standing symbol of the old regime, was removed from the chairmanship of the SUP headquarters meetings in San Francisco with the stipulation that henceforth a new chairman would be elected from the floor at every meeting. In San Pedro the SUP membership voted to ban the *Seamen's Journal*—now irreverently dubbed the "Seamen's Urinal"—from the union hall. John McGovern, secretary of the West Coast Marine Firemen, was expelled, as was Carl Carter, the Sailors' Union agent in Portland.[20] Carter had been one of the SUP's most ardent Red-baiters. During the 1934 strike he had characterized MWIU members as "finks and skunks." Soon after the strike he had launched a virulent public attack on Harry Bridges. In an open letter that the SUP official submitted to newspapers up and down the coast, Carter declared,

> We do not need no foreign element or any foreigner to tell us Americans what is best to do. The best thing that you can do is to go back to the land from whence you came and if it be that you have no country advise that you go to the devil. . . .
>
> If we had you here in Portland we would know how to put the skids under you and get you out of the country. . . .
>
> Let me advise that should you ever come to Portland and happen to drop in to see me, it is more than probable that my fist would find contact with your jaw, and I know of many others who have a desire to do likewise. We believe in Unionism but not Communism.

In an action that vividly symbolized the sensibility of the new era, the sailors voted to expel a veteran member of their own union for engaging in a tirade against a longshoreman.[21]

It is surely no coincidence that soon after Scharrenberg's expulsion, Bill Caves was reinstated as a member in good standing of the Sailors' Union and a number of the most prominent spokesmen for the MWIU were admitted to membership in several of the ISU affiliates. Caves had been the chairman of the ISU joint strike committee in 1934 until he was suspended for his strident advocacy of cooperation with the MWIU. Whereas Scharrenberg was a symbol of the old order, Caves was a symbol of the new, and his friendly ties with the Communist party were undoubtedly well known. Lundeberg was already influential enough in the SUP that this conscious opening to the Left could not have proceeded as it did without his cooperation and support. It was partly for this reason that Scharrenberg thundered against the domination of the Sailors' Union by the "Darcy-Bridges-Lundeberg clique."[22]

Moreover, Lundeberg and his associates spoke out openly against Red-baiting, which they characterized as a weapon of the shipowners. When Furuseth refused to accept the SUP expulsion of Scharrenberg because, in his words, "Andrew Furuseth takes no orders from Communists," San Francisco Sailors' patrolman Charlie Cates responded, "Who is [Furuseth] representing? If he is working for the seamen he had better change his tactics. . . . We are not going to let any individual or group of officials break us up with the well-known 'red scare.' " A week later Cates, who was one of Lundeberg's most aggressive allies, published a scathing article in the *Voice* denouncing "The Methods of the Red Baiter." This was also the time when the Sailors' Union of the Pacific enthusiastically endorsed the formation of a labor party and lent its support to the United Labor party campaign in San Francisco. Again, although Lundeberg himself did not play a prominent role in this campaign, it is unlikely that the SUP would have acted as it did without his cooperation.[23]

Thus, if by the end of the summer of 1935 there was a significant and relatively open disagreement between Bridges and Lundeberg, it was not over communism or a labor party or craft-versus-industrial unionism. It was a tactical disagreement on a trade union question, namely, whether to hold the line or retreat in the Maritime Federation's support of the British Columbia waterfront strikers.

It is quite likely that this breach could have been healed if other matters had not intervened to create a more significant and lasting conflict. But when the longshoremen voted in late September to renew their arbitration award for another year, the unity that had appeared to be impregnable during the summer of 1935 suddenly became very fragile indeed. For as Bridges acknowledged several years later, the unilateral renewal of the longshore award "disregarded entirely the interests of the seamen."[24]

The Maritime Federation advocated a policy whereby all agreements with the shipowners would expire simultaneously and no union would ratify a contract—or, in case of a strike, return to work—until all other unions had settled. This principle of solidarity had been a powerful weapon in the Big Strike, but it had finally been breached by the longshoremen when they voted unilaterally to accept arbitration and return to work. In the period following the strike the stevedores had received a favorable arbitration award, and they had further strengthened their position through job action. The seamen's arbitration award had been much less satisfactory, and even the significant gains won through job action had not closed the gap between the two crafts. Thus, the Sailors' Union, in particular, was determined to win the six-hour day in port and to bring seamen's wages and overtime pay closer to the level of the stevedores. SUP spokesmen maintained that steam schooner men who handled lumber in port performed "the same work as longshoremen for less than one-third of longshore pay." But as in 1934, their ability to wage this battle successfully depended in large measure on the solidarity of the dockworkers. And as Bridges acknowledged, "As long as the information was out in advance that the longshoremen had renewed their contracts, that put the seamen at a great disadvantage."[25]

Not surprisingly, the seafarers reacted with outrage at the news of the longshoremen's vote. Lundeberg called it a violation of the basic principles of the Maritime Federation. An even stronger criticism came from Herb Mills, a Bridges ally and member of the Communist party, who called the ILA "the weak sister of the Maritime Federation." As for Bridges and the ILA militants, they opposed renewing the longshore awards but were caught between the conservative policy of the union's Pacific District executive committee on the one side and the overwhelming vote of the ILA rank and file on the other. As Henry Schmidt once admitted, "When the majority of the rank and file of the ILA . . . express [their opinion] through a ballot, that's law to us."[26]

The seamen faced their own dilemma: either to renew the ISU awards and live with a number of humiliating inequities for another year, or fight alone in a perhaps fruitless battle to wrest major concessions from the employers. In this situation Lundeberg's stance of no retreat became attractive to an increasing number of militants within the Sailors' Union. And job action, which had been widely regarded as a tactic to force concessions from the shipowners, now became their normative—indeed, sacred—strategy. Moreover, as the Firemen and the Cooks and Stewards gradually opted for a policy of caution and federation unity, and as Bridges's allies in the SUP endorsed his belief that unfavorable circumstances necessitated a policy of consolidation and strategic retreat to preserve what had already been won, the SUP militants increasingly took their case to the rank-and-file sailors, and to the steam schooner men in particular.

Once again, as had so often been the case in the past, it appeared that the sailors would have to fight their own battles because others had failed to stand by them. As Lundeberg recalled, the seamen had gone back to work with the longshoremen in 1934 to "maintain unity, although they went back with nothing in the way of gains for themselves. Instead, they were forced to fight inch by inch through job actions up and down the coast in order to establish conditions." Lundeberg the federation president was about to give way to Lundeberg the embattled sailor. And for the first time, the aggressive and articulate group of SUP activists who coalesced around him began to speak the language of doctrinaire syndicalism.[27]

The fulcrum for this group was job action. In the fall of 1935 the theory and practice of job action convulsed the Maritime Federation and nearly tore it asunder. The Lundeberg group sparked the debate, and the actions that they initiated on a number of steam schooners provided much of its immediacy and sense of urgency. One of the most fascinating moments in this developing crisis came at a headquarters meeting of the Sailors' Union in mid-October, where a resolution introduced by rank-and-filer Arthur Ward, with the endorsement of several of Lundeberg's closest allies, was hotly debated for two hours and then "laid on the table" pending further discussion. The controversial resolution not only echoed the ideas and style of the IWW, but Ward himself was a direct link with the Wobbly past, having been imprisoned during the criminal syndicalism trials of the early 1920s. Ward's resolution epitomized the peculiar amalgam of economic direct action, industrial unionism, antagonism toward all forms of bureaucratic authority, and the equation of union democracy with rank-and-file insurgency on the job that was to characterize the program of the Lundeberg group in the coming months. In particular, the Ward resolution was an attack on the policies advocated by Harry Bridges and his allies in the seamen's unions. Bridges, who rightly sensed a growing danger to federation unity, had just taken the lead in calling for an emergency convention of the Maritime Federation. His allies among the seafarers were attempting to negotiate a new collective bargaining agreement with the shipowners and were getting nowhere. Sam Usinger, one of the endorsers of Ward's resolution, had just rebuked them publicly for assuming that the seamen could win anything "by sitting at a lacquer finished round table with a pitcher of lemonade thereon" or by imitating "the Silk Shirt Patriarch's manner." "The boys are hungry for job action," Usinger declared, and Ward came forward with a program based squarely on that assumption.[28]

He began by pointing out that the seamen had been inundated with "legal advice, conventions, delegations, and committees," which had resulted only in a "leaking treasury bucket" and "a dose of silent contempt from the shipowners." The legal advice on the 1935 arbitration award had cost in the vicinity of $6,000 "for an agreement which could have been drawn up by a law clerk or a rank and file member." Scornfully, Ward pointed out that after expending a great deal of time and money in pursuit of a new contract, the best the seamen's negotiating committee could come up with was "two worthless propositions"—to renew the current award, or to accept arbitration. Moreover, the Bay Area District Council of the Maritime Federation had recommended yet another convention, which, in Ward's eyes, would mean the same people discussing the same problem, with the rank and file again footing the bill. He charged that the seamen aboard ship resented "the mania on the part of a few men . . . to convene, arbitrate, negotiate and reconvene. . . . We have convened away in railroad fares, salaries etc., a sizeable fighting and education fund which would contribute to *the only power a Union or a Federation has: economic direct action on the job.*"

Job action was "the great negotiator," the source of all the seamen's gains, the only weapon that could compel the shipowners to listen. And, he said, when they were finally ready to listen, "we [should] elect a rank and file committee—which *does not* mean a committee of elected officers, to do our talking for us."

In the meantime, Ward proposed that the proper course for the seamen to follow was to nonconcur in the call for an emergency convention of the Maritime Federation; to initiate an educational campaign to strengthen the federation "so that *finally it will become THE union of the Marine Industry*"; and to begin a program of job action—"wherever it will affect the ILA and the strength of the Maritime Federation the least and where it will hurt the shipowners the most, which place at the present time is the steam schooners."[29]

Right after the heated discussion of Ward's resolution the Sailors' Union patrolmen in San Francisco began agitating among steam schooner crews to take action aboard ship with the goal of winning the six-hour day in port and the payment of one dollar per hour in cash for all overtime work. This was clearly a case of spark-plug unionism, where a militant minority took the lead and called on their fellow workers to come along. Charlie Cates announced that "steam schooner men on several ships are taking a stand" and "asking for . . . moral support from sailors aboard steam schooners." The crews of six or seven ships were soon involved, and several smaller companies gave in to the men's demands. The *Voice of the Federation* declared on October 17 that "job action is taking place in the Bay region with keen effect at the present time."[30]

However, while this activity met with some success, it also provoked a storm of protest and debate, with more heat coming from the maritime unions than the employers. The Marine Cooks and Stewards' Association (MCS) ordered its members to stay aboard ship when the steam schooners were tied up, and both the MCS and the Marine Firemen passed resolutions condemning disorganized job action. Moreover, at a mass meeting of the ISU affiliates in San Francisco, a majority of the seamen present went on record as "opposing disorganized strikes called by a single organization." Longshoremen were ordered to work any vessels tied up by the dispute, with the full support of Bridges and the *Waterfront Worker*. Both argued that the SUP "direct actionists" were confused about basic facts of trade unionism because, under the guise of job action, they were in fact calling strikes that involved not only other shipboard crafts but, in some cases, longshoremen and teamsters as well. Bridges accused the sailors of going "outside the provisions of their agreement," a peculiar charge coming from a man with his well-earned reputation for placing solidarity ahead of contracts, and considering that the SUP's agreement with the shipowners had already expired. More to the point, the *Waterfront Worker* warned that "if the few individuals in the Sailors' Union who are responsible for initiating all the disputes" were allowed to continue unchecked, there would be a "grave danger" of a split within the ranks of the ISU and the federation. As evidence of this danger, the paper quoted the alleged statement of one of the direct actionists that if the rest of the crafts did not come off the ships in support of the sailors, "then they are a bunch of finks and we will strike without their support anyway!"[31]

Who were these activists whose course aroused such a storm of protest? Were they hard-core syndicalists? It has been an article of faith in many studies of the West Coast seamen that there was a more or less coherent anarcho-syndicalist group in the SUP, and that it played an important role for a time, especially in strengthening Lundeberg's natural propensity toward syndicalism. William Schneiderman of the California Communist party identified a distinctive group of Lundeberg associates "as far back as 1935," and characterized them as "in the main sincere, militant rank and file elements strongly influenced by syndicalist tendencies, who had the typical I.W.W. approach regarding 'economic action as opposed to political action.' " Less partisan observers have painted a similar portrait. But no one has ever identified the members of this group or rooted their alleged role in concrete historical practice. They have been entirely overshadowed by the personality and career of Lundeberg, even though they were instrumental in helping to shape his program and in rallying the SUP rank and file behind his leadership at a time when his position was far from entrenched or secure.[32]

Unfortunately we know very little about these men, but there is enough information about some of them to develop a rudimentary collective portrait. Charlie Cates was certainly one of their most outspoken representatives. A relatively young man of obscure background, he became an SUP patrolman in San Francisco, where he established a reputation as an effective militant. It is possible that he had been a boxer at one time. In any case, he was famous for his ability and willingness to use his fists. But he was no mere slugger. His regular columns in the *Voice* bear the mark not only of forceful advocacy but of principled commitment as well.[33]

Carl "Shingles" Tillman was a native of Sweden, and like Lundeberg he spoke with a thick Scandinavian accent. He apparently had relatively little sea time, but was nonetheless popular with the large Scandinavian element among the SUP membership. A shingle weaver and lumberjack by background, it is probable that during his years in the Northwest woods he picked up some of the syndicalist ideology that had long permeated the area. During the 1934 strike he was a militant activist in Portland. On one occasion during the strike, when the shipowners were attempting to move hot cargo by rail, Tillman "laid down on the railroad tracks and dared them to come ahead." After the strike, he was one of the leaders in the battle to win union control of hiring. He also played an active role in the effort to expel Scharrenberg from the SUP. Apparently he worked closely with the Communist party in several of these campaigns. Elected an SUP patrolman in San Francisco in the fall of 1935, he soon became the leading spokesman for the Sailors' Union in the Maritime Federation. In this role he often tangled verbally with Bridges and his many allies, who sardonically dubbed him the Great Emancipator because of his long orations in opposition to prevailing federation policy.[34]

Lloyd E. (Sam) Usinger was yet another of the San Francisco patrolmen.

Although less well known than either Cates or Tillman, his letters and reports in the *Voice of the Federation* indicate that of the three, he had the most explicit commitment to syndicalism. He publicly condemned the capitalist system, stated that the goal of the seamen was to own the ships, and called on his fellow workers to "form a one-big-union where poverty and unemployment shall be unknown." Although closely aligned with Lundeberg, Usinger was apparently somewhat undisciplined and individualistic. One former sailor remembered him as an "anarchist" and a "wild man." He recalled seeing Usinger pick up a typewriter and throw it at an SUP official during an argument in the union hall. Early in 1936 he was sentenced to six months in jail as a result of charges arising from "a minor, early morning brawl" with another member of the SUP. The fact that the shipowners' attorney made a point of attending his trial and aiding the prosecution's efforts to gain a conviction and jail sentence is a testament to his reputation on the waterfront.[35]

Among other Lundeberg associates, Austen Hansen, a Dane, was a member of the influential SUP publicity committee and an ardent advocate of job action and industrial unionism who called upon his fellow workers to "continue forward until labor gets the full product of its toil." Emil Miljus had allegedly been a member of the MWIU and the Communist party before joining the Sailors' Union and lining up with Lundeberg. Ed Coester, a veteran of six years on steam schooners, had been an SUP member intermittently since 1928. In the summer of 1935 he was elected to the job of port agent in Portland, and unlike the others he remained a leading SUP official for many years. His attraction to Lundeberg seems to have been more personal than ideological. H. M. Bright, an Australian, may have been influenced by the One Big Union movement that fellow Aussie Harry Bridges had encountered as a young sailor. The Australian seamen had a reputation for internationalism, and Bright spoke out forcefully on the need for international working-class solidarity.[36]

With a few possible exceptions, then, the record of these men was not one of doctrinaire anarcho-syndicalism, and it certainly was not yet one of strong anticommunism (whereas the Wobblies, syndicalism's organized remnant, had long been rabidly anti-Communist). It is even probable that one or two of these men had been members of the Communist party in the recent past, or at least had worked closely with Communists in the pursuit of common objectives on the waterfront. Insofar as they already had a developed syndicalist commitment, it had not always precluded political activity. However, the events of the fall of 1935, beginning with the longshoremen's renewal of their arbitration award, propelled the Lundeberg group in the direction of a sometimes contradictory but nonetheless dogmatic stance that included hostility to politics, advocacy of industrial unionism, and a deep craft loyalty to the embattled sailors. Moreover, as Bridges, his maritime union allies, and the various organs of the Communist party became more critical of the course advocated by these SUP activists, they in turn moved more in the direction of anticommunism. In the case of Lundeberg himself, his pugnacity, inflexibility, and bulldog tenacity made it virtually certain that once he disagreed sharply and openly with Bridges and the Communists, he would become their sworn enemy.

The protest triggered by the steam schooner job actions, and the calling of an emergency convention of the Maritime Federation to consider this problem and several others, forced the SUP syndicalists into a temporary retreat. For one thing, it was clear that the majority of the rank-and-file sailors did not yet support the position of the Lundeberg group on job action and the need for independent initiative by the Sailors' Union. On October 21 Harry Bridges was warmly received by the SUP membership at a meeting that voted to concur with the call for a Maritime Federation emergency convention and to suspend all job actions in the meantime. While this vote was in effect a repudiation of the extreme position taken by several of Lundeberg's closest allies in their support of the Ward resolution, Lundeberg himself did not oppose the calling of an MFPC convention. On October 20 he wrote to federation Secretary-Treasurer Fred Kelley: "In view of all the unrest on the coast it might be a good idea to hold a special convention . . . to try to straighten some of these problems out and also get a little more cooperation and friendly spirit on the coast." But a few days later he expressed ambivalence and a certain amount of resignation in the face of the controversy and hostility besetting the federation. He wrote to Kelley: "Some times I think it will be allright to have [a convention] and other times I don't. Anyway I've ceased worrying about it. I am not saying anything one way or the other. You and I have had enough grief for a long time to come."[37]

When it came to a debate on the principle of job action, however, Lundeberg and his allies expressed no ambivalence and no willingness to retreat. A *Voice* editorial entitled "Job Action, Or Else—" defended this tactic as "a spontaneous demonstration of the will of the men," but conceded that committees within the marine unions and the Maritime Federation should be set up to guard against cases of "indiscriminate, unorganized or unjustified job action." The editorial triggered an explosion of criticism and debate, with Lundeberg himself leading the ranks of job action's uncompromising defenders. He declared: "Job action is never indiscriminate, unorganized, or unjust." It "is not spontaneous. Neither is it emotional." Significantly, he placed the rights of men on the job in opposition to the prerogatives of union committees and officials and even to decisions reached by democratic procedure at union meetings. "The workers on the job . . . know best when the time is right for job action," he said. "Those who try to put job action in committees' hands or in conferences are people who are trying their damndest to kill the seamen's strongest weapon." In an obvious reference to the condemnation of the steam schooner job actions expressed at a mass meeting of ISU affiliates in San Francisco, he argued that "the rank and file will always use this weapon no matter what one individually primed meeting might say."[38]

It had been commonplace to posit a contradiction between the rank and file on the one hand and old-guard union officials like Joe Ryan and Paul Scharrenberg on the other. But now Lundeberg and his allies were suggesting an inherent contradiction between the workers and their union leaders, even those who were widely regarded as the embodiment of rank and file. According to the SUP delegation to the Maritime Federation emergency convention, trade union officials, because of their official status, "can not lend themselves openly to supporting specific instances of job action and must of necessity take a more conservative stand." Therefore, all decisions regarding job action "must be left to the men on the job." Moreover, any attempt to separate the decision-making process from the workers at the point of production smacked of the condescension represented by "Seamen's [Church] Institutes, Y.M.C.A.'s, [and] Arbitration Boards." As Lundeberg put it, "THE MEN ON THE SHIPS ARE CAPABLE OF PICKING THE RIGHT TIME AND PLACE. Give the rank and filers a little credit."[39]

The emergency convention of the Maritime Federation met in mid-November and adopted in slightly amended form a job action resolution introduced by Harry Bridges. The Bridges position basically constituted a middle ground between those elements who demanded that "all job action shall cease," as one resolution put it, and the SUP delegation's position calling for recognition of the right of workers to resort to job action whenever they deemed it necessary. The amended resolution defined job action in carefully limited terms and declared that where its use threatened to "jeopardize the Maritime Federation as a whole," the matter should be referred to the MFPC district councils "for further action and adjustment."[40]

After the convention, the *Voice of the Federation* bravely declared that solidarity had been its keynote, and many of the delegates proceeded on the assumption that genuine unity had been achieved. But beneath the surface appearance of unity, the breach between the sailors and the other maritime crafts was widening and relations between the Lundeberg group and its opponents were becoming increasingly hostile. During the convention the SUP delegation had warned that adoption of Bridges's job action resolution would constitute "one of the biggest victories for the shipowners on this coast," while the *Western Worker* had responded in kind by declaring that "Harry Lundeberg does not consciously play the shipowners' game, but the results of his individualistic actions may well be the same." The Communist party newspaper accused Lundeberg of making a strong appeal for unity at the MFPC convention and then going to a Sailors' Union meeting and threatening "open violence" against "a majority of the rank and file" because they allegedly disagreed with his policies.[41]

At this time Lundeberg was running for the top office in the SUP against Herb Mills, who was the union's dispatcher in San Francisco, a close ally of Bridges, and a member of the Communist party. Lundeberg sharpened the tone of his campaign and the overall controversy by responding to the *Western Worker* with a long open letter that was surprisingly mild toward the Communist party newspaper but sharply critical of his opponents in the Sailors' Union, whom he accused of deliberately misinforming both the *Western Worker* and the membership of the SUP. He characterized his critics as "a few individuals on the beach, who never go to sea, and whose strike records . . . would certainly not bear the closest investigation," and he accused "this handful of so-called sailors" of trying to ram arbitration down the seamen's throats "by hook or by crook."[42]

Although Lundeberg refrained from criticizing the Communist party, even in the face of provocation, some of his followers began for the first time to employ the rhetoric of anticommunism. Charlie Cates, who had scathingly criticized "The Methods of the Red Baiter," now declared in an election leaflet: "Do you want your union piloted by a political dictatorship group of the minority? Will you take for your important officers the johnny come latelys: who have been in your *union for only a dog watch,* who shout so loudly in your meetings: Will you elect disappearing officials that have been on a million committees for Ethiopia? Steady as she goes—nothing to the left—nothing to the right."

Cates, at least, was not willing to limit his attacks on the opposition to words alone. At a turbulent Sailors' Union meeting in December, he "dumped" Herb Mills, the leading symbol within the union of opposition to the Lundeberg group, while Mills was chairing the meeting. The hostility was becoming so intense that an SUP member warned another Bridges ally in the union to "bring your boxing gloves when you arrive" in San Francisco.[43]

In mid-October it had seemed that Lundeberg and his allies represented a minority not only within the Maritime Federation as a whole but in their own Sailors' Union as well. At an SUP meeting attended by three hundred members, only four men had voted against ending the steam schooner job actions initiated by the militant San Francisco patrolmen. But the unwillingness of the shipowners to engage in meaningful collective bargaining, and the persistence of the syndicalists, gradually turned the tide in favor of the Lundeberg group. In January 1936 Lundeberg was elected Sailors' Union secretary by a better than three-to-one margin. Even before his election, in mid-December 1935, an SUP meeting had voted to renew and extend the campaign of job actions to win the six-hour day on the steam schooners. Since the Maritime Federation emergency convention had declared that any job action should be limited to a single ship, dock, or warehouse, unless the rest of the maritime unions agreed otherwise, SUP representatives took great pains to present this action as "a Sailors' problem" that could be handled by the sailors themselves. "Remember," a widely circulated leaflet warned, "this shall not be a strike. There will be no picket lines. Do not involve any other organizations."[44]

Whether the SUP militants actually believed that such a broad-gauged action could avoid involving other maritime crafts is perhaps a moot point, because the shipowners quickly dragged other unions into the fray by laying up the steam schooners and locking out entire crews as the vessels docked in Pacific Coast ports. By the end of the year approximately fifty steam schooners were tied up, their crews idle. While this conflict was only one among many on the turbulent Pacific Coast waterfront, it served to deepen the overall crisis and to sharpen the breach between the embattled sailors and the other maritime crafts, thereby intensifying the antagonism between Bridges and Lundeberg.

On the employers' side, it is clear that their response to the steam schooner job actions was not unpremeditated. Most of the shipowners remained unwilling to concede the passing of the long era of nearly absolute employer hegemony on the waterfront. While they paid lip service to the principle of orderly collective bargaining, even this painful concession implied a relative equality that they were loathe to grant in practice. In any case, when they did think in terms of the give-and-take of bargaining, they envisioned a relationship with conservative trade unionists like Ryan and Scharrenberg. In contrast, Bridges and Lundeberg seemed bent on "overthrow[ing] the existing form of government." Thus, to the shipowners, every battle over prerogatives, every job action—even the famous demand for "ham and eggs"—had overtones of the final conflict. ". . . the time to make a stand is now and not later," said Roger Lapham of the American-Hawaiian Steamship Company. "Better fight in the middle of the room and not wait until you have reached the window sill."[45]

For months before the steam schooner controversy came to a head, maritime employers had been meeting with representatives of the San Francisco Chamber of Commerce, the Industrial Association, and similar groups on both coasts in order to come up with a unified plan to break the power of the maritime unions and rid them of their radical leadership. Harry Bridges warned his fellow unionists of the existence of such a plan, or "suspension program," which would involve the cancellation by the employers of all arbitration awards. He stated that the shipowners' intention was "to lay up their ships and tell the government that they are unable to operate . . . because of the exorbitant demands of the unions and the fact that the unions are continually interfering with interstate commerce." According to Louis Stark of the *New York Times,* the shipowners had already approached the Depart-

ment of Justice demanding that the Maritime Federation leadership be prose-
cuted under the Sherman Antitrust Act "for conspiracy to restrain and interfere with interstate commerce." An attorney for the shipowners had presented the Justice Department with "voluminous records and exhibits" in
support of the charge that the federation was an illegal conspiracy. Stark also
reported that "employers on the Pacific Coast virtually have completed formation of a coastwide 'vigilante' organization to protect their interests in the
event they find themselves unable to obtain redress from the government . . .
well-informed sources in San Francisco indicate that the employers are ready
for a 'show-down.' "[46]

As if the shipowners' increasingly unified determination to precipitate a
showdown with the maritime unions did not pose enough of a problem, the
executive board of the International Seamen's Union was also indicating a
readiness to launch a frontal attack on its Pacific Coast affiliates. Not surprisingly, the most strident advocate of such a course was Paul Scharrenberg,
whose appetite for combat had been fed by his expulsion from the SUP and by
the persistent refusal of the Sailors' Union to reinstate him, in spite of
frequent orders to that effect by the ISU executive board. As the first ISU
convention in six years approached, Scharrenberg issued a public call for
decisive action against the West Coast insurgents. "Only by a prompt declaration of war upon the wrecking crew," he said, "can we hope to reestablish the
reputation of our International Union as a responsible organization. Only by
prompt action can we hope to rally the timid loyal members. One or more
charters must be revoked. One or more new District Unions must be organized, and those who have taken the lead in recent disruptive activities must
be barred from membership in any District Union of the International Seamen's Union."

With a tone of resignation, Assistant Secretary of Labor McGrady admitted
that the Department of Labor "has spent more time trying to bring peace and
order on the Pacific Coast than on any other labor situation in this country."
Only a few months earlier, with the release of the *Point Clear* and the
apparent end of one major crisis, McGrady had exulted: "We look for no more
trouble in the Pacific Coast shipping industry for the next two years." Now
with a new crisis mounting and Louis Stark's ominous words ringing in his
ears, he was forced to swallow his earlier optimism and implicitly acknowledge that the government's mediation efforts had met with defeat.[47]

In this explosive context, the Sailors' Union's renewed campaign for the
six-hour day on the steam schooners provoked a bitterly critical response from
many elements within the Maritime Federation. Both the Marine Cooks and
Stewards and the Marine Firemen attacked the SUP for violating the job
action resolution passed by the federation emergency convention. Bridges,
after outlining the employers' plans for a showdown, argued that this was an
occasion where the unions faced the necessity of strategic retreat. Even within

the Sailors' Union, there were influential voices who claimed that Lundeberg and his "clique" failed to "take into consideration the powerful forces of capital and realize that we have to be united on the coast when we fight them."[48]

But in the face of this torrent of criticism Lundeberg and his allies refused to concede a thing. Tillman blamed the sailors' predicament on the ILA's unilateral decision to renew the longshore awards, declaring, moreover, that "if it had not been for the Seamen in [the] 1934 strike, the ILA would have been beaten." In response to Bridges's statement that the steam schooner crisis would have to be resolved by the Maritime Federation as a whole, Lundeberg declared that "no organization . . . can compel the Sailors to work if they do not wish to." As for Bridges's call for strategic retreat, he stated that "there can be no retreat in the steam schooner action."[49]

By mid-April Bridges was ruling out job action as a weapon of the Maritime Federation and stating that the ILA could no longer continue to become involved every time "a ship is pulled by a couple of drunks from the crew." While Bridges and his allies increasingly demanded a unified program of action, Lundeberg's reply was indicative of both his policy and the pugnacious and irreverent image that was becoming his trademark. "F——— you guys," he exclaimed. "When the S.U.P. wants to strike it'll strike."[50]

The emergence of the Sailors' Union as an independent force had profound consequences in other areas as well. Whereas previously the alliance between the Sailors and the San Francisco Longshoremen had formed the dynamic core of the Maritime Federation's left wing, the development of "syndicalists" and "Communists" as antagonistic forces diluted the strength of the Bridges group on many political questions and legitimized anticommunism within the Maritime Federation. At the MFPC's 1936 convention a resolution favoring a farmer-labor party was narrowly defeated when the Lundeberg group united with the federation's conservative elements against the Communists and their allies. Lundeberg and his associates had supported the United Labor party in 1935, and they easily could have swung the vote in favor of the farmer-labor party resolution. Now, however, they expressed opposition to any working-class involvement in politics.[51]

On the question of communism and Red-baiting, there was a similar evolution toward an intransigence that contrasted sharply with the position that the Lundeberg group had taken during the Maritime Federation's halcyon days. The personalities of Bridges and Lundeberg, and the fact that the Communist party openly sided with Bridges and criticized his opponents, perhaps made it inevitable that Lundeberg would become an outspoken anti-Communist. But he was not alone. Within the Maritime Federation, William Fischer, a Portland longshoreman who succeeded Lundeberg as president and became his close ally, served as the most outspoken foe of Bridges and his "Communist" associates. Soon after becoming president in early 1936, Fischer was criticized as a Red-baiter. He responded, "I have no fight with the Comrades; but I will not permit them to run our organization if I can help it." Fischer considered himself an advocate of industrial unionism, and his Wobbly background perhaps made him hostile to politics of any stripe. He sought an editor of the *Voice of the Federation* who would agree "not to inject anything political" into the paper. By June of 1936, however, the "comrades" had become "rats" in Fischer's estimation, and he was warning his allies, "You fellows will have to watch the [*Voice*] and don't let the rats slip anything over. They are scheming all the time."[52]

A part of the historian's task is to penetrate beneath the surface of the epithets and accusations that ultimately prevailed, in order to grasp the valid perceptions and authentic concerns that both Communists and syndicalists articulated in the early stages of their debate. The sailors had urgent grievances, and they wanted to settle them by applying the methods that had been so successful during the 1934 strike and after. They argued with some justification that the longshoremen had abandoned them at certain crucial points, and that the sailors must continue the fight, alone if necessary. However, Bridges, with the support of other crafts, increasingly came to believe that sustained pressure from the shipowners, the government, and the international unions threatened to isolate the maritime workers and thus required a policy of caution, consolidation, and even strategic retreat where necessary. Both sides had legitimate arguments to make. The problem was that in the whirlwind of events and tangle of personalities, political and strategic tendencies became dogmatic obsessions, foreclosing any possibility of uniting the two sides of this thorny contradiction by means of a process of dialogue and accommodation.

Even though neither Bridges nor Lundeberg had much interest in theory, their argument echoes some of the important themes that the Left had debated periodically for more than half a century. The strength of the Lundeberg group was their focus on the immediate concerns of the men on the job who chafed under the weight of continued grievances and resented the employers' constant chiseling away at hard-won gains. Their concept of democracy was localistic, spontaneous, and geared to hammering out a consensus in the course of action rather than through plebiscites, meetings, and conventions. They recalled to some degree the "vague but attractive formula of 'mass action' " around which much of the American Left had coalesced during the upheavals of 1919; and their emphasis on the workplace as the focal point of transformation and democratic renewal reflected the best aspects of the syndicalist tradition.[53]

However, in their zeal for combat the Lundeberg group displayed a weakness that also had its roots in the history of American syndicalism, especially as reflected in the IWW's frequently expressed contempt for fellow workers who were unwilling to join them on the battle lines every time a call was issued. In the midst of the first steam schooner crisis, when a majority of the rank and filers at an ISU mass meeting had condemned disorganized job action, one of the militants had allegedly called his fellow seamen a "bunch of finks" and declared that "we will strike without their support anyway." Likewise, undaunted by the adverse sentiment expressed through democratic procedure, Lundeberg had stated publicly that "one individually primed meeting" could not stem the tide of job action.[54]

Bridges, on the other hand, believed that any viable trade union policy had to be founded upon a broad consensus. Therefore, he labored tirelessly in his own San Francisco local and up and down the coast to win support for his program. Unlike the syndicalists, who at first showed little interest in the implications of their ideas beyond the maritime industry, he constantly sought to broaden the base of working-class unity, even if it meant placing limits on the exuberant militancy that had become the marine workers' trademark. Increasingly, he came to believe that spontaneous actions by small groups of workers on the job threatened the overall interests of the ILA and the federation and he declared in November 1935 that Local 38-79 was "taking steps to discipline members, and to protect the interests of the union at large." Soon afterward he warned the MFPC District Council in San Francisco of the necessity to build closer ties with uptown unionists who feared the waterfront unions' penchant for " 'pulling men off the job' without first trying to settle disputes by other means." In July 1936 he stated that "the policy of the ILA will be for coast-wise action on all questions of major importance and . . . a referendum vote will be necessary before the ILA will take action."[55] (As we shall see in the next two chapters, Bridges and Lundeberg would eventually reverse their positions, in practice if not in theory, as dramatically new circumstances came to the fore. Although he continued to advocate a policy of discipline and uniformity, the longshore leader proved reluctant to crack down on dockworkers who engaged in militant action on the job. Meanwhile, Lundeberg veered sharply away from his defense of spontaneous activism and increasingly sought to place restrictions on shipboard militancy.)

Although the unity of the Maritime Federation had been fatally compromised by early 1936, the organization managed to retain a significant measure of viability for at least another year and through the course of a major maritime strike of ninety-nine days' duration. Ironically, some credit for this development must go to the shipowners; for every time they attempted to make a stand, it served mainly to weld the warring elements in the Maritime Federation into a seemingly invincible force. One of the clearest examples of this dynamic came in April 1936, with the *Santa Rosa* incident. East Coast wildcat strikers declared this Grace line vessel hot, claiming that her crew was composed of scabs, and called upon the Maritime Federation to boycott the ship when it docked in West Coast ports. The federation's San Francisco District council dispatched pickets to greet the vessel. However, after investigating the circumstances under which the *Santa Rosa* had sailed from New York, the San Francisco ILA local declared that "this was a bum beef" and voted not to join the picket lines. At precisely this moment, the employers used the boycott of the *Santa Rosa* as a pretext to launch their suspension program—against the San Francisco ILA local! As it became clear that the shipowners' objective was to destroy the hiring hall and force the removal of a leadership group that had been elected by an overwhelming margin, the entire coast—not only the marine unions but conservative AFL officials from uptown organizations—rallied behind the embattled San Francisco Longshoremen. After a week the employers were forced to beat a humiliating retreat, maritime unity was apparently solidified, and Bridges's reputation for coolness and steadfast leadership in times of crisis was vastly enhanced.[56]

The next—and last—great expression of Maritime Federation unity came with the ninety-nine-day strike that began on October 30, 1936. Again employer intransigence played an important role in pulling the feuding waterfront factions together around their common slogan, "An Injury to One Is an Injury to All." In the negotiations preceding the strike, the shipowners demanded substantial changes in the 1934 and 1935 arbitration awards. They expressed bitter opposition to the union-controlled hiring hall and the six-hour day, declared their willingness to arbitrate these issues, and called on the unions to do likewise. Above all, they continued to attack the maritime union leadership and the unions' combative stance as subversive of basic American principles. Employers used a quickie strike over the issue of safety aboard ship to charge the maritime unions with "a determined campaign . . . to destroy discipline on American merchant ships—a campaign to *nullify the authority of the Master* and other officers, and to substitute for it *rule by the crew.*" As a coastwide strike loomed, the press reported that the Big Three shipping lines—Matson, Dollar, and American-Hawaiian—had "believed for some time that there could never be peace on terms satisfactory to them as long as Bridges and Lundeberg, or men of their philosophy and tactics, continued in control of the unions."[57]

The maritime workers emphatically refused to submit fundamental issues such as the hiring hall to arbitration. As a representative of the Marine Cooks and Stewards put it, "The union cannot and should not be asked to arbitrate its very existence." But the unions were eager to engage in collective bargaining in the hope of consolidating the gains they had won through job action up and down the coast. According to federal mediator Edward McGrady, the big stumbling block was the seamen's hiring halls, which they had achieved through systematic defiance of arbitrators' rulings. The seafaring unions wanted this victory recognized in a signed agreement. But as McGrady noted,

"The shipowners absolutely refused to concede the present system of shipping." When he asked the seamen to compromise on this issue, they were equally adamant in their refusal.

As the original strike deadline approached, McGrady's report to the Roosevelt administration was steeped in pessimism. He predicted that "if this strike takes place—it will be worse [than 1934] because the ship owners have joined with organizations consisting of farmers, wholesale businessmen, manufacturers, and industrialists, from the Canadian borderline down to San Pedro. All of them are determined 'to smash radicalism and communism,' but, in reality, to destroy the maritime unions. They believe the fight might as well take place now and have it over with." The major shipping lines were indeed ready, even eager, for a confrontation. Their public relations gambit was the demand for arbitration; their strategy was to "fold their arms until business losses in coast cities, plus privation to thousands of wage-earners produce a public opinion favorable to strikebreaking." With Roosevelt running for reelection in the face of bitter employer opposition, McGrady feared that the shipowners' strategy had another dimension. He reported that they would welcome the conflict and disruption of a prolonged strike because "they would like also to defeat the present Administration."[58]

At 11:48 P.M. on October 29 the White House received a telegram from McGrady, who reported despondently that not one of the shipowners he had depended on to achieve a peaceful settlement had come through. "Everything humanly possible was done," he said, "but when our alleged friends fail us we have not much chance to succeed."

The strike began at midnight. From the very beginning it was a vivid testament to the growth of the unions' power since 1934. In the Big Strike the longshoremen had walked out first and had been joined gradually by other crafts. Many seamen had enrolled in the unions only after the strike began and some had not joined at all. This time, however, the entire coast was organized and forty thousand maritime workers walked out together. Given the employers' folded-arms strategy, there were no scabs and there was little violence. Initially 136 vessels were tied up in Pacific Coast ports; this number would grow by nearly 100 as other ships completed their voyages and the crews walked off. The Dollar line had managed to keep some of its vessels sailing in 1934, but when the *President McKinley* docked on the fiftieth day of the 1936 strike, an employer spokesman lamented the end of a thirty-six-year tradition. "It has been said that the sun never sets on the British flag—so it was with Dollar ships," he noted, "until today."[59]

The most significant advance over 1934 came with the spread of the strike to seamen on the Atlantic and Gulf coasts. The West Coast unions had sought a nationwide tie-up in 1934, but had been thwarted by the ILA's Ryan and by the top officials of the ISU. Since that time, however, the Pacific Coast example had sparked a growing struggle among Eastern and Gulf seamen to throw off the yoke of employer domination and the corruption and stagnation of the ISU officialdom. The first major breakthrough came with the so-called mutiny on the S.S. *California,* when an obscure bosun's mate named Joseph Curran emerged as the spokesman for an East Coast crew that "sat down" aboard ship in San Pedro harbor to demand West Coast wages and conditions for all seamen. The firing of Curran and sixty-three shipmates when the vessel returned to New York provoked the Spring Strike of 1936. ISU officials branded the strikers as outlaws and expelled their leaders from the union. The insurgents formed the Seamen's Defense Committee and prepared for a general shipping strike in the fall. When the Pacific Coast ports shut down on October 30 nearly thirty thousand Atlantic and Gulf Coast seafarers walked off the ships under the leadership of the Seamen's Defense Committee.

These men fought against overwhelming odds. They faced the combined opposition of shipowners, police, their own union, and Ryan's ILA. Ryan even declared that his longshoremen would strike any shipping companies that came to terms with the "outlaw" seamen. More formidable than the threat of a counterstrike, however, was the active presence of Ryan's goons. The ILA president testified before a congressional committee, "We went to the [shipowners] and said, 'Give us money; we are going to fight them.' We got the money and drove them back with bats where they belonged." Curran recalled that in New York "You'd go down to lonesome, faraway docks, and if you'd find a picket missing you'd look around and find his body in an alley."[60]

The ISU officials had their own "beef squads." They were particularly active in the Gulf, where an escalating rank-and-file rebellion among seamen and the fragile presence of a Maritime Federation of the Gulf made the waterfront a volatile and dangerous place. As longshoreman Gilbert Mers recalled, "Wearing a federation button could get you crippled for a brief period, maybe a lengthy one." The center of beef squad activity was in Houston, where gun-toting, ISU troubleshooter Wilbur Dickey terrorized striking seamen. When a group of strikers attempted to take control of the union hall, Dickey shot a young Wobbly named Johnny Kane in the stomach and killed him. One eyewitness recalled that "Kane went down and before Dickey had time to fire again four or five guys began scramblin' with him. A Greek, a West Coast man, takes Dickey's nose in his mouth and grinds it off between his teeth. The pain was so great that Dickey drops his gun. Johnny is dyin' on the ground and I see the Greek spit Dickey's nose out. The crowd worked Dickey all around the yard into the gutter with everybody kickin' him. I even saw little shoe-shine boys take a kick at him." Nearly two thousand people attended Johnny Kane's funeral. The procession of several hundred automobiles was over two miles long. As the marine workers filed by the grave site, each of them placed a Gulf Maritime Federation button on the casket "as a mute promise that the martyred Kane will not have died in vain, and that the fight for a National Maritime Federation . . . will be carried on."[61]

Altogether, twenty-seven seamen were killed in Atlantic and Gulf Coast ports during the Fall Strike. Although the strikers eventually gained important concessions from the employers, many of them were gradually worn down by the violence of their foes. One strike leader recalled that "out of 30,000 members that registered in the beginning of the strike, we wound up . . . with less than 3,000 men left up and down the entire Coast. Presumably, the rest of the guys finked out." But even the men who "finked out" were becoming thoroughly disgusted with their union officials' reactionary stance. The Fall Strike was to be another nail in the ISU's coffin. Meanwhile, Joe Curran and a number of Communist maritime workers were gaining valuable experience and increasing recognition as the battle-tested leaders of the East Coast seamen.[62]

The dream of a national maritime federation had been gathering momentum ever since the historic events of 1934, and the Fall Strike seemed to be an additional step in this direction. But Harry Lundeberg and his allies were wary of Curran's ambition and downright hostile to the Communists who surrounded him. The "outlaw" Seamen's Defense Committee had a much larger constituency than the three West Coast seamen's unions combined, and Lundeberg feared that the East Coast insurgents would attempt to gobble up the SUP and would provide yet another beachhead for Communist control of the waterfront.[63]

Harry Bridges saw matters in an entirely different light. He welcomed the emergence of the Curran group and believed that the Atlantic Coast strike confronted the West Coast unions with an opportunity to expand their influence and an obligation to assist embattled fellow workers. Having recently been elected president of the ILA's Pacific Coast District, Bridges invaded Ryan's bailiwick. On an unauthorized and highly controversial tour of eastern port cities, he encouraged longshoremen to defy the ILA president and honor the seamen's picket lines. He called Ryan a "shipowners' agent and strikebreaker." Ryan in turn called Bridges a "punk" and removed him from the payroll of the international union. But Ryan's opposition only enhanced the irrepressible Aussie's stature. In New York he spoke to an overflow crowd of maritime workers and their sympathizers in Madison Square Garden. He was the last speaker at a long meeting, but when he was introduced the crowd of eighteen thousand leaned forward as one to hear his every word. Louis Adamic declared, "I have never heard a better organized, more effective, more intelligent, or more sincere speech than Bridges made on this occasion." He characterized the West Coast leader as "an extraordinary man . . . driven on a straight course by a great passion."[64]

When Bridges returned home he quickly became involved in another round of controversy. The newspapers were full of speculation that the sailors and marine firemen were on the verge of a settlement with the employers. Even the *Voice of the Federation* ran a banner headline declaring, "Strike End Looms," at a time when several unions, including the ILA, had not even begun negotiating with the shipowners. Bridges was furious. He implied that Lundeberg and the sailors were about to abandon the united front of striking unions. He demanded that the editor of the *Voice,* a Lundeberg ally, be fired. He announced that a West Coast settlement should be contingent upon a satisfactory resolution of the Atlantic Coast seamen's dispute.

The employers were—or professed to be—surprised and outraged at Bridges's call for East-West solidarity. "The Eastern fight is not Bridges' fight," said T. G. (the workers called him Tear Gas) Plant, the shipowners' chief spokesman. Plant attacked Bridges as a "mere wrecker," driven by "false ambition" and "desire for personal glorification." At the same time, the American League against Communism, an organization supported by several influential employer spokesmen, called upon San Franciscans to rout Bridges and the Reds: "On the East Coast, the GOOD AMERICAN UNION LEADERS can keep out the Communists. On the West Coast the COMMUNISTS ARE IN! Bridges is the dictator! It's up to the public to GET THEM OUT! IT'S UP TO YOU!"[65]

Instead of closing ranks around the embattled longshoreman as they had done in the face of previous shipowner assaults, elements within the Maritime Federation joined in the chorus of denunciation. Barney Mayes, who was deposed as *Voice of the Federation* editor at the insistence of Bridges and his allies, accused the Communist party of trying to "crucify me because I have resisted their attempts to dictate the policies of the *Voice.*" Mayes had worked closely with the renowned Dunne brothers and other Trotskyist leaders of the 1934 Minneapolis teamsters' strike. Within the Maritime Federation he had aligned himself with Lundeberg, William Fischer, and others who were combatting the influence of Bridges and the Communists. Upon becoming editor of the *Voice,* Mayes had allegedly declared, "We are going to stop using this paper to eulogize one man." Now he charged "I am opposed to the Communist Party, not because of its 'radicalism,' but because I consider it a reactionary force and an enemy of militant industrial unionism. In spite of the radical phraseology of the Communist Party, its line has shifted so much to the right that if Samuel Gompers were alive today he would have to fight them from the left."[66]

Mayes's allies added to the crescendo. Austen Hansen and the SUP publicity committee issued a bulletin accusing Bridges and a "disruptive faction" of sabotage and slander. The bulletin concluded: "[Bridges] must remember that even Napoleon met his Waterloo! And he has been warned publicly today to keep his hands and his nose out of the sailors' business." Harry Lundeberg disavowed "all personal attacks on any other leader while a strike situation exists," but nonetheless chimed in with a blast at "disgruntled factionalists," "disappointed 'glory' seekers," and "self-appointed 'Commissars.' "

A semblance of unity was restored when the SUP announced that the sailors would not take a vote on their agreement until the basic demands of all other unions had been met. (Lundeberg maintained that this had been the SUP's intent all along.) The strike then dragged on for another month and a half; it ended on February 4, 1937. On the surface the settlement was a major victory for the entire Maritime Federation. The sailors and other unlicensed seafaring crafts won recognition of the hiring hall and significant concessions in the realm of wages, hours, and overtime pay. The ILA also made important advances, but for the most part the longshoremen had struck to defend the gains of 1934 and to aid the seamen in their struggle for parity with the dockworkers.[67]

However, even the afterglow of victory could not obscure one ominous fact. The friction between Bridges and Lundeberg had become front-page news. Although this conflict would not undo the gains won through the Big Strike and its ninety-nine-day sequel, it was moving—inexorably—to the center stage of waterfront labor relations. Soon the formation of the National Maritime Union on the East Coast, and the escalating battle between the AFL and the CIO nationwide, would harden the lines of cleavage on the West Coast, cripple the Maritime Federation, and cast a lasting shadow on the bright achievements of the Pentecostal era.

Before examining the succession of events that propelled this friction toward the breaking point, we should pause and seek to place the Pentecostal era in a broader context. Was it perhaps a loud but ephemeral tempest that had little impact on other workers and even less bearing upon developments in the larger society? One historian has characterized the West Coast maritime workers as at best "an anachronistic enclave of working-class identity" that was marginal to begin with and was "soon to fade into even more marginal status." It is true that in the mid-thirties the number of longshoremen on the Pacific Coast did not much exceed fourteen thousand, and the number of seafaring workers—including licensed officers—was about twenty-three thousand. The Maritime Federation had more than forty thousand members at its peak, but this included warehousemen, shipyard craftsmen, and other workers who were not, strictly speaking, part of the marine labor force. Compared to the industrial legions in auto, steel, and mining, the maritime work force was small indeed and the West Coast segment was less than a fifth of the national total.[68]

However, the significance of these workers cannot be judged only in terms of their numbers. The major cities on the West Coast were port cities; shipping was vital to their economic well-being. And the maritime workers were strategically located in the industrial infrastructure. As they demonstrated again and again, their strikes had an extraordinary impact on the economic life of the entire region. Had they remained isolated, they could have been crushed. But the ferment generated by the Great Depression and the New Deal made other workers and other sections of the population receptive to the militant tactics and even the radical outlook that so often permeated the waterfront in the 1930s. Far from being a marginal force, the insurgent marine unionists were the pacesetters for an entire generation of workers on the Pacific Coast, and their impact went beyond the labor movement and influenced the development of politics and society.

Even before the San Francisco general strike, the ILA had begun to forge ties with workers in the warehouse industry, and these ties became the basis for the famous March Inland. Waterfront warehousemen were an important link in the chain of transportation and distribution. They had long labored under conditions similar to those of the longshoremen; and as unskilled—often casual—laborers who had their own shape-up in close proximity to the docks, they were a potential source of strikebreakers during waterfront labor disputes. Thus, partly out of self-interest, the ILA began organizing warehousemen during the 1934 strike.

Louis Goldblatt, who was to become one of the key figures in the March Inland, recalled how a few activists "took the dust off" an old ILA charter that had been issued in 1919 and constituted themselves as the nucleus of Weighers, Warehousemen and Cereal Workers' Union, Local 38-44. They waged a whirlwind organizing campaign among waterfront warehousemen and then moved uptown, reaching out to workers in other warehousing, and even manufacturing, concerns. As one organizer put it, "Our jurisdiction can take us into any place where a [hand] truck is pushed and . . . where storaging and warehousing is done." In spite of bitter and prolonged employer resistance in the uptown warehouses, the campaign was a spectacular success. Local 38-44 walked out for its own demands during the 1936–37 strike and used the time off the job to extend its organizing drive. The union recruited at least a thousand new members during the strike, and soon afterward Henry Schmidt acknowledged that the Warehousemen had surpassed the San Francisco Longshoremen as the largest local in the ILA Pacific Coast District.[69]

There was much more than territorial ambition at stake in the March Inland. In "bring[ing] the waterfront further up-town," as one organizer put it, the ILA was not only extending the range of unionism but was building organizations that were dramatically different from those that had survived the lean years between 1919 and 1934. The employers charged that the March Inland meant the extension of subversive principles and organizations. The Industrial Association warned of a "conspiracy to fasten marine control on all San Francisco business"; and a group of warehouse owners characterized the campaign as an attempt by "a handful of radical leaders" to "dominate business—to dominate the whole labor movement, and to dominate politically." "It is not organized labor as the City has known it," declared men who a decade before had combined to undermine even the most conservative AFL unions.[70]

As the warehouse campaign continued to penetrate further inland, the maritime workers also helped stoke the fires of insurgent unionism in the lumber camps and sawmills. In September 1936 a Federation of Woodworkers was formed in the Pacific Northwest, with a contingent of marine workers in attendance. Although the impetus for this organization came from within the lumber industry, the ties between lumber and maritime workers were close and conditions in the two industries tended to breed a similar ideological orientation. The new woodworkers' federation elected a Communist from British Columbia as president, and the *Voice* proudly proclaimed that it was "modeled on the Maritime Federation."[71]

It remained for Roger Lapham, president of the American-Hawaiian Steamship Company, to paint the most alarming portrait of the marine workers' objectives. Speaking to the U.S. Chamber of Commerce in Washington, D.C., he declared, "We know that Bridges' aim is to extend his control to the Gulf and the Atlantic and that he hopes to have a maritime federation which will supplant all A. F. [of] L. unions in shipping. Once having secured that control, the next step will be control of all trucks. . . . If that move is successful, the next step is to secure control of the railroad unions. Once that is secured, Bridges and his group will control the distribution of the country and whoever controls distribution rules the country."[72]

Although Lapham's remarks were laced with half-truths and outright distortions, a number of marine union leaders did dream of organizing far beyond the waterfront. Some visions of the Maritime Federation's natural constituency included an interlocking chain of workers from the ships and docks to the trucks and warehouses and from there all the way to the canneries and fields. Another version focused on workers in "all forms of transportation, passenger as well as freight, both on land and sea and even in the air." Was the object to "overthrow the Government" or "rule the country," as Lapham charged? Certainly not in some classic insurrectionary sense. In fact, part of the motivation was defensive. Bridges argued that because itinerant agricultural workers were easily mobilized as strikebreakers, the ILA, "if only from a selfish standpoint, is concerned with the drive to bring organization to those who work in the fields." But there was also a deeply felt impulse toward solidarity and a genuine desire to see the power of workers "magnified a thousand-fold." Some of the waterfront syndicalists were quite outspoken about the necessity of acting "together as an organized class that will rightfully control production"; while the advocates of political action seemed to be imbued with a social-democratic vision of "organizing a worker political party." Both groups shared the common belief that organizing at the point of production would somehow create "an army of undefeatable workers." Louis

Goldblatt, who was closely associated with the Communists in the ILA, declared, "We are beginning to organize for something bigger than the ILA itself—the organization of the transportation [and] distribution workers. Once such a union is formed . . . we will become really invincible."[73]

Of course, this dream never squared with reality. The Maritime Federation eventually foundered on the rocks of internal discord, and in spite of remarkable achievements, the March Inland failed to realize the inflated hopes of its architects. However, the vision of the marine workers bore fruit in more elusive but still significant ways. For their insurgency triggered a wave of organizing and ferment among a generation of workers on the West Coast. According to California labor journalist and historian David Selvin, the 1934 waterfront strike "set off an incredible period of union organization. . . . Unions came to life that had been little more than charters on the wall of a meeting hall." His observation has been corroborated by many participants in these historic events. Louis Goldblatt recalled,

> A lot of organization was literally stimulated by the waterfront. I remember, for example, there was an old Clinton Cafeteria down at lower Market Street. . . . The culinary workers had made some progress in organization, but not enough; a number of us decided to get in the act. That meant, oh, maybe 50 or 60 of us going in there one morning, occupying every seat, ordering a cup of coffee and sitting there; that's all. Three or four hours of that and the company gets the idea pretty quick that unless they recognize the union their chances of business could be pretty thin.
>
> Like barber shops on the waterfront; all had to organize at once. The idea that they could operate non-union was completely unacceptable. Everybody got in the act. These things stimulated the organizations throughout the city. It also resulted in us making some awfully good friends and supporters.

Even the San Francisco Labor Council, once the domain of rock-ribbed conservatives like John O'Connell and Paul Scharrenberg, became the center of vibrant activity and discussion. Goldblatt declared that the debates on the expulsion of the CIO and its affiliates in 1937 constituted "perhaps the finest chapter in the history of the Labor Council" (a remarkable statement considering that Goldblatt and his union were expelled). The excitement generated by these debates "resulted in an enormous attendance, not only by delegates; there would be nights when there were almost as many people outside the Labor Council as there were inside. People came because it was the best show in town and without charge."[74]

This ferment and growth extended far beyond the storm center of San Francisco and even penetrated the open-shop citadel of Los Angeles. Journalist Carey McWilliams recalled attending a meeting of piece-rate workers who shelled walnuts for a large growers' cooperative in East Los Angeles.

> I was the only male in the hall, in which fifteen hundred women of all ages, shapes, sizes, and nationalities had gathered. Questions had to be translated into

several different languages, the audience being a bizarre mix of Armenians, Russian Americans, Mexican Americans, and other ethnics. . . . As I wrote to [Louis] Adamic: "You should have been there if only to have gotten the *feel* of the meeting, its tension and excitement. . . ."

Women and girls stood on benches, crowded the aisles and doorways, applauded every time they heard the word organize. It was the one English word all of them understood. The spirit that animated that meeting was the spirit of the New Deal, which had reached full tide with the rebirth of the labor movement.

Among workers in the Golden State the "spirit of the New Deal" derived much of its energy from sources independent of Franklin Roosevelt and his administration. McWilliams unhesitatingly declared that the 1934 maritime strike "transformed the labor and political scene in California."[75]

8

AFL versus CIO: "We found brother slugging brother"

Labor relations on the Pacific Coast waterfront remained turbulent throughout the 1930s, until a new set of conditions emerged during World War II. But late in the decade it became increasingly evident that militant activity was not necessarily an expression of expanding unity and heightened class consciousness. On the contrary, after the marathon strike of 1936–37, acrimonious disputes between unions began to overshadow the conflict between workers and employers. By 1938 longshoremen and seamen were shedding each other's blood in San Francisco, and the Maritime Federation was staggering from the blows. (It would expire in 1941.) At the same time, the raging controversy between the AFL and the CIO led to new arenas of conflict and the creation of new alliances, which only served to sharpen the divisions on the waterfront. This fratricidal warfare did not undermine the economic gains of individual unions, but it did make a mockery of the dream of One Big Union and the slogans of solidarity that had been forged in the heat of battle in 1934.

In many ways the experience of West Coast maritime workers was only a microcosm of larger developments within the American working class. In 1936 and 1937 auto, rubber, and steel workers affiliated with the Committee for Industrial Organization (CIO) spearheaded one of the great bursts of working-class insurgency in American history. But they came up against a determined counteroffensive led by the most rabidly antiunion sections of American capital. In the midst of this epic battle the AFL moved to suspend and then expel the unions associated with the CIO on the charge that it functioned as "a rival and dual organization within the family of organized labor." Henceforth, jurisdictional conflict between unions would be almost as prolonged and violent as the struggle between workers and employers.[1]

The Committee for Industrial Organization was formed in November 1935 at the initiative of the United Mine Workers' John L. Lewis, with the stated goal of organizing millions of unorganized workers into industrial unions under the banner of the American Federation of Labor. Fearing that Lewis was building a rival center of power from which to challenge the entrenched leadership of the federation, AFL President William Green warned that the CIO would create "discord, division, misunderstanding, and confusion," and asked that it be disbanded. Lewis adamantly refused, telling the Mine Workers' convention that the "members of the Executive Council of the American Federation of Labor will be wearing asbestos suits in hell before that committee is dissolved."[2]

The AFL old guard wasted little time responding to Lewis's challenge. In the summer of 1936 the executive council suspended the ten unions that had affiliated with the CIO, and then in March 1937 ordered the expulsion of all CIO affiliates from AFL state and city federations. This order was followed by an unprecedented wave of fratricidal warfare that spread from coast to coast. Green charged that the CIO "[has] ripped and torn asunder our movement in many places," and declared, "we have men at each other's throats on the Pacific coast and elsewhere, fighting each other just like animals did in the days of the jungle."[3]

In spite of his self-serving perspective, Green was not far wrong about the level of conflict. In Portland, Oregon, the Brotherhood of Carpenters picketed sawmills organized by the CIO-affiliated International Woodworkers of America (IWA). Teamsters refused to deliver lumber to the mills and overturned trucks driven by IWA members. The AFL patrolled the rivers in small boats, and steam schooner sailors refused to bring cargoes of logs across the waterborne picket lines. In Westwood, California, an IWA organizing campaign "was broken by an armed mob." Bands of men armed with guns and clubs roamed the streets, rounded up known CIO members, and after a brief "trial," ordered them out of town. Between five and six hundred people, including wives and children, were thus deported.[4]

In New Orleans, where local authorities sided with the AFL, the city witnessed a sustained campaign of police and vigilante violence. The NMU's Blackie Myers recalled that "cops were meeting all trains and busses on the lookout for CIO organizers." Myers evaded this police dragnet by getting "a little Cajun girl to waltz off [the bus] with me, and I squeezed this twist right past them." But eventually he was arrested on a trumped-up vagrancy charge and sentenced to twenty-nine days in jail. Another organizer reported that "our halls have been raided about a dozen times in the last 10 days." In one instance, "the chief of police led a raid on the NMU hall for the purpose of seizing leaflets which we had been distributing" and "arrested 120 of our

people." When the CIO encroached on AFL jurisdiction by organizing previously unorganized teamsters and striking for union recognition, the AFL
equipped strong-arm men with baseball bats and unleashed them on the CIO
picket lines. This tactic failed to break the strike, so "the police started
wholesale arrests of our pickets," organizer Bob Robertson reported. Robertson himself had his spine fractured in two places. Another CIO official, Felix
Siren, was taken to police headquarters, where he was spread-eagled on the
floor and beaten for about fifteen minutes by an officer who stood six-foot-
four and weighed close to 250 pounds. After his release, Siren was ordered
out of town and told that he "had no business coming down to New Orleans in
the first place, telling the 'niggers' about their rights."[5]

Through all of this mayhem, both the AFL and the CIO continued to win
converts. (Organized labor gained nearly three million new members from
1935 to 1939.) Finally, in 1938, after the failure of several rounds of peace
negotiations, Lewis and his aides ratified what had become a practical fact by
officially transforming the CIO into a new labor federation, the Congress of
Industrial Organizations.[6]

The AFL-CIO split did not cause the divisions within the Maritime Federation. But it became the instrument for deepening these cleavages and render-
ing them permanent. Harry Lundeberg, in particular, seized upon the conflict
as a means of furthering his own strategic and ideological objectives.
Although he labored in Bridges's shadow, Lundeberg would play a far more
volatile role in the unraveling of the Maritime Federation. He was becoming—perhaps had always been—a peculiar combination of white-hot
hatred and cold calculation. Thus the monumental force of his anticommunism also served the pragmatic purpose of defending the SUP's jurisdiction in
an uncertain economic environment.

Sailors on the Pacific Coast had often confronted a swollen labor market. In
the middle and late 1930s, there were 23,000 members of the seafaring unions
but a maximum of 16,300 jobs at any one time. The practice of job rotation
equalized available work, but the membership's commitment to this innovation would be severely tested if the job market were to shrink even further.
Already the vital lumber trade faced potentially devastating competition from
railroads and long-haul trucking. By the late 1940s the devastation would be
nearly complete. Meanwhile, the reappearance of jurisdictional battles with
longshoremen on the steam schooners awakened ancient fears and heightened
craft sensibilities; and the emergence of the National Maritime Union raised
the specter of additional encroachments on the SUP's troubled terrain. In
Lundeberg's mind, Harry Bridges, Joe Curran, and their respective unions all
became tainted with communism and committed to the destruction of the
SUP. Since they also affiliated with the CIO, he would come to regard the
organization as an instrument of Communist trade union objectives and
therefore an enemy to be fought at every turn. Conversely, the once-despised

AFL old guard would become a powerful ally in his recurring warfare against rival waterfront unions. Increasingly, the rhetoric of syndicalism would rationalize the pursuit of business unionism.[7]

Initially, however, Lundeberg greeted the formation of Lewis's committee with genuine enthusiasm, in part because it came at a time when he faced a parallel crisis of his own. In January 1936, as the AFL-CIO controversy was gathering momentum, the leadership of the International Seamen's Union revoked the charter of the SUP, expelling the Sailors from both the ISU and the AFL. The international union justified this action on the grounds that the SUP was harboring dual unionists (Communists), violating agreements with employers, and refusing to reinstate Paul Scharrenberg as a member in good standing in spite of numerous orders to do so. The ISU initiated legal proceedings to seize all of the SUP's property; it forced the removal of SUP delegates from AFL central labor councils, and announced its intention to organize a new sailors' affiliate on the West Coast.

But the embattled SUP launched a fierce counterattack. Its lawyers successfully warded off ISU challenges in the courts, and the union leadership waged a dramatically effective campaign to have every member sign a card pledging his continued loyalty. Of great symbolic value was the continued and outspoken allegiance of two of the union's pioneers: Nicholas Jortall, a founding member of the Coast Seamen's Union in 1885; and Walter Macarthur, the eminently respectable white-shirt sailor. At the SUP's fifty-first anniversary celebration, Macarthur denounced the men in control of the international as union-busters, and scornfully dismissed their effort to build a new sailors' affiliate on the coast. "The mountain labored," he said, "and brought forth a mouse!"

The ISU was forced to seek a face-saving compromise. Its leadership offered to reissue a charter to the SUP, but only on the condition that the Sailors abide by the terms of a new ISU constitution that weakened the autonomy of its affiliated unions, strengthened the hand of the international officers, and included other provisions that were deeply offensive to the West Coast militants. Characteristically, Lundeberg and his allies refused to accept this offer. The new constitution had been ratified at the ISU convention after the expulsion of SUP delegates whose votes might have defeated it. Thus they denounced it as illegal, and argued that the document was all the more unacceptable because it seemed to prohibit affiliation with the Maritime Federation of the Pacific. While expressing a desire to rejoin both the ISU and the AFL on an honorable basis, the SUP leaders eagerly embraced the Committee for Industrial Organization and became outspoken advocates of industrial unionism. They even proposed a merger of the SUP with the Marine Cooks and Stewards and the Marine Firemen to form one seamen's union on the West Coast.[8]

Harry Bridges and his allies responded to these developments far more cautiously than Lundeberg. While denouncing the ISU for revoking the sailors' charter, Bridges maintained that reaffiliation with the AFL—"the only organized body of workers in the nation"—was an absolute necessity that would require certain compromises with the ISU leadership. He argued that the ISU was operating from a position of weakness and therefore would not make an issue of the SUP's allegiance to the Maritime Federation. Moreover, he pointed to the West Coast ILA as proof that progressives could work within even the most reactionary AFL unions. Above all, Bridges and his associates argued that affiliation with the AFL was a matter of principle. As Henry Schmidt put it, "Any program for establishing independent Unions [is] a bit unpopular as far as the I.L.A. is concerned; we're still for the A.F. of L., the recognized Labor Movement in America."[9]

In articulating their views, Bridges and Schmidt had an agressive ally in the Communist party, which had finally discarded its policy of dual unionism and was now firmly committed to working within the AFL. Although the Communists offered virtually unequivocal support to Lewis and the AFL's industrial union bloc, they warned against the danger of "withdrawals or splits or expulsions." The *Maritime Worker,* a Party publication on the San Francisco waterfront, greeted the prediction that the CIO would evolve into a new labor federation with the statement that "nothing could be further from the truth." Communists aggressively campaigned for the reaffiliation of the sailors with the ISU on the terms offered by the international union; and Bridges echoed a common opinion among CP members and sympathizers when he warned the Sailors' Union against standing outside the AFL and expressing a "'holier than thou' attitude."[10]

In auto and steel, the Communists threw themselves into the campaign for industrial unionism with great enthusiasm. But in the maritime industry they displayed a new sensitivity to the long history of craft separation and called for a step-by-step movement toward the formation of an industrial union. The first step, they argued, must be "the strengthening of the individual craft unions and the advancement of the fight for democracy and progressive policies in these unions." By following this path, said Roy Hudson, "the workers will soon be able to achieve a National Maritime Federation"; and on the basis of that experience they would presumably see the necessity of "amalgamating all their forces into one powerful, compact industrial union." It was this cautious, incremental approach that led *Voice* editor Barney Mayes to condemn the Communist party as "an enemy of militant industrial unionism." But Party members eagerly embraced this new line and denounced criticism from Trotskyists, Wobblies, and the SUP leadership as "idle talk" and the "spittoon philosophizing of sectarians."[11]

Given the Communists' record of dual unionism and ultraleft posturing during the Third Period, it is hardly surprising that some seamen responded to their new stance with surprise and anger. One Lundeberg ally in the SUP declared, "It is strange that the very ones who holler the loudest today about staying within the A.F. of L. and who advise that we take the charter back at any price are the self same group who up to about a year ago were knocking the A.F. of L., the Sailors' Union, and everybody in general. They used to be unanimous about breaking up the A.F. of L. unions on the coast. Now they are holier than the holiest."[12]

An SUP meeting warned that "anyone aiding or abetting the reactionary I.S.U. officials in their war against the Sailors' Union of the Pacific [will] be classed as enemies of the S.U.P." In the eyes of Lundeberg and his supporters, it had come to this: the Communists and Bridges were acting in concert with "the Scharrenberg machine"; they were sabotaging the campaign for militant industrial unionism; they were "enemies of the S.U.P." But the CIO seemed to offer a principled program and a reliable ally. Like the SUP, it stood foursquare for industrial unionism. Like the SUP, its affiliated unions were being pushed out of the AFL. Throughout 1936 and well into 1937, Lundeberg seemed to believe that he and his sailors had everything to gain by aligning themselves with the CIO. And important forces within the CIO apparently reciprocated this enthusiasm. Len De Caux, the editor of the *CIO News* and a Bridges ally, recalled that CIO director John Brophy initially favored Lundeberg over Bridges on the West Coast because he regarded the longshoreman as "too AFL-minded."[13]

In the midst of the 1936–37 maritime strike, autoworkers sat down in two Fisher Body plants in Flint, Michigan, touching off a nationwide confrontation with the powerful General Motors Corporation. The United Auto Workers held GM's plants for forty-four days, with the full support of John L. Lewis and the CIO. The UAW's victory brought hundreds of thousands of workers into the new auto union. It was followed by a quieter but equally historic development when U.S. Steel, bastion of the open shop, signed a contract with Lewis and the Steel Workers Organizing Committee. Suddenly the CIO had moved from grandiose idea to established fact. It had defeated the GM colossus in open combat; it had brought U.S. Steel to terms without a strike. It seemed to be a victorious army on a long march through America's industrial heartland; and at every way station eager recruits were coming forward to enlist in the campaign.

As the dust settled from their own ninety-nine-day strike, maritime workers took stock of the CIO's seemingly relentless advance in the winter and spring of 1937. At first, Lundeberg and other SUP spokesmen were more enthused than ever. When the leadership of the now disintegrating ISU offered to restore the SUP charter on the Sailors' terms, Lundeberg greeted their capitulation with disdain and moved to take a referendum vote on affiliating with the CIO. The new SUP newspaper, *West Coast Sailors,* asked: "Do we want to accept the old ISU crew and the AFL representatives? Or do we . . . want to follow under the banner of the CIO and the ideals of progressive industrial unionism?"[14]

With this referendum as a bargaining chip, Lundeberg hoped Lewis would grant him a charter that would make the SUP the nucleus of a national seamen's union. But even as he negotiated with Lewis, Lundeberg witnessed a series of developments that would dramatically alter his attitude toward the new federation. First and foremost, there was the emergence of the National Maritime Union (NMU) and its bid for affiliation with the CIO. The collapse of the East Coast rank-and-file seamen's strike in 1937 had not marked the end of the insurgent movement. On the contrary, the bankruptcy of the ISU officials was now more apparent than ever to the majority of seamen on the Atlantic and Gulf coasts. And in the course of the spring and fall strikes, a stable corps of new leaders had emerged. The group was headed by Joe Curran, a veteran sailor with a rough exterior and more than his share of natural ability and native cunning. Richard Boyer described him as a man with "a head like a block of granite, a loud, angry voice, and the attitude of someone struggling against an impulse towards mayhem." In spite of this ferocious demeanor, he was immensely popular with the rank and file. Curran was surrounded by Jack Lawrenson, Blackie Myers, and Ferdinand Smith— all of them Communists, experienced seamen, and gifted mass leaders. Also present were crimson-Red MWIU veterans Al Lannon and Tommy Ray, providing the benefit of their considerable organizing skill and an additional touch of controversy. (For years Ray was attacked as the "commissar" behind Curran.)[15]

Ironically, the AFL executive council played a role in rescuing the ISU insurgents from the defeat they had suffered in their recent "outlaw" strike. In response to the spectacular momentum of the CIO, the AFL leaders finally began listening to the long-standing charge that the top officials of the International Seamen's Union were corrupt, incompetent, and undemocratic. By endorsing the rank-and-file demand for fair elections, they strengthened the insurgents' claim to legitimacy.

But the AFL's intervention was too little, too late. The pace of events relentlessly drove the East Coast militants toward the formation of a new union. For one thing, ISU officials sought to block every attempt by the rank-and-file movement to work within the channels of the International Seamen's Union. "Emperor" David Grange even secured a court injunction forbidding the insurgents from using the ISU's name. Gradually, the Curran forces began demanding that the shipowners recognize their Rank-and-File Committee instead of the "paper leadership" of the ISU. They backed up their demand with a series of job actions, particularly on the vessels of the International Mercantile Marine Company (IMM). According to Elinore Herrick of the National Labor Relations Board, New York harbor was soon in a state of "indescribable turmoil." On May 4, 1937, in order to restore "the foreign and domestic commerce of the United States and the peace of the community," the IMM agreed to secure its crews from the Rank-and File Committee's new hiring hall in New York City. The next day Curran announced the formation of the National Maritime Union. NMU spokesmen made it clear that they intended to cast their lot with the CIO.[16]

The SUP leadership regarded the NMU with contempt and distrust from the very beginning. They criticized the new union because it did not immediately establish a carbon copy of the SUP's referendum democracy, and because NMU officials willingly embraced seamen who had been finks during the recent strikes. They continually belittled the uneven but often heroic struggle waged on the East Coast. At the very moment when Atlantic Coast seamen were engaging in a wave of sit-downs and job actions, Lundeberg was declaring that conditions on intercoastal vessels—"those crumby tubs that come drifting in here from the East Coast"—had been improved only as a result of struggle waged by the Pacific Coast unions. "We filled those ships with West Coast men and doused them with job action until the owners finally knew we meant business. . . . In not one instance were the conditions on those ships improved on the East Coast! Always on the West Coast!"[17]

Basically, the SUP spokesmen were unwilling to acknowledge the greater complexity of the East Coast situation. The Atlantic and Gulf Coast seamen were a much larger and more heterogeneous group than their West Coast counterparts. Race, nationality, and regional loyalties had proven far more divisive in the East than in the West. Moreover, the great battles that had galvanized the consciousness of the West Coast rank and file had not had the same impact on the Atlantic Coast. The most heroic of the eastern strikes had ended in defeat. After a sustained display of courage, the majority of the men had "finked out" during the recent Fall Strike. To treat them as pariahs would have placed the new union in opposition to the majority of its potential constituency and would perhaps have driven many seamen back into the arms of the ISU.

All of these facts were perfectly plain, and they dictated a strategy of cautious consolidation among the diverse ranks of the East Coast seamen. But the SUP leaders were blind to this reality. Their view was colored by jurisdictional rivalry, by West Coast provincialism and lingering Wobbly sectarianism, and above all by hatred of the Communist "commissars" who were a vital part of the Curran group. The depth of this hatred is evident from Harry Lundeberg's response to a meeting with Joe Curran in April 1937, shortly before the formation of the NMU. Curran approached Lundeberg to acknowledge his discontent with the Communists' insistence on working within the ISU. He had come to believe that a new union was necessary. He wanted Lundeberg's advice and the SUP's support for such a move.

It must have been an extraordinary meeting, because Curran had the reputation of being as strong-willed and self-righteous as Lundeberg; and as chief rivals for the leadership of the nation's seamen the two men had exchanged many an insult in the recent past. Gilbert Mers, who was the only other person present, recalls: "Curran made his pitch. He was looking for allies, he said, and he would most of all like an alliance with the SUP. He was becoming more and more convinced that the theory of capturing the ISU machinery was not going to work to the benefit of the seamen. He believed that the seamen should form a new union. He sought Lundeberg's and the SUP's support for such a move."

Lundeberg interrupted with the charge that Curran's collaboration with the Reds made him an unworthy ally. Curran readily acknowledged that he had aligned himself with the Communist faction in the East Coast rank-and-file movement, but pointed out that his goal now was to win support for a program that was diametrically opposed to the Party line. Mers then joined the fray. He and Curran argued that a better program, and not Red-baiting, was the only principled way to oppose the Communists. They pointed out that conditions on the Atlantic and Gulf coasts were different from those on the Pacific. But to no avail. Lundeberg "wouldn't budge." By the spring of 1937 he was implacably hostile to the Communists and, perhaps, to any potential rival on the waterfront no matter what his ideological bent. At the moment when he was reaching out to embrace the CIO, the Sailors' Union leader had made anticommunism the linchpin of any alliance.[18]

As for Curran, Lundeberg may have left him with no place else to go, but the Communists made it easier for him when they recognized the inevitable and enthusiastically embraced the campaign to build the National Maritime Union. In spite of the SUP leadership's contempt, the NMU rapidly developed into a major force on the waterfront. Speaking to the Maritime Federation convention in June 1937, Jack Lawrenson estimated that as ships docked in eastern and Gulf ports, men were transferring their books to the new union at the rate of three thousand a week. To secure formal recognition of this process, the NMU had already petitioned the NLRB for representation elections at several steamship companies. In what Irving Bernstein has called "an expression of the death wish," the ISU requested elections on sixty additional lines, allowing the NMU to consolidate its gains in spectacular fashion. At International Mercantile Marine, the NMU received 2,563 votes to the ISU's 170. At the Luckenbach Steamship Company, the tally was NMU 436, ISU 8; on the Black Diamond line the ISU received only a single vote. Altogether the NMU polled 18,947 votes and secured recognition from fifty-two shipping lines, while the ISU received 3,015 votes and carried only six lines. By the end of the year the new union would claim 47,325 dues-paying members on the Atlantic and Gulf coasts, about six times the membership of the SUP. Even so, the NMU's attitude toward its West Coast counterpart remained conciliatory, until the SUP made it clear that conciliation was impossible.[19]

Meanwhile, the momentum of events was also pulling Harry Bridges in the direction of the CIO. Bridges had always praised the CIO, while insisting that its stated goal of organizing the unorganized must be accomplished within the framework of the AFL. Moreover, he had worked long and hard to maintain friendly ties with many AFL representatives on the West Coast, in the hope of winning them for a policy of amalgamation and evolution toward industrial unionism. In the course of a prolonged and sometimes violent jurisdictional dispute between the CIO-affiliated Industrial Union of Marine and Shipbuilding Workers (IUMSWA) and several AFL Metal Trades unions, Bridges had consistently sided with the AFL. The top officials of the Marine and Shipbuilding Workers were members of the Socialist party, but Bridges allegedly attacked them as "Trotskyites" and declared that "the I.U.M.S.W.A. NATIONALLY has got to be broken." The union's leadership complained bitterly to John L. Lewis that "the controlling elements in the Maritime Federation are fanatically devoted to a policy that runs counter to everything that the CIO is trying to accomplish." They charged that "every kind of lying propaganda, professional thugs, newspaper statements and slander has been used to break down our organization," and that "all these actions have been promoted and pushed by the ILA and the Maritime Federation under the personal direction of Harry Bridges." Bridges, in particular, "has stated his policy very clearly, 'to bring the CIO unions back into the AF of L,' " and "try to bore from within" the federation, with the goal of establishing "industrial unionism by amalgamation sometime in the distant future." Finally, after ILA Ship Scalers and IUMSWA members had come to blows on San Francisco's Matson docks in March 1937, John Brophy wired Bridges with the complaint that "this action will not help [the] union movement and assuredly is not advancing the program and policies of the CIO."[20]

At the ILA's Pacific District convention in April, Bridges reaffirmed his support for the CIO and its objectives, but stated that the ILA would remain within the AFL. By June, however, with industrial warfare raging in many of the nation's steel towns, Bridges and his allies seemed to throw caution to the winds. According to one of his critics, the longshoreman "tried to drive everyone . . . into the AF of L . . . , right up until April and May of this year. Then overnight he suddenly switched to the CIO and tried to stampede everyone into it." The *Voice of the Federation* now characterized the AFL as "a dead corpse" and equated it with "reaction, fascism, and barbarism." Bridges returned from a conference with John L. Lewis to announce that "the tremendous march of the C.I.O. in the middle west and East is sweeping everything before it." He called upon his fellow unionists to set aside "petty differences" and help "organize the greatest trade union movement this nation has ever seen."[21]

Obviously, Lundeberg did not welcome the news that his chief rival was no longer "too AFL-minded." But he could take comfort from the reports of SUP official Bob Stowell, whom he had dispatched to Washington, D.C., to confer with Lewis and other "people that count." Stowell indicated that the Sailors could depend on the support of an impressive array of forces in their quest for a CIO charter. In the first place there was CIO Vice President Sidney Hillman, who did not share Lewis's equanimity about working with Communists. "I've already got some powerful factors at work," Stowell wrote, "getting it over to Lewis that to play with Bridges and Curran is to invite trouble and criticism for himself." Second, there was John R. Steelman, a high-ranking Department of Labor representative who was officially neutral but in reality was encouraging the SUP to engage in a nationwide organizing campaign. Third, and more surprising, was the apparent support of Joe Ryan. Stowell reported that "Joe Ryan has been here talking to Lewis." The ILA president apparently told Lewis that he could easily imagine a situation where the East Coast ILA and a CIO-affiliated SUP would "find themselves in the same camp." Clearly Ryan was toying with the CIO in the hope that the SUP could be used as a weapon to destroy the Communist-led National Maritime Union on the Atlantic and Gulf coasts.[22]

Finally, Stowell reported on the activities of an even more unlikely ally, the shipowners. The SUP official had several friendly meetings with a representative of the United Fruit Company who assured him that a growing number of East Coast shipping lines were favorably disposed toward the Sailors' Union. The jurisdictional battle between the ISU and the NMU was tying up one ship after another, and Stowell reported that the constant "gorilla warfare . . . has gotten the operators into a place where they would go for the devil himself if he could straighten this mess out." But it was not simply a matter of turning to the "devil himself," for Stowell also reported that the "West Coast owners have given us a great boost with the East Coast owners."[23]

Why would the Pacific Coast shipowners be singing the praises of Harry Lundeberg? Only a few months earlier they had been determined to remove him from the leadership of the SUP. They had repeatedly expressed the belief that peaceful collective bargaining was impossible on the West Coast as long as he and "men of [his] philosophy and tactics" remained at the helm of the maritime unions. But something must have happened during the 1936–37 strike to change their minds. Twenty years later Roger Lapham recalled that in the midst of the strike, Assistant Secretary of Labor Edward McGrady had come to the American-Hawaiian offices and said, "Lundeberg would like to talk to you." First, the sailor spoke with Thomas G. Plant, an American-

Hawaiian executive and spokesman for the Waterfront Employers' Association. "Tom took him up to my office," said Lapham. "Had an hour or two with him." Then Lapham conferred with Lundeberg, and "in no time at all they had an agreement worked out." Implicitly or explicitly, Lundeberg must have given the owners assurances that a long-term accommodation was possible, and this apparently had paved the way for the employers' sudden reversal on the strike's "big stumbling block," union control of hiring. Stowell gave an indication of the new attitude on both sides when he wrote, "These people back here have faith in Harry, and now that I have come in here and don't go around raising hell and calling everyone fakers and preaching the overthrow of the existing order of things, they think maybe the SUP is OK."[24]

In the final analysis, however, the issue of a CIO charter would be decided by John L. Lewis. What did he think? Lewis had led Lundeberg to believe that the Sailors would receive a charter. But there is no evidence that he agreed to Lundeberg's terms, and in the meantime circumstances had changed dramatically. First, there was Bridges's apparent willingness to bring the West Coast ILA into the CIO. This made Lundeberg and the SUP less important as an opening wedge on the Pacific Coast. Second, the seamen's situation was ripening day by day. With the imminent collapse of the ISU, the emergence of the National Maritime Union, and the existence of at least six other seafaring organizations that were potential CIO affiliates, Lewis sought to bring as many of these unions together as he could. He must have recognized that Lundeberg could not play a unifying role among these diverse forces. Moreover, while the SUP was the best organized of the seafaring unions, the membership of the fledgling NMU was already far larger. As for the Communists in the NMU and Bridges's ILA, Lewis was supremely confident of his ability to use the Reds for his own purposes. As he allegedly put it to an anxious CIO colleague, "Who gets the bird, the hunter or the dog?"[25]

While Stowell was plotting SUP strategy in Washington, CIO Director John Brophy came to Portland to address the Maritime Federation convention. He recalled that the delegates were men who "had been through the union wars, they had studied the problems of organized labor, and many had been steeped in the radical press for years. They missed very little." Brophy spoke for an hour in the morning and answered a barrage of questions for most of the afternoon. In regard to the longshoremen, he stated that the West Coast ILA could receive a CIO charter immediately, without waiting for the Ryan-controlled Atlantic and Gulf Coast districts to come along. Among the seamen, however, there were progressive organizations on both coasts, and therefore "the important thing is for those groups to come together in unity and make a joint application to the C.I.O." Above all, Brophy emphasized what seemed to him a sensible and basic principle, namely, that the majority must rule. Here his experience as a coal miner had not prepared him to understand the waterfront's long legacy of craft separation and the jurisdictional fears and jealousies that were now regaining momentum. As he said at one point, "Craft unionism [versus] industrial unionism has never been an issue in the Mine Workers Union. Miners accept industrial unionism as naturally as they breathe." When one delegate expressed the fear that within the CIO "smaller organizations [would] be governed by the dictates of the larger one," Brophy replied, "I don't get the point of emphasizing differences. The majority may impose its will on the minority. That is the rule in any association."[26]

Lundeberg and the SUP delegates listened to Brophy with increasing skepticism and hostility. Unlike the coal miner, the sailors were all too familiar with what they regarded as the tyranny of the majority. They saw it in the numerical superiority that gave the longshoremen so much leverage in the Maritime Federation, and in the lengthening shadow of the NMU. Although Lundeberg continued to pay lip service to the ideals of industrial unionism, he was becoming increasingly preoccupied with the right of his men to autonomy and self-determination in any larger affiliation they might opt for. And the SUP leader was finally coming to the point of stating openly that "the question of amalgamating seamen and shoreworkers . . . is definitely out. The seamen must at all times have the right to run their own business without the domination of shoreworkers."[27]

Right after Brophy spoke to the Maritime Federation convention, Lundeberg wired Lewis to inform him that the vote on the affiliation of the SUP with the CIO was being terminated. This placed Lundeberg in an embarrassing position. He had predicted, and virtually everyone assumed, that the Sailors' Union referendum would result in an overwhelming endorsement of the CIO. But the SUP leadership saw the sailors' vote more as a bargaining chip than as an exercise in rank-and-file democracy. They were prepared to enter the CIO only on their own terms, which meant that they would be free to dominate or even exclude Bridges, Curran, and the Communists. (Brophy recalled that in two long conversations with Lundeberg, the sailor "stuck to it that he would not join [the CIO] if Bridges did.") Lewis, however, had no interest in excluding potential allies. He wanted to cast the net of CIO affiliation as widely as possible. Thus he proposed a CIO-sponsored maritime conference for early July 1937 in Washington, D.C., where delegates from every marine union except the disintegrating ISU and the Ryan leadership of the ILA would seek to resolve their differences and move toward the formation of a national maritime federation. After such a meeting, Lewis would issue as many CIO charters as circumstances required.[28]

At the time, Lewis was deeply involved in the bloody Little Steel strike and in fending off charges that the CIO was a Communist-inspired attempt at insurrection. Thus the task of preparing for a CIO maritime conference fell to Brophy and Mervyn Rathborne, a college-educated Englishman who was president of the American Radio Telegraphists Association. Rathborne was then a member of the Communist party, but Frances Perkins remembered him fondly as a "pink-cheeked, blond-haired, blue-eyed Englishman, who looks more like a boy at Winchester than like a grown man working for his living." He and Brophy were reputed to be the brains behind the CIO maritime conference. The plan they developed, which the conference participants eventually endorsed, had two key objectives: first, to bring as much of the ILA as possible into the CIO; and second, to create one national seamen's union through a merger of the existing seafarers' organizations. Although reasonable enough in theory, the practical effect of the Brophy-Rathborne proposal was to further alienate Joe Ryan and Harry Lundeberg from the CIO. At Bridges's insistence, the document declared that a CIO-affiliated long-shoremen's union would "actively cooperate with all maritime unions at all times," and would resolve matters of national importance by a referendum of the entire ILA membership. For Ryan, acceptance of such terms could have been tantamount to suicide. If he ever remotely contemplated joining the CIO, Bridges's attempt to remold the national ILA in the image of its Pacific Coast district quickly dissuaded him.[29]

Lundeberg faced a knottier problem. On the surface, the Brophy-Rathborne proposal seemed to embody principles that he and his associates claimed as their own. But in reality it threatened to wreck the SUP on the shoals of ideological and jurisdictional conflict. Whereas Lundeberg had hoped that the CIO would rescue the Sailors' Union from its growing isolation, it now appeared that CIO affiliation would align him with maritime unionists whom he despised and distrusted. Moreover, a national seamen's union in which the majority ruled would favor the East Coast and would perhaps mean the liquidation of the SUP as an autonomous entity. As Bob Stowell wrote from Washington, "This is a case where the very life of the union is at stake. If we are gobbled up by that group, with voting strength centered in the East, all our jurisdictional problems will be immediately settled—in favor of the people who are trying to encroach on our jurisdiction."[30]

As the date of the CIO maritime conference approached, Stowell warned Lundeberg in a letter, "WE'VE GOT TO DO SOMETHING AND DO IT PRETTY DAMNED SOON." On July 4, three days before the conference was scheduled to begin, he suggested a bold plan whose implementation would have presented the CIO with a dramatic ultimatum. "The stage is all set for us to take over the works," he wrote,

IF WE GO INTO ACTION RIGHT AWAY. . . . The solution is for us to immediately launch [a] national organization campaign. . . . The first step would be to vote to remain independent for the time being unless Lewis offers us the charter right away. Second step would be to change the name of the Union to allow for national organization, something like Sailors Union of the Pacific, Atlantic and

Gulf. Third step would be a whirlwin[d] publicity campaign on the East Coast and East Coast ships before these [NLRB] elections are held back here.

But Lundeberg was not yet prepared to follow such a course. For the moment he chose to remain aloof. The Sailors' Union virtually abstained from participating in Lewis's maritime conference, thereby shattering any hope of creating a national seamen's union under the auspices of the CIO.[31]

John Brophy recalled in later years that when Lewis sent him to Portland to address the Maritime Federation convention, "he just told me to go out there and try to get both Bridges and Lund[e]berg, but to take either one if it had to be a choice." The contemporary record indicates, however, that it was much more than a matter of taking potluck. Lewis and Brophy labored diligently and skillfully to bring a broad coalition of maritime unions into the CIO. They succeeded with Bridges because he now shared their objectives; he also represented a larger base and could claim a more formidable set of allies than Lundeberg. In this sense, as Brophy acknowledged, "there was no choice on the Coast." By July the CIO director was prepared to swallow his reservations about the controversial Aussie. Ignoring the not so distant past, he announced that "Harry Bridges has cooperated very completely with us to advance the program of the C.I.O." Brophy declared, moreover, that any attempt to Red-bait the longshore leader would be "very speedily repudiated by us."[32]

Although Bridges was the man the CIO was looking for on the coast, he did not come easy; for "he was very tough, just as tough as Lewis." First, he demanded that Lewis appoint him West Coast director of the CIO. Then he insisted upon approaching Ryan with a proposal to bring the entire ILA into the new federation. Although he attached conditions that Ryan could not possibly accept, Bridges was not merely being coy or deceitful. Rather, he was deeply concerned about questions of democratic procedure and institutional legitimacy. According to Louis Goldblatt, he even made "a straightforward proposition to Joe Ryan to take a national referendum in the ILA on whether to go into the CIO. If the majority voted [no], we wouldn't go in either." Of course, Ryan couldn't accept such an offer. He had never allowed a referendum on anything. But it was characteristic of Bridges that he sought to pursue his objectives in the broadest possible arena. In the early days he had rejected the MWIU, in spite of his sympathy for the Communists, because he saw that the Red union was isolated and sectarian. Likewise, with the formation of Lewis's Committee for Industrial Organization, he had tempered his enthusiasm for the CIO's goals with the recognition that in the eyes of millions of workers the AFL still wore the mantle of legitimacy. Now that the CIO's momentum seemed irresistible, and the AFL's stance utterly reactionary, he was prepared to join the CIO. But he wanted to pursue this historic course in a way that would persuade the greatest possible number of workers and their unions to do likewise.

Unfortunately, however, Bridges's powers of persuasion were limited by "the political complexion of his most ardent supporters," and by his own abrasive style. Richard Neuberger noted his habit of referring to trade union opponents as "Trotskyite stooges" and "Hearst agents." And Benjamin Carwardine, San Francisco organizer for the Marine and Shipbuilding Workers' union, warned that "opposition to the CIO on the west coast is now based on personal opposition to Bridges, and even more, on antagonism to the Communist Party." Carwardine was exaggerating only slightly when he declared that "all the enemies of Bridges and his faction have now automatically become enemies of the CIO."[33]

Bridges and his allies emerged from the Washington, D.C., maritime conference with a quickened sense of hope and determination, and more than a few illusions about the irresistible power of their movement. Almost immediately a campaign was launched "to organize all Longshoremen into the C.I.O.," which meant confronting Joe Ryan in his heavily fortified New York stronghold. Mervyn Rathborne, secretary of the new CIO Maritime Committee, asked Lewis to bankroll a staff of twenty-five organizers on the Atlantic and Gulf Coast waterfronts. B. B. Jones, a San Francisco longshoreman and Communist party member, was dispatched to New York, and veteran Communist Al Lannon took leave of the NMU to head up the campaign with Jones. By late August they claimed that CIO groups were functioning in at least nine New York ILA locals, and Rathborne was reporting on favorable developments from Portland, Maine, to the Gulf of Mexico. He told Lewis, "Our progress to date has convinced us that the International Longshoremen's Association on the Atlantic and Gulf Coasts can be moved into the C.I.O. as a result of two or three months intensive work."[34]

But it was not to be. Ultimately, the CIO failed in its attempt to create national unions of seamen and stevedores. In spite of some flashes of excitement, the Atlantic and Gulf longshoremen remained largely insulated—sometimes forcibly so—from the appeal of the CIO. Even on the Pacific Coast, where the overwhelming majority of ILA members voted to join the CIO and form the International Longshoremen's and Warehousemen's Union (ILWU), dockworkers in Tacoma and two other Northwest ports refused to abandon the AFL. Among the West Coast seamen, it appeared that the dream of One Big Union was giving way to the fear of amalgamation. John Brophy was forced to send a letter assuring the president of the Maritime Federation that the CIO had "no intention of issuing a charter to longshoremen and seafaring crafts jointly" or of combining licensed officers and unlicensed maritime workers in the same union. But his reassuring words did not stem the tide of confusion and doubt, especially since it had become clear that the CIO was competing with the AFL for the allegiance of organized workers and their unions. The Maritime Federation had often criticized William Green and the AFL executive council as splitters and wreckers who were "sabotag[ing] the organization of the unorganized." Now, however, charges of disruption and even dictatorship were aimed at Lewis and the CIO. A San Pedro longshoreman warned that Lewis "is a dictator in his sphere, just as Hitler, Mussolini, and Stalin are in theirs." In August V. J. Malone, the secretary of the Marine Firemen's union, resigned from the CIO Maritime Committee because, he said, "a definite split has been caused in the West Coast maritime circles, and I do not want to do anything that will widen the breach." Malone informed Lewis that he would "consist[e]ntly endorse the C.I.O. program of [organizing] the unorganized, but when the program causes a breach in the organized, then I feel that I should have no part in it."[35]

In spite of Malone's defection, however, there were important gains for the CIO. The National Maritime Union, Marine Cooks and Stewards, Marine Engineers, Inlandboatmen, and Radio Telegraphists all voted to affiliate. For the moment, only Ryan's longshoremen and the Masters, Mates, and Pilots stayed with the AFL. The Pacific Coast Marine Firemen withdrew from the AFL, but Malone and his allies in the union were determined to remain independent of the CIO, even though the membership had voted over-whelmingly for CIO affiliation in a coastwide referendum. In the case of the SUP's referendum, the ballots were never counted; apparently they were burned. With characteristic belligerence, Lundeberg and his cohorts warned the CIO that anyone daring to tamper with the SUP's jurisdiction on the West Coast would be "shipped back to [John L. Lewis] in a 'wooden overcoat.' "[36]

For nearly a year after the CIO maritime conference SUP officials maintained that independence from both the AFL and the CIO was the only intelligent and principled course. While jealously guarding the jurisdictional claims of the West Coast sailors, the SUP declared itself a principled advocate of industrial unionism, in contrast to what it now characterized as the spurious pretense of the CIO. In a testament to unblinking self-righteousness, Lunde-berg and his associates argued that seamen "have been in the vanguard of the movement towards industrial unions for years," while the CIO was "com-pletely nullifying the industrial aspect" of unionism by allowing a host of local agreements in auto, rubber, and steel. Moreover, declared an SUP pamphlet, "the CIO has done nothing on the West Coast but create confusion and disunity." Thus, the union's recommendation to its membership was to "chart a course which will keep us as far away as possible" from the jurisdictional warfare between the rival federations.[37]

But as other maritime unions aligned themselves with one side or the other, Lundeberg discovered that the fruits of independence were isolation and weakness. The need for reliable allies became especially clear during a major dispute with the NMU in April 1938. When the Shepard line freighter *Sea Thrush* docked in San Francisco on April 19, it was manned by an NMU crew, even though the SUP claimed jurisdiction over all Shepard line vessels. The company was headquartered on the East Coast, but it sailed to Pacific Coast ports. The Sailors' Union maintained that it had first organized Shepard line ships in 1935 and had won a closed shop agreement in April 1937. Soon thereafter, however, the National Labor Relations Board had conducted representation elections on all East Coast shipping lines, and the NMU had routed the ISU in the Shepard line vote. (The SUP's name had not even appeared on the ballot.) The company then began hiring crews from the NMU hall, and the beef came to a head in San Francisco. The Sailors' Union declared the ship hot and greeted the *Sea Thrush* with a picket line at the pier.[38]

In the fratricidal climate of 1938, the CIO longshoremen could not stand by and watch CIO seamen forced off the vessel by a rival union. Thus the San Francisco stevedores crashed a massive SUP picket line of five hundred men. In the major riot that ensued it was fist against fist and baseball bat against cargo hook, with Lundeberg personally directing the sailors' side of the battle and supplying most of the bats.[39] After fifteen minutes of fighting, and numerous injuries, the longshoremen finally broke through the picket line and worked the ship. That was the end of the physical confrontation, but the damage to the dream of One Big Union was irreparable. As a Maritime Federation official put it, "Who struck the first blow no one will ever know and each side blames the other. The fact remains that regardless of who was right or who was wrong we found brother slugging brother. Men who were the best of friends before became bitter enemies later. Men who had suffered side by side and stood shoulder to shoulder on other picket lines now were battering each other down." The Sailors' Union withdrew from the Maritime Federation in June. Although the organization survived until 1941, it would never again be the instrument that Lundeberg, Bridges, and other militants had envisioned in 1935.[40]

The Shepard line beef finally convinced Lundeberg that independence was "no longer a sane course to steer." Jurisdictional warfare required loyal allies with substantial physical and financial resources, and various AFL affiliates had proven their mettle in the battles around the *Sea Thrush* and other Shepard line ships. ILA longshoremen had honored the SUP's picket lines in Tacoma, and the Teamsters had helped to beef up the Sailor's Union defenses in San Francisco. In addition, AFL central labor councils, which had expelled SUP delegates at the ISU's insistence in 1936, were now giving the Sailors "unqualified backing."[41]

In May 1938 the SUP leadership proposed a coastwide referendum on affiliation with the AFL, which they now characterized as "rejuvenated and

. . . once again a fighting force." "The A.F. of L. has adhered to the true principles of Labor," declared the leadership's resolution, "while the CIO has degenerated into the machine of a political party." Lundeberg made it clear that there was more at stake than the status of the West Coast sailors, as he called on the membership to "get ready for the new Seamen's Union of America, conducted on rank and file principles and backed by the progressive labor movement in America." Some SUP members undoubtedly balked at including such AFL luminaries as Joe Ryan and Seattle Teamsters' union boss Dave Beck in "the progressive labor movement of America." Lundeberg himself had often denounced Ryan as a strikebreaker, and the elegantly tailored Beck was famous for his declaration that "some of the finest people I know are employers." But Lundeberg now argued that "we can not be sentimental. Any Union, struggling for existence, must reinforce itself with available allies; not those that correspond to the IDEAL, but those ready to hand."[42]

The Seattle Sailors' branch opposed the leadership's recommendation by "an overwhelming standing vote." But it was approved by the other branches and carried by a big margin at the San Francisco headquarters meeting. In the coastwide referendum, 2,144 men favored affiliation with the AFL, while 927 voted to remain independent. The orphan SUP was about to adopt a parent.[43]

Lundeberg was in a strong position to dictate his terms for reaffiliation because, as he observed, the AFL was "in pretty rotten shape" among seamen. With the collapse of the ISU, Green had gathered the relatively small number of Atlantic and Gulf seamen who refused to join the NMU into a federal labor union, under the direction of some of the least savory hangovers from the ISU's palace guard. Lundeberg accused these men of "quite a lot of chiseling and racketeering," and complained that they were making "a laughing stock of the name of the A.F. of L." In October Green and the executive council met most of Lundeberg's terms. They dismantled their insipid federal labor union, buried the corpse of the ISU, and chartered the Seafarers' International Union of North America (SIU), with Lundeberg as president and the SUP as its nucleus. The SUP of course retained full autonomy in its internal affairs. In addition, Atlantic, Gulf, and Great Lakes districts were to be created and granted autonomy within a year. In these districts, the union would include deck, engine, and stewards' divisions, on the model of the NMU, which the SIU was meant to disrupt and ultimately destroy. The AFL pledged to support the new organization financially, and Green responded generously to Lundeberg's pleas for assistance.[44]

Once he decided to rejoin the AFL, Lundeberg went on the offensive. He was determined to defend and extend the jurisdiction of his sailors, to build an AFL seamen's union that would challenge the CIO in every one of the nation's ports, and to take the fight inland as well. Thus he sought to mold his sailors into an armada of volunteer organizers—and warriors—to serve as shock troops in the jurisdictional battles that were convulsing the West Coast and much of the nation. His growing anticommunism now became an all-encompassing mania; he justified his every action—including "goon squads, gun-play, black jacks, etc."—in these terms. Since in his mind the CIO had become an instrument of the Communist party, it was necessary to destroy the rival labor federation.[45]

These themes become especially clear in a series of letters and progress reports Lundeberg sent to William Green over a period of several years. In them fact and fantasy, special pleading, and dogmatic obsession merge to provide an accurate reflection of Lundeberg's worldview. He reported that in the bitter, often violent conflict between the AFL Brotherhood of Carpenters and the International Woodworkers of America in the Pacific Northwest, "we have been able to help quite a lot with effective work through our Seamen who sail the ships into the Lumber and Sawmill towns." He reminded Green that Alaska was close to the Soviet Union and was therefore of vital interest to the AFL not only from a trade union standpoint but from the standpoint of national security as well. Should the CIO succeed in its organizing campaign, he warned, "the Communist party of America will have enough stooges placed in various parts of Alaska to sabotage this country." But with typical bravado he reported that "the whole territory of Alaska could be organized into the A.F.L. in a short time with the aid of the Seamen." He even argued that Bridges's longshoremen "could be swung back to the A.F. of L." Summing up his organizing—and disorganizing—efforts over a three-year period, he informed Green that

the fight with the C.I.O. on the Pacific Coast has been hot and heavy. . . . The attitude of most A.F. of L. Unions has been that they would like to see the C.I.O. eliminated. But when it comes to actual fighting which, from time to time, might result in a busted nose or a broken arm, these Unions will not give any support outside of sympathy. . . . Without bragging, we can truthfully say that we have carried the brunt of the fight against the C.I.O. on the Pacific Coast. This has been tough and will continue to be tough until this Communist-controlled element is cleaned out.[46]

As president of an organization that claimed national jurisdiction, Lundeberg did not limit his field of vision to the Pacific Coast. In fact, some of his most belligerent and controversial forays came on the Atlantic and Gulf coasts, particularly in the Gulf. Here an anti-Communist faction within the NMU was spearheading a determined campaign to wrest leadership of the union from the Curran group. Called the Mariners' Club, or "Sea Gulls," this faction was made up of an odd assortment of conservative unionists, disgruntled office-seekers, and left-wing militants who shared the anticommunism of the Wobblies. Lundeberg seized upon this dissident movement to further his goal of disrupting the CIO and building his Seafarers' International

Union. To shore up his forces in the Gulf, he made peace with some of the ISU officials he had accused of "chiseling and racketeering" and making a "laughing stock" of the AFL. Finn Schefstad, a former associate of "Emperor" David Grange, had herded scabs through picket lines on the New Orleans waterfront during the Fall Strike of 1936–37. ISU troubleshooter Wilbur Dickey had shot and killed rank-and-file militant Johnny Kane in Houston during the same strike. Both of these men, along with several other notorious "fink herders" from the old regime, were placed on the SIU payroll in the Gulf.[47]

Apparently Lundeberg was prepared to sponsor and finance "organizing" activities that led to numerous physical confrontations and, directly or indirectly, to murder. In September 1939 an NMU official named Philip Carey was killed—beaten with chains and shot in the back—outside a New Orleans bar. William McCuistion, a former MWIUer who had become one of the Dies Committee's star anti-Communist witnesses, was arrested in 1940 and tried for the murder in January 1941. In a city where the press regularly denounced the CIO as an instrument of the Communist party, and with Congressman Dies playing an active role in his defense, McCuistion was acquitted without taking the witness stand. Some members of the jury apparently acknowledged his role in the murder but said they had acquitted him because he was "doing valuable work for the Dies Committee." McCuistion and three SIU organizers, who were implicated in the case and tried in 1942, received a number of cash payments from Lundeberg during the period surrounding the murder and the two trials.[48]

Lundeberg may have had no idea that men in the pay of the ISU would resort to murder (if indeed they did). But he was not one to shy away from violence. On the contrary, he was a proud participant in numerous jurisdictional brawls, and he wore his scars with pride. Explaining his absence from the AFL convention in 1940, he wrote to Green, "My jaw was smashed badly . . . by a piece of lead, or a blunt instrument during a recent fight we had with a CIO-Communist Party force" on the San Francisco waterfront. (Actually, he was leading a group of SUP members through an ILWU ship scaler's picket line.) With regard to the violence that led to the Carey murder, he asked Green to realize that "organizing in the Gulf, particularly in the seamen's field is no picnic, due to the fact that all kinds of tactics are used, such as goon squads, gun-play, black jacks, etc., which seems to be the order of the day. . . . This is indeed a strange way to organize, but . . . nowadays one must organize and deal with people as we find them—and according to circumstances."

Lundeberg, promised the AFL president that "within another month to six weeks—with hard work and fighting—the whole Gulf should be under the banner of the A.F. of L." But the results of his efforts did not justify such optimism, and Green eventually cut back on the AFL's financial support. By

February 1940 the SIU claimed three thousand members in the Gulf, six thousand on the East Coast, and eighteen hundred on the Great Lakes. Even if these figures are accurate, they indicate that the SIU was no more than an irritant to the National Maritime Union, which retained the allegiance of the vast majority of the Atlantic and Gulf Coast seamen.[49]

On the Pacific Coast, however, Lundeberg's SUP remained the most dynamic alternative to the unionism of Bridges and the ILWU. Although the rhetoric of syndicalism remained more or less constant, in practice the SUP was moving toward the hardheaded business unionism of Andrew Furuseth and the AFL. Thus it was fitting that when Furuseth died in January 1938, Lundeberg and the members of the Sailors' Union forgave him for recommending their expulsion from the ISU and adopted the legendary old man as the patron saint of the SUP.[50]

The new relationship with the employers, and the imperatives of jurisdictional warfare, required that the SUP membership march in step, unencumbered by the discordant strains of spontaneous insurgency aboard ship. More and more, it appeared necessary to impose program and discipline from the top. In a remarkable turnaround, Lundeberg began waging an aggressive campaign to eliminate unauthorized job actions. He had asserted in 1935 that "the workers on the job . . . know best when the time is right for job action"; those who attempted to place limits on its use were "trying their damndest to kill the seamen's strongest weapon." But the Sailors' Union chief began discarding his syndicalist principles during the 1936–37 strike. The new departure was highlighted by a July 1937 editorial in the *West Coast Sailors* under the title "Can We Discipline Ourselves?" The editorial warned against "the actions of irresponsible individuals" and concluded that "the Union will not tolerate bum beefs arising out of drunken brawls, and will take firm, disciplinary action against individuals . . . who do not heed the welfare of the union as a whole." A resolution passed later in the year instructed "all ships crews and ships delegates not to tie up or delay the sailing of any ship in any port whatsoever unless so authorized" by the membership at a headquarters meeting. In a radical departure from their previous position, Lundeberg and his associates took the stand that beefs should be "settled by the officials who have been duly elected for just such purposes." When a steam schooner crew pulled a job action in June 1938, Lundeberg rushed to the scene, and as he later reported, "I told them that it was damn foolishness to stick around and picket or sitdown aboard the ship to get what they had coming, because that was my job—to get that for them and to handle their beef, and instead of contacting me to do the work, they were sitting down and grand-standing on a so-called picket line."

This trend toward the suppression of spontaneous militancy and shipboard democracy culminated in 1942 with a policy change that removed the membership's right to elect ships' delegates. Henceforth port agents and patrolmen would have the prerogative of appointing a delegate aboard ship "as they know the best men fitted to be delegate and the best interests of the SUP." The *West Coast Sailors* argued that the new policy would eliminate "the drunken type of delegate."[51]

While men who engaged in militant action aboard ship were increasingly characterized as drunks, those who offered more than an occasional gripe at union meetings were labeled commies. The charge of communism served to delegitimize and intimidate anyone who dared to challenge Lundeberg and other elected officials. Those who refused to be deterred by this accusation were often subjected to more direct means of intimidation. SUP beef squads became a familiar part of the waterfront scene. As Seattle port agent Maxie Weisbarth acknowledged, "Guys that talk off the point, to stir up trouble," are asked to "sit down," and if they don't, "we get a couple of guys [to] throw them out." One young sailor received forty stitches in his face after a "couple of guys" worked him over.[52]

Lundeberg's anticommunism took an especially macabre turn in the summer of 1938. At issue was the status of six SUP members who were fighting with the International Brigades in Spain. At first the SUP leadership had enthusiastically supported the loyalist cause, but by 1938 their increasingly fanatical anticommunism made such support impossible. A long article by Sam Usinger in the *West Coast Sailors* argued that "the Communists have sabotaged and sold out the workers in Spain, in the interests of the Fascists and the Landowning class." Usinger apparently had spent several months in Barcelona in the company of Spanish anarchists and disenchanted Americans like William McCuistion. He concluded that "it is just another Bosses' war" and asked the SUP newspaper to print his report in the hope that "you can save someone else from going over to Spain and getting butchered for the Party."

Meanwhile, upon hearing of the SUP's departure from the Maritime Federation, Joe Bianca and five other Sailors' Union members wrote a spirited letter from Spain lamenting the "shameful situation" in their union. They warned that the next step for the SUP would be "an open alliance with the shipowners," unless the membership removed Lundeberg and his allies from office. Lundeberg responded by having the six men expelled from the SUP for "anti-union activity"—the specific charge was membership in the Communist party—and nonpayment of dues. Ironically, this letter informing the "Internationals" of their expulsion arrived in Spain too late for four of the six to read it. In the Ebro River campaign, one of the bloodiest battles of the Spanish civil war, Joe Bianca was killed by a piece of shrapnel. After two years and innumerable battles as a machine gunner, he had seemed indestructible. His death caused widespread shock and led to the official statement that "the Lincoln Washington Battalion has lost its best soldier." During the same offensive, Jack Eggen, a hero of the 1934 strike, died when a bullet struck him between the eyes. William Slivon, a union activist who had served as a picket captain during the 1936–37 strike, was killed instantly when a mortar exploded at his feet. As for the other three SUP members, two were hospitalized with serious wounds and one was missing in action. Joe Bianca and his shipmates deserved a better fate. But for Lundeberg and his syndicalist allies the internationalism of the Pentecostal era had given way to the urgent task of isolating "the Stalinist infection before it reached epidemic proportions."[53]

If ideological tests were the rationale for expelling Communists from the Sailors' Union, racial criteria prevented blacks and other minorities (except Hawaiians) from joining in the first place. Under Lundeberg's leadership, the SUP relentlessly upheld the white supremacist traditions that it had inherited from Furuseth, Scharrenberg, and other representatives of the old guard. Russel Ryvers, a black chief steward and veteran of forty years in the maritime industry, recalled that when he got a deck job on a Weyerhaeuser steam schooner in 1924, the "firemen and sailors ganged up on me. They walked off the ship in Everett, Washington, and forced the company to put me off." When the unions seized full control of hiring after the 1934 strike, blacks were often barred from even entering the Sailors' and Marine Firemen's halls. (Black seamen retained an enclave in the stewards' department and increasingly were welcomed as members of the Marine Cooks and Stewards' Union.)[54]

This blatant discrimination did not cause much controversy during the 1930s, in part because there were few if any jobs available for newcomers to the marine crafts. With the coming of War War II, however, the merchant marine expanded dramatically. Between 1941 and 1945 the number of deep-sea jobs increased from fifty-five thousand to two hundred thousand. The War Shipping Administration operated training schools "on a nondiscriminatory basis," graduating more than a hundred thousand candidates for maritime employment. In spite of considerable pressure from the federal government's Fair Employment Practices Committee (FEPC), the SUP adamantly refused to accept black seamen in its ranks. One black applicant was told by a Sailors' Union representative that "they didn't ship colored boys on the West Coast"; and a federal agency reported that "[a union official] called this office and said the the S.U.P. was not hiring Negroes and were not going to hire them." He accused the federal government of "attempting to 'cram Negroes down [our] throats.' " After the war, according to an SUP veteran, Lundeberg actively fanned the flames of the sailors' prejudice, in part to further his jurisdictional warfare against the racially integrated Marine Cooks and Stewards. "Racist types [found that they] could make a name for themselves [in the SUP] and win the favor of the leadership" by encouraging hostility between sailors and cooks.[55]

The Seafarers' International Union, with Lundeberg as president and the SUP as its model, followed a similar course. The union took advantage of the wartime situation to expand its membership considerably in direct competition with the NMU, whose left-wing leadership was aggressively committed to nondiscriminatory policies. SIU spokesmen were eager to highlight the difference between the two unions in this regard. Secretary-Treasurer John Hawk declared, "This is not a Kosher organization or one interested in social reform. . . . We are not going to become like the N.M.U." Some SIU organizers even boasted of their ties to the Ku Klux Klan. In spite of government pressure, the union's policies remained rigidly segregationist. An FEPC examiner reported that the SIU "has a separate hiring hall and separate dispatcher for Negroes. It assigns them only to the stewards' department, and then only if the stewards' department is all-Negro." When the FEPC ordered the union to cease its racist practices, it simply ignored the order.[56]

In explaining their discriminatory policies, Lundeberg and his allies claimed to be defending the liberty of "many thousands of brave loyal men" in the face of unwarranted government interference. This use of the language of voluntarism was very common during the late thirties and the war years, when the AFL became increasingly alarmed about the vast extension of the administrative state. Because the National Labor Relations Board, in particular, dared to define the boundaries of union jurisdiction and often seemed to favor industrial over craft unions, the AFL leadership was soon attacking its policies as incompatible with the historic practice of autonomous trade unionism. The federation's most outspoken voluntarists warned that boards and commissions like the NLRB were becoming "judges, juries, and executioners," and declared that in supporting President Roosevelt and the New Deal, "we have been too willing to accept gains at the price of lost liberty and lost capacity for self-determination and self-action." Many AFL unionists, including the SIU's John Hawk, cooperated with congressional investigating committees launched by conservatives and segregationists who were attempting to sabotage the NLRB, the FEPC, and the New Deal in general. Lundeberg himself developed a warm relationship with outspoken anti–New Dealers such as U.S. Senators Robert Taft of Ohio and William Knowland of California.[57]

For Lundeberg and other SIU-SUP spokesmen, the language of voluntarism merged easily with the rhetoric of white supremacy. The practice of discrimination was rationalized as the defense of "the fundamental rights of American citizenship," the sanctity of the home, and the purity of the race. John Hawk maintained that "neither the President nor the FEPC or any other committee would be able to force a white man to live with a Negro." Likewise, the Marine Firemen expressed the fear that federal policy would flood their union with blacks. Reaffirming their determination to "stay a white union," the Firemen declared that their "social affairs and . . . living quarters" were not subject to regulation by "the President and other liberal minded men." "There is nothing in the statement of any of these men which says that we shall take anyone of another race into our homes and beds." Lundeberg himself chided a group of liberal critics: "You theorists talk a lot about mixing with Negroes. But do you eat and sleep with them?"

Taking a slightly different tack, Sailors' Union official Maxie Weisbarth acknowledged that there were no blacks in the SUP "because Negroes aren't sailors. It's not their kind of work. They're cooks, yes. But they don't *like* deck work. Do I think they could do deck jobs? Them? Work? Real work? They don't like to work." These attitudes proved so persistent that the regional director of the Equal Employment Opportunity Commission in San Francisco would conclude in 1972, "There has been little, if any, change in the racial practices and racial composition of the Sailors' Union of the Pacific since the FEPC hearings during World War II."[58]

It is hardly surprising that Lundeberg and the SUP attracted criticism from a wide spectrum of trade union and political opinion. The secretary-treasurer of the California State Federation of Labor (AFL) accused him of "consistently support[ing] anti-labor candidates who have voted against everything of benefit to labor and the working people of the nation." The left-wing Marine Cooks and Stewards blasted him as "one of the greatest fakers and union wreckers of our day." Even the independent Marine Firemen described the SUP as a union living in "the shadow of the blackjack." However, the SUP remained democratic in form, and for the most part, Lundeberg retained the active support of the Sailors' Union membership, for at least three reasons. First, he and other spokesmen were careful to present their policies in the militant language of the Pentecostal era. They claimed to be the legitimate heirs of a left-wing labor movement that traced its lineage back to the Wobblies. Especially in the late thirties, they argued that they were criticizing the Communists and the CIO from the left. Lundeberg cultivated friendly ties with the remnants of the IWW and placed a number of Trotskyists in important positions in both the SUP and the Seafarers' Union. Thus, while the leadership's policies were increasingly cast in the mold of business unionism, the union's rhetoric remained militant, even radical.[59]

Also, Lundeberg proved to be a master at defending the economic interests of the West Coast sailors. In his syndicalist days he had bragged that his goal was to "squeeze the shipowners and capitalists and make them lose dough." He never entirely abandoned that stance, even though he became increasingly friendly with the employers and concerned about the economic well-being of the shipping industry. In practice, he did indeed "squeeze the shipowners" to improve the wages and conditions of his men. Two students of labor relations have estimated that between 1935 and 1948, "he was the champion gain-producer of the [maritime] industry. Indeed there were few unionists in the entire country who could claim as much so far as [improvements in] basic wage rates were concerned."[60]

Finally, in a shrinking labor market, Lundeberg fought ferociously to defend the jobs of the West Coast sailors and even to extend their jurisdiction. His critics charged that as employment declined, he tried to keep his own membership working "by raiding other unions." Thus, in 1940 he led his men across ILWU ship scalers' picket lines in an attempt to seize the scalers' work for members of the SUP. In 1949 he attempted to sabotage a strike called by the Communist-led Canadian Seamen's Union (CSU). He signed contracts with employers who had previously recognized the CSU and ordered his sailors to crash the Canadian seamen's picket lines. This move provoked bloodshed in ports from Halifax to Vancouver and precipitated a state of national emergency in Great Britain when British longshoremen refused to unload ships manned by SUP strikebreakers. Again, when "Communist" leaders of the Marine Cooks and Stewards were attacked by both the CIO and the federal government, Lundeberg shamelessly raided the MCS, declaring, "We make no bones about it, we aim to run that fink hall right off the waterfront."[61]

As SUP propagandists portrayed this crusade, the heroic sailors were often outnumbered but never outfought in their numerous battles with "finks and political le[e]ches," "yellow rats," and "Spics" armed with "shivs." Lundeberg himself became not only "the most progressive labor leader the world has ever seen" but a kind of Superman of the sea. In the Shepard line beef, it was alleged that a "Commy RAT" wielding a hunk of iron aimed a death blow at the back of his head, "while two more planted assassins moved in from each side of him"—all to no effect. In the 1940 brawl with ILWU ship scalers in San Francisco, the *West Coast Sailors* claimed that with the indestructible Lunchbox in the lead, twenty-four sailors "with their bare hands went through a cut-throat gang of Communist party hatchetmen . . . armed with knives, knucks, lead pipes, etc. and went to work!"

This was militant unionism of a sort, but "fight[ing] capitalism to a finish" was no longer its objective. Henceforth the shipowners were vilified only insofar as they were too weak-kneed to eliminate rival unions, or "Commie saboteurs," from American ships. The enemy now was communism, the CIO, and the very same men who had been valued fellow workers in the heyday of maritime insurgency.[62]

9

Porkchops and Politics: Unions and the Popular Front

Despite the continuing barrage of accusations that the marine union leadership wanted to Sovietize the waterfront and rule the country, it is clear in retrospect that the millennial fervor of the syndicalist renaissance cooled in the late 1930s. This drift to the right must be viewed in the larger context, not only of the union movement becoming divided against itself, but of other, external factors that were pushing labor toward moderation. As the unions entered into written agreements with employers and witnessed new forms of state intervention in the realm of collective bargaining, they were hemmed in by new constraints. In the volatile world of maritime labor relations, arbitration became an important means of resolving disputes. Economists Clark Kerr and Lloyd Fisher observed that among the longshoremen, arbitration was "almost continual." Each arbitration award was made part of the contract until it became "a monstrosity containing little that reflected a meeting of minds and much that was judicially imposed." Meanwhile, the National Labor Relations Board had received "one of the broadest grants of power and discretion that Congress had ever entrusted to an administrative agency." Nationwide the NLRB settled two thousand strikes and averted eight hundred more. The board also played a key role in defining the boundaries of union jurisdiction. Its decision that the entire coast, rather than individual ports, constituted the appropriate bargaining unit for dockworkers was a vital factor in the emergence of the International Longshoremen's and Warehousemen's Union and the demise of the ILA on the Pacific Coast.[1]

In addition, the attitudes of unorganized and newly organized workers were also a vital constraining factor. While a certain amount of militant rhetoric was necessary to establish credibility with the rank and file, a more important test was the ability to deliver on the promise of improved wages and conditions. In the competition for the allegiance of ever broadening numbers of workers, union organizers could hardly afford to emphasize politics at the expense of porkchops.[2]

Ironically, the Communist party also played an important role in orienting the maritime unions toward a more moderate stance. The political line and practice of American Communists shifted dramatically to the right during the Popular Front era. The clearest barometer of this shift was the Party's changing attitude toward Franklin Roosevelt and the New Deal. In October 1934 the *Daily Worker* characterized Roosevelt as "the leading organizer and inspirer of Fascism in this country." Even as the Communist line was changing, the president remained the object of scorn. In January 1936 the Party declared that "it would be sheer madness to depend upon Roosevelt." Earl Browder derided him as a man who "roars like a lion and acts like a rabbit. " His promises, said Browder, "are in the ash can already." The *Daily Worker* called for a "big vote for a Farmer-Labor Party in 1936, even if Roosevelt is defeated."[3]

But as the advance of fascism in Europe grew more dangerous, and as American Communists developed valuable ties with the CIO and other authentic mass organizations, the Party began to champion Roosevelt and the New Deal as vital components of the Popular Front in the United States. Gradually, even the Popular Front (based upon workers, farmers, and the middle class) gave way to a broader conception, the Democratic Front, which was designed to include "important sections of the upper middle class and certain liberal sections of the bourgeoisie." The rhetoric of class against class was relegated to the closet. The struggle was now between "the people" and the "Economic Royalists," or simply between "progress" and "reaction." Browder hailed the Democratic Front as the crowning example of the "maturity of our Party in American political life," and declared in mid-1938 that "it is a thousand times better to have a liberal and progressive New Deal, with our democratic rights, than to have a new Hoover, who would inevitably take our country onto the black and sorrowful road of fascism and war."[4]

These themes found increasingly clear expression in the maritime unions in which Communists played a significant role. Articles and editorials in the *Voice of the Federation* showered praise upon Roosevelt and the New Deal, emphasized the importance (often the priority) of electoral politics, and defined the marine workers' struggle in terms of broad national goals that even conservatives should have found unobjectionable. In discussing the relations between labor and capital, Communists and their allies in the Maritime Federation now spoke in language that was far removed from that which had characterized the syndicalist renaissance in its heyday. Whereas the *Voice* had once celebrated the aggressive wave of job actions and quickie strikes that had marked the battle for conditions aboard ship, the paper now hailed the marine cooks and stewards who were *"faithfully* doing their duty" and "maintaining the public welfare" by providing polite, efficient service to ships' passengers.[5]

Of course, conflict with the employers continued throughout this period, but the unions were careful to declare their desire for peace. During a prolonged dispute between the Matson line and the marine unions, Maritime Federation Secretary Bruce Hannon denounced the company's "continued policy of chiseling and violating conditions and agreements" as "a major threat to the peace and good relations established on the front." The unions had sought "every possible means of peaceful adjustment," Hannon claimed. When the 1939 collective bargaining agreements were about to expire, Maritime Federation President H. F. McGrath raised a similar cry: "We Want Peace But The Shipowners Want War!" "All responsible men will sit around a conference table and try to negotiate differences," said McGrath. "But not the shipowners—not this year." Instead they bragged that "from now on it's going to be boxing gloves with Bridges." (The timing of this threat was hardly accidental. With the enthusiastic support of the employers, the federal government had recently begun the first of four efforts to deport Bridges as an undesirable, i.e., Communist, alien. The deportation hearing was held during the summer of 1939, on Angel Island in San Francisco Bay.) The Maritime Federation leaders saw the employers' hostility as evidence of a campaign not only against Bridges and the marine unions, but against Roosevelt, the New Deal, and the nation's economic well-being. Hannon declared that Matson's hostile stance was "no foundation on which to build a merchant marine or establish recovery." And a *Voice* editorial called for support of legislation that would "strengthen the American Merchant Marine," along with "commerce, industry, and the National Defense program." At times it even appeared that Keynesian analysis was in vogue, as the *Voice* characterized the membership of the Maritime Federation as "forty thousand consumers," and quoted—with no evidence of disagreement—Roosevelt's declaration that "we must give our people a stake in our system of free economic enterprise."[6]

The infatuation with Roosevelt was especially striking. An ILWU member from Seattle called FDR "the greatest friend organized labor ever had." *Voice* editorials readily agreed, characterizing him as "a great human being and a great President," and "a man who has Organized Labor's interest topmost in his mind." During the Labor Day parades of 1938 and 1939, maritime workers marched behind banners that proclaimed "We Want Roosevelt in 1940," and a telegram from the engine and stewards' departments of the S.S. *Mariposa* implored the president to "disregard the [anti-]third term tradition." In San Francisco's Labor Day parade, the plea was even set to music, as marchers sang,

>   Mr. Roosevelt won't you please run again.
>   You're right in the middle
>   Of solving the riddle.
>   Mr. Roosevelt, won't you do it again.

After all, said Howard Costigan of the left-liberal Washington Commonwealth Federation, FDR was "the best business agent [organized labor] has ever had in the White House."[7]

As the political mood of the country shifted to the right in 1937 and 1938, and as employers sought to stem the tide of union gains, the *Voice* often implied that labor was no longer fighting to achieve its own autonomous objectives but was battling to defend Roosevelt and his program. Even when employers and workers locked horns, the bone of contention was really Roosevelt and the New Deal. In August 1938 a *Voice* editorial asked, "Why are the employers creating strife and unrest in labor's ranks now?" and answered, "Because they are out to smear Roosevelt and the New Deal. . . . They think, by smashing the unions, that they can smash Roosevelt." Labor's task was "to keep the New Deal alive," and the only way to do that was "for the trade unions of this country—and particularly of this Coast—to stand solid in the face of employers' attacks."[8]

When eighty-five thousand men and women marched up San Francisco's Market Street on Labor Day 1938, the *Voice* saw this vast outpouring as a demonstration by workers that "they would fight to the last ditch in upholding *President Roosevelt's program* for no speed-ups and the retention of the American Standard of Living." More than Harry Bridges, or even John L. Lewis, this Hudson Valley patrician and graduate of Groton and Harvard had become the symbolic leader of organized labor. Roosevelt defined labor's program; workers fought in the ditches to defend it. Even on May 1, symbol among Communists of the "final conflict," when the international working class would become the human race, the historic theme of class against class was deemphasized. Instead, a Seattle May Day parade, initiated by the Maritime Federation, was billed as "a mass rally behind President Roosevelt's peace program."[9]

Parades and picket lines were among the tried-and-true weapons of labor and the Left, but by 1938 the *Voice* was emphasizing the importance—and, increasingly, the priority—of electoral politics. Although the 1938 elections generally represented a sharp setback for the Roosevelt administration and New Deal liberalism, the states of California and Washington were dramatic exceptions. Culbert Olson, a Democrat with a record of supporting Popular Front causes, defeated incumbent Republican Frank Merriam in the California gubernatorial race, and one of the new governor's first acts in office was to free Tom Mooney from prison. The *Voice* hailed the "gigantic revolt against Republican misrule" that had freed Mooney and reminded its readers that the revolt "had to take place at the ballot box." To the north, the Washington Commonwealth Federation elected numerous candidates to office on the Democratic party ticket, prompting Howard Costigan to predict that the "1939 legislature is a cinch to be the most liberal in the history of the state."[10]

Maritime Federation spokesmen and New Deal politicos agreed that these gains were a result of organized labor's willingness to set aside jurisdictional battles and unite politically behind the Democratic party. "Labor is the Democratic Party," said Washington Congressman Warren Magnuson. "The union men . . . form the backbone of the New Deal." California's Democratic Governor Olson declared that the future of the United States "depends less and less on the captains of finance, more and more on organized labor." Where liberal and left candidates were defeated, as in Wisconsin, the *Voice* pointed to two problems: "the formation of a third party," which "split the progressive forces"; and the "fanatical opposition" of William Green and some sectors of the AFL to liberal candidates who were identified with the CIO. "This election shows the need for unifying the labor movement," said the *Voice,* and "this can best be done by carrying . . . our fight into the halls of Congress and the state legislatures."[11]

Much of the above rhetoric suggests the emergence of a social-democratic orientation among reform politicians and labor spokesmen. But the Communists proved increasingly reluctant to push this ground swell in the direction of third-party politics. As early as June 1937 the Communist party central committee had declared that "insofar as mass trade unions and other progressive groups . . . are not ready at present to join in the formation of the Farmer-Labor Party, we should encourage them to systematic and organized activity within the Democratic Party." By early 1939 even William Z. Foster, the symbol among Communists of left opposition to Browder's policies, was praising Roosevelt and issuing stern warnings about the "third party danger," which "is much used by demagogues to split and paralyze the people's forces."[12]

To be sure, Party publications continued to chide the president for "conciliating and placating the reactionaries." During the bloody Little Steel strike, when CIO unionists were gunned down by city and state administrations that had been elected with labor support, Roosevelt's response to fanatically anti–New Deal employers, and to embattled steelworkers who had overwhelmingly voted his column in 1936, was "a plague on both your houses." Soon thereafter, the *Communist* declared with apparent satisfaction that labor finally seemed to be shedding its illusions about the president and moving toward "more political independence." In the same breath, however, the Party asserted that greater independence meant "a *more* conscious and *stronger* alliance between labor and Roosevelt."[13]

Liberal and left-wing critics scoffed at this "dialectical" reasoning and pointed out that the Communists had pushed the struggle for socialism "so far to the background that one needs a telescope to see it at all." Indeed, many years later Earl Browder would declare that the Party had "relegated its revolutionary socialist goals to the ritual of chapel and Sundays on the pattern long followed by the Christian Church. On the weekdays it became the most single-minded practical reformist party that America ever produced." However, in the heyday of the Popular Front, after years of sectarian isolation, it was a dizzying experience for Communists to march in step with the workers as they embraced the Roosevelt presidency and the New Deal. In the trade unions, Communists tended to emphasize alliance at the expense of independence, to tail after the perception that the president "honestly has the interest of the workers at the basis of his policies." But at the time, taunts of revisionism seemed a small price to pay for daring to bask in the bright light of the political mainstream. "It was as though a new day had dawned," George Charney recalled. "We were not only Communists, we were Americans again."[14]

In retrospect, the question is not whether the Communists should have supported Roosevelt and the New Deal, but how. Clearly, the Socialist party derived no benefit from its strident contention that the immediate choice was socialism or fascism. The party's membership declined throughout the second half of the decade until by 1939 it was almost extinct. Moreover, several highly publicized experiments with labor-based politics in the late thirties offered little solace to the Communists' left-wing critics. In Detroit, a five-man Labor slate contending for seats on the city's Common Council was soundly defeated. In Akron, Ohio, a Democratic mayoralty campaign that was widely perceived as a quest for union power went down to defeat, in spite of the fact that Democratic registrants outnumbered Republicans by almost three to one and "Akron probably had more union members per capita than any other city in the United States." The Detroit and Akron examples suggest that electoral campaigns that appealed largely to the working-class vote fared poorly. In the context of a badly divided labor movement, even unionized workers did not demonstrate overwhelming support for labor tickets.[15]

Communists in the Popular Front era were correct to emphasize that insurgent electoral politics had to be constructed upon a broader foundation than labor. However, like many of their contemporaries, they too easily assumed that a steady evolution toward fundamental political realignment was taking place. The *Nation,* for example, expressed confidence that a large majority of Americans would eventually unite under the banner of "a really powerful farmer-labor party," and the Communists convinced themselves that a revamped Democratic party could embody this objective. Earl Browder, who had once exclaimed happily that "mass disintegration of the traditional party system has begun," now boasted that Communists were learning to take their place within the two-party system. When they finally retreated from this position, and embarked on a sharply different course, it was not on the basis of an independent analysis of American conditions, but at the behest of the Comintern.[16]

The Popular and Democratic fronts withered in the aftermath of the Nazi-Soviet pact of August 23, 1939. News of the pact came as a "complete shock" to American Communists; it left many of them "limp and confused." In about a month's time, however, they were to learn that the differences between fascism and bourgeois democracy had become insignificant, and that Party advocacy of an alliance between the Soviet Union and the Western powers against fascist aggression was no longer appropriate. The European conflagration that erupted on September 1 was characterized as the "Second Imperialist War," and the Communists were soon advocating a policy of strict neutrality. It took longer to abandon Roosevelt. But as the president slowly but surely committed himself to the Allied cause, and developed bipartisan ties with Republican critics of the New Deal who were also fervently pro-British, he became—once again—an object of the Communists' wrath. By mid-1940 a Party luminary was declaring that Roosevelt was "not a barrier to, or guarantee against, the establishment of fascism." He was not even a "lesser evil" than his Republican opponent in the presidential campaign. The alternative to Roosevelt was the recasting of a united front "built *primarily from below,* on a class struggle basis."[17]

On the waterfront, Communists and their allies readily fell into line. The most authoritative voice was surely that of Bill Bailey, whose antifascist credentials were impeccable. Not only had he fought valiantly as a member of the Abraham Lincoln Battalion in Spain, but in the summer of 1935 he had run a gauntlet of German sailors and gun-wielding New York City detectives to tear the swastika from the bow of the German liner *Bremen,* as a crowd of demonstrators cheered wildly on the dock below. Now Bailey was charged with the responsibility of putting antifascism aside and articulating the new line. "The war in Europe has changed its character so much during the past two weeks," he said in late September, "that it is now definitely the 'Second Imperialist War,' " and "cannot in the least be supported by the working people of the world. . . . We maritime workers must insist that all American ships keep out of the war zones. We have absolutely no business there."[18]

After Bailey's opening salvo, others quickly followed. In early October the Marine Cooks and Stewards' Association resolved that the European conflict was "no longer a war against aggression but an imperialist war, Daladier and Chamberlain being as much at fault as either Hitler or the Nazi party." A. E. Harding, president of the Maritime Federation's Washington district council, dismissed "high sounding labels, such as 'A War to Destroy Hitlerism,' " as "just so much poppycock." A CIO spokesman in Portland stated that the real battle in Europe was not the "war between Hitler and Chamberlain," but the "fight between labor and capital." "And it's that here, too," he said, "which means that we've got to fight [capital] if we're going to hold on to what we have." With the renewal of the language of class struggle, the Popular Front was dead.[19]

Tracing the twists and turns of the Communist political line is a necessary task, but it would be wrong to assume a one-dimensional model where a handful of Communists in the leadership of the unions imposed their will on a duped or acquiescent rank and file. In reality, the relationship between leaders and members was far more complex, and Communists generally sought to build unions in ways that maximized the opportunity for democratic decision making. In a study of the left-led United Electrical Workers (UE), Ronald Filippelli has challenged the common accusation that Communist influence in unions resulted largely from "deception and manipulation. From the beginning," he asserts, "UE's structure provided for a broad participation by the membership." Specifically, "the major responsibility for bargaining proposals and strategy lay with the local unions. All UE negotiating committees were elected, contracts were ratified by referendum, and strikes were called and concluded by membership votes."

Likewise, Maritime Federation officials declared that their constituent unions "are run by their members, not by 'Communists' 'reds' or 'radicals.' It is a peculiarity of the Pacific Coast maritime unions that officials must submit every action of the slightest importance to a majority vote of the membership." Louis Adamic echoed this claim when he studied maritime labor relations in April 1936; and three and a half years later, *San Francisco Chronicle* labor reporter Arthur Eggleston marveled at the extent to which waterfront labor had broken with the autocratic structure and practice of old-line AFL unions. "Referendum election of officers, referendum votes on agreements, referendum votes on practically everything of importance and extremely easy methods of recalling officers constitute a grave threat to the less risky method of machine and convention control," he wrote. Insofar as Communists and Party sympathizers played an important role in the marine unions, then, it was necessarily within the framework of democratic form and procedure.[20]

The Party may have come closer to achieving a mass membership in marine than in any other area of industrial concentration. In the wake of an intensive recruiting drive in late 1937 and early 1938, it was reported that maritime ranked first among all of the basic industries with 603 new Party recruits (compared with 552 in the much larger steel industry). But Communists made up a relatively small percentage of the membership of even the smallest marine unions. Moreover, imbued with energy and direction and often blessed with strategically placed allies, they tended to be concentrated disproportionately at the leadership levels. From the standpoint of Communist union officials, who routinely faced aggressive and well-financed campaigns by anti-Communist opponents, Party members quite naturally appeared to be the best qualified candidates for union office, perhaps the only ones who could be relied upon to defend the Left's embattled strongholds. It is hardly an exaggeration to assert that in some left-led unions, notably the Marine Cooks and Stewards and the National Maritime Union, Party membership became a prerequisite for officeholding.[21]

A consequence of this development was that the Communist orbit attracted not only the most radical workers, but also opportunists who saw the Party as a vehicle for advancing their own careers. Joe Curran reported that when he visited San Francisco on the eve of the 1936-37 strike, a Communist union official "strongly urged me . . . to join the Party, stating that it was the only way I would get anywhere in the movement." (The official, John E. Ferguson of the Marine Firemen's union, soon switched sides and became an outspoken anti-Communist and star witness for the Dies Committee.) Curran may not have heeded this advice, but many others did. Journalist Murray Kempton, himself a veteran of a brief sojourn in the National Maritime Union, concluded that "membership in the waterfront section of the Party had become more necessary for the careerist in the NMU than the Rotary Club could ever hope to be in more ordinary societies." Somewhat more charitably, former Party member Joseph Starobin observed that it "proved easier to become a leader of 'masses' than to build a 'mass base.' "[22]

This lopsided concentration of Reds at the top levels of the unions makes it that much easier to distort the relationship between union leaders and the rank and file. In the case of the West Coast Longshoremen, a long-standing obsession with the dynamic personality and left-wing politics of Harry Bridges had led to an underestimation of the independence and initiative of the dockworkers themselves. Roger Lapham, president of the American-Hawaiian Steamship Company, recalled the shipowners' belief that every candidate for a job on the docks was "thoroughly screened by Bridges. We used to think that only a Communist could get on as a new longshoreman." In the same vein, labor economist Walter Galenson wrote in 1960 that "whatever the truth was with respect to the Communist Party status of Bridges, there is no doubt whatsoever that the ILWU was under the complete domination of this organization." Of course, Bridges made no bones about his respect for the Communist party and his agreement with many of its policies. But the ILWU members did not let their admiration and affection for the outspoken Limo interfere with their capacity for independent judgment. Charles Larrowe recalls an occasion when Bridges made an eloquent plea to the members of the San Francisco longshore local. When he had finished, the rank and file gave him a standing ovation and then, almost unanimously, voted down his proposal. Over a period of years the longshore locals of the ILWU resolutely fought Bridges on a number of issues and often elected local officers who were outspokenly opposed to his political views.[23]

There is one notable area, though, where the persistence of the Left bore fruit in spite of considerable opposition in the ranks of the workers. Communists and their allies played a vital role in pushing the unions they led toward a break with white supremacist ideology and practice. The constitution of the old Marine Cooks and Stewards' Association had stated that the union was formed in part "to relieve ourselves of the degrading necessity of competing with an alien and inferior race." Although the specific reference was to Chinese and Japanese seamen, blacks were almost entirely excluded as well until after the 1934 strike. Gradually, as Communists became the leading force in the union, the MCS began admitting nonwhites, and a few even achieved prominent leadership positions. With the coming of World War II and the dramatic expansion of the merchant marine, nonwhites quickly became a majority in the union. By 1950 the membership was approximately one-third white and 45 to 50 percent black, with the remaining 15 to 20 percent drawn from other minorities. When the SUP raided the Marine Cooks and Stewards in the late forties and early fifties, black workers rallied to the defense of their union. They had not forgotten that the MCS was one of the very few organizations that accepted them fully when they migrated to the West Coast during the war. In the words of economist Jane C. Record, "Many of these men, largely from the South, found in the [MCS] hiring hall the most satisfying social experience of their lives."[24]

Although the much larger National Maritime Union never had as high a percentage of black members as the MCS, its leadership worked hard to build a racially integrated union. NMU veteran Johnny Gladstone has recalled that "sentiments of rank-and-file sailors on [the race] question [were] not much different between the SUP, SIU, and NMU. . . . Anti-Negro sentiment always existed as an undercurrent; often it was accompanied by anti-Semitism. . . . the big difference is that in the SUP and SIU it was encouraged, while in the NMU it was more than discouraged—it was not tolerated."

During the war, leaders of the National Maritime Union pressured the employers and the government to end Jim Crow hiring practices. By 1944 they had negotiated contracts with 125 shipping companies stipulating that there would be no employment discrimination against nonwhite NMU members. Meanwhile, the union waged an extensive educational campaign against racism in its own ranks. According to Gladstone, who was a ship's carpenter and Communist party member in the 1940s, "Some of the finest Communist cadres and rank and filers fought the issue out relentlessly. But it was never easy. . . . It was one hell of an enormous job [which] required constant vigilance."[25]

In the Longshoremen's union, as well as the MCS and the NMU, it was Communists and Party sympathizers who led the attack on the legacy of Jim Crow. The Pacific Coast ILA locals had long excluded nonwhites, but a major breakthrough occurred during the Big Strike when the San Francisco local opened its doors to black longshoremen. Henry Schmidt acknowledged that "many, many of our members were opposed to those people coming in." But thanks in large measure to the leadership of left-wing militants like Schmidt and Bridges, the San Francisco ILA overcame the forces of inertia and prejudice within its ranks and established impressive guidelines for racial integration. Immediately after the strike Bridges announced that black labor would never again find the doors of the San Francisco longshore local closed. Reviewing the union's record ten years later, economist Herbert Northrup reported that "segregated gangs are not permitted, and the union's no-discrimination policy is strictly enforced."[26]

When the Pacific Coast District of the ILA became the ILWU, the union's top leaders were firmly committed to emulating the San Francisco example throughout the organization. The ILWU's well-known opposition to racial discrimination was an important factor in the union's expansion into Hawaii, not only on the waterfront but among sugar and pineapple plantation workers as well. The triumph of the ILWU in Hawaiian agriculture brought about a degree of fraternization across racial lines that few had thought possible. As in the Marine Cooks and Stewards, black and other minority workers resolutely defended their union and provided a solid base of support for left-wing ILWU leaders who were under sharp attack from other unionists and the federal government.

Unlike the MCS and the National Maritime Union, however, the ILWU had a strong tradition of local autonomy that made it impossible for the Left to impose its will throughout the organization. A number of ILWU locals, most notably the longshore local in Portland, refused to admit blacks to membership and defended their stance by appealing to the union's tradition of autonomy. The Portland local included an active left-wing faction, but it was consistently outflanked on the race issue by a vocal segregationist minority. In the face of Portland's continuing obstinacy, the international officers faced an unhappy choice between competing principles. They also confronted a major tactical hurdle, because forcing the issue might have driven the Portland local into the eager embrace of the ILA, Harry Lundeberg, and Dave Beck. Thus, it was not until the 1960s that the international was able to compel the Portland longshoremen to accept black workers into their ranks.[27]

The logic of the Popular and Democratic fronts clearly pointed in the direction of class collaboration and "responsible" unionism. To be sure, Communists participated in and led many bitter strikes in the late 1930s. But the Party was increasingly sensitive about maintaining a viable working relationship with New Dealers and the top leadership of the CIO at a time when the average citizen was allegedly "becoming fed up on unions and union tactics." More and more, the tendency was to see strikes only as a last resort. Thus, when the great victory in the Flint sit-down strike of 1937 triggered an exuberant wave of shop-floor insurgency in the auto industry, Communists who had always championed militancy now warned against "foster[ing] strikes and labor trouble." "The union can only grow on the basis of established procedure and collective bargaining," said one of the Party's leading spokesmen in Flint. At the national level, the politburo denounced unauthorized strikes as "against the interests of the workers."[28]

On the waterfront, left-wing spokesmen dutifully committed themselves to "peace and good relations." But somehow the theory never seemed to penetrate the workaday world, because the number of strikes involving marine workers remained legendary. According to economists Kerr and Fisher, it was "an unmatched record of labor-management controversy." There were nearly fourteen hundred work stoppages on the West Coast waterfront from 1930 to 1948, with the greatest concentration in the middle and late thirties. Only four of these strikes were major coastwide walkouts. The rest were quickies, where in most instances the initiative came from the rank and file.[29]

Bridges had expressed ambivalence about the unrelenting wave of job actions as early as the fall of 1935. By April 1936 he was declaring that the longshoremen could no longer support sailors' work stoppages every time "a ship is pulled by a couple of drunks from the crew." As Western regional director of the CIO, he affirmed that "we are definitely committed as a national policy to the strict observance of contracts both in letter and spirit." However, Bridges refused to embrace the Communist party's blanket condemnation of outlaw strikes. Instead, he offered a vital qualification to the principle of contractual sanctity. "[N]o union in any industry," he said, "can allow itself . . . to be used as a strike-breaking agency." When workers were on strike against employers, other unionists simply could not be expected to cross their picket lines. This was a principle that Bridges defended far and wide. Len De Caux remembered that his speech at the CIO's founding convention "drew platform rebuke for plugging class solidarity more than contractual sanctity."[30]

Although defending rank-and-file militancy, Bridges increasingly emphasized that it was useful only when harnessed to the unions' strategic objectives. He told a convention of lumber and sawmill workers, "We get into enough [strikes]. We gamble our entire organization sometimes for the protection of one or two men . . . but we're not dumbbell enough to gamble it when there's a good chance of losing." In the day-to-day routine on the docks, however, the longshoremen's actions were governed more by reflex than strategy. For them job action had become a way of life. Henry Schmidt, who served three terms as president of the San Francisco longshore local in the thirties, recalled that "the guys got very arbitrary. They would call a slowdown or work stoppage themselves without consulting anybody. . . . I would have to tell them, 'Fellows, some day you may own these ships, and then you can do whatever you please, but there are still shipowners and we have an award. It doesn't say that you can do these things.' 'Ahhh,' they'd say, they'd give you hell."[31]

Even when the focus of job action shifted from the economic to the political realm, the initiative and solidarity of rank-and-file workers was impressive. This was vividly demonstrated in 1939, when longshoremen from San Pedro to the Northwest ports refused to load ships carrying scrap iron to Japan. The campaign began in December 1938, when schoolchildren from San Francisco's Chinatown set up picket lines on the Embarcadero. Their picket signs declared that "Imperial Japan Needs American Scrap Iron . . . to Kill Chinese Children. Boycott Japan!" According to the *San Francisco Examiner*, longshoremen "refused to cross the . . . picket line, and many of them joined in the march themselves." Soon three Chinese crew members walked off the ship, followed by three Greek seamen who declared their sympathy with the protestors' cause. In the face of employer demands that agreements be honored and the ship loaded, Henry Schmidt replied, "Our union wants to live up to its contract, yet . . . [w]e cannot ask self-respecting men to push those Chinese children out of the way and load iron that will be used to slaughter their countrymen."[32]

The initial crisis was eased after four days, when the youthful demonstrators agreed to withdraw their picket lines. Schmidt declared that "the movement is just beginning," but pointed to congressional action as the means of resolving the issue. "That's the only way you can do it," he said. The dockworkers, however, continued to wage their campaign at the point of production. Matters came to a head in San Pedro, where a local arbitrator ruled that men who refused to load scrap iron were violating the union's contract with the employers and must be punished. Bridges replied defiantly that "if we have to choose between [penalizing longshoremen for honoring picket lines] and putting up a battle on this Coast we will choose the latter because we will retain our self-respect even though we might get a beating in the process." He reminded the arbitrator, "We are a social organization as well as a union organization," and that commitment to principle would take precedence over "the technical wording of an agreement."

Citing Bridges's words as evidence of the need for a firm response, the arbitrator ruled that sixty-one San Pedro longshoremen who had refused to load scrap iron would be suspended without pay for a week. The ILWU refused to accept this ruling, and instead distributed the suspended men among a large number of work gangs. As employer representatives prevented the penalized longshoremen from working, entire gangs would walk off the job, and a partial tie-up of Los Angeles harbor ensued.[33]

Another significant example of the rank and file's capacity for independent judgment and initiative came during the 1940 presidential election campaign, when the Communist party was outspokenly critical of Franklin Roosevelt, and for his own reasons, John L. Lewis supported the candidacy of Republican nominee Wendell Willkie. Lewis was a hero to millions of American workers, but they did not agree with his bitter indictment of the New Deal's failings, nor could they bring themselves to support Willkie against Roosevelt. Lewis claimed that "Willkie has the common touch. . . . He has worked with his hands, and has known the pangs of hunger." But he was also a Wall Street lawyer and utility magnate who had been an articulate and impassioned critic of the New Deal. The San Francisco CIO council no doubt spoke for many workers in declaring that "it takes a wild stretch of the imagination to interpret Wendell Willkie as anything but a reactionary stooge." When the Republican nominee campaigned in industrial areas, he heard workers booing and heckling, and saw them spit on the sidewalks and turn their backs as his motorcade passed by. When Lewis endorsed Willkie in a nationwide radio address, Ohio coal miners hung their union president in effigy and denounced him as a "Judas, Traitor, Dictator." All across the country workers repudiated Lewis's stand not because they resented the attempt of a labor leader to influence their political decisions, but rather because they believed that Lewis was betraying the interests of the working class. For better or worse, American workers had adopted Franklin Roosevelt and his party as their own. Political analyst Samuel Lubell concluded in 1940 that "the New Deal appears to have accomplished what the Socialists, the I.W.W., and the Communists never could approach. It has drawn a class line across the face of American politics."[34]

How did Communist party members and sympathizers in the maritime unions respond to this turn of events? In the past Harry Bridges had openly deviated from the Party's stance on electoral politics. In 1934, when Communists were denouncing former Socialist Upton Sinclair as "Hitler-like" and a "dangerous Social-Fascist," Bridges and the San Francisco ILA supported Sinclair's bid for governor of California on the Democratic ticket. In early 1936, when the Party was blasting FDR and calling for the formation of a farmer-labor party "even if Roosevelt is defeated," Bridges was stating his apprehension that the shipowners planned to "cause disruption and strife in the Maritime Industry, on the eve of the Presidential elections," because they hoped to replace Roosevelt with a "reactionary administration." After the Maritime Federation of the Pacific expressed such fears openly, thereby implying support for the president's reelection, the Communist party responded with a public attack on this "incorrect" stance. "Such ideas are dangerous and will disarm the workers," said Roy Hudson, "because they create illusions about the role of Roosevelt in combating the growing fascist offensive of the shipowners."[35]

By 1940, however, Bridges was far more ready to accommodate himself to the changing flow of the Party's political line. In the wake of the Lewis speech attacking Roosevelt and endorsing Willkie, he declared, "We got our union and our conditions by fighting for them all the way down the line against the attempted betrayals and sell-out of President Roosevelt and the New Deal." The ILWU leader predicted that U.S. participation in the European war would mean the destruction of the trade unions and the imposition of a fascist dictatorship in the United States. "With the re-election of President Roosevelt," he said, "we are well on our way toward that kind of a set-up."[36]

Although Bridges refused to join Lewis in endorsing Willkie, he declared that "it took the courage of a lion to do what Lewis did the other night." But the maritime workers were not impressed. In fact, after Lewis's radio address, a number of locals that had withheld support from Roosevelt now came forward to endorse him by overwhelming margins. The San Francisco Longshoremen, Bridges's own local, called for the president's reelection, while the San Pedro and Seattle locals reaffirmed their earlier endorsement of Roosevelt. Longshoremen from Aberdeen, Portland, and Stockton, Warehousemen from San Francisco, and the left-leaning Marine Cooks and Stewards' branches in San Francisco and San Pedro also entered the president's column.[37]

Three of the big four longshore locals passed an additional resolution: they called upon Bridges to resign as president of the ILWU. Earlier in the year, the outspoken Aussie had told Byron Darnton of the *New York Times*, "Our union is just as democratic as we can make it. Any guy can get up on the floor and call Harry Bridges all kinds of a bum, and I got to take it." This was no mere rhetoric. After his election to the presidency of the fledgling ILWU, Bridges had proposed that "the present recall provisions be liberalized and strengthened, making it easier to immediately suspend or remove any official" who abused his authority. Now, with three locals calling him "all kinds of a bum," Bridges responded that their demand for his resignation was "in full keeping with the democratic structure of our organization." He pointed out that if 15 percent of the members signed petitions demanding his removal from office, he would be subject to a recall election.[38]

Although this particular storm over Bridges soon subsided, there would be many more, and most of them would be related to his increasingly flamboyant embrace of the Communist party line. After Germany invaded the Soviet Union in June 1941, and even more so when the United States declared war on the Axis powers, the Communists became aggressive advocates of building a broad national front, with Roosevelt as the revered commander in chief. "We are pledged to uphold the President, the Commander-in-Chief," Bridges told an ILWU convention after the United States entered the war, "and nobody in this convention or in this union has any right to complain about the actions of the President." Like Roosevelt, the Communists were determined to subordinate every other concern to the quest for military victory, which meant labor-management cooperation for full production on the home front.

Earl Browder told a group of New York unionists that "we have to find out how to make the capitalist system work." To aid in this endeavor, the NMU started a leadership training school that taught union members "how to get along with their bosses." Two journalists who observed the school in session, and adjudged it "downright spectacular," summarized its curriculum as "Readin', Writin', and No Strikin'." Bridges went a step beyond "No Strikin'." He told the San Francisco CIO council that if union officials continued to stress wages and hours, "we're slackers and selling out our unions and our country." Instead, the union movement must emphasize winning the war. "How? Production," he declared. "I'd rather say speedup, and I mean speedup. . . . To put it bluntly, I mean your unions today must become instruments of speedup of the working class of America."[39]

The workers' response was equally blunt. At a mass meeting in Los Angeles, when Bridges proposed an increase in the number of sacks per sling load, a rank-and-file longshoreman confronted him with the statement that "I never thought that I'd hear Harry Bridges tell us to give up our conditions just because of a little old war." Characterizing Bridges's proposal as "horse shit," the longshoreman declared, "Just because your pal Joe Stalin is in trouble, don't expect us to give up our conditions to help him out." As for the shipowners, if they wanted more sacks loaded, "they can come down here and load them." When he finished speaking, three thousand longshoremen rose to their feet, stomping, clapping, and laughing.

"Harry laughed, too," recalled a union member who was there, but for the most part he was undeterred by rank-and-file opposition. Believing that the wartime alliance between the United States and the Soviet Union would also undergird the monumental task of postwar reconstruction, the Communists raised the possibility of extending the wartime no-strike pledge into the postwar period. At a time when the pledge was under bitter attack from many workers and local union officials, Bridges embraced this idea of extended class collaboration and articulated it in a way that was more simplistic and absolute than Browder and other Party leaders had intended. This only added fuel to the fire. In 1945 Milton Murray, president of the American Newspaper Guild, charged that "Harry Bridges is not a leader of labor. He is a misleader, and . . . a wrecker of honest trade unionism." Prominent in Murray's bill of particulars was Bridges's "quisling pronouncement that he favored continuation of the no-strike pledge after the war."[40]

The furor surrounding the 1940 presidential election and Bridges's conduct during the war reveals much about the relationship between leaders and the rank and file in the "Communist-dominated" ILWU. A number of top ILWU officials did indeed agree with the line of the Communist party on many national and international issues. But the membership continued to exercise independent judgment, and the union's structure facilitated the development of local autonomy and a turbulent local democracy. The practical results were not always pleasing to the leadership. Henry Schmidt remembered the job actions of the late 1930s as "a constant headache"; and the irascible Bridges was sometimes infuriated by criticism from the ranks. But as he acknowledged, "I got to take it."[41]

Conclusion

"Labor on the March"—How Far?

Journalist Edward Levinson had the luxury (and the handicap) of writing the labor history of the 1930s as it was being made. In his *Labor on the March,* which he completed in December 1937, Levinson portrayed the CIO as "a new gospel," and he saw the millions of CIO buttons sprouting on workers' overalls, shirtwaists, and caps as "badges of a new independence." For Levinson and many other Americans, "labor was on the march as it had never been before in the history of the Republic." This sense of excitement, innovation, and upheaval also pervades Irving Bernstein's impressive scholarly study, *Turbulent Years,* which appeared in 1970, and it has been central to the recollections of many participants in the great events of the thirties. Jim Cole, a black packinghouse worker, told a contemporary interviewer that the CIO's triumph over the legacy of racial and ethnic antagonism in Chicago's stockyards was "the greatest thing in the world." Likewise, a worker from Connecticut's Brass Valley has stated that in the heyday of unionism, "one person's cause was everyone's cause," and unions became a vital focal point of many workers' lives. "I can recall going to union meetings where the hall was always overflowing," he said. "We used to make it a point to get there early, so we'd get a seat."[1]

Recent studies of labor in the 1930s, however, have discovered more inertia than militancy, more myopia than class consciousness, more division than unity. Indeed, a student of Akron's fabled rubber workers has concluded that where it existed, union militancy was a sign of weakness, not strength; while in his memoir of the thirties literary critic Malcolm Cowley wonders whether the militancy of the sit-down strikes was "aroused by anything nobler than the hope of driving a new Buick."[2]

How do the maritime workers relate to the emerging portrait of labor's not so "turbulent years?" What did they accomplish in the course of the 1930s?

And why, after such a promising start, did they fail to build a united labor movement on the waterfronts of the Pacific Coast? Clearly their militancy was more than episodic. It flickered in 1933, reached a peak intensity in the Big Strike of 1934, and continued to burn—often brightly—for the rest of the decade. Can this "irresponsible" enthusiasm be construed as a sign of weakness? Whatever its effect on the long-term decline of waterborne commerce relative to rail and truck transport, the militancy of the 1930s led to major victories in the realm of wages, hours, and working conditions. Moreover, the continuing solidity of the maritime unions stands in marked contrast to the experience of more heralded organizations in the mass-production industries, whose membership figures plunged almost as rapidly in 1938 and 1939 as they had risen in 1936 and 1937.[3]

The sustained burst of self-activity among longshoremen and seamen involved far more than porkchops and the parochial possibilities of the moment on the job. From March 1935 to the summer of 1939 there were frequent demonstrations and even work stoppages that emcompassed political and international themes. The employers' chief spokesman complained of more than fifty such actions in an eighteen-month period. As late as 1939, a Bloody Thursday orator would declare, "We will not be stopped until we have won the thing we are entitled to: The earth and the fullness thereof."[4]

"The earth and the fullness thereof" was not to be theirs, but the era of insurgent unionism did bring about a dramatic transformation of the maritime workers' living and working conditions. Between 1935 and 1948, their wage gains were truly remarkable. They far exceeded the increases won by workers in comparable sectors of the transportation industry and may have been on a par with those of such national pacesetters as building tradesmen and bituminous coal miners. In the area of working conditions, the transformation was equally significant. The longshoremen's control of the pace of work became legendary. As late as 1961 an astute observer would characterize work on the West Coast docks as "the most attractive way of life for a casual laborer in the United States, if not in the entire world." Among the seamen, the semifeudal hierarchy of seafaring life became a thing of the past. In spite of explicit contractual language protecting the shipowners' prerogatives, seamen won control of hiring through a series of job actions up and down the coast. Aboard ship, sailors often refused to work when officers were standing over them. Labor activist and historian Stan Weir was especially impressed by the example of a bosun who ordered a chief mate to "get off the deck and back on the bridge where you belong." Weir remembered his shipmates in the SUP as "a highly conscious group of men" who were prepared to back up such bold initiatives with job action when necessary.[5]

Why did the dream of One Big Union and a unified, class-conscious labor movement remain unfulfilled? There are many reasons, but the persistence of craft antagonisms and the divisive impact of the conflict between the AFL and the CIO seem most significant. The maritime unions often demonstrated real solidarity with workers in other industries, even in other countries; and the longshoremen, especially in San Francisco, became a widely acclaimed symbol of working-class pride and militancy. But their expressions of pride sometimes reflected a stubborn craft identity. They became, in their own eyes, the "Lords of the Docks," the "most militant and organized body of men the world has ever seen." A publication of the San Francisco longshore local declared, "There is no question about it, the workers not only in America, but throughout the world are interested in what the West Coast longshoremen have done and . . . are doing." A San Franciscan who had returned recently from a visit to Finland reported that the Finns "were eager for news of the West Coast longshoremen. In many instances, the first question asked was, *'How are the West Coast longshoremen doing?'* "[6]

This tendency toward narrow self-congratulation might have been harmless enough, if it had been merely rhetorical. But in September 1935 the Longshoremen unilaterally renewed their collective bargaining agreement with the shipowners, thereby leaving the seamen in the lurch and making a mockery of the Maritime Federation's rallying cry. This was the moment when the "muck of ages" loosened the bonds of solidarity and set in motion the trend toward fragmentation and fratricide. The Sailors, especially, felt betrayed by men whom they had regarded as their closest allies. Soon the SUP militants distanced themselves from the Longshoremen and became the other dynamic pole around which the contending forces in the Maritime Federation coalesced. By 1940, the Sailors were declaring themselves the rightful nucleus of any industrial union of maritime workers. Why? Because they claimed to be in the line of apostolic succession that began with "the first seafarers, the Phoenicians," from whom "we have inherited the right to maintain and sail anything that floats on water. To be technical—handling cargo included," they warned their rivals on the docks.[7]

Animosity between longshoremen and seamen was nothing new. But the escalating war between the AFL and the CIO dramatically enlarged the scope of the conflict and made the divisions on the waterfront more rigid and permanent. It is surely not a denigration of Harry Lundeberg's talent or zeal to suggest that he could not have become the force that he did without the material and institutional resources the AFL provided. With the aid of Teamster and ILA muscle and money supplied by the AFL executive council, he was able to strengthen the position of the once vulnerable SUP and significantly expand his own influence as well. In the process he discarded much of his syndicalist baggage and even managed to embrace Joe Ryan as "a great fighter [who] kept the Reds out of New York harbor." Although the Norwegian immigrant always presented himself as "yewst a sailor," he was to become a success story of almost legendary proportions—the president of an international union, the associate of prominent elected officials, a resident of one of the nation's most affluent suburbs, and a popular symbol of Cold War anticommunism.[8]

On the other side of the waterfront divide, Harry Bridges played a more complex role in labor's civil war and reaped a more contradictory harvest. Initially he and his Communist allies were determined to anchor the maritime unions, and accomplish the CIO's stated objectives, within the confines of the AFL. In the spring of 1937, eighteen months after the CIO's founding, their commitment to the decaying ISU and other AFL craft unions remained so tenacious that an ally like Joe Curran was looking elsewhere for leadership and some CIO partisans were accusing Bridges and "his CP gang" of "trying to drive us off the water-front." When he finally embraced the CIO without reservation, Bridges enhanced his own stature considerably—as West Coast director of the new federation and president of an international union. But a formidable array of enemies joined forces to limit the ILWU to the Pacific Coast and to slow the momentum of its march inland. Nonetheless, Bridges could claim of his Longshoremen and Warehousemen, "We built the CIO on the West Coast and in doing it we built a hell of a lot of AFL unions" as well.[9]

Although Bridges's reach far exceeded his grasp, many participants in the labor movement continued to regard him as a preeminent symbol of insurgent unionism—indeed, in some quarters, as "the morning star of the long-anticipated revolution." Len De Caux recalled the "unsinkable Harry Bridges," whose speeches "included radical phrases such as even the reds avoided." Dorothy Day, a pacifist and leader of the Catholic Worker movement, believed he was "a Communist in his political affiliations," but still characterized him as "one of the best labor leaders in the country." Even a left-wing critic credited him with having given "great leadership to the workers of the West Coast." With some justification, however, others viewed him as a "factional leader" whose abrasive personal style and close ties with the Communist party helped to turn potential allies into enemies of the CIO. Within the organization his critics would complain that "almost every appointment made by Bridges has been either a Communist or a Communist sympathizer."[10]

Bridges's stubborn (but not absolute) adherence to the Party line not only affected the development of the CIO; it also cost him and his union dearly. Beginning soon after the Big Strike, he became the object of a sustained campaign that Supreme Court Justice Frank Murphy characterized as a "relentless crusade to deport an individual because he dared to exercise that freedom which belongs to him as a human being and is guaranteed him by the Constitution." The seemingly "everlasting Bridges case" was not resolved until the mid-1950s. In the meantime, the CIO expelled the ILWU and ten other unions on the charge that they were Communist-dominated organizations. Somehow Bridges and the ILWU survived this onslaught and achieved recognition as an honest, democratic union that won for its members "the best conditions of any longshoremen in the world." For cold warriors, the contrast between the "Communist-dominated" ILWU and the vociferously anti-Communist but racket-ridden ILA must have been embarrassing indeed.[11]

Edward Levinson portrayed the schism in the labor movement as a case of the CIO's democratic industrial unionism versus the craft autocracy of the AFL executive council. Developments on the West Coast waterfront, however, suggest that the reality was more complex. In terms of temperament and avowed ideology, there was an enormous gulf between the AFL's William Green and Harry Lundeberg. The sailor's crude, irreverent style must have been personally repellent to the conservative, well-mannered AFL president; and his lingering IWWism was an embarrassing reminder of earlier heresies. At the time the two men were negotiating a rapprochement, Lundeberg remained an outspoken advocate of industrial unionism and referendum democracy. Moreover, even though Green denounced sit-down strikes and contract-breaking as "abhorrent to all American principles," many of the SUP's militant activists continued to regard job action as a vital component of rank-and-file unionism. But the AFL leadership was determined "to push the C.I.O. into the Pacific Ocean"; and Lundeberg was a useful instrument in the pursuit of this goal. In return, the sailor had objectives of his own. The pressure of competition with the CIO compelled Green to make concessions to Lundeberg's unionism that might have been unthinkable in other circumstances. Thus, for several years after reaffiliation with the AFL, the SUP remained a haven for IWW dual unionists, recruited other avowed revolutionaries, and continued its advocacy of industrial unionism.[12]

In practice, of course, Lundeberg was concerned mainly with defending the interests of deck sailors on the West Coast. But through the agency of the Seafarers' International Union of North America, and with the aid of other AFL affiliates, he extended his domain and challenged rival unions wherever he encountered them, on all the major waterways of the United States and Canada. In this sense, he was typical of many AFL "craft unionists"—in the Carpenters, Machinists, and Teamsters unions, for example—who took advantage of the ferment of the 1930s to continue expanding their jurisdiction far beyond its original craft base.[13]

As for the CIO, it could legitimately claim to be an unprecedented force for industrial unionism in some sectors of the economy, and some of its affiliates were models of trade union democracy. However, on the Pacific Coast, the new federation met with little success in pursuing its stated goal of organizing the unorganized. To be sure, there were important victories among lumber workers and metal miners, and some short-lived successes among the cannery and agricultural workers of California's farm factories. But for the most part, the CIO planted its banner in areas where long-established unions claimed jurisdiction and sometimes where workers had been organized for many years. When the decision was made to challenge the AFL across the board, Lewis, like Green, found himself making concessions that went against the grain of his stated principles. Nowhere was this more true than on the waterfront, where the CIO made significant headway but the pattern of entrenched craft unions remained largely in place. The Marine Cooks and Stewards' Association, which claimed a membership of eighty-two hundred, was one of the smallest unions in the CIO. Although the MCS represented only a single maritime craft in one coastal region of the United States, the union clung stubbornly to its independence and rejected pressure from Bridges and others to become an autonomous division of the NMU. Likewise, the Pacific Coast Marine Firemen, who were even smaller than the MCS, expressed the fear that within the NMU, or Lundeberg's Seafarers, they would become "nothing more than a despised and doglike auxiliary."[14]

The *Pacific Coast Longshoreman,* voice of the Tacoma ILA local and an additional handful of AFL loyalists, could claim with some effect that the issue between the CIO and the AFL "is not industrial unionism versus craft unionism . . . and [the CIO's] purpose is not to organize the unorganized workers." Unions like the SUP and the Tacoma ILA, both proud and venerable organizations that cherished their autonomy and adhered to the voluntarist traditions of the AFL, saw the CIO as a steamroller and charged that the marriage of convenience between the autocratic Lewis and the Communists was "the first step toward a dictatorship or a totalitarian government."[15]

In retrospect, it is easy to dismiss these accusations as examples of the paranoia of the moment. Even a tiny craft union like the MCS could retain its independence within the CIO; the Communists showed far more respect for trade union democracy than their enemies acknowledged; and Lewis, who was indeed an autocrat, had the wisdom to tolerate a good deal of democratic ferment in CIO affiliates (other than his Mine Workers) as long as the greater good of the federation was not disrupted. True or not, however, the bitter charges and countercharges between rival organizations reveal something of the enormous energy that was expended in labor's civil war. As late as June 1940, the Los Angeles waterfront was in chaos over jurisdictional disputes between the competing federations. When the Consolidated Steel Corporation agreed to hire only AFL members at its Long Beach shipyard, the CIO retaliated by picketing AFL-organized restaurants and bars in San Pedro, closing down sixty-seven establishments. In return, members of AFL culinary unions picketed the docks and tied up thirteen ships. This kind of fratricidal warfare would continue to plague the waterfront for another decade and a half, until the AFL-CIO merger in 1955.[16]

It is tragic that the militancy of the marine workers turned inward and resulted in "civil war amongst men who [had] stood together and fought side by side for years." Even so, the achievements of the Pentecostal era remained real and durable. To some degree they were possible because of conditions that were specific to the decade of the Great Depression and the New Deal. But the maritime workers' own subculture was a vital ingredient in the fuel that propelled them forward during the 1930s, and it drew upon wellsprings that were deeply embedded in the historical experience of the waterfront labor force. This subculture was nurtured in the isolation of sailortowns, in the harsh conditions of work aboard ship and along shore, in the encounter with diverse ways of life in the world's port cities. It was replenished by migrants from Australia, Great Britain, and Scandinavia, and from the lumber camps and sawmill towns of the Pacific Northwest. The contradictory force of this experience pulled men toward cynicism and hope, cosmopolitanism and provincialism, revolutionary syndicalism and craft unionism. It is true that the remnants of this once vibrant subculture barely exist today beyond a few shrinking enclaves. But to deny the richness of the past because of the paucity of the present would be to deny history its discontinuity and would, in this instance, reflect what E. P. Thompson has called "the enormous condescension of posterity." I hope this study has avoided that condescension and has captured some of the drama and the motive force of a powerful historical moment that transformed the lives of a generation of workers on the waterfronts of the Pacific Coast.[17]

Notes

Introduction

1. For the classic scholarly overview of the New Deal era as a time of widespread labor militancy, see Irving Bernstein, *Turbulent Years: A History of the American Worker, 1933–1941* (Boston: Houghton Mifflin, 1970). Two articles that exemplify the more recent emphasis in its most sweeping form are Melvyn Dubofsky, "Not So 'Turbulent Years': Another Look at the American 1930s," *Amerikastudien* 24 (Jan. 1979): 5–20; and Sidney Verba and Kay Lehman Schlozman, "Unemployment, Class Consciousness, and Radical Politics: What Didn't Happen in the Thirties," *Journal of Politics* 39 (May 1977): 291-323. Carefully researched studies that reach similar (although more limited) conclusions about the "not so turbulent" thirties include John Bodnar, "Immigration, Kinship, and the Rise of Working-Class Realism in Industrial America," *Journal of Social History* 14 (Fall 1980): 45–65; Ray Boryczka, "Militancy and Factionalism in the United Auto Workers, 1937–1941," *Maryland Historian* 8 (Fall 1977): 13–25; Peter Friedlander, *The Emergence of a UAW Local, 1936–1939: A Study in Class and Culture* (Pittsburgh: University of Pittsburgh Press, 1975); Nelson Lichtenstein, "Auto Worker Militancy and the Structure of Factory Life, 1937–1955," *Journal of American History* 67 (Sept. 1980): 335–53; Daniel Nelson, "Origins of the Sit-Down Era: Worker Militancy and Innovation in the Rubber Industry, 1934–38," *Labor History* 23 (Spring 1982): 198–225; Daniel Nelson, "The CIO at Bay: Labor Militancy and Politics in Akron, 1936–1938," *Journal of American History* 71 (Dec. 1984): 565–86; Ronald W. Schatz, *The Electrical Workers: A History of Labor at General Electric and Westinghouse, 1923–60* (Urbana: University of Illinois Press, 1983); and Robert H. Zieger, "The Limits of Militancy: Organizing Paper Workers, 1933–35," *Journal of American History* 63 (Dec. 1976): 638–57.

2. Silas B. Axtell, comp., *A Symposium on Andrew Furuseth* (New Bedford, Mass.: Darwin Press, 1948), p. 81.

3. Plant quoted in Howard Kimeldorf, "Reds or Rackets: The Making of Radical and Conservative Unions on the Waterfront" (manuscript accepted for publication by the University of California Press), p. 44. On the longshoremen, I have relied mainly

on the following: Charles B. Barnes, *The Longshoremen* (New York: Survey Associates, 1915); E. J. Hobsbawm, "National Unions on the Waterside," in Hobsbawm, *Labouring Men: Studies in the History of Labour* (New York: Basic Books, 1964), pp. 204–30; Charles P. Larrowe, *Shape-up and Hiring Hall: A Comparison of Hiring Methods and Labor Relations on the New York and Seattle Waterfronts* (Berkeley: University of California Press, 1955); Raymond Charles Miller, "The Dockworker Subculture and Some Problems in Cross-Cultural and Cross-Time Generalizations," *Comparative Studies in Society and History* 11 (June 1969): 302–14; Herb Mills, "The San Francisco Waterfront: The Social Consequences of Industrial Modernization," in *Case Studies on the Labor Process*, ed. Andrew Zimbalist (New York: Monthly Review Press, 1979), pp. 127–55; and William W. Pilcher, *The Portland Longshoremen: A Dispersed Urban Community* (New York: Holt, Rinehart and Winston, 1972). Kimeldorf, "Reds or Rackets," is an excellent study of the contrast between the cosmopolitanism of West Coast dockworkers and the conservatism and insularity of their New York counterparts.

4. The literature on this subject is voluminous. In England, especially, the work of E. P. Thompson has sparked a vigorous and sometimes bitter debate among historians and others. From the vast literature, I will cite only the following works that I have found particularly instructive: E. P. Thompson, *The Making of the English Working Class* (New York: Pantheon, 1963); E. P. Thompson, "Eighteenth-Century English Society: Class Struggle without Class?" *Social History* 3 (May 1978): 133–65; E. P. Thompson, *The Poverty of Theory and Other Essays* (New York: Monthly Review Press, 1980); Raymond Williams, *Marxism and Literature* (New York: Oxford University Press, 1977); Perry Anderson, *Arguments within English Marxism* (London: Verso, 1980); Richard Johnson, "Three Problematics: Elements of a Theory of Working-Class Culture," in *Working-Class Culture: Studies in History and Theory*, ed. J. Clarke, C. Critcher, and R. Johnson (New York: St. Martin's, 1980), pp. 201–37; and Gareth Stedman-Jones, "History and Theory," *History Workshop Journal*, no. 8 (Autumn 1979): 198–202. On the continual recomposition of the working class and the persistence of internal divisions, see Richard Edwards, *Contested Terrain: The Transformation of the Workplace in the Twentieth Century* (New York: Basic Books, 1979), and David M. Gordon, Richard Edwards, and Michael Reich, *Segmented Work, Divided Workers: The Historical Transformation of Labor in the United States* (New York: Cambridge University Press, 1982).

5. Thompson, *The Making of the English Working Class*, p. 10.

6. "Interview with Herbert Gutman," *Radical History Review*, no. 27 (May 1983): 215; Gareth Stedman-Jones, "Working-Class Culture and Working-Class Politics in London, 1870–1900; Notes on the Remaking of a Working Class," *Journal of Social History* 7 (Summer 1974): 460–508; Standish Meacham, *A Life Apart: The English Working Class, 1890–1914* (Cambridge, Mass.: Harvard University Press, 1977); John Bodnar, *Workers' World: Kinship, Community, and Protest in an Industrial Society, 1900–1940* (Baltimore: Johns Hopkins University Press, 1982); Tamara K. Hareven and Randolph Langenbach, *Amoskeag: Life and Work in an American Factory City* (New York: Pantheon, 1978); Bruce Nelson, "Immigrant Enclaves versus Class Consciousness: Miners and Steel Workers in Pennsylvania, 1900–1940," *Reviews in American History* 11 (Dec. 1983): 576–81. On the 1919 steel strike, see Jeremy Brecher, *Strike!* (San Francisco: Straight Arrow Books, 1972), pp. 118–28,

and David Brody, *Labor in Crisis: The Steel Strike of 1919* (Philadelphia: Lippincott, 1965); on the great eruptions in the textile industry, see Melvyn Dubofsky, *We Shall Be All: A History of the Industrial Workers of the World* (New York: Quadrangle/New York Times Book Co., 1969), pp. 227–62, and Bernstein, *Turbulent Years*, pp. 298–315.

For attempts at a typology of working-class culture and consciousness in the United States, see Bruce Laurie, *Working People of Philadelphia, 1800–1850* (Philadelphia: Temple University Press, 1981), and Alan Dawley and Paul Faler, "Working-Class Culture and Politics in the Industrial Revolution: Sources of Loyalism and Rebellion," *Journal of Social History* 9 (Summer 1976): 466–80. For a provocative study of the impact of ethnic and regional subcultures on the consciousness of autoworkers in the 1930s, see Friedlander, *The Emergence of a UAW Local*.

7. Bruce Nelson, " 'Pentecost' on the Pacific: Maritime Workers and Working-Class Consciousness in the 1930s," *Political Power and Social Theory* 4 (1984): 157.

8. On the relationship between "inherent" and "derived" ideas, I have benefited from the discussion in George Rudé, *Ideology and Popular Protest* (New York: Pantheon, 1980), especially pp. 28–29, 35–36. Rudé emphasizes that "among the 'inherent' beliefs of one generation, and forming part of its basic culture, are many beliefs that were originally derived from outside by an earlier one"; and also that "the derived or more 'structured' ideas are often a more sophisticated distillation of popular experience and the people's 'inherent' beliefs." The statement about the "final importance" of the "political front" was made by Harry Bridges in 1939. See *Daily Proceedings of the Second Constitutional Convention of the Congress of Industrial Organizations*, San Francisco, Oct. 10–13, 1939, p. 67.

9. For a recent survey of the decline of syndicalism and the rise of communism in the labor movement, see Larry Peterson, "Revolutionary Socialism and Industrial Unrest in the Era of the Winnipeg General Strike: The Origins of Communist Labour Unionism in Europe and North America," *Labour/Le Travail*, no. 13 (Spring 1984): 115–31. Peterson emphasizes the Communists' success at incorporating syndicalist leaders and practices into their movement. On the IWW in the United States, the best study is Dubofsky, *We Shall Be All*.

10. The pioneering recent interpretation of syndicalist tendencies in the labor movement is David Montgomery, "The 'New Unionism' and the Transformation of Workers' Consciousness in America, 1909–22," in Montgomery, *Workers' Control in America: Studies in the History of Work, Technology, and Labor Struggles* (New York: Cambridge University Press, 1979), pp. 91–112. Another valuable introduction to the mood of syndicalism is Richard Hyman's foreword to the 1975 edition of *The Frontier of Control: A Study in British Workshop Politics*, by Carter L. Goodrich (1920; reprint ed., London: Pluto Press, 1975), especially pp. vii–xix. Other studies that have helped to shape my thinking on this subject include Mike Davis, "The Stop Watch and the Wooden Shoe: Scientific Management and the Industrial Workers of the World," *Radical America* 9 (Jan.–Feb. 1975): 69–95; James E. Cronin, "Labor Insurgency and Class Formation: Comparative Perspectives on the Crisis of 1917–1920 in Europe," in *Work, Community, and Power: The Experience of Labor in Europe and America, 1900–1925*, ed. James E. Cronin and Carmen Sirianni (Philadelphia: Temple University Press, 1983): 20–48; Carmen Sirianni, "Workers' Control in Europe: A Comparative Sociological Analysis," in ibid., pp. 254–310; Bernard

H. Moss, *The Origins of the French Labor Movement, 1830–1914: The Socialism of Skilled Workers* (Berkeley: University of California Press, 1976); William Rosenberg, "Workers and Workers' Control in the Russian Revolution," *History Workshop Journal*, no. 5 (Spring 1978): 89–97; Steve Smith, "Craft Consciousness, Class Consciousness: Petrograd 1917," *History Workshop Journal*, no. 11 (Spring 1981): 35-56; and Chris Goodey, "Factory Committees and the Dictatorship of the Proletariat (1918)," *Critique*, no. 3 (Autumn 1974): 27–47.

11. Moss, *Origins of the French Labor Movement*, p. 154; [Tom Mann], *Tom Mann's Memoirs* (1923; reprint ed., London: MacGibbon and Key, 1967), p. 206; Emile Pouget, "Syndicalism in France," *International Socialist Review* 15 (Aug. 1914): 100–105; Helen Marot, *American Labor Unions* (New York: Henry Holt, 1914), p. 250. See also Robert Rives La Monte, "The New Socialism," *International Socialist Review* 13 (Sept. 1912): 212–16.

12. Hyman, "Foreword," p. x; George P. West, "Andrew Furuseth and the Radicals," *Survey*, Nov. 5, 1921, p. 209.

13. James E. Cronin has argued that in addition to the process of capitalist rationalization on the job, urbanization—and the development of working-class neighborhoods and urban social networks in particular—also played a vital role in the shaping of working-class consciousness and activity during this period. See Cronin, "Labor Insurgency and Class Formation," p. 40.

14. On Italy, see Gwynn A. Williams, *Proletarian Order: Antonio Gramsci, Factory Councils, and the Origins of Italian Communism, 1911–1921* (London: Pluto Press, 1975), and Paolo Spriano, *The Occupation of the Factories: Italy, 1920* (London, Pluto Press, 1975); on Scotland, see James Hinton, *The First Shop Stewards' Movement* (London: Allen and Unwin, 1973); on Germany, see Barrington Moore, Jr., *Injustice: The Social Bases of Obedience and Revolt* (White Plains, N.Y.: M. E. Sharpe, 1978), especially pp. 275–353.

15. Montgomery, *Workers' Control in America*, p. 94; Steve Fraser, "Dress Rehearsal for the New Deal: Shop-Floor Insurgents, Political Elites, and Industrial Democracy in the Amalgamated Clothing Workers," in *Working-Class America: Essays on Labor, Community, and American Society*, ed. Michael H. Frisch and Daniel J. Walkowitz (Urbana: University of Illinois Press, 1983), p. 227; Brody, *Labor in Crisis*, p. 113; *Nation* and Interchurch World Movement *Report* quoted in Brecher, *Strike!*, pp. 101, 120. Fraser has noted that the syndicalist impulse that flourished among New York clothing workers was a "complex and ambiguous phenomenon" that "often extended no farther than the horizon created by their own tiny shops." Fraser, "Dress Rehearsal for the New Deal," p. 228.

16. On the role of skilled workers in the workers' movement of this era, see the articles by Cronin, Goodey, Montgomery, and Sirianni cited in note 10.

17. Charles Ashleigh, "The Floater," *International Socialist Review* 15 (July 1914): 35, 37.

18. Joseph Conlin has argued that the Wobblies did not consider themselves syndicalists, and that the term was applied to them mainly by their enemies. They did indeed carry on extended polemics with such converts to syndicalism as William Z. Foster and Tom Mann over the question of "dual unionism" versus "boring from within." But in the final analysis, their strategic orientation and ultimate goals had a great deal in common with syndicalism and must be given greater weight than tactical

disagreements in evaluating the IWW's relationship to the syndicalist movement. See Joseph Robert Conlin, *Bread and Roses Too: Studies of the Wobblies* (Westport, Conn.: Greenwood Press, 1969), pp. 8–40, and the opposite point of view expressed by Dubofsky in *We Shall Be All*, pp. 146–70.

19. Montgomery, *Workers' Control in America*, pp. 105–7; Dubofsky, *We Shall Be All*, p. 170.

20. Robert James Lampman, "Collective Bargaining of West Coast Sailors, 1885–1947: A Case Study in Unionism" (Ph.D. diss., University of Wisconsin, 1950), p. 174; Betty V. H. Schneider, *Industrial Relations in the West Coast Maritime Industry* (Berkeley: University of California, Institute of Industrial Relations, 1958), p. 41; Rose Pesotta, *Bread upon the Waters* (New York: Dodd, Mead, 1944), p. 90.

1. Foc' sle and Sailortown: The Life, Work, and Subculture of Merchant Seamen

1. Elmo Paul Hohman, *History of American Merchant Seamen* (Hamden, Conn.: Shoe String Press, 1956), pp. 28–29.

2. Richard B. Morris, *Government and Labor in Early America* (1946; reprint ed., New York: Octagon Books, 1965), p. 263; Olmsted quoted in Jesse Lemisch, "Jack Tar in the Streets: Merchant Seamen in the Politics of Revolutionary America," *William and Mary Quarterly*, 3d ser., 25 (July 1968): 378.

3. Frederick Law Olmsted, *The Cotton Kingdom: A Traveller's Observation on Cotton and Slavery in the American Slave States*, ed. Arthur M. Schlesinger (1861; reprint ed., New York: Alfred A. Knopf, 1953), pp. 452–53; Joseph P. Goldberg, *The Maritime Story: A Study in Labor-Management Relations* (Cambridge, Mass.: Harvard University Press, 1958), p. 37.

4. Dana quoted in Hyman Weintraub, *Andrew Furuseth: Emancipator of the Seamen* (Berkeley: University of California Press, 1959), p. 3.

5. National Seamen's Union of America (NSUA), *The Red Record: A Brief Resume of Some of the Cruelties Perpetrated upon American Seamen at the Present Time* (San Francisco: Coast Seamen's Journal, [1895?]), pp. 2, 8, 10, 15.

6. Richard Henry Dana, Jr., *Cruelty to Seamen: Being the Case of Nichols and Couch* (1839; reprint ed., Berkeley: privately printed, 1937), pp. 8, 9; NSUA, *The Red Record*, p. 11.

7. Weintraub, *Andrew Furuseth*, pp. 3, 39; NSUA, *The Red Record*, p. 1.

8. For examples of the persistence of buckoism after the passage of the La Follette Seamen's Act of 1915, see: *Seamen's Journal*, Feb. 1923, p. 10; *Marine Workers Voice*, Oct. 1929, p. 3; N. Sparks, *The Struggle of the Marine Workers* (New York: International Publishers, 1930), pp. 32–33; Richard O. Boyer, *The Dark Ship* (Boston: Little, Brown, 1947), pp. 122–27; Joseph Curran, "The Reminiscences of Joseph Curran," Oral History Collection, Columbia University, 1964, pp. 27–31.

9. Furuseth quoted in Jerold S. Auerbach, "Progressives at Sea: The La Follette Act of 1915," *Labor History* 2 (Fall 1961): 345; Curran quoted in Boyer, *The Dark Ship*, p. 186; Hugh Mulzac, *A Star to Steer By* (New York: International Publishers, 1963), p. 99; Robinson quoted in "Seven Seamen," *Fortune* 16 (Sept. 1937): 122.

10. George McPherson Hunter, "Destitution among Seamen," *Survey*, Aug. 3, 1912, p. 618; "Seven Seamen," p. 122; A British Marine Officer, "Can America

Produce Merchant Seamen?" *Atlantic Monthly* 104 (Dec. 1909): 799; Tony Lane, " 'Philosophical Anarchists': British Merchant Seamen and Their Attitudes to Authority, 1850–1910" (unpublished paper), p. 3.

11. "Seven Seamen," p. 132; Charles Rubin, *The Log of Rubin the Sailor* (New York: International Publishers, 1973), p. 143.

12. Rubin, *Log of Rubin the Sailor,* pp. 118, 124; Murray Kempton, *Part of Our Time: Some Monuments and Ruins of the Thirties* (New York: Simon and Schuster, 1955), p. 87.

13. Goldberg, *The Maritime Story,* pp. 12–14; [Walter Macarthur], "The Boarding-Houses," in Walter Macarthur, Correspondence and Papers, c. 1905–1944, carton 1, Bancroft Library, University of California, Berkeley; Walter Macarthur to Victor A. Olander, Jan. 23, 1932, in ibid.

14. Captain E. W. Mason to Walter Macarthur, Mar. 18, 1932, in Macarthur papers, carton 1; Judith Fingard, *Jack in Port: Sailortowns of Eastern Canada* (Toronto: University of Toronto Press, 1982), p. 241; Judith Fingard, " 'Those Crimps of Hell and Goblins Damned': The Image and Reality of Quebec's Sailortown Bosses," in *Working Men Who Got Wet,* ed. Rosemary Ommer and Gerald Panting (St. John's: Maritime History Group, Memorial University of Newfoundland, 1980), pp. 330–31; *Coast Seamen's Journal* quoted in Peter B. Gill [with Ottilie Dombroff Markholt], "The Sailors' Union of the Pacific from 1885 to 1929" (unpublished manuscript, Seattle, 1942, in Bancroft Library, University of California, Berkeley), pp. 158–59, hereafter cited as Gill, "Sailors' Union of the Pacific."

15. Marine Workers Industrial Union, *The Centralized Shipping Bureau* (New York: Marine Workers Industrial Union, 1934), pp. 13–14. Alexander, a Communist, was one of the chief architects of Baltimore's Centralized Shipping Bureau in 1934. Seamen registered and shipped on a rotary basis, at a hall that they themselves directed, thus breaking the hold of the crimps, until the shipowners retaliated by boycotting the port of Baltimore. Later in the same year the great West Coast maritime strike gave the union hiring hall a momentum it was never to relinquish, and the crimping system was finally destroyed. For more on the Centralized Shipping Bureau, see chapter 3.

16. Paul S. Taylor, *The Sailors' Union of the Pacific* (New York: Ronald Press, 1923), p. 18. The view of the seaman as childlike and irresponsible was widespread. The particular quote is from Rev. Samuel Boult, chaplain of the New York Port Society. See "The Hard Lot of the Sailor," *Survey,* May 13, 1911, p. 266.

17. *Waterfront Worker,* Dec. 10, 1934, p. 6; Al Richmond, *A Long View from the Left: Memoirs of an American Revolutionary* (Boston: Houghton Mifflin, 1973), p. 166. On the seamen's indictment of the Seamen's Church Institute, see also Sparks, *Struggle of the Marine Workers,* pp. 20–22.

18. Hiller B. Zobel, *The Boston Massacre* (New York: W. W. Norton, 1970), pp. 191, 214; Carl Bridenbaugh, *Cities in Revolt: Urban Life in America, 1743–1776* (New York: Alfred A. Knopf, 1955), pp. 114–17, 309; Lemisch, "Jack Tar in the Streets," passim.

19. Morris, *Government and Labor in Early America,* p. 265; Fingard, *Jack in Port,* p. 95.

20. Helen Lawrenson, *Stranger at the Party: A Memoir* (New York: Random House, 1975), pp. 220–21. Helen Lawrenson's husband, Jack Lawrenson, was a

seaman, a Communist party member (until 1945), and a vice president of the National Maritime Union for more than a decade.

21. U.S. Congress, House, Committee on Merchant Marine and Fisheries, *Hearings on Bills Relating to the Rights and Duties of Seamen,* 54th Cong., 1st sess., 1896 (Washington, D.C.: Government Printing Office, 1896), pp. 38, 45.

22. Weintraub, *Andrew Furuseth,* pp. 109, 162.

23. Morris, *Government and Labor in Early America,* p. 265; Hohman, *American Merchant Seamen,* p. 7; Fingard, *Jack in Port,* p. 51.

24. Lemisch, "Jack Tar in the Streets," pp. 396, 407, and passim. In an even more revealing article, Lemisch reported on the conduct of American seamen in British naval prisons during the American Revolution. Here, especially on the prison ships in New York harbor, they were confronted with "crowding, filth, disease, and death. Contemporaries estimated that close to 12,000 died there during the war." With death a more likely fate than liberation through a prisoner exchange, and in spite of constant inducements to defect and join the British navy, Lemisch found that only 8 percent of the prisoners chose to defect, and of these perhaps as many as 50 percent were "Old Countrymen," born in the British Isles. Moreover, the prisoners, as one put it, "adventured to form themselves into a republic, framed a constitution and enacted wholesome laws with suitable penalties" for those who deviated from the revolutionary norm. Jesse Lemisch, "Listening to the 'Inarticulate': William Widger's Dream and the Loyalties of American Revolutionary Seamen in British Prisons," *Journal of Social History* 3 (Fall 1969): 9, 17, 21, and passim.

25. Kempton, *Part of Our Time,* p. 95; Boyer, *The Dark Ship,* p. 198.

26. Bernard Raskin, *On a True Course: The Story of the National Maritime Union of America, AFL-CIO* (New York: National Maritime Union of America, 1967), p. 64; Boyer, *The Dark Ship,* p. 114.

27. Peter H. Wood, *Black Majority: Negroes in South Carolina from 1670 through the Stono Rebellion* (New York: Alfred A. Knopf, 1974), p. 286; Thompson, "Eighteenth-Century English Society," pp. 150, 157, 163.

28. Mulzac, *A Star to Steer By,* p. 95. Recent studies that emphasize the seaman's capacity for rationality and prudent calculation include Fingard, *Jack in Port;* Lewis R. Fischer, "A Dereliction of Duty: The Problem of Desertion on Nineteenth Century Sailing Vessels," in Ommer and Panting, eds., *Working Men Who Got Wet,* pp. 53–70, and Lane, " 'Philosophical Anarchists.' "

29. Lane, " 'Philosophical Anarchists,' " pp. 15–16; United States Maritime Commission, *Economic Survey of the American Merchant Marine* (Washington, D.C.: Government Printing Office, 1937), p. 45.

30. Fischer, "A Dereliction of Duty," pp. 55, 63, 65; Fingard, *Jack in Port,* pp. 69, 142–43. In an article entitled "Resistance to Slavery," George M. Fredrickson and Christopher Lasch offer an interesting comparison between slavery and other "total institutions" such as prisons and mental hospitals. In all such institutions "conventional politics are nonexistent." In seeking a more viable model than that of Sambo-like quiescence or that of constant rebellion, Fredrickson and Lasch point to "virtuosos, neither docile nor rebellious, who spend their lives in skillful and somewhat cynical attempts to beat the system at its own game." Although the world of the seamen did not constitute a "total institution," there seem to be clear parallels between the allegedly

irresponsible behavior of seamen in periods of quiescence and the behavior of the "virtuosos" described by Fredrickson and Lasch. See George M. Fredrickson and Christopher Lasch, "Resistance to Slavery," in *American Slavery: The Question of Resistance*, ed. John H. Bracey, Jr., August Meier, and Elliott Rudwick (Belmont, Calif.: Wadsworth Publishing Co., 1971), pp. 179–92.

31. Peter DeLottinville, "Joe Beef of Montreal: Working Class Culture and the Tavern, 1869–1889," *Labour/Le Travailleur*, no. 8–9 (Autumn-Spring 1981–82), p. 24; Richard C. McKay, *South Street: A Maritime History of New York* (New York: G. P. Putnam's Sons, 1934), p. 413; Herman "Dutch" Thomas, "Seamen Ashore: Waterfronts of the World," *Hawsepipe* 1 (Mar.–Apr., 1982): 16.

32. Herman Melville, *Redburn, His First Voyage* (1849; reprint ed., London: Penguin Books, 1976), p. 263; Lawrenson, *Stranger at the Party*, pp. 217, 220; Jack London, *John Barleycorn* (1913; reprint ed., New York: Greenwood Press, 1968), pp. 37–42. An insightful discussion of the saloon as a social center and an agency for reinforcing working-class values is Jon M. Kingsdale, "The 'Poor Man's Club': Social Functions of the Urban Working-Class Saloon," *American Quarterly* 23 (Oct. 1973): 472–89.

33. Albert Richard Wetjen, "Ships, Men and the Sea," *Collier's*, Mar. 7, 1925, p. 25.

34. "The Maritime Unions," *Fortune* 16 (Sept. 1937): 123. *Fortune* characterized seamen as "the true proletariat of the Western world, the homeless, rootless, and eternally unmoneyed . . . men who have no stake in the system beyond this month's voyage, who have been all over the world and seen none of it beyond its dull ubiquitous Sailortowns, who have become a part of it nowhere. Four out of five of them have no wives and three out of five have no addresses."

35. *Voice of the Federation*, Oct. 10, 1935, p. 5; interview with Tommy Ray, May 31, 1979.

36. Bridges quoted in Charles P. Larrowe, *Harry Bridges: The Rise and Fall of Radical Labor in the United States* (New York: Lawrence Hill, 1972), p. 5; Mulzac, *A Star to Steer By*, pp. 38–39; Myers's experience described in Boyer, *The Dark Ship*, pp. 217–32; Rubin, *Log of Rubin the Sailor*, pp. 74–78.

37. Interview with Harold Johnson, Aug. 4, 1984; interview with Tommy Ray, May 31, 1979; Len De Caux, *Labor Radical—From the Wobblies to CIO: A Personal History* (Boston: Beacon Press, 1970), pp. 499–500.

38. Nathan Glazer, *The Social Basis of American Communism* (New York: Harcourt, Brace and World, 1961), pp. 114, 218; Robert Eugene Randolph, "History of the International Longshoremen's and Warehousemen's Union, 1945–1951" (M.A. thesis, University of California, Berkeley, 1952), p. 224; Albert Lannon, [Jr.], "Red Diaper Baby: A Personal Political Memoir" (unpublished autobiography, n.p., n.d.), p. 2.

39. Richmond, *Long View from the Left*, pp. 209–10; *New York Times*, Sept. 13, 1935, p. 12; Oct. 4, 1935, p. 18; Joseph Young to Tom Kozar, Aug. 1979, copy in author's possession.

40. Interview with Joe Stack, Nov. 26, 1978.

41. Richmond, *Long View from the Left*, pp. 200–201.

42. In an essay review of recent publications on the IWW, William Preston has offered a stinging critique of a " 'social sore' theory of American radicalism that

explains unrest solely as a product of bad conditions (presumably unique ones)." See Preston, "Shall This Be All?: U.S. Historians versus William D. Haywood *et al.,*" *Labor History* 12 (Summer 1971): 435–53. See also Barrington Moore's *Injustice,* a challenging and insightful study of the relationship between material conditions and popular protest. Moore argues that "misery in some objective sense is quite insufficient to provoke a popular outbreak" (p. 321).

43. Jane Cassels Record, "The San Francisco Waterfront: Crucible of Labor Factionalism" (unpublished paper, University of California, Institute of Industrial Relations, Berkeley, 1952), pp. 9–10.

44. Lawrenson, *Stranger at the Party,* p. 212; Boyer, *The Dark Ship,* p. 240; interview with Charles Rubin, Oct. 6, 1979.

45. Goldberg, *The Maritime Story,* p. 34; Mulzac, *A Star to Steer By,* p. 60; Weintraub, *Andrew Furuseth,* p. 140.

46. Hohman, *American Merchant Seamen,* pp. 116–17.

47. *Seamen's Journal,* Oct. 19, 1921, p. 9; Lampman, "Collective Bargaining of West Coast Sailors," pp. 49–51.

48. Interview with Dan Boano, Feb. 25, 1979.

49. "The Last Serfs," *Nation,* Feb. 2, 1927, p. 107.

50. Thompson, *Making of the English Working Class,* pp. 167, 185; Paul Avrich, *Kronstadt 1921* (Princeton: Princeton University Press, 1970). The statement about "fight[ing] capitalism to a finish" was widely attributed to Harry Lundeberg, a militant Sailors' Union of the Pacific member from Seattle who became the first president of the Maritime Federation of the Pacific. Lundeberg's career will be discussed at length in chapters 7 and 8.

51. John Steinbeck, *Of Mice and Men* (New York: Covici Friede, 1937), p. 28; *Seamen's Journal,* Oct. 26, 1921, p. 6; Eugene O'Neill, *The Long Voyage Home: Seven Plays of the Sea* (New York: Modern Library, 1946), p. 49.

52. Ray quoted in Kempton, *Part of Our Time,* p. 90.

53. *Seamen's Journal,* Oct. 26, 1921, p. 6.

54. Interview with Charles Rubin, Oct. 6, 1979.

55. Frank Paterno, "Trade Union Unity: Pennsylvania Strike," *Voice of the Federation,* Jan. 23, 1936, p. 2.

2. Craft Unionism and Syndicalist Unionism, 1885–1930

1. Weintraub, *Andrew Furuseth,* p. 58. Olander served as secretary-treasurer of the International Seamen's Union for many years; Scharrenberg was editor of the *Seamen's Journal* for more than two decades. On Scharrenberg's low opinion of the rank and file and his "decidedly middle-class" life-style, see Mary Ann Burki, "Paul Scharrenberg: White Shirt Sailor" (Ph.D. diss., University of Rochester, 1971), pp. 32–33, 35.

2. Weintraub, *Andrew Furuseth,* p. 11; Taylor, *Sailors' Union of the Pacific,* p. 47; Ira B. Cross, *A History of the Labor Movement in California* (Berkeley: University of California Press, 1935); pp. 157, 168; Alexander Saxton, *The Indispensable Enemy: Labor and the Anti-Chinese Movement in California* (Berkeley: University of California Press, 1971), pp. 194–99; sailors' spokesmen quoted on p. 199.

3. Weintraub, *Andrew Furuseth,* pp. 16–19.

4. Walter Macarthur to Victor A. Olander, Jan. 23, 1932, in Macarthur papers; Weintraub, *Andrew Furuseth,* pp. 12–13.

5. Furuseth's statement is in *Proceedings of the Twenty-fourth Annual Convention of the International Seamen's Union of America,* Philadelphia, Jan. 10–20, 1921, pp. 21–22, hereafter cited as ISU, *Proceedings.*

6. Taylor, *Sailors' Union of the Pacific,* pp. 9–10; interview with Bob McElroy, Aug. 19, 1981; interview with John P. Olsen, Oct. 22, 1981; telephone interview with Jim Kendall, July 16, 1981; Lampman, "Collective Bargaining of West Coast Sailors," p. 43n; See also "Nationality of Members of the International Seamen's Union of America," *Monthly Labor Review* 12 (Feb. 1921): 430–31.

7. Taylor, *Sailors' Union of the Pacific,* pp. 9–10, 140; Sailors' Union of the Pacific Delegation to the Emergency Convention of the Maritime Federation of the Pacific, "Answer to Resolution Introduced by Brother Harry Bridges, Local 38-79 Referring to Job Action," in International Longshoremen's and Warehousemen's Union, Subject files relating to seamen and maritime unions, c. 1936–76, carton 12, Bancroft Library, University of California, Berkeley, hereafter cited as ILWU files relating to seamen and maritime unions.

8. Taylor, *Sailors' Union of the Pacific,* p. 107; Gill, "Sailors' Union of the Pacific," p. 320; Auerbach, "Progressives at Sea," pp. 353–54; Goldberg, *The Maritime Story,* pp. 33–40; David Brody, *Steelworkers in America: The Nonunion Era* (Cambridge, Mass.: Harvard University Press, 1960), pp. 77, 82.

9. Axtell quoted in Gill, "Sailors' Union of the Pacific," p. 462.

10. Weintraub, *Andrew Furuseth,* p. 135. For a more positive view of the effectiveness of the Seamen's Act, see Paul S. Taylor, "Eight Years of the Seamen's Act," *American Labor Legislation Review* 25 (Mar. 1925): 52–63.

11. La Follette quoted in Weintraub, *Andrew Furuseth,* p. 132.

12. Silas B. Axtell to Friends of Furuseth Legislative Association, Dec. 25, 1946, in William Denman, Correspondence and Papers, c. 1900–1959, Bancroft Library, University of California, Berkeley; "Address by Carl Lynch before Furuseth Club," printed in *Congressional Record,* Mar. 14, 1946, p. 2; William Denman, "Andy Furuseth—The Abe Lincoln of the Sea" (unpublished manuscript, 1948), in Denman papers; Gompers quoted in Auerbach, "Progressives at Sea," p. 350; West, "Andrew Furuseth and the Radicals," p. 207.

13. Weintraub, *Andrew Furuseth,* pp. 2–19, 48–51; Taylor, *Sailors' Union of the Pacific,* pp. 175–76.

14. Weintraub, *Andrew Furuseth,* pp. 85, 91–92, 192.

15. George P. West, "Andrew Furuseth Stands Pat," *Survey,* Oct. 15, 1923, pp. 88–90; Andrew Furuseth, "Work Is Worship," in *A Symposium on Andrew Furuseth,* comp. Silas B. Axtell (New Bedford, Mass.: Darwin Press, 1948), p. 180.

16. Weintraub, *Andrew Furuseth,* p. 173; Walter Macarthur to Victor A. Olander, Jan. 23, 1932, in Macarthur papers; Sparks, *Struggle of the Marine Workers,* pp. 44–46; Goldberg, *The Maritime Story,* p. 96.

17. Weintraub, *Andrew Furuseth,* pp. 68, 157–58; Auerbach, "Progressives at Sea," p. 359; Gill, "Sailors' Union of the Pacific," p. 394; Sparks, *Struggle of the Marine Workers,* p. 44.

18. Weintraub, *Andrew Furuseth*, p. 23; Axtell, *A Symposium on Andrew Furuseth*, p. 81; *Seamen's Journal*, Nov. 23, 1921, p. 6; Apr. 1935, p. 8; West, "Andrew Furuseth and the Radicals," p. 209.

19. *Seamen's Journal*, Sept. 21, 1921, p. 9; Walter Macarthur to Ira B. Cross, Mar. 13, 1935, in Macarthur papers, carton 1.

20. "History of [the Marine Cooks and Stewards'] Union," p. 45, in National Union of Marine Cooks and Stewards (NUMCS), Records, c. 1935–55, carton 2, Bancroft Library, University of California, Berkeley; Auerbach, "Progressives at Sea," pp. 346–47; Saxton, *The Indispensable Enemy*, pp. 172, 244–47; Roger Daniels, *The Politics of Prejudice: The Anti-Japanese Movement in California and the Struggle for Japanese Exclusion* (Berkeley: University of California Press, 1962), pp. 27–28, 126 (n. 34); Burki, "Paul Scharrenberg: White Shirt Sailor," p. 164; *Seamen's Journal*, June 1929, p. 9.

21. *Seamen's Journal*, Sept. 26, 1900, p. 6; May 1, 1901, p. 6; Feb. 1929, p. 3; [Morris Watson], "No Colored Allowed to Work Here," pt. 1, p. 1, in ILWU files relating to seamen and maritime unions, carton 13.

22. Weintraub, *Andrew Furuseth*, p. 113; Auerbach, "Progressives at Sea," p. 357; Walter Macarthur to Ira B. Cross, Mar. 13, 1935, in Macarthur papers, carton 1; *Seamen's Journal*, May 29, 1901, p. 1.

23. *Seamen's Journal*, May 8, 1901, p. 7; Weintraub, *Andrew Furuseth*, p. 173; Auerbach, "Progressives at Sea," p. 352.

24. Gill, "Sailors' Union of the Pacific," pp. 525–28; Robert Bruere and Heber Blankenhorn quoted in ibid., p. 529 (emphasis added).

25. Goldberg, *The Maritime Story*, p. 94; *Seamen's Journal*, Nov. 17, 1920, p. 6.

26. Goldberg, *The Maritime Story*, p. 94; *Seamen's Journal*, Jan. 19, 1921, p. 8; Gill, "Sailors' Union of the Pacific," pp. 529–30.

27. Riggers and Stevedores' Union to San Francisco Labor Council, Nov. 5, 1914, in San Francisco Labor Council, AFL-CIO, Correspondence and Papers, 1906–65, carton 15, Bancroft Library, University of California, Berkeley, hereafter cited as SFLC papers; Robert Edward Lee Knight, *Industrial Relations in the San Francisco Bay Area, 1900–1918* (Berkeley: University of California Press, 1960), p. 272; Waterfront Workers' Federation, *The Longshoremen's Strike: A Brief Historical Sketch of the Strike Inaugurated on June 1, 1916, in Pacific Coast Ports of the United States* (San Francisco: Waterfront Workers' Federation, 1916), p. 5.

28. Riggers and Stevedores' Union, "Resolution Adopted by This Union," July 27, 1919, SFLC papers, carton 15; Waterfront Employers' Union, *"Full and By": A Message from the Waterfront Employers Union* (San Francisco: [Waterfront Employers' Union], Office of the Secretary, 1921), pp. 5, 8; Robert Coleman Francis, "A History of Labor on the San Francisco Waterfront" (Ph.D. diss., University of California, Berkeley, 1934), pp. 164–65; *San Francisco Daily News*, Sept. 27, 1919, p. 1; Sept. 30, 1919, p. 1; San Francisco Chamber of Commerce to John A. O'Connell, Nov. 19, 1919, SFLC papers, carton 15.

29. *San Francisco Daily News*, Sept. 29, 1919, p. 4; Francis, "History of Labor on the San Francisco Waterfront," p. 167.

30. Francis, "History of Labor on the San Francisco Waterfront," pp. 174–76.

31. David Jay Bercuson, "The One Big Union in Washington," *Pacific Northwest*

Quarterly 69 (July 1978): 127–31, 134; Gill, "Sailors' Union of the Pacific," pp. 367–69.

32. *Seamen's Journal,* Sept. 24, 1919, p. 6.

33. Gill, "Sailors' Union of the Pacific," pp. 580–81. Furuseth in turn characterized Thompson as "an editor of whose discretion we have no definite knowledge," and moved immediately to revoke the *Journal's* historic status as the voice of the International Seamen's Union. ISU, *Proceedings* (1921), pp. 133–34.

34. *New York Times,* May 4, 1921, p. 1; Goldberg, *The Maritime Story,* pp. 99–101; Gill, "Sailors' Union of the Pacific," p. 556.

35. Gill, "Sailors' Union of the Pacific," pp. 563–65.

36. Mulzac, *A Star to Steer By,* p. 97; *New York Times,* May 10, 1921, pp. 1, 3; May 19, 1921, p. 17; May 21, 1921, p. 1; May 22, 1921, p. 19.

37. Gill, "Sailors' Union of the Pacific," pp. 567–68; *Seamen's Journal,* Sept, 21, 1921, p. 6.

38. Gill, "Sailors' Union of the Pacific," p. 568; West, "Andrew Furuseth and the Radicals," p. 207; Larrowe, *Shape-up and Hiring Hall,* pp. 91–92; *Seamen's Journal,* July 13, 1921, p. 6.

39. West, "Andrew Furuseth Stands Pat," p. 86; *Seamen's Journal,* July 20, 1921, p. 1.

40. Andrew Furuseth to Thomas A. Hanson, July 13, 1921, in Victor A. Olander, Papers, 1898–1942, box 89, Chicago Historical Society Library; West, "Andrew Furuseth and the Radicals," pp. 208–9; Gill, "Sailors' Union of the Pacific," p. 584; Hyman Weintraub, "The I.W.W. in California, 1905–1931" (M.A. thesis, University of California, Los Angeles, 1947), p. 223.

41. *Seamen's Journal,* Sept. 21, 1921, pp. 6–7; Nov. 16, 1921, p. 6; *San Francisco Chronicle,* Sept. 10, 1921, p. 1; West, "Andrew Furuseth Stands Pat," p. 88; Sailors' Union of the Pacific, "Minutes," Sept. 26, 1921, and Nov. 14, 1921, in Paul Scharrenberg, Correspondence and Papers, carton 1, Bancroft Library, University of California, Berkeley.

42. West, "Andrew Furuseth and the Radicals," p. 209; *Seamen's Journal,* July 18, 1900, p. 7; Sept. 26, 1900, p. 6. On the Wheatland riot, Carleton Parker, and the California Commission of Immigration and Housing, see Cletus E. Daniel, *Bitter Harvest: A History of California Farmworkers, 1870–1941* (Ithaca: Cornell University Press, 1981), pp. 88–91, and Carleton H. Parker, *The Casual Laborer and Other Essays* (1920; reprint ed., Seattle: University of Washington Press, 1972).

43. J. Vance Thompson to Mr. Geo. L. Bell, n.d. (emphasis added), in Simon J. Lubin, Correspondence and Papers, 1912–36, carton 1, Bancroft Library, University of California, Berkeley.

44. J. Vance Thompson to Mr. Geo. L. Bell, Feb. 25, 1917; Mar. 26, 1917; Thompson, "Continued Report on I.W.W. Activities" [summer 1917]; Thompson, untitled report from San Francisco, July 6, 1917, all in Lubin papers, carton 1.

45. *Seamen's Journal,* July 6, 1921, p. 6; July 13, 1921, p. 6; July, 20, 1921, p. 1.

46. *Seamen's Journal,* July 20, 1921, p. 6; Aug. 10, 1921, p. 9; Aug. 17, 1921, p. 8.

47. West, "Andrew Furuseth Stands Pat," p. 86; West, "Andrew Furuseth and the Radicals," p. 209; Gill, "Sailors' Union of the Pacific," pp. 580–81.

48. Gill, "Sailors' Union of the Pacific," p. 584; interview with Ken Austin, Oct. 3, 1981; interview with Harry Bridges, Oct. 6, 1981; Arthur Emil Albrecht, *International Seamen's Union of America: A Study of Its History and Problems,* Bulletin of the United States Bureau of Labor Statistics, Miscellaneous Series No. 342 (Washington, D.C.: Government Printing Office, 1923), p. 100; *Industrial Solidarity* quoted in Gill, "Sailors' Union of the Pacific," pp. 593–94.

49. Weintraub, "The I.W.W. in California," pp. 225–26; *Western Worker,* July 15, 1932, p. 3.

50. Industrial Workers of the World, General Defense Committee, *California the Beautiful and the Damned* (Chicago: General Defense Committee, n.d.), pp. 11–12; Weintraub, "The I.W.W. in California," p. 226. The IWW declared, "It must be borne in mind that out of all the persons convicted under the criminal syndicalism law not one has been convicted for DOING anything. No crime, in the sense of a deed or even a word, has ever been charged against any one of them." In August 1923 the *Nation* pointed out that Judge Charles Busick of Sacramento had gone even further than the criminal syndicalism law by granting an injuction that made membership in the IWW contempt of court, thus making it possible to imprison Wobblies without the formality of a jury trial. *Nation,* Aug. 1, 1923, p. 100.

51. Goldberg, *The Maritime Story,* p. 125; West, "Andrew Furuseth Stands Pat," p. 87; "Upton Sinclair Defends the Law," *Nation,* June 6, 1923, p. 647; Upton Sinclair, "Protecting Our Liberties," *Nation,* July 4, 1923, p. 10; Mary Reed, "San Pedro," *Nation,* July 9, 1924, p. 45.

52. Weintraub, "The I.W.W. in California," pp. 227–28; Louis B. Perry and Richard S. Perry, *A History of the Los Angeles Labor Movement, 1911–1941* (Berkeley: University of California Press, 1963), pp. 183–84; West, "Andrew Furuseth Stands Pat," p. 87. See also George P. West, "After Liberalism Had Failed," *Nation,* May 30, 1923, p. 629; and Art Shields, "The San Pedro Strike," *Industrial Pioneer,* June 1923, pp. 14–18.

53. Reed, "San Pedro," pp. 45–46; Weintraub, "The I.W.W. in California," pp. 236–46, the *Industrial Worker* quoted on p. 246; West, "Andrew Furuseth Stands Pat," pp. 86–87; Harry Bridges interview. West offered a spirited defense of the IWW against Furuseth's accusations in "Andrew Furuseth Stands Pat," p. 87.

54. Ken Austin interview; Herman "Dutch" Thomas, "Seamen Ashore," *Hawsepipe* 1 (Nov.–Dec. 1981): 9; Pilcher, *The Portland Longshoremen,* p. 38. See also Jeremy R. Egolf, "The Limits of Shop Floor Struggle: Workers vs. the Bedaux System at Willapa Harbor Lumber Mills, 1933–35," *Labor History* 26 (Spring 1985): 195–229. Although he does not mention seamen, Egolf emphasizes (on p. 203) that "interoccupational mobility among 'stump farmers,' dock and mill workers, loggers and shingle weavers facilitated solidarity among workers."

55. Carlos A. Schwantes, *Radical Heritage: Labor, Socialism, and Reform in Washington and British Columbia, 1885–1917* (Seattle: University of Washington Press, 1979), pp. 20, 153; Murray Morgan, *The Last Wilderness* (New York: Viking Press, 1955), p. 140; Harvey O'Connor, *Revolution in Seattle: A Memoir* (New York: Monthly Review Press, 1964), p. 61; Tom Scribner, *Lumberjack* (Davenport, Calif.: Redwood Ripsaw, 1966), p. 1. Robert E. Ficken argues that by 1917 the larger lumber operators in the Northwest had improved conditions in the logging camps in order to

reduce turnover and increase efficiency. See Ficken, "The Wobbly Horrors: Pacific Northwest Lumbermen and the Industrial Workers of the World, 1917–1918," *Labor History* 24 (Summer 1983): 325–26.

56. Vernon H. Jensen, *Lumber and Labor* (New York: Farrar and Rinehart, 1945), pp. 30, 107; Morgan, *The Last Wilderness,* pp. 133–34, 211.

57. O'Connor, *Revolution in Seattle,* p. 80; Scribner, *Lumberjack,* p. 1. See also Robert L. Tyler, *Rebels of the Woods: The I.W.W. in the Pacific Northwest* (Eugene: University of Oregon Books, 1967), pp. 85–94. For a more skeptical view of the IWW's achievements, see Ficken, "The Wobbly Horrors," pp. 340–41.

58. Lampman, "Collective Bargaining of West Coast Sailors," p. 174n; *Voice of the Federation* (Supplement), Aug. 20, 1936, pp. 1, 8; Ken Austin interview; Pilcher, *The Portland Longshoremen,* pp. 38, 42.

59. Ian Turner, *Industrial Labour and Politics: The Dynamics of the Labour Movement in Eastern Australia, 1900–1921* (Canberra: Australian National University, 1965), pp. 141–59; Joe Harris, *The Bitter Fight: A Pictorial History of the Australian Labour Movement* (Brisbane: University of Queensland Press, 1970), p. 249.

60. Turner, *Industrial Labour and Politics,* pp. 153–54; Ian Bedford, "The One Big Union, 1918–1923," in Ian Bedford and Ross Curnow, *Initiative and Organization* (Melbourne: F. W. Cheshire, 1963), p. 18.

61. Bedford, "The One Big Union," p. 31.

62. Harry Bridges interview; telephone interview with Frank Paton, Sept. 21, 1981; Maritime Federation of the Pacific Coast, *Proceedings of the Special Convention of the Maritime Federation of the Pacific Coast,* San Francisco, Nov. 12–22, 1935, Session of Nov. 13, pp. 8–10.

63. Larrowe, *Harry Bridges,* pp. 36–37.

64. Goldberg, *The Maritime Story,* pp. 118–21, quoted on p. 118; Weintraub, *Andrew Furuseth,* p. 159.

65. Weintraub, *Andrew Furuseth,* pp. 190–91; *ISU Pilot,* June 7, 1935, pp. 6–7; Sept. 13, 1935, p. 4; *Daily Worker,* Aug. 31, 1935, p. 5; Rubin, *Log of Rubin the Sailor,* p. 191; Philip Taft, "The Unlicensed Seafaring Unions," *Industrial and Labor Relations Review* 3 (Jan. 1950): 197.

66. Weintraub, *Andrew Furuseth,* p. 190; Irving Bernstein, *The Lean Years: A History of the American Worker, 1920–1933* (Boston: Houghton Mifflin, 1960), pp. 85–86; *Seamen's Journal,* Mar. 1930, p. 98.

67. Wytze Gorter and George H. Hildebrand, *The Pacific Coast Maritime Shipping Industry, 1930–1948,* vol. 2: *An Analysis of Performance* (Berkeley: University of California Press, 1954), p. 177.

68. United States Maritime Commission, *Economic Survey of the American Merchant Marine,* p. 35; "The U.S. Merchant Marine," *Fortune* 16 (Sept. 1937): 164, 169; Lampman, "Collective Bargaining of West Coast Sailors," p. 124.

69. Gorter and Hildebrand, *The Pacific Coast Maritime Shipping Industry,* vol. 2, pp. 259–60; Lampman, "Collective Bargaining of West Coast Sailors," pp. 126–29; [William A. Hurst and Lynn Mah], *Waterborne Trade of California Ports* (San Francisco: Federal Reserve Bank of San Francisco, 1951), p. 8. Roger Lapham, president of the American-Hawaiian Steamship Company, recalled that "we had

something like 13 or 14 competitors in the trade. We were for conferences to bring in non-conference lines as well as what we termed the industrial carriers. U.S. Steel had a large fleet. They wouldn't join the conference. Finally they agreed to more or less follow conference rates. Then Bethlehem Steel Company put some ships in the trade. They wouldn't join the conference. There were some out-and-out rate-cutters." Roger Lapham, "An Interview on Shipping, Labor, San Francisco City Government, and American Foreign Aid," conducted by Corinne L. Gilb, University of California, Berkeley, General Library, Regional Cultural History Project, 1957, p. 66.

70. "The U.S. Merchant Marine," pp. 61, 169; "Marine Subsidies," *Fortune* 16 (Sept. 1937): 65.

71. Felix Riesenberg, Jr., *Golden Gate: The Story of San Francisco Harbor* (New York: Tudor Publishing Co., 1940), pp. 238, 241–44, 298–302; "With Matson down to Melbourne," *Fortune* 16 (Sept. 1937): 105, 170, 172, 174.

72. Lampman, "Collective Bargaining of West Coast Sailors," pp. 131–34, Furuseth quoted on p. 132.

73. Lampman, "Collective Bargaining of West Coast Sailors," pp. 136–39; Waterfront Employers' Union, *"Full and By,"* p. 23.

74. Perry and Perry, *A History of the Los Angeles Labor Movement,* pp. 21, 200–201; Selig Perlman and Philip Taft, *History of Labor in the United States, 1896–1932,* vol. 4: *Labor Movements* (New York: Macmillan, 1935), p. 491; Bernstein, *The Lean Years,* pp. 146–48, quoted on p. 147.

75. Robert W. Cherny, "Securing 'Industrial Freedom': The American Plan in San Francisco" (paper delivered at the annual meeting of the Organization of American Historians, Los Angeles, Apr. 1984), pp. 1–8, Senate Committee on Education and Labor quoted on p. 1; Ray Stannard Baker, "A Corner in Labor: What Is Happening in San Francisco Where Unionism Holds Undisputed Sway," *McClure's Magazine* 22 (Feb. 1904): 366–78; Saxton, *The Indispensable Enemy,* pp. 241–42; Robert W. Dunn, *The Americanization of Labor: The Employers' Offensive against the Trade Unions* (New York: International Publishers, 1927), p. 49; Cross, *A History of the Labor Movement in California,* p. 254; Riesenberg, *Golden Gate,* p. 304.

76. At times the policy of slashing wages proved self-defeating, and the employers were forced to offer higher rates in order to retain a necessary core of experienced and skilled seamen. Goldberg, *The Maritime Story,* p. 113; William S. Hopkins, "Employment Exchanges for Seamen," *American Economic Review* 25 (June 1935): 252.

77. Walter J. Petersen, *Marine Labor Union Leadership* (San Francisco, 1925), pp. 46, 50, 52.

78. Lampman, "Collective Bargaining of West Coast Sailors," p. 148; Paul S. Taylor and Norman Leon Gold, "San Francisco and the General Strike," *Survey Graphic* 23 (Sept. 1934): 405; Hopkins, "Employment Exchanges for Seamen," p. 255.

79. Hopkins, "Employment Exchanges for Seamen," pp. 254–55; Gill, "Sailors' Union of the Pacific," pp. 645–50, 661.

80. George Larsen quoted in Weintraub, *Andrew Furuseth,* p. 159; *Seamen's Journal,* Apr. 1936, p. 136; Walter Galenson, *The CIO Challenge to the AFL: A History of the American Labor Movement, 1935–1941* (Cambridge, Mass.: Harvard University Press, 1960), p. 436.

3. Red Unionism: The Communist Party and the
Marine Workers Industrial Union

1. For the traditional view of the American Communist party, focusing on its subservience to the Soviet Union and the development of line and leadership at the top, see Theodore Draper, *The Roots of American Communism* (New York: Viking Press, 1957); Theodore Draper, *American Communism and Soviet Russia* (New York: Viking Press, 1960); Irving Howe and Lewis Coser, *The American Communist Party: A Critical History (1919–1957)* (Boston: Beacon Press, 1957); Max M. Kampelman, *The Communist Party vs. the C.I.O.: A Study in Power Politics* (New York: Frederick A. Praeger, 1957); Harvey Klehr, *The Heydey of American Communism: The Depression Decade* (New York: Basic Books, 1984). The most systematic apologia is William Z. Foster, *History of the Communist Party of the United States* (New York: International Publishers, 1952). New departures include Paul Buhle, "Jews and American Communism: The Cultural Question," *Radical History Review*, no. 23 (Spring 1980): 9–33; Maurice Isserman, "The 1956 Generation: An Alternative Approach to the History of American Communism," *Radical America* 14 (Mar.–Apr. 1980): 43–51; Maurice Isserman, *Which Side Were You On? The American Communist Party during the Second World War* (Middletown, Conn.: Wesleyan University Press, 1982); and Mark Naison, *Communists in Harlem during the Depression* (Urbana: University of Illinois Press, 1983). See also Nelson Lichtenstein, "The Communist Experience in American Trade Unions," *Industrial Relations* 19 (Spring 1980): 119–31; James R. Prickett, "New Perspectives on American Communism and the Labor Movement," *Political Power and Social Theory* 4 (1984): 3–36; and the rejoinder to Prickett by Dorothy Healey, "False Consciousness and Labor Historians," ibid., pp. 281–88.

The memoirs of individual Party members have been the most valuable source for demystifying the Communist party and understanding the lives and aspirations of its active members. Among the most useful of these recollections are George Charney, *A Long Journey* (Chicago: Quadrangle Books, 1968); Peggy Dennis, *The Autobiography of an American Communist: A Personal View of a Political Life, 1925–1975* (Westport, Conn.: Lawrence Hill; Berkeley: Creative Arts, 1977); Steve Nelson, James R. Barrett, and Rob Ruck, *Steve Nelson, American Radical* (Pittsburgh: University of Pittsburgh Press, 1981); Nell Irvin Painter, *The Narrative of Hosea Hudson: His Life as a Negro Communist in the South* (Cambridge, Mass.: Harvard University Press, 1979); and Richmond, *Long View from the Left*. See also Vivian Gornick, *The Romance of American Communism* (New York: Basic Books, 1977). Theodore Draper offers a stinging critique of the new generation of historians in "American Communism Revisited," *New York Review of Books*, May 9, 1985, pp. 32–37, and "The Popular Front Revisited," *New York Review of Books*, May 30, 1985, pp. 44–50. Maurice Isserman attempts to place their work in context in "Three Generations: Historians View American Communism," *Labor History* 26 (Fall 1985): 517–45.

2. *Four Fighting Years: A Short History of the Marine Workers Industrial Union* (New York: Marine Workers Industrial Union, [1934]), pp. 2–3; *Seamen's Journal*, Sept. 1928, p. 7; *Marine Workers Voice*, Oct. 1928, p. 4. See also Jerry King, Ralph Emerson, Fred Renaud, and Lawrence McRyn, *We Accuse (From the Record)* (New York: n.p., 1940), p. 6.

3. Fernando Claudin, *The Communist Movement: From Comintern to Cominform* (New York: Monthly Review Press, 1975), p. 55; Draper, *The Roots of American Communism*, pp. 198–99, 248, 274; Bert Cochran, *Labor and Communism: The Conflict that Shaped American Union*, (Princeton: Princeton University Press, 1977), p. 21.

4. Draper, *American Communism and Soviet Russia*, pp. 285–97, 396; Cochran, *Labor and Communism*, p. 43.

5. *Marine Workers Voice*, Oct. 1928, pp. 1, 4; Dec. 1928, p. 2; Jan. 1930, pp. 1, 7; Mar. 1930, p. 2; "Unity of Seamen, Longshoremen and Harbor Workers for an Industrial Union Based on Ship, Dock and Fleet Committees," Sailors' Union of the Pacific, Central Archive, MWIU file.

6. *Four Fighting Years*, p. 5; *New York Times*, Apr. 26, 1930, p. 39; interview with Tommy Ray, May 31, 1979. *Marine Workers Voice*, Oct. 1929, p. 2; U.S., Congress, House, Special Committee on Un-American Activities, *Investigation of Un-American Propaganda Activities in the United States: Hearings before a Special Committee on Un-American Activities*, 76th Cong., 1st sess., vol. 11 (Washington, D.C.: Government Printing Office, 1940), p. 6546, hereafter cited as Dies Committee, *Hearings*.

7. In spite of the apparent logic of dual unionism in some industries by 1928, I am persuaded that the decision to create new industrial unions in the United States came from S. A. Lozovsky and other leaders of the international Communist movement. Apparently, spokesmen for the American Party bitterly opposed this policy until it was forced on them in the summer of 1928. According to Lozovsky, American delegates to the Comintern "argued furiously, they argued foaming at the mouth, they accused me of schism," when he proposed the formation of a dual union to compete with the United Mine Workers. Eventually, American Communists created a new labor federation, the Trade Union Unity League, which announced that "the fascist AFL is the enemy of the working class." As late as February 1932 Lozovsky was still declaring: "But that we want to break up the reformist trade unions, that we want to weaken them, that we want to explode . . . the trade union apparatus and to destroy it—of that there cannot be the slightest doubt." On the logic of dual unionism, see Prickett, "New Perspectives on American Communism and the Labor Movement," pp. 8–11; Lozovsky quoted in Theodore Draper, "Communists and Miners, 1928–1933," *Dissent* 19 (Spring 1972): 373; see also Harvey A. Levenstein, *Communism, Anticommunism, and the CIO* (Westport, Conn.: Greenwood Press, 1981), pp. 7–18.

8. *New York Times*, Apr. 27, 1930, p. 26; Apr. 28, 1930, p. 11; *Daily Worker*, Apr. 26, 1930, pp. 1, 5; Apr. 28, 1930, p. 1; Apr. 30, 1930, p. 2; Roy Hudson, unpublished manuscript on the history of the MWIU, n.d., p. 4, hereafter cited as Hudson, "History of the MWIU"; interview with Roy Hudson, Oct. 29, 1981; *Marine Workers Voice*, Sept. 1929, p. 2.

9. Interview with Roy Hudson, Oct. 29, 1981; MWIU preamble reprinted in Marine Workers Industrial Union, *The Point Gorda Strike: Report of Ship Delegate George Clark at the National Committee Meeting of the Marine Workers Industrial Union* (New York: Marine Workers Industrial Union, [1932?]), p. 3; *New York Times*, Apr. 28, 1930, p. 11; *Daily Worker*, Apr. 28, 1930, p. 1.

10. National Maritime Union of America, *Two Years: A Record of Struggle and Achievement of the East Coast Seamen* (New York: National Maritime Union of America, 1939), sec. 3 (pages not numbered). On workaways, Harry Alexander

stated: "These workaways (some ships carried as high as eight workaways) crowded the crews' quarters, washrooms, and mess rooms. On some ships it was impossible to feed the crew and workaways at one sitting and that caused a lot of fights during meal hours—a stranger looking on would think that the seamen were a bunch of pigs." MWIU, *Centralized Shipping Bureau*, p. 15.

11. *Marine Workers Voice*, Mar. 1933, p. 3; Studs Terkel, *Hard Times: An Oral History of the Great Depression* (New York: Pantheon, 1970), p. 19; Curran, "Reminiscences," p. 41. On the activity of the unemployed during the depression, see Roy Rosenzweig, "Organizing the Unemployed: The Early Years of the Great Depression, 1929–1933," *Radical America* 10 (July–Aug. 1976): 37–60.

12. "Longshore Labor Conditions in the United States—Part I," *Monthly Labor Review* 31 (Oct. 1930): 1–20; "Longshore Labor Conditions in the United States—Part II," *Monthly Labor Review* 31 (Nov. 1930): 11–25; *The Hook*, Apr. 1, 1935, p. 2.

13. Curran, "Reminiscences," pp. 38–39.

14. Bodnar, *Workers' World*, p. 19.

15. Sterling D. Spero and Abram L. Harris, *The Black Worker: The Negro and the Labor Movement* (New York: Columbia University Press, 1931), p. 202; *The Hook*, Mar. 11, 1935, p. 1; Ernest Poole, "The Ship Must Sail on Time" *Everybody's Magazine* 19 (Aug. 1908): 176; Lawrenson, *Stranger at the Party*, pp. 207–11.

16. Interview with Al Richmond, Apr. 6, 1983.

17. "Once upon a Shop Floor: An Interview with David Montgomery," *Radical History Review*, no. 23 (Spring 1980): 41; Frank Marquart, *An Auto Worker's Journal: The UAW from Crusade to One-Party Union* (University Park: Pennsylvania State University Press, 1975), p. 35; Martin Glaberman, *Wartime Strikes: The Struggle against the No-Strike Pledge in the UAW During World War II* (Detroit: Bewick Editions, 1980), p. 73.

18. Spero and Harris, *The Black Worker*, pp. 183, 199; Oscar Ameringer, *If You Don't Weaken* (New York: Henry Holt, 1940), pp. 196–202, 214–19; William H. Harris, *The Harder We Run: Black Workers since the Civil War* (New York: Oxford University Press, 1982), p. 19; David M. Katzman, "Black Longshoremen" (paper delivered at the annual meeting of the Organization of American Historians, San Francisco, Apr. 1980), pp. 10–13.

19. *The Hook*, Sept. 1934, p. 1; Gilbert Mers, "One Step at a Time, Many Backward" (autobiography scheduled for publication by Singlejack Books, San Pedro, Calif.), p. 363. Mers's autobiography contains numerous insights on race relations among longshoremen in the Gulf Coast ports.

20. Interview with J. R., May 28, 1979; Al Richmond to author, Aug. 24, 1982; Donald T. Critchlow, "Communist Unions and Racism: A Comparative Study of the Responses of the United Electrical Radio and Machine Workers and the National Maritime Union to the Black Question during World War II," *Labor History* 17 (Spring 1976): 230–44; Jane Cassels Record, "The Rise and Fall of a Maritime Union," *Industrial and Labor Relations Review* 10 (Oct. 1956): 81–92.

21. *Marine Workers Voice*, Nov. 1932, p. 1; Mar. 1933, p. 3; *Daily Worker* article reprinted in Dies Committee, *Hearings*, 11: 6593–95.

22. Interviews with Roy Hudson, Oct. 29, 1981, and Apr. 1, 1982; *Four Fighting Years*, p. 31. See also the editorial on "Political Action" in *Marine Workers Voice*, Jan. 1934, p. 4.

23. Interview with Roy Hudson, Nov. 23, 1981.

24. Steve Nelson et al., *Steve Nelson*, pp. 40, 76; Curran, "Reminiscences," p. 36; interview with George Cullinan, Dec. 12, 1979; interview with Bill McCarthy, Sept. 30, 1980.

25. The estimate of fifteen thousand members appears in *Two Years*, sec. 4 (pages not numbered). Joe Curran stated at the Dies Committee hearings in 1938 and again in his oral history interview with Columbia University in 1964 that the MWIU had fourteen thousand members and the ISU only eight hundred during the early thirties. William McCuistion also informed the Dies Committee that the "maximum membership" of the MWIU was "about 14,000." See Dies Committee, *Hearings*, 11: 6458, 6645; Curran, "Reminiscences," p. 33. Hudson's estimate appears in Hudson, "History of the MWIU," pp. 13–14; his estimate is corroborated by that of another MWIU veteran (interview with J.R., May 28, 1979).

26. Hudson, "History of the MWIU," p. 14; *Seamen's Journal*, June 1, 1935, p. 3; "Statement of Oscar Carlson, Secretary, Marine Firemen's, Oilers' and Watertenders' Union to Seamen Members of the International Seamen's Union of America and Particularly to Members of the Marine Firemen, Oilers' and Watertenders' Union (Aug. 22, 1935)," in Al Lannon, Papers, c. 1930–68, in author's possession, courtesy of Albert Lannon, Jr.; Curran, "Reminiscences," p. 36.

27. Mike Pell, *Six Seamen: Different Men under Different Systems* (New York: International Publishers, 1933), p. 12; interview with Bill Bailey, Jan. 24, 1979; Al Lannon to E. S. B., n.d., in Lannon papers; Rubin, *Log of Rubin the Sailor*, p. 141.

28. Richmond, *Long View from the Left*, pp. 115, 197, 206–7; interview with Al Richmond, Apr. 6, 1983; Bill Bailey, "The Kid from Hoboken" (unpublished autobiography, 1980), p. 96; "Full Proceedings of Special National Council, [National Maritime Union], Jan. 6–10 [1947], in *Pilot*, Feb. 12, 1947, p. 19.

29. William E. Leuchtenburg, *Franklin D. Roosevelt and the New Deal, 1932–1940* (New York: Harper and Row, 1963), pp. 280–81.

30. Richmond, *Long View from the Left*, pp. 175–76; Richard Krebs [Jan Valtin], *Out of the Night* (New York: Alliance Book Corp., 1941), pp. 361–63; Dies Committee, *Hearings*, 11: 6548; Larry Hennessey, "I Faced Death on the Waterfront," *Bluebook* 95 (Oct. 1952): 54. See also King et al., *We Accuse*, pp. 14–17.

31. McCuistion testified before the Dies Committee that the basis of the Communist program in maritime was "to get control of the marine industry as a means of controlling the war industries." The following exchange between Congressman Dies and McCuistion reveals the purpose as well as the underlying theme of McCuistion's testimony:

"The CHAIRMAN. Now, I want to ask you what would happen in case of a war between the United States and Soviet Russia with the seamen on ships in control of the Communists?

"Mr. McCUISTION. There would immediately be a series of strike actions against the shipment of war materials to the Soviet Union. This has already happened in 1919. . . . In my opinion the American seamen would oppose it and they would not be able successfully to carry out the strike. . . . But the Communists on the ships, as I say, one man can sink a ship at the dock, or in midocean, and that has happened."

During the height of the Cold War, Hennessey chimed in with the observation that "the huge port [of New York] offers hundreds of different forms of sabotage: Atomic bombs planted at strategic places could disrupt the port for months." Dies Committee, *Hearings,* 11: 6753; Hennessey, "I Faced Death on the Waterfront," p. 55. See also Charles Yale Harrison, "Stalin's American Merchant Marine," *American Mercury* 51 (Oct. 1940): 135–44; and William McFee, "Seagoing Soviets," *Saturday Evening Post,* Sept. 21, 1940, pp. 27, 83–88.

32. Dies Committee, *Hearings,* 11: 6544, 6552, 6589; Al Richmond to author, Aug. 24, 1982.

33. Interviews with Roy Hudson, Oct. 29, 1981, and Nov. 23, 1981; interview with Sam Darcy, Dec. 19, 1979; interview with Al Richmond, Sept. 17, 1982.

34. Hudson, "History of the MWIU," p. 6; Richmond, *Long View from the Left,* pp. 168–73; Kempton, *Part of Our Time,* pp. 86–89.

35. *Daily Worker,* July 25, 1932, p. 3; Aug. 2, 1932, p. 2; *New York Times,* July 23, 1932, p. 56; July 31, 1932, p. 20; Curran, "Reminiscences," p. 24; Dies Committee, *Hearings,* 11: 6565; Richmond, *Long View from the Left,* p. 170.

36. *Daily Worker,* July 25, 1932, p. 3; *Marine Workers Voice,* Mar. 1933, p. 2; Richmond, *Long View from the Left,* pp. 173–79, Mink quoted on pp. 176–77.

37. Dies Committee, *Hearings,* 11: 6626; interview with Bill Bailey, Jan. 24, 1979; the Waterfront Section's admonition against throwing the "pulp junk" overboard is reprinted in Dies Committee, *Hearings,* 11: 6619; *Marine Workers Voice,* Dec. 1933, p. 1.

38. Interview with Roy Hudson, Oct. 29, 1981; Rubin, *Log of Rubin the Sailor,* p. 249.

39. Elizabeth Wickenden to William Plunkert, Apr. 2, 1934, Federal Emergency Relief Administration [FERA], State File (Maryland), RG 69, No. 420, National Archives [NA]; Elizabeth Wickenden to Janet Long, July 13, 1934, ibid. I am indebted to Jo Ann E. Argersinger, "Assisting the 'Loafers': Transient Relief in Baltimore, 1933–1937," *Labor History* 23 (Spring 1982): 226–45, for alerting me to the existence of material in the National Archives on the Baltimore seamen's struggle.

40. MWIU, *Centralized Shipping Bureau,* p. 17; interview with Roy Hudson, Oct. 29, 1981; *Marine Workers Voice,* Jan. 1934, p. 3; Feb. 1934, pp. 1–2.

41. Joseph La Combe to William J. Plunkert, Apr. 22, 1934, FERA, RG 69, No. 420, NA; "Report on Baltimore Seamen Situation by Mr. Harman," Apr. 2, 1934, ibid; Elizabeth Wickenden to William Plunkert, Apr. 2, 1934, ibid.

42. Interview with Roy Hudson, Oct. 29, 1981; MWIU, *Centralized Shipping Bureau,* p. 22; Dies Committee, *Hearings,* 11: 6627.

43. Interview with Roy Hudson, Oct. 29, 1981; MWIU, *Centralized Shipping Bureau,* pp. 8, 18.

44. Joseph La Combe to William J. Plunkert, Apr. 22, 1934, FERA; *Marine Workers Voice,* Mar. 1934, p. 3; interview with Roy Hudson, Oct. 29, 1981; MWIU, *Centralized Shipping Bureau,* p. 18. The Scottsboro Boys were nine black youths who were sentenced to death by the state of Alabama on the charge of raping two white girls, one of whom later recanted her testimony and served as a witness for the defense. Thanks mainly to the aggressive intervention of the Communist party, the campaign to free the Scottsboro Boys became a major preoccupation among leftists and civil rights advocates in the 1930s. The best source on this celebrated case is Dan T. Carter, *Scottsboro: A Tragedy of the American South,* rev. ed. (Baton Rouge: Louisiana State University Press, 1979).

45. Eastern and Gulf Sailor's Association, reports from New York branch, Sept. 20, 1933; Dec. 5, 1933; Feb. 14, 1934; report from Boston branch, Jan. 17, 1934, Sailors' Union of the Pacific, Central Archive, Eastern and Gulf Sailor's Association file; Frank R. Stockl to President Roosevelt, Mar. 15, 1934, FERA, RG 69, No. 420, NA; Elizabeth Wickenden to William Plunkert, Apr. 2, 1934, ibid; William Plunkert to Aubrey Williams, Apr. 2, 1934, ibid; MWIU, *Centralized Shipping Bureau*, p. 24; *Marine Workers Voice*, Apr. 1934, p. 3.

46. MWIU, *Centralized Shipping Bureau*, pp. 24–25; Harry Greenstein to William J. Plunkert, May 2, 1934, FERA, RG 69, No. 420, NA; interview with Bill Bailey, Jan. 24, 1979.

47. Interview with Roy Hudson, Oct. 29, 1981.

48. *Waterfront Worker*, Aug. 28, 1934, p. 6; Jan 21, 1935, p. 4; Dies Committee, *Hearings*, 11: 6615. Officials of the International Seamen's Union were eager to assist in the destruction of the MWIU. In the aftermath of the 1934 strike, they reported MWIU members to the shipowners and demanded in the name of patriotism and anticommunism that they be removed from the ships and replaced with ISU men. A Sailors' Union official offered an enthusiastic description of this campaign: "WE PULL ALL the marine comicals off an[d] this is the way we do it. As soon as one of the crew or the patrolman reports that there is a wrecker aboard any ship, the agent from the firemen and I go down to the ship and verify the fact and then we go to the agents of the company and ask them if they are still hiding behind the skirts of the communists. Of course that doesn't set so very well with them and they deny having anything to do with that party and then we have them. *We show them that they are employing them and ask them in the name of patriotism to let them go. It has worked successfully every time so far.*" R. J. Evans to E. R. Stowell, Nov. 6, 1934, SUP Central Archive, San Pedro correspondence, 1934 (emphasis added).

49. *New Yorker*, Nov. 28, 1936, p. 31.

4. Prelude to the Pentecostal Era: Communists and Longshoremen in San Francisco

1. Lampman, "Collective Bargaining of West Coast Sailors," p. 48; *Western Worker*, July 15, 1932, p. 3; [George Larsen] to Carl E. Carter, Apr. 6. 1934, SUP Central Archive, Portland correspondence, 1934; "Ernest G. Ramsay: Reminiscences of a Defendant in the Shipboard Murder Case," in *The Shipboard Murder Case: Labor, Radicalism, and Earl Warren, 1936–1941*, an oral history conducted by Miriam Feingold Stein (Berkeley: Regional Oral History Office, Bancroft Library, University of California, 1976), pp. 6–7.

2. Bernstein, *Turbulent Years*, p. 257.

3. Francis, "History of Labor on the San Francisco Waterfront," pp. 174–76, 183; *Constitution and By-laws of the Longshoremen's Association of San Francisco and Bay Districts* (San Francisco, 1919), p. 4, SFLC papers, carton 11; E. Ellison to J. A. O'Connell, Dec. 18, 1919, SFLC papers, carton 22; *Labor Clarion*, Oct. 3, 1924, p. 12; Bridges quoted in William Martin Camp, *San Francisco: Port of Gold* (Garden City, N.Y.: Doubleday, 1947), p. 447; Paul Eliel, "Labor Problems in Our Steamship Business," *Yale Review*, 2d ser. 26 (Spring 1937): 515.

4. John A. O'Connell, "Transforming a Company Union," *American Federationist*

37 (Jan. 1930): 61–62; Francis, "History of Labor on the San Francisco Waterfront," pp. 183–86; Henry Schmidt, *Secondary Leadership in the ILWU, 1933–1966,* an oral history conducted 1974–81 by Miriam F. Stein and Estolv Ethan Ward (Berkeley: Regional Oral History Office, Bancroft Library, University of California, 1983), p. 113. The Blue Book was finally seated in the San Francisco Labor Council in February 1929. The organization was unseated in May 1931 because of its persistent refusal to affiliate with the International Longshoremen's Association. *Labor Clarion,* May 22, 1931, p. 10; official correspondence on the question of admitting the Blue Book to the Labor Council appears in SFLC papers, carton 11.

5. Interview with John P. Olsen, Oct. 22, 1981. One day in 1927, while working on the Luckenbach dock, Harry Bridges complained of not receiving full pay for actual time worked. According to Bridges, "The company refused to pay me, and I complained to the 'Blue Book' union delegate, with the final result that I never received my money for the time I worked and I lost my job in the bargain." Camp, *San Francisco: Port of Gold,* pp. 447–48.

6. Mayhew quoted in Bernstein, *Turbulent Years,* p. 254.

7. Bridges quoted in Larrowe, *Harry Bridges,* p. 8; Eugene Gordon, "War on the Waterfront," *New Masses,* Mar. 6, 1934, p. 15; [ILA Local 38-79], *The Truth about the Waterfront: The I.L.A. States Its Case to the Public* (San Francisco: International Longshoremen's Association, Local 38-79, [1935], p. 6; Redfern Mason, "Autobiography" (unpublished manuscript, c. 1941), p. 360, in Redfern Mason, Correspondence and Papers, c. 1895–1939, Bancroft Library, University of California, Berkeley.

8. [ILA Local 38-79], *The Maritime Crisis: What It Is and What It Isn't* (San Francisco: International Longshoremen's Association, Local 38-79, [1936]), pp. 11, 13. Bill Rutter, a veteran of the 1934 strike, stated in 1975: "I've seen ships come in here loaded with bulk sulphur. That is one of the roughest cargoes to handle because of bothering your eyes, and I've seen two hundred people shape up there trying to get a job. Twenty-five would probably be hired and they were the old time sulphur people. When these fellows went in, that big crowd on the outside of the gate didn't disappear right away. Somebody might break their leg or something and that would be a chance for them to grab that job." Rutter quoted in Frederic Chiles, "General Strike: San Francisco, 1934—An Historical Compilation Film Storyboard," *Labor History* 22 (Summer 1981): 439.

9. *Waterfront Worker,* Dec. 1932, p. 2; Feb. 11, 1935, p. 2; *Western Worker,* July 17, 1933, p. 4. Employer spokesman Paul Eliel acknowledged in retrospect that "men in need of money had to cash their brass employment checks through usurers at rates of interest running as high, in some instances, as 10% per week. In other cases gang bosses had to be placated and jobs purchased either through 'kick-backs' or other favors. . . . such practices were common enough along the San Francisco waterfront so that, over a term of years, most of the workers were bound to encounter conditions of this kind." Eliel, "Labor Problems in Our Steamship Business," p. 516.

10. Interview with Sam Darcy, Dec. 19, 1979; *Western Worker,* June 1, 1932, p. 6; July 31, 1933, p. 2; Aug. 7, 1933, p. 4.

11. *Western Worker,* Mar. 5, 1934, p. 1; Mar. 12, 1934, p. 2; May 7, 1934, p. 4; May 14, 1934, p. 2.

12. Daniel, *Bitter Harvest,* pp. 130–34; Klehr, *The Heyday of American Commu-*

nism, pp. 26, 32–35; Decker quoted in Ella Winter, *And Not to Yield: An Autobiography* (New York: Harcourt, Brace and World, 1963), p. 191 (see Winter's own assessment on the same page); Sam Darcy to author, Feb. 9, 1982; Darcy interview; Earl Browder, "The American Communist Party in the Thirties," in *As We Saw the Thirties: Essays on Social and Political Movements of a Decade,* ed. Rita James Simon (Urbana: University of Illinois Press, 1967), p. 234; Joseph R. Starobin, *American Communism in Crisis, 1943–1957* (Cambridge, Mass.: Harvard University Press, 1972), pp. 65, 73, 114–15; Isserman, *Which Side Were You On?,* pp. 23–25, 192–96; Orrick Johns, *Time of Our Lives: The Story of My Father and Myself* (New York: Stackpole, 1937), pp. 324–25.

13. Sam Darcy, "The Declining American Federation of Labor," *International Press Correspondence,* Aug. 28, 1930, p. 835; Daniel, *Bitter Harvest,* p. 134; Darcy interview; Sam Darcy, "The Great West Coast Maritime Strike," *Communist* 13 (July 1934): 679–80.

14. "Vote Communist" (election leaflet), in SFLC papers, carton 27; Richmond, *Long View from the Left,* pp. 162–63; Harry Jackson and Nat Ross, "Methods of Work and Some Tasks of the Party in the South," *Daily Worker,* July 2, 1932, p. 6; Painter, *Narrative of Hosea Hudson,* pp. 89–90, 110, 112–15; Darcy interview; Dies Committee, *Hearings,* 11: 6580–81; Earl Browder, "The Struggle for the United Front," *Communist* 13 (Oct. 1934): 952; inteview with [name withheld], 1970.

15. Interview with Roy Hudson, Nov. 23, 1981.

16. *Marine Workers Voice,* Oct.–Nov. 1933, pp. 1–2; Jan. 1934, p. 4; Feb. 1934, p. 4.

17. Bernstein, *Turbulent Years,* pp. 252–53; Larrowe, *Harry Bridges,* pp. 3–8; Bruce Minton and John Stuart, *Men Who Lead Labor* (New York: Modern Age Books, 1937), pp. 175–77; Estolv E. Ward, *Harry Bridges on Trial* (New York: Modern Age Books, 1940), pp. 160–62; interview with Harry Bridges, Oct. 6, 1981.

18. Frances Perkins, *The Roosevelt I Knew* (New York: Viking Press, 1946), p. 316; Bernstein, *Turbulent Years,* p. 256; U.S. National Longshoremen's Board, "Proceedings before the National Longshoremen's Board . . . to Arbitrate Controversies between the Waterfront Employers and the International Longshoremen's Association, Local 38, of the Pacific Coast District," San Francisco, Aug. 8–24, 1934, pp. 166–67, 170; hereafter cited as National Longshoremen's Board, "Proceedings."

19. *Labor Clarion,* Sept. 5, 1924, p. 4. Bridges recalled: "Around 400 of us paraded up Market Street on Labor Day. And the company agents stood on the sidewalk and took all our names down, all those they knew or could recognize. We were blacklisted for the next couple of years." Peter Trimble, "Harry Bridges," *Frontier* 2 (Jan. 1951): 6.

20. Minton and Stuart, *Men Who Lead Labor,* pp. 179–80; interview with Henry Schmidt, Oct. 14, 1981; Larrowe, *Harry Bridges,* p. 16.

21. Ward, *Harry Bridges on Trial,* pp. 123–24; 145–46; Bridges interview; Theodore Dreiser, "The Story of Harry Bridges," *Friday,* Oct. 4, 1940, pp. 6–7. Although Bridges came to believe that the MWIU could not succeed among longshoremen, he continued to support the Red union in preference to the ISU among seamen (whereas Darcy apparently favored abandoning the MWIU altogether and attempting to work entirely within the AFL maritime unions). During the 1934 strike Bridges "was active . . . in inducing seamen to join the M.W.I.U. and actually conducted groups of seamen

to M.W.I.U. headquarters for that purpose." U.S. Immigration and Naturalization Service, Department of Justice, *In the Matter of Harry Renton Bridges: Memorandum of Decision,* File no. 55973/217 (Washington, D.C.: Government Printing Office, 1941), p. 98; Sam Darcy to author, May 12, 1981.

22. Jim Kendall quoted in Chiles, "General Strike: San Francisco, 1934," p. 443.

23. Larrowe, *Harry Bridges,* pp. 13–15; Bernstein, *Turbulent Years,* pp. 259–60; Charles A. Madison, *American Labor Leaders: Personalities and Forces in the Labor Movement,* 2d ed. (New York: Frederick Ungar, 1962), p. 407; Cochran, *Labor and Communism,* p. 61.

24. "The Shop Paper—An Organ of Struggle," *Party Organizer* 6 (Feb. 1933): 76–78; Darcy interview; Darcy, "The Great West Coast Maritime Strike," p. 665; *Waterfront Worker,* June 1933, p. 5.

25. Richmond, *Long View from the Left,* p. 215; Sam Darcy, "The San Francisco General Strike—1934," *Hawsepipe* 2 (Sept.–Oct., 1982): 1, 7; Johns, *Time of Our Lives,* p. 325; Sam Darcy to author, May 12, 1981; interview with Miriam Dinkin Johnson, Aug. 2, 1984.

26. Darcy interview; *Marine Workers Voice,* Mar. 1933, p. 3.

27. *Waterfront Worker,* Dec. 1932, p. 1 and passim; Feb. 1933, p. 1; Mar. 1933, p. 1. Tom Mooney, a militant unionist and socialist, was convicted of the bombing that killed ten people during the San Francisco Preparedness Day parade of 1916. The case was fraught with controversy, and the trade union movement assumed Mooney's innocence. The effort to free him became a rallying cry in labor and radical circles around the world. He was eventually pardoned by Governor Culbert Olson of California in 1939. See Richard H. Frost, *The Mooney Case* (Stanford, Calif.: Stanford University Press, 1968).

28. *Party Organizer* 6 (Jan. 1933): 26; and ibid. (Feb. 1933): 78; *Western Worker,* Jan. 30, 1933, p. 2.

29. *Marine Workers Voice,* Mar. 1933, p. 3; *Waterfront Worker,* Apr. 1933, pp.1–2.

30. *Waterfront Worker,* May 1933, p. 5; June 1933, p. 5; July 1933, p. 2.

31. Bernstein, *Turbulent Years,* pp. 33, 41, Brophy quoted on p. 41; O'Connor quoted in Staughton Lynd, "The Possibility of Radicalism in the Early 1930s: The Case of Steel," *Radical America* 6 (Nov.–Dec. 1972): 39; Henry Schmidt interview.

32. *Waterfront Worker,* July 1933, p. 3; *San Francisco Call-Bulletin,* Mar. 31, 1934, p. 3; *American-Citizen Longshoreman,* Nov. 30, 1936, in SFLC papers, carton 27; Larrowe, *Harry Bridges,* pp. 12–13. "Meeting Called to Order . . . Sept. 28, 1931"; J. C. Bjorklund to Lee J. Holman, Feb. 26, 1932; [Lee J. Holman] to John C. Bjorklund, Mar. 1, 1932; in International Longshoremen's and Warehousemen's Union, Archives, Anne Rand Research Library, San Francisco, Case Files, Coast 1933, folder on early ILA Organization, 1931–33.

33. Francis, "History of Labor on the San Francisco Waterfront," p. 188; the phrase "elementary sense of self-preservation" is Theodore Draper's in Draper, "Communists and Miners, 1928–1933," p. 391.

34. *Waterfront Worker,* July 1933, p. 1; Aug. 15, 1933, p. 5.

35. *Waterfront Worker,* July 1933, pp. 1, 6; Aug. 1933, p. 4; Aug. 15, 1933, p. 1.

36. *Western Worker,* July 17, 1933, p. 4 (emphasis added).

37. Bridges interview; Darcy interview. Darcy stated that "Bridges and the

longshoremen were innocent of this fight." On Bridges's earlier recollections about the origins of the *Waterfront Worker* and his relationship to the paper, see U.S. Immigration and Naturalization Service, *In the Matter of Harry Renton Bridges*, pp. 88–97.

38. Darcy, "The Great West Coast Maritime Strike," p. 666. That the Communist party was not fully reconciled to the subordinate role of the MWIU among West Coast longshoremen is evident from Roy Hudson's report at the Party's eighth national convention, April 2–8, 1934. Only a month before the Big Strike, he stated that while the Communist-led Cannery and Agricultural Workers Industrial Union "captured" the farm workers, "1200 longshoremen joined the ILA. It does not help to say we are beginning to do opposition work there. If there had been a real organization, if the Party had mobilized its forces and given more guidance to marine, we would be more in the leadership, we would have organizational control of the longshoremen, who at one time refused to load munition[s] against the Soviet Union." Roy Hudson, "The Work of the Marine Union," *Party Organizer* 7 (May–June 1934): 29.

39. Lee J. Holman to General Hugh Johnson, July 18, 1933; and Pacific Coast Labor Bureau [PCLB], "Labor Case Report[s]" on Winblad, Hessler, and others are in ILWU Archives, Case Files, Coast 1933, folder on PCLB Reports on Misc. Disputes.

40. N.R.A. Board of Adjustment to Joseph C. Sharp, Sept. 2, 1933, in ILWU Archives, Case Files, Coast 1933, folder on PCLB Reports on Misc. Disputes; Bernstein, *Turbulent Years,* p. 261; *Waterfront Worker,* Sept. 15, 1933, pp. 1, 3; Larrowe, *Harry Bridges,* pp. 18–21, Bridges quoted on p. 21.

41. Creel quoted in Bernstein, *Turbulent Years,* p. 261.

42. Bridges interview; Henry Schmidt interview; Schmidt, *Secondary Leadership in the ILWU,* pp. 57–58; *Dispatcher,* May 4, 1984, p. 4; U.S., Congress, House, Special Committee on Un-American Activities, *Investigation of Un-American Propaganda Activities in the United States: Hearings before a Special Committee on Un-American Activities,* 75th Cong., 3d sess., vol. 3 (Washington, D.C.: Government Printing Office, 1938), p. 1726.

43. Sam Darcy to author, Feb. 9, 1982; Schmidt, *Secondary Leadership in the ILWU,* p. 59.

44. *Waterfront Worker,* Aug. 15, 1933, p. 1.

45. Bridges quoted in Larrowe, *Harry Bridges,* p. 17; *Western Worker,* May 7, 1934, p. 5.

46. *Western Worker,* Sept. 4, 1933, p. 1.

47. Darcy, "The Great West Coast Maritime Strike," pp. 666–67; *Western Worker,* Mar. 12, 1934, pp. 1, 5.

48. Larrowe, *Harry Bridges,* p. 27; *San Francisco Call-Bulletin,* Mar. 31, 1934, p. 3; *Labor Clarion,* Apr. 13, 1934, p. 7; Apr. 27, 1934, p. 11; *San Francisco Chronicle,* June 5, 1934, p. 1; Darcy, "The Great West Coast Maritime Strike," p. 684; "Longshoremen! Watch the Labor Fakers Scamper," *Waterfront Bulletin,* n.d., Scharrenberg papers, carton 3; *American-Citizen Longshoreman,* Nov. 30, 1936, p. 2.

49. Bernstein, *Turbulent Years,* p. 263; *Western Worker,* Apr. 23, 1934, p. 5; May 7, 1934, pp. 1, 5. Viewing the longshoremen's situation from the vantage point of the conservative leadership of the Sailors' Union of the Pacific, an SUP official wrote: "They tell me [the ILA] meetings are conducted by mob rule with the so-called rank and file movement raising the roof, and devoted mainly to criticizing of those in office. A somewhat similar situation to what we had in 1921, only worse. It is hard to

conceive of anything stable and successful resulting under such conditions." [George Larsen] to P. B. Gill, Apr. 26, 1934, SUP Central Archive, Seattle correspondence, 1934.

50. Mike Quin, *The Big Strike* (Olema, Calif.: Olema Publishing Co., 1949), pp. 240–42; Creel quoted in Larrowe, *Harry Bridges*, p. 28.

51. Henry Schmidt interview.

5. The Big Strike

1. Axtell, *Symposium on Andrew Furuseth*, p. 81.

2. The term was popularized by Mike Quin in *The Big Strike*. On the extraordinary eruptions of 1934, see Bernstein, *Turbulent Years*, pp. 217–317. For narratives of the 1934 maritime and general strike, see ibid., pp. 252–98; Charles P. Larrowe, "The Great Maritime Strike of '34," Pt. 1, *Labor History* 11 (Fall 1970): 403–51, and Pt. 2, *Labor History* 12 (Winter 1971): 3–37, hereafter cited as Larrowe-1 and Larrowe-2; and Quin, *The Big Strike*.

3. Quin, *The Big Strike*, pp. 104–5; *San Francisco Chronicle*, July 6, 1934, p. 1.

4. *San Francisco Chronicle*, May 12, 1934, p. 2; May 18, 1934, p. 17; *Los Angeles Times*, May 13, 1934, p. 6; Ronald Magden and A. D. Martinson, *The Working Waterfront: The Story of Tacoma's Ships and Men* (Tacoma, Wash.: International Longshoremen's and Warehousemen's Union, Local 23, 1982), p. 110; Michael Egan, " 'That's Why Organizing Was So Good': Portland Longshoremen, 1934: An Oral History" (senior thesis, Reed College, 1975), p. 51; Roger D. Lapham, "Pacific Maritime Labor Conditions as They Affect the Nation" (address to the Chamber of Commerce of the United States, Washington, D.C., Apr. 30, 1936), in Roger Lapham, "An Interview on Shipping," p. 412. Egan's Reed thesis includes an interview with Harry Pilcher, an Everett longshoreman and Communist party member, who participated in the events on the Seattle waterfront. Pilcher recalled (p. 51): "By Friday [the third day of the strike] they had scabs on every dock in Seattle. Us fellows from Everett and Tacoma got together and we rounded up all of the militant men we could find in Seattle. And Saturday morning we hit the docks in force. . . . I'd say at least a thousand unemployed came down and backed us up. . . . we got through that Saturday and there wasn't any scabs left on the Seattle waterfront."

5. Donald Mackenzie Brown, "Dividends and Stevedores," *Scribner's* 97 (Jan. 1935): 54–55; Schmidt, *Secondary Leadership in the ILWU*, p. 99.

6. Jerold S. Auerbach, *Labor and Liberty: The La Follette Committee and the New Deal* (New York: Bobbs-Merrill, 1966), pp. 177–78; Ivan F. Cox to Robert F. Wagner, Feb. 5, 1934, SFLC papers, carton 11; Perry and Perry, *History of the Los Angeles Labor Movement*, pp. 366–67; U.S., Congress, Senate, Subcommittee of the Committee on Education and Labor, *Report, Violations of Free Speech and Rights of Labor*, Report no. 1150, 77th Cong., 2d sess. (Washington, D.C.: Government Printing Office, 1942), pt. 2, pp. 131, 134–35; hereafter cited as La Follette Committee, *Report*.

7. *Los Angeles Daily News* quoted in Larrowe-1, p. 410; Lew Levenson, "California Casualty List," *Nation*, Aug. 29, 1934, pp. 243–45; [American League against War and Fascism (Los Angeles Committee)], *California's Brown Book* (Los Angeles: American League against War and Fascism, 1934), pp. 4–5.

8. *Los Angeles Times,* May 16, 1934, sec. 2, pp. 1, 10.

9. *Voice of the Federation,* June 28, 1935, p. 4; interviews with Bob McElroy, May 31, 1979, and Feb. 3, 1981.

10. Perry and Perry, *History of the Los Angeles Labor Movement,* p. 367; *Foc'sle Head,* July 2, 1934, p. 2; *Voice of the Federation,* June 14, 1935, p. 2.

11. Schmidt quoted in *Voice of the Federation,* June 21, 1935, p. 4; *San Francisco Chronicle,* July 10, 1934, p. 1; Chiles, "General Strike: San Francisco, 1934," p. 457; Quin, *The Big Strike,* p. 129; anonymous recollection in ILWU Archives, Case Files, Coast 1934, 1934 Strike Personal Interviews; interview with Roy Hudson, Oct. 29, 1981; Paul Eliel, *The Waterfront and General Strikes, San Francisco, 1934: A Brief History* (San Francisco: Hooper Printing Co., 1934), p. 128.

12. [George Larsen] to P. B. Gill, Apr. 26, 1934, SUP Central Archive, Seattle correspondence, 1934.

13. Francis, "History of Labor on the San Francisco Waterfront," pp. 12, 182–83; ILA Local 38–79, executive board minutes, Oct. 9, 1933, ILWU Archives; Darcy, "The Great West Coast Maritime Strike," pp. 671–72.

14. Larrowe, *Harry Bridges,* p. 38; Theodore Durein, "Scabs' Paradise," *Reader's Digest* 30 (Jan. 1937): 21; Herbert R. Northrup, *Organized Labor and the Negro* (New York: Harper and Brothers, 1944), pp. 152–53; *San Francisco Chronicle,* May 10, 1934, p. 4; May 13, 1934, p. 3; May 16, 1934, p. 3.

15. Schmidt, *Secondary Leadership in the ILWU,* p. 228. In an interview with the author on Oct. 14, 1981, Schmidt recalled, "All of a sudden, fourteen or fifteen black [longshore]men walked into the office and said, 'Well, we're here. Do you want us?' "

16. Walter Macarthur to Mr. Michelson, Jan. 31, 1936, in Macarthur papers, carton 1; Bridges quoted in Larrowe-1, p. 416; Caves's statement appears in a letter he wrote on Aug. 26, 1938, in "Case of Ferdinand Smith, Vice-President of National Maritime Union of America [Sept. 23, 1938]," p. 17, in ILWU files relating to seamen and maritime unions, carton 12.

17. [George Larsen] to P. B. Gill, Apr. 26, 1934; Nov. 17, 1933; Nov. 23, 1933; George Larsen to John A. Feidje, Dec. 12, 1933; to Carl E. Carter, Feb. 17, 1934; Apr. 6, 1934; Apr. 20, 1934; Carl E. Carter to George Larsen, Mar. 29, 1934, SUP Central Archive, Portland correspondence, 1934.

18. [George Larsen] to John A. Feidje, Oct. 12, 1933; [George Larsen] to Carl E. Carter, Mar. 1, 1934; Mar. 15, 1934; Apr. 6, 1934, SUP Central Archive, Portland correspondence, 1934.

19. "Minutes of Meeting of District Committee[,] International Seamen's Union of America," May 9, 1934, SUP Central Archive, 1934 strike file; [George Larsen] to C. E. Carter, May 11, 1934, ibid., Portland correspondence, 1934.

20. *Waterfront Worker,* Oct. 22, 1934, p. 7; May 21, 1934, p. 3; *San Francisco Chronicle,* May 13, 1934, p. 3; Darcy, "The Great West Coast Maritime Strike," p. 670.

21. Interview with Harold Johnson, Aug. 4, 1984.

22. SUP, minutes of headquarters meeting, San Francisco, May 15, 1934; [George Larsen] to P. B. Gill, May 24, 1934, SUP Central Archive, Seattle correspondence, 1934.

23. On the teamsters, see Robert McClure Robinson, "A History of the Teamsters in the San Francisco Bay Area, 1850–1950" (Ph.D. diss., University of California,

Berkeley, 1951), pp. 223–63; Paul Eliel, *The Waterfront and General Strikes,* p. 50. Eliel stated: "Had it not been for this stand of the Teamsters' Union the strike of longshoremen would undoubtedly have collapsed within a week or ten days at the most."

24. Sam Darcy, "The San Francisco Bay Area General Strike," *Communist* 13 (Oct. 1934): 995; Bulcke quoted in Joseph Blum and Lisa Rubens, "Strike," *San Francisco Sunday Examiner and Chronicle, California Living Magazine,* July 8, 1984, p. 12; Quin, *The Big Strike,* p. 148. The San Francisco newspapers generally refrained from offering an exact estimate of the number of participants in the general strike. The number of organized workers on strike in San Francisco appears to have been close to fifty thousand. The press did estimate that between forty-two and forty-seven thousand workers struck in the East Bay. However, these figures almost certainly did not include the apparently significant number of unorganized workers who also walked off the job. Therefore, the Communists' estimate of some hundred and twenty-five thousand participants may well be accurate. See William F. Dunne, *The Great San Francisco General Strike: The Story of the West Coast Strike—The Bay Counties' General Strike and the Maritime Workers' Strike* (New York: Workers' Library, 1934), p. 3.

25. J. Paul St. Sure, "Some Comments on Employer Organizations and Collective Bargaining in Northern California since 1934," an interview conducted by Corinne Gilb for the Institute of Industrial Relations Oral History Project, University of California, Berkeley, 1957, p. 69–70, 72–73.

26. George Larsen to Andrew Furuseth, May 18, 1934, SUP Central Archive, 1934 strike file; "Seven Seamen," p. 123.

27. *Waterfront Worker,* May 21, 1934, p. 4.

28. Frances Perkins to Franklin D. Roosevelt, July 15, 1934, in Franklin D. Roosevelt, Papers as President, Official File, 1935–45, 407-B, box 11, Franklin D. Roosevelt Library, Hyde Park, N.Y., hereafter cited as FDR Official File; Quin, *The Big Strike,* pp. 98–99; Eliel quoted in Larrowe-1, p. 444.

29. Interview with Al Richmond, Sept. 17, 1982; "The Maritime Unions," p. 132; George P. West, "Labor Strategist of the Embarcadero," *New York Times Magazine,* Oct. 25, 1936, p. 7; Perkins, *The Roosevelt I Knew,* p. 316; Richard L. Neuberger, "Bad-Man Bridges," *Forum* 101 (Apr. 1939): 198–99.

30. Madison, *American Labor Leaders,* p. 409; Ward, *Harry Bridges on Trial,* p. 105; *Voice of the Federation,* Apr. 23, 1936, p. 3.

31. John P. Olsen interview; Eliel quoted in Larrowe-2, pp. 17–18; Landis quoted in Ward, *Harry Bridges on Trial,* p. 230.

32. Emory Scott Land, "The Reminiscences of Emory Scott Land," Oral History Collection, Columbia University, 1963, p. 191; Louis Adamic, *My America, 1928–1938* (New York: Harper and Brothers, 1938), p. 375; *San Francisco Examiner,* Aug. 30, 1935, p. 8; West, "Labor Strategist of the Embarcadero," p. 7.

33. *Waterfront Worker,* Feb. 11, 1935, p. 6; Oct. 15, 1934, p. 6.

34. John P. Olsen quoted in Chiles, "General Strike: San Francisco, 1934," p. 465.

35. Minton and Stuart, *Men Who Lead Labor,* p. 199; Neuberger, "Bad-Man Bridges," p. 199; Darcy interview; "Herbert Resner: The Recollections of the Attorney for Frank Conner," in Stein, *The Shipboard Murder Case,* pp. 13–14; *Voice of the Federation,* July 19, 1936, p. 4.

36. "The Maritime Unions," p. 137; Matthew Josephson, "Red Skies over the Waterfront," *Collier's*, Oct. 5, 1946, pp. 17, 89–90; Bernstein, *Turbulent Years*, p. 266; Larrowe, *Shape-up and Hiring Hall*, pp. 16–17; U.S., Congress, Senate, Committee on Interstate and Foreign Commerce, *Waterfront Investigation: New York–New Jersey*, 83d cong., 1st sess., Report no. 653 (Washington, D.C.: Government Printing Office, 1953), pp. 7–13.

37. *San Francisco Chronicle*, June 17, 1934, pp. 1, 2; June 18, 1934, p. 1.

38. Quin, *The Big Strike*, pp. 84–85; Henry Schmidt interview; *San Francisco Chronicle*, June 29, 1934, p. 1.

39. Quin, *The Big Strike*, pp. 52–53.

40. Eliel quoted in Larrowe-1, pp. 43–44.

41. Darcy interview; Starobin, *American Communism in Crisis*, p. 258; John Brophy, *A Miner's Life*, ed. John O. P. Hall (Madison: University of Wisconsin Press, 1964), p. 275. Brophy was the CIO's first director and, after John L. Lewis, the person most crucial to the organization during its formative stages. A deeply religious Roman Catholic, Brophy eventually became a staunch anti-Communist. In 1938, however, he stridently attacked those who raised the cry of "Communist" within the CIO, lambasting the "social and intellectual bankruptcy of their methods" and even accusing them of treason. *Labor Herald*, Aug. 25, 1938, p. 2, in John Brophy, Papers, 1917–63, Department of Archives and Manuscripts, Catholic University of America, Washington, D.C.

42. Eliel, *The Waterfront and General Strikes*, p. 128; Darcy interview.

43. Even the San Francisco ILA local passed an anti-Communist resolution, in response to strong pressure from the Labor Council. The resolution declared that any ILA member who refused "to disavow all connections with the Communist element on the waterfront . . . shall be held to trial on charges of insubordination and if found guilty shall be expelled from Local 38-79." Although the resolution was "unanimously concur[r]ed in" at a membership meeting, it seems to have had no effect on the strike committee's close working relationship with the MWIU, the International Labor Defense, and other Communist-led organizations and individuals. Ivan F. Cox to John O'Connell, June 26, 1934, in SFLC papers, carton 11.

44. *Foc'sle Head*, June 28, 1934, p. 2.

45. *Foc'sle Head*, May 18, 1934, p. 1; June 22, 1934, pp. 1, 2; July 2, 1934, p. 2; "A Synopsis of the Events Leading up to and Following the Attempt to Suspend W. W. Caves, from the Office of Chairman of the Strike Committee, Sailors' Union of the Pacific," SUP Central Archive, 1934 strike file; interview with Bob McElroy, May 31, 1979. Eventually Caves was removed from the strike committee. The minutes of a special meeting on June 24 recorded the decision "to suspend W. W. Caves from the strike committee, because he has not been around for three days, and because his attitude and general disposition seems to inject a spirit of dissension in the committee." SUP Strike Committee, minutes of special meeting, San Francisco, June 24, 1934, SUP Central Archive, 1934 strike file.

46. *San Francisco Chronicle*, June 21, 1934, p. 4; *Foc'sle Head*, June 25, 1934, p. 1; Johnson and Merriam quoted in *Nation*, Aug. 29, 1934, p. 228 (emphasis added).

47. Miriam Allen De Ford, "San Francisco: An Autopsy on the General Strike," *Nation*, Aug. 1, 1934, p. 122; ibid., p. 113; John Terry, "The Terror in San Jose," *Nation*, Aug. 8, 1934, p. 162.

48. *San Francisco Chronicle,* July 18, 1934, p. 1; *San Francisco Examiner,* July 18, 1934, p. 1; "Who Owns the San Francisco Police Department?" *Nation,* Aug. 29, 1934, pp. 228–29; Quin, *The Big Strike,* pp. 162–63; Lorena Hickok to Aubrey W. Williams, Aug. 15, 1934, in *One Third of a Nation: Lorena Hickok Reports on the Great Depression,* ed. Richard Lowitt and Maurine Beasley (Urbana: University of Illinois Press, 1981), p. 305; Robert Cantwell, "War on the West Coast: I. The Gentlemen of San Francisco," *New Republic,* Aug. 1. 1934, p. 309; Sam Darcy to author, May 12, 1981. There may have been some workers, even a few strikers, involved in the reign of terror. With sorrow and anger, the *Waterfront Worker* acknowledged the apparent truth of the rumor that "some I.L.A. men were in the posse that helped smash the workers meeting places." *Waterfront Worker,* Sept. 14, 1934, p. 2; Oct. 1, 1934, p. 7.

49. Darcy, "The San Francisco Bay Area General Strike," p. 999.

50. *San Francisco Chronicle,* July 19, 1934, p. 1. Three days earlier the *Chronicle* (July 16, 1934, p. 2) had reported that Bridges recommended the "immediate establishment of food distribution depots in every section of the city." "If the people can't get food," the paper reported Bridges as saying, "the maritime workers and longshoremen will lose the strike."

51. Paul Eliel stated that as the last marchers broke ranks, "a general strike, which up to this time had appeared to many to be a visionary dream of a small group of the most radical workers, became for the first time a practical and realizable objective." Eliel, *Waterfront and General Strikes,* p. 128.

52. John F. Neylan to F. C. Atherton, Aug. 16, 1934, in John Francis Neylan, Correspondence and Papers, c. 1911–60, Bancroft Library, University of California, Berkeley, box 56. On the role of the San Francisco newspapers in the general strike, see Earl Burke, "Dailies Helped Break General Strike," *Editor and Publisher,* July 28, 1934, p. 5; and Evelyn Seeley, "War on the West Coast: II. Journalistic Strikebreakers," *New Republic,* Aug. 1, 1934, pp. 310–12.

53. John A. O'Connell to William Green, July 2, 1934, SFLC papers, carton 31; Frances Perkins to Franklin D. Roosevelt, July 15, 1934, in FDR Official File, 407-B, box 11; Casey quoted in Taylor and Gold, "San Francisco and the General Strike," p. 409; interview with Sam Kagel, July 18, 1984; "Henry Melnikow, and the National Labor Bureau: An Oral History," interview conducted by Corinne Lathrop Gilb, Institute of Industrial Relations, University of California, Berkeley, 1959, pp. 181–82, 189, 197–98; Carl Lynch to Strike Committees, I.S.U. of A., July 18, 1934, SUP Central Archive, 1934 strike file.

54. Quin, *The Big Strike,* pp. 176–77, 179.

55. Paul S. Taylor, "The San Francisco General Strike" (typescript, n.d.), p. 16, in Paul S. Taylor, material relating to agricultural and maritime strikes in California, 1933–42, Bancroft Library, University of California, Berkeley, carton 3; Quin, *The Big Strike,* p. 180.

56. Larrowe, *Harry Bridges,* p. 87; the phrase "all the muck of ages" is from Karl Marx and Friedrich Engels, *The German Ideology,* quoted in Glaberman, *Wartime Strikes,* p. 126.

57. John Cooper to George Larsen, July 26, 1934, SUP Central Archive, 1934 strike file.

58. "Proceedings, Special Meeting, Sailors' Union of the Pacific, Maritime Hall

Building, San Francisco, July 29, 1934," in Scharrenberg papers, carton 6, p. 1; hereafter cited as SUP, "Proceedings . . . July 29, 1934."

59. Ibid., pp. 4–5.

60. Ibid., pp. 8, 11–13.

61. *San Francisco Chronicle,* June 30, 1934, p. 2.

62. Johnson quoted in ibid., July 18, 1934, pp. 1, 5.

63. SUP, "Proceedings . . . July 29, 1934," pp. 14–15; the nicknames ridiculing Furuseth appeared in the *Foc'sle Head,* June 29, 1934, p. 1; July 12, 1934, p. 2.

64. SUP, "Proceedings . . . July 29, 1934," p. 14.

65. *San Francisco Chronicle,* July 31, 1934, p. 7.

6. The Syndicalist Renaissance

1. *Nation,* Aug. 1, 1934, p. 122; SUP, "Proceedings . . . July 29, 1934," p. 5.

2. Crocker quoted in SUP, "Proceedings . . . July 29, 1934," p. 10.

3. Ibid., p. 5; Karl Marx and Friedrich Engels, *Manifesto of the Communist Party* (Peking: Foreign Languages Press, 1972; the original German text appeared in 1848), p. 42: "Now and then the workers are victorious, but only for a time. The real fruit of their battle lies, not in the immediate result, but in the ever-expanding union of the workers."

4. Schmidt and Rutter quoted in Chiles, "General Strike: San Francisco, 1934," pp. 461, 463.

5. *Waterfront Worker,* Oct. 22, 1934, p. 4; Feb. 11, 1935, p. 4; Gregory Harrison, *Maritime Strikes on the Pacific Coast: A Factual Account of the Events Leading to the 1936 Strike of Marine and Longshore Unions* (San Francisco: Waterfront Employers Association, 1936), pp. 9, 14; "Ernest G. Ramsay: Reminiscences of a Defendant in the Shipboard Murder Case," in Stein, *The Shipboard Murder Case,* p. 4.

6. *Pacific Seaman,* Sept. 22, 1934, p. 1; *San Francisco Chronicle,* Sept. 21, 1934, p. 6; *Waterfront Worker,* Oct. 1, 1934, p. 5.

7. *Waterfront Worker,* Oct. 29, 1934, p. 7.

8. Ibid., Apr. 22, 1935, p. 4.

9. Ibid., Mar. 18, 1935, p. 7.

10. Foisie and Plant quoted in Richard Alan Liebes, "Longshore Labor Relations on the Pacific Coast, 1934–1942" (Ph.D. diss., University of California, Berkeley, 1942), p. 304; Almon E. Roth, *Merchant Marine Labor Problems on the Pacific Coast* (n.p., [1938]), p. 12; Almon E. Roth, *"Men and Ships": A Clinical Study in Human Relationships on One of the World's Most Turbulent Waterfronts* (n.p., [1938]), p. 9. Reviewing the history of organized slowdowns, Paul Eliel stated in 1941: "The employers contend—and there is ample data to support them in general if not in detail—that the costs of handling cargo on the Pacific Coast have doubled since 1934. Only a fractional part of this is due to changes in wage rates. The greatest share can be charged to the fact that the number of tons of cargo handled per man-hour is little more than half of what it was in the earlier year." Paul Eliel, "Labor Peace in Pacific Ports," *Harvard Business Review* 19 (Summer 1941): 432.

11. *Waterfront Worker,* Feb. 11, 1935, p. 5; Jan. 28, 1935, pp. 4, 6; *Voice of the Federation,* Oct. 10, 1935, p. 5.

12. *Waterfront Worker,* Oct. 15, 1934, p. 2; Dec. 3, 1934, p. 2; Dec. 10, 1934, p. 7.

13. Harrison, *Maritime Strikes on the Pacific Coast,* p. 21.

14. *Waterfront Worker,* Oct. 22, 1934, p. 4.

15. *Waterfront Worker,* Sept. 14, 1934, p. 5; *Voice of the Federation,* Apr. 21, 1936, p. 4.

16. *Waterfront Worker,* Mar. 25, 1935, p. 7.

17. *Waterfront Worker,* June 24, 1935, p. 7; Apr. 8, 1935, p. 6; *Voice of the Federation,* July 5, 1935, p. 4.

18. Barnes, *The Longshoremen,* p. 18; *Voice of the Federation,* Feb. 6, 1936, p. 4.

19. ILA Local 38-79, *The Truth about the Waterfront,* p. 12; Mers, "One Step at a Time, Many Backward," p. 431.

20. *San Francisco Examiner,* Oct. 14, 1935, p. 4A; Harrison, *Maritime Strikes on the Pacific Coast,* pp. 21–22.

21. ILA Local 38-39, *The Truth about the Waterfront,* p. 13.

22. Harrison, *Maritime Strikes on the Pacific Coast,* p. 18.

23. *Pacific Seaman,* Sept. 1, 1934, pp. 3–4.

24. Hobsbawm, *Labouring Men: Studies in the History of Labour,* p. 209; Miller, "The Dockworker Subculture and Some Problems in Cross-Cultural and Cross-Time Generalizations," pp. 306, 308–9.

25. *Seamen's Journal,* Feb. 1935, p. 3; May 1935, p. 6.

26. *Voice of the Federation,* July 19, 1935, p. 4; *Seamen's Lookout,* Feb. 1935; *ISU Pilot,* Feb. 27, 1935, p. 3.

27. Lundeberg quoted in Goldberg, *The Maritime Story,* p. 140; *Voice of the Federation,* July 19, 1935, p. 4.

28. *Voice of the Federation,* Sept. 20, 1935, p. 4; Nov. 4, 1935, p. 2; *ISU Pilot,* Nov. 7, 1935, p. 5.

29. In his recent memoir of the 1930s, literary critic Malcolm Cowley asks, "As for the American workers, did they share our [i.e., the intellectuals'] hope of building a new society? They were encouragingly militant, as they had proved in the sitdown strikes, but was their militance aroused by anything nobler than the hope of driving a new Buick?" Malcolm Cowley, *The Dream of the Golden Mountains: Remembering the 1930s* (New York: Viking Press, 1980), p. 316.

30. *San Francisco Chronicle,* Sept. 4, 1934, p. 1; *Waterfront Worker,* Sept. 14, 1934, p. 7.

31. The poem appeared in the "Anti-hearst Examiner," SFLC papers, carton 31; *Voice of the Federation,* Sept. 6, 1935, p. 2; Louis Goldblatt, *Working Class Leader in the ILWU, 1935–1977,* interview conducted by Estolv Ethan Ward (Berkeley: Regional Oral History Office, Bancroft Library, University of California, 1983), p. 109.

32. *Voice of the Federation,* July 5, 1935, p. 2; Sept. 6, 1935, pp. 1–2.

33. Ibid., July 12, 1935, p. 1; *American Seaman,* July 11, 1935, pp. 1, 5. See also San Francisco Bay Area District Council #2, Maritime Federation of the Pacific, "Minutes" (hereafter cited as SFBA DC#2, MFPC, "Minutes"), July 9, 1935, in Maritime Federation of the Pacific Coast, files, 1935–41, International Longshoremen's and Warehousemen's Union, Anne Rand Research Library, San Francisco,

hereafter cited as MFPC files. Characteristically, the Hearst press estimated a much smaller number of marchers. *San Francisco Examiner,* July 6, 1935, p. 1.

34. *Voice of the Federation,* July 12, 1935, p. 1.

35. *Voice of the Federation,* June 3, 1937, p. 10; *Los Angeles Times,* May 29, 1937, p. 1.

36. *Western Worker,* Dec. 26, 1935, p. 1; *Voice of the Federation,* Dec. 27, 1935, p. 3.

37. Roger Lapham, "Pacific Maritime Labor Conditions as They Affect the Nation," in Lapham, "An Interview on Shipping," p. 411; *West Coast Sailors,* Jan. 3, 1947, p. 8, *Waterfront Worker,* Oct. 22, 1934, p. 2; Dec. 24, 1934, p. 4.

38. Washington District Council #1, Maritime Federation of the Pacific Coast, "Minutes" (hereafter cited as WDC #1, MFPC, "Minutes"), July 3, 1936, in MFPC files.

39. *Waterfront Worker,* July 1933, p. 6; Mar. 25, 1935, p. 4; *San Francisco Chronicle,* Mar. 3, 1935, pp. 1, 3; *Western Worker,* Mar. 7, 1935, p. 1; *Voice of the Federation,* Sept. 17, 1936, p. 5; WDC #1, MFPC, "Minutes," Aug. 28, 1936.

40. *Voice of the Federation,* Oct. 17, 1935, p. 3; Oct. 24, 1935, p. 1; Nov. 21, 1935, p. 4; *Western Worker,* Dec. 19, 1935, p. 1.

41. *Voice of the Federation,* July 29, 1937, p. 1; Aug. 5, 1937, p. 1.

42. Joint Marine Modesto Committee, *The Modesto Frame-up* (San Francisco: Joint Marine Modesto Committee, [1936]).

43. Robert Dallek, *Franklin D. Roosevelt and American Foreign Policy, 1932–1945* (New York: Oxford University Press, 1979), pp. 110–19; *Voice of the Federation,* Oct. 24, 1935, p. 6; Nov. 21, 1935, p. 4; Sept. 26, 1935, p. 5; Sept. 13, 1935, p. 5.

44. *Voice of the Federation,* Oct. 10, 1935, p. 6.

45. *San Francisco Chronicle* editorial quoted in *Voice of the Federation,* Oct. 24, 1935, p. 6.

46. Roth, *"Men and Ships,"* pp. 3–4, 6.

47. *Voice of the Federation,* Oct. 24, 1935, p. 6.

48. *San Francisco Examiner,* Oct. 5, 1935, p. 1.

49. *Voice of the Federation,* Nov. 6, 1935, p. 2.

50. Ibid., Mar. 26, 1936, p. 6.

51. SFBA DC#2, MFPC, "Minutes," Sept. 17, 1935; *Voice of the Federation,* Sept. 13, 1935, p. 6.

52. *Waterfront Worker,* Mar. 18, 1935, p. 6.

53. On the Associated Farmers of California and the criminal syndicalism trial, see Daniel, *Bitter Harvest,* pp. 251–54.

54. Carey McWilliams, *Factories in the Field: The Story of Migratory Farm Labor in California* (1939; reprint ed., Santa Barbara, Calif.: Peregrine Publishers, 1971), pp. 241–43; *Western Worker,* Sept. 12, 1935, p. 2; *Voice of the Federation,* Aug. 30, 1935, p. 6.

55. Adamic, *My America,* p. 372; SFBA DC#2, MFPC, "Minutes," Oct. 29, 1935; *Voice of the Federation,* Aug. 30, 1935, p. 1; Sept. 6, 1935, p. 1; Sept. 13, 1935, p. 1.

56. *San Francisco Chronicle,* Mar. 3, 1935, pp. 1, 3; *San Francisco Examiner,*

Mar. 3, 1935, p. 3; *Waterfront Worker,* Mar. 18, 1935, p. 8; *The Mooney Case,* p. 469; *Nation,* Sept. 12, 1934, p. 285; Lillian Symes, "California, There She Stands!," *Harper's* 170 (Feb. 1935): 366.

57. SFBA DC#2, MFPC, "Minutes," Sept. 17, 1935; *Voice of the Federation,* July 5, 1935, p. 4; Dec. 27, 1935, p. 5.

58. *Voice of the Federation,* Nov. 27, 1935, p. 5; Aug. 30, 1935, p. 5; Nov. 14, 1935, p. 5.

59. *Voice of the Federation,* Feb. 13, 1936, p. 1. Of course, Lincoln was not nearly as anticapitalist as the ILA members implied. He exalted the independence of small producers who worked for themselves in shops and on farms, taking (in his words) "the whole product to themselves, and asking no favors of capital on the one hand, nor of hirelings and slaves on the other." On Lincoln's ideology, see Eric Foner, *Politics and Ideology in the Age of the Civil War* (New York: Oxford University Press, 1980), p. 32; and *Free Soil, Free Labor, Free Men: The Ideology of the Republican Party before the Civil War* (New York: Oxford University Press, 1970), pp. 29–32.

60. Alfred Haworth Jones, "The Search for a Usable Past in the New Deal Era," *American Quarterly* 23 (Dec. 1971): 714–18, 722–24. For the argument that American culture was fundamentally conservative in the 1930s, see Warren Susman, Introduction to *Culture and Commitment, 1929–1945,* ed. Warren Susman (New York: George Braziller, 1973), especially pp. 8–9. See also Richard H. Pells, *Radical Visions and American Dreams: Culture and Social Thought in the Depression Years* (New York: Harper and Row, 1973).

61. *Voice of the Federation,* Dec. 27, 1935, p. 3; Oct. 3, 1935, p. 6.

62. *Voice of the Federation,* June 11, 1936, pp. 1, 6; Harry Lundeberg, "To the Members of All Unions Affiliated with the Maritime Federation of the Pacific Coast," June 6, 1935, in MFPC files.

63. *Voice of the Federation,* Feb. 13, 1936, p. 2; ILA local 38-79, *The Truth about the Waterfront,* pp. 11–12.

64. See Alan Trachtenberg, *The Incorporation of America: Culture and Society in the Gilded Age* (New York: Hill and Wang, 1982), especially pp. 73–78, 234.

65. *New Masses,* Jan. 1, 1935, p. 6; *Daily Worker,* Dec. 26, 1935, p. 5; Earl Browder, *Who Are the Americans?* (New York: Workers' Library, 1936), pp. 12–13; Earl Browder, *Lincoln and the Communists* (New York: Workers' Library, 1936), pp. 5, 8; Roy B. Hudson, *True Americans: A Tribute to American Maritime Workers Who Fought for World Democracy in the Trenches of Spain* (New York: Waterfront Section, Communist Party, 1938), p. 11.

66. Alex Bittelman, "The Supreme Court, the New Deal and the Class Struggle," *Communist* 14 (July 1935): 595.

67. George Charney, *A Long Journey* (New York: Quadrangle Books, 1968), pp. 73–74, 77. See also Maurice Isserman, "The 1956 Generation: An Alternative Approach to the History of American Communism," *Radical America* 14 (Mar.–Apr. 1980): 43–51; Steve Nelson et al., *Steve Nelson, American Radical,* pp. 174–76; and Roy Rosenzweig, " 'United Action Means Victory': Militant Americanism on Film," *Labor History* 24 (Spring 1983): 274–88.

68. Thomas Bell, *Out of This Furnace* (1941; reprint ed., Pittsburgh: University of

Pittsburgh Press, 1976), p. 410. Friedlander, *The Emergence of a UAW Local,* pp. 122–27, includes a provocative and insightful discussion of the way in which black and immigrant workers in the auto industry saw the Socialist and Communist parties as vehicles of cultural integration.

69. *Waterfront Worker,* June 17, 1935, p. 5 (emphasis added); July 1, 1935, p. 7.

70. William Z. Foster, "Syndicalism in the United States," *Communist* 14 (Nov. 1935): 1056; Thomas Ray to author, Dec. 28, 1978.

71. See, for example, WDC#1, MFPC, "Minutes," Mar. 27, 1936; *Voice of the Federation,* Mar. 19, 1936, p. 3. The latter example concerns a proposal to send a delegate from ILA Local 38–79 to the Soviet Union as part of "a large delegation of Union representatives from all ports of the U.S.A." The *Voice* reported that "the proposition, after much discussion, was tabled. It was pointed out by those who opposed it that there was much business concerning our own affairs on the San Francisco Waterfront to be discussed, which are more urgent."

72. *Voice of the Federation,* July 5, 1935, p. 4; Sept. 12, 1935, p. 4; July 12, 1935, p. 2.

73. *Voice of the Federation,* Mar. 26, 1936, p. 4; *Waterfront Worker,* Oct. 29, 1934, p. 7; James Joll, *The Anarchists* (Boston: Little, Brown, 1964), p. 204; Jane C. Record, "Ideologies and Trade Union Leadership: The Case of Harry Bridges and Harry Lundeberg" (Ph.D. diss., University of California, Berkeley, 1954), p. 40.

74. *Voice of the Federation,* Jan. 23, 1936, p. 3; Draper, *The Roots of American Communism,* p. 16.

75. Eric Leif Davin and Staughton Lynd, "Picket Line and Ballot Box: The Forgotten Legacy of the Local Labor Party Movement, 1932–1936," *Radical History Review,* no. 22 (Winter 1979–80): 43–44, 55. See also Kenneth Waltzer, "The Party and the Polling Place: American Communism and an American Labor Party in the 1930s," *Radical History Review,* no. 23 (Spring 1980): 104–29.

76. *Western Worker,* Nov. 11, 1935, p. 2; *Voice of the Federation,* Aug. 30, 1935, pp. 1–2; Sept. 6, 1935, p. 2.

77. SFBA DC#2, MFPC, "Minutes," July 16, 1935.

78. *Voice of the Federation,* Oct. 13, 1935, p. 1; Sept. 6, 1935, p. 2; Aug. 30, 1935, p. 6.

79. *Western Worker,* Nov. 4, 1935, p. 2; *Voice of the Federation,* Sept. 6, 1935, p. 2; *San Francisco Chronicle,* Oct. 27, 1935, p. 1.

80. *San Francisco Chronicle,* Nov. 6, 1935, p. 1; *Western Worker,* Nov. 11, 1935, p. 2. The action of Vandeleur and his associates on the San Francisco Central Labor Council may have been out of step with the sentiments of many unions and central labor bodies in 1935, when independent political activity reached a peak. But it was a clear forerunner of the fratricidal conflict that was to wreck labor's initiatives toward independent politics in 1937 and 1938. See Mike Davis, "The Barren Marriage of American Labour and the Democratic Party," *New Left Review,* no. 124 (Nov.–Dec. 1980): 54–58.

7. The Rise and Fall of the Maritime Federation

1. Darcy, "The Great West Coast Maritime Strike," p. 667; Harvey Schwartz, *The March Inland: Origins of the ILWU Warehouse Division, 1934–1938* (Los Angeles:

University of California, Institute of Industrial Relations, 1978), pp. 109, 235; interview with Sam Darcy, Dec. 19, 1979.

2. *Waterfront Worker,* Jan. 7, 1935, p. 2; Feb. 4, 1935, pp. 1–2; Marine Federation of Seattle, "Minutes," Jan. 20, 1935, in MFPC files. After the formation of the coastwide Maritime Federation, the Seattle group became Washington District Council #1 of the MFPC.

3. *Voice of Action,* Mar. 8, 1935, and May 7, 1935, quoted in Lampman, "Collective Bargaining of West Coast Sailors," p. 164; *Seamen's Journal,* May 1935, p. 9.

4. Lampman, "Collective Bargaining of West Coast Sailors," p. 166; interview with Harold Johnson, Aug. 4, 1984. On Lundeberg's role as an SUP militant between the 1934 strike and his election to the presidency of the MFPC, one of his associates in the Sailors' Union stated: "Harry Lundeberg was one of the first men to start the fight for shipping through the Union Hall, and as patrolman for the Sailors' Union helped the crews win their demands on 52 vessels in less than three months time by organized job action and forcing finks off the ships, etc." *Voice of the Federation,* Nov. 21, 1935, p. 5.

5. Ironically, Friedl had worked closely with the San Pedro police in harassing, and sometimes terrorizing, militant members of the Marine Firemen's union. But apparently he was too bold in flaunting his violent tendencies and his arsenal of weapons. Al Quittenton, a San Pedro sailor, recalled that during the tanker strike in the spring of 1935 Friedl had stood on a dock in broad daylight firing a rifle at scabs aboard a ship in the harbor. Another seaman claimed that Friedl "advocated violence in every form, not only toward strike-breakers, but toward anyone opposing him." While police were raiding his apartment in an apparent search for weapons, Friedl appeared at the door with gun in hand and was shot down. Interview with Al Quittenton, May 11, 1981; *Western Worker,* July 1, 1935, p. 1; July 18, 1935, p. 3; *Voice of the Federation,* June 28, 1935, pp. 1–2; July 5, 1935, p. 2; *Seamen's Journal,* Aug. 1935, pp. 10–11. On William Fischer, see *Voice of the Federation* (Supplement), Aug. 20, 1936, pp. 1, 8.

6. Stephen Schwartz, "The Year 1934: A Chapter from the History of World Labor" (unpublished paper), pp. 18–21; Record, "Ideologies and Trade Union Leadership," p. 42; Frank J. Taylor, "Roughneck Boss of the Sailors' Union," *Saturday Evening Post,* Apr. 18, 1953, pp. 22–23, 180–83.

7. Schwartz, "The Year 1934," pp. 21–23; Benjamin Stolberg, *The Story of the CIO* (New York: Viking Press, 1938), p. 190; Philip Taft, "Strife in the Maritime Industry," *Political Science Quarterly* 54 (June 1939): 234; Darcy interview; Record, "Ideologies and Trade Union Leadership," pp. 42–43.

8. [Paul Scharrenberg?], "A Short Biography of Harry Lundeberg," in Scharrenberg papers, carton 2; *Voice of the Federation,* Nov. 21, 1935, p. 5.

9. Darcy interview; *Voice of Action,* May 3, 1935, quoted in Lampman, "Collective Bargaining of West Coast Sailors," p. 166.

10. Taylor, "Roughneck Boss of the Sailors' Union," p. 23; Bernstein, *Turbulent Years,* p. 576; Harry von Morpurgo, "The Legendary Life of Harry Lundeberg" (unpublished manuscript), in Scharrenberg papers, carton 2, pp. 1–2, 5, 14; *Washington Post,* Sept. 7, 1947, p. 6B.

11. Bernstein, *Turbulent Years,* p. 577.

12. William Fischer to F. M. Kelley and Harry Lundeberg, Mar. 4, 1936, in MFPC files.

13. La Follette Committee, *Report,* pt. 7, p. 1056.

14. *New York Times,* July 31, 1935, p. 9; Aug. 11, 1935, sec. 4, p. 7; SFBA DC#2, MFPC, "Minutes," Sept. 23, 1935.

15. SFBA DC#2, MFPC, "Minutes," Sept. 23, 1935; Sept. 24, 1935.

16. Ibid., July 1, 1935; Aug. 6, 1935; Aug. 12, 1935.

17. Scharrenberg, "Reminiscences"; Knight, *Industrial Relations in the San Francisco Bay Area,* pp. 275–76, 348–49; Daniel, *Bitter Harvest,* pp. 273–74; "Address of Paul Scharrenberg to the 20th Annual Convention of the American Legion, Department of California, Santa Monica, September 16, 1938," in Scharrenberg papers, carton 1; *Seamen's Journal,* Aug. 1935, p. 1; Sept. 1935, p. 1.

18. *Voice of the Federation,* Feb. 13, 1936, p. 6; Mar. 26, 1936, p. 2; *Seamen's Lookout,* Feb. 1935, p. 3; Scharrenberg's response to the trial committee is cited in E. R. Stowell to V. A. Olander, Feb. 8, 1936, in ILWU files relating to seamen and maritime unions, carton 12. Stowell expressed the opinion that "a great deal of our trouble and his can be traced to his failure to appear [before the trial committee] at that time, and to his method of refusal."

19. *San Francisco Examiner,* June 5, 1935, p. 6; *San Francisco Chronicle,* June 6, 1935, pp. 1, 3; "Communist Maritime Activities," in Mr. Morton to Paul Scharrenberg, June 21, 1935, Scharrenberg papers, carton 1. Lundeberg's claim that he called for Scharrenberg's expulsion in 1932 appears in a handwritten note in Scharrenberg papers, carton 1. It is apparently a quote from Lundeberg's testimony before a government committee, but I have been unable to locate the source of the quote.

20. *Western Worker,* Apr. 8, 1935, p. 1; June 1, 1935, p. 1; *Voice of the Federation,* June 14, 1935, p. 1; Oct. 31, 1935, p. 6; *Seamen's Journal,* July 1935, p. 12; Aug. 1935, p. 10; Scharrenberg, "Reminiscences," p. 118. See also the SUP documents, "Trial of Paul Scharrenberg" and "*The True Story* about the Expulsion of *Paul Scharrenberg* from the Sailors Union of the Pacific," in ILWU files relating to seamen and maritime unions, carton 12. At the beginning of the tanker strike, the *Western Worker* presented the calling of the strike as an act of rank-and-file insurgency: "The pressure of the seamen finally forced action." *Western Worker,* Mar. 14, 1935, p. 1.

21. Sailors' Union of the Pacific, Portland branch, report, May 26, 1934, in SUP Central Archive, Portland correspondence, 1934; *Voice of Action,* Jan. 18, 1935, p. 3.

22. *Western Worker,* June 27, 1935, p. 1; *Seamen's Journal,* Aug. 1935, p. 1.

23. *Voice of the Federation,* Sept. 13, 1935, p. 5; Sept. 20, 1935, p. 5.

24. Larrowe, *Harry Bridges,* p. 105.

25. *Voice of the Federation,* Dec. 19, 1935, p. 5; Larrowe, *Harry Bridges,* p. 105.

26. SFBA DC#2, MFPC, "Minutes," Sept. 28, 1935; *Voice of the Federation,* Mar. 26, 1936, p. 3.

27. Lundeberg quoted in Larrowe, *Harry Bridges,* p. 112.

28. *Voice of the Federation,* Oct. 10, 1935, p. 6; on Ward's IWW background, see Weintraub, "The I.W.W. in California," pp. 113–14.

29. "Resolution," Oct. 13, 1935, introduced by Arthur C. Ward, endorsed by C. Taylor, Austen Hansen, S. Sorenson, H. M. Bright, and L. E. Usinger, in ILWU files relating to seamen and maritime unions, carton 12.

30. *Voice of the Federation,* Oct. 17, 1935, pp. 1, 2; *San Francisco Examiner,* Oct. 19, 1935, p. 3.

31. SFBA DC#2, MFPC, "Minutes," Oct. 22, 1935; *Waterfront Worker,* Oct. 21, 1935, p. 8; Nov. 4, 1935, p. 8.

32. William Schneiderman, *The Pacific Coast Maritime Strike* (San Francisco: Western Worker Publishers, 1937), p. 10.

33. Interview with Al Quittenton; telephone interview with Jim Kendall; Britt Webster to Al Quittenton, Dec. 25, 1935, in ILWU files relating to seamen and maritime unions, carton 13; *Voice of the Federation,* Oct.–Dec. 1935, passim.

34. Telephone interview with Frank Paton; John McGovern to Paul Scharrenberg, July 15, 1940, in Scharrenberg papers; *West Coast Sailors,* Apr. 22, 1938, p. 3; *Voice of the Federation,* July 19, 1935, p. 5; "Sworn Statement of William C. McCuistion," May 14, 1940, in Scharrenberg papers, carton 2; Harry Bridges interview; Jim Kendall interview; Al Quittenton interview.

35. *Voice of the Federation,* Sept. 13, 1935, p. 4; Oct. 10, 1935, p. 6; Feb. 13, 1936, p. 5; SFBA DC#2, MFPC, "Minutes," Dec. 20, 1935; Britt Webster to Al Quittenton, Dec. 25, 1935; Frank Paton interview.

36. *Voice of the Federation,* Oct. 17, 1935 (Bright); Oct. 24, 1935, p. 4 (Hansen); July 9, 1936, p. 4 (Hansen); "Communist Maritime Activities," in Scharrenberg papers, carton 1 (Miljus); on Coester, see handwritten note by Scharrenberg in ibid.

37. *Western Worker,* Oct. 24, 1935, p. 2; Harry Lundeberg to F. M. Kelley, Oct. 20, 1935, and Oct. 24, 1935, MFPC files.

38. *Voice of the Federation,* Oct. 24, 1935, p. 6; Oct. 31, 1935, p. 4.

39. Sailors' Union of the Pacific Delegation to the Emergency Convention of the Maritime Federation of the Pacific, "Answer to Resolution Introduced by Brother Harry Bridges, Local 38–79, referring to job action," in ILWU files relating to seamen and maritime unions, carton 12; *Voice of the Federation,* Oct. 31, 1935, p. 4.

40. Maritime Federation of the Pacific Coast, *Proceedings of the Special Convention of the Maritime Federation of the Pacific Coast,* San Francisco, Nov. 12–22, 1935, Session of Nov. 20, p. 15; *Voice of the Federation,* Nov. 27, 1935, p. 6.

41. SUP Delegation, "Answer to . . . Harry Bridges," in ILWU files relating to seamen and maritime unions, carton 12; the *Western Worker* editorial was reprinted in the *Voice of the Federation,* Nov. 21, 1935, p. 2.

42. *Voice of the Federation,* Nov. 21, 1935, p. 2.

43. Leaflet, "Issued by a Group of Rank and File," [Dec. 1935], in ILWU files relating to seamen and maritime unions, carton 12; Britt Webster to Al Quittenton, Dec. 25, 1935.

44. *Voice of the Federation,* Jan. 16, 1936, p. 3; Sailors' Union of the Pacific, "Resolution" (leaflet, San Francisco, Dec. 16, 1935), in ILWU files relating to seamen and maritime unions, carton 12.

45. La Follette Committee, *Report,* pt. 7, p. 1065; R. D. Lapham to Hon. Frances Perkins, Apr. 13, 1935, in Lapham, "An Interview on Shipping," pp. 406–7.

46. SFBA DC#2, MFPC, "Minutes," Jan. 7, 1936; *New York Times,* Dec. 31, 1935, p. 2. A spokesman for the San Francisco Chamber of Commerce warned that the Maritime Federation "is reaching out. It has taken in the warehouse people; it has taken in people who work in canneries; it has taken in people who work in sugar refineries. It is reaching into the lumber industry. Their power is so evident that right at the moment nobody can ship any lumber up and down this Pacific Coast." He neglected to mention the fact that part of the reason nobody could ship any lumber up and down the coast

was because the employers had, in effect, declared a lockout on all the lumber schooners. La Follette Committee, *Report,* pt. 7, p. 1065.

47. Paul Scharrenberg, "To the Executive Board of the International Seamen's Union of America," Dec. 2, 1935, Scharrenberg papers, carton 1; *San Francisco Chronicle,* Oct. 2, 1935, p. 1; Jan. 1, 1936, p. 13.

48. SFBA DC#2, MFPC, "Minutes," Dec. 27, 1935, and Jan. 7, 1936; Britt Webster to Al Quittenton, Dec. 25, 1935.

49. SFBA DC#2, MFPC, "Minutes," Jan. 7, 1936.

50. Ibid., Apr. 21, 1936; Lundeberg quoted in Larrowe, *Harry Bridges,* p. 112.

51. *Voice of the Federation,* June 11, 1936, pp. 1, 6. See also Carl Tillman's statement in opposition to Bridges's proposal for a congressional investigation of the maritime industry, in SFBA DC#2, MFPC, "Minutes," Mar. 10, 1936.

52. William Fischer to W. J. Stack, Apr. 6, 1936; Fischer to F. M. Kelley, Mar. 9, 1936; Fischer to F. M. Kelley, June 27, 1936; in MFPC files.

53. Draper, *The Roots of American Communism,* pp. 88–91.

54. *Waterfront Worker,* Oct. 21, 1935, p. 8; *Voice of the Federation,* Oct. 31, 1935, p. 4.

55. *Proceedings of the Special Convention of the Maritime Federation of the Pacific Coast,* San Francisco, Nov. 12–22, 1935, Session of Nov. 13, p. 10; SFBA DC#2, MFPC, "Minutes," Apr. 21, 1936, and July 31, 1936.

56. SFBA DC#2, MFPC, "Minutes," Apr. 13–21, 1936; WDC #1, MFPC, "Minutes," Apr. 17, 1936; *Voice of the Federation,* Apr. 16, 1936, pp. 1, 6; Adamic, *My America,* pp. 373–75.

57. "S.S. President Hoover Incident" (broadside issued by the Coast Committee for the Shipowners, [Sept. 1936]), in Paul S. Taylor, material relating to agricultural and maritime strikes in California, carton 3; Goldberg, *The Maritime Story,* p. 155.

58. "Broadcast No. 1 of the Voice of the Maritime Unions," Nov. 26, 1936, in "San Francisco Waterfront Strikes, 1936–37: A Collection of Pamphlets, Broadsides, etc.," Graduate Social Science Library, University of California, Berkeley; Edw. F. McGrady to the President, Sept. 20, 1936, in FDR Official File; Goldberg, *The Maritime Story,* pp. 156, 320.

59. [Edward] McGrady to Marvin H. McIntyre, Oct. 29, 1936, in FDR Official File. *San Francisco Chronicle,* Oct. 31, 1936, p. 2; Dec. 19, 1936, p. 12.

60. "Statement of John M. Franklin, President of the International Mercantile Marine Company, Concerning Mutiny of the Crew of the S.S. California of the Panama Pacific Line," [Mar. 1936], in SFLC papers, carton 17; Goldberg, *The Maritime Story,* pp. 154, 159; Boyer, *The Dark Ship,* pp. 143–44, 200.

61. Mers, "One Step at a Time, Many Backward," p. 326; Boyer, *The Dark Ship,* p. 250; *Voice of the Federation,* June 18, 1936, p. 6; Dec. 24, 1936, p. 1.

62. Goldberg, *The Maritime Story,* p. 161.

63. *Voice of the Federation,* Nov. 26, 1936, p. 7.

64. Ibid., Dec. 3, 1936, p. 3; Louis Adamic, "Harry Bridges Comes East," *Nation,* Dec. 26, 1936, p. 753.

65. *Voice of the Federation,* Dec. 17, 1936, p. 1; *San Francisco Chronicle,* Dec. 23, 1936, p. 2; American League against Communism, " 'Red' Bridges—Read Out of National" (leaflet), in Neylan papers, box 95.

66. *Voice of the Federation,* Dec. 24, 1936, p. 4; Jan. 7, 1937, p. 8.

67. *San Francisco Examiner,* Dec. 24, 1936, p. 2; *San Francisco Chronicle,* Dec. 24, 1936, p. 12; *Voice of the Federation,* Dec. 24, 1936, pp. 1, 11; Bernstein, *Turbulent Years,* pp. 583–84; Goldberg, *The Maritime Story,* pp. 161–62; Larrowe, *Harry Bridges,* pp. 114–16; Roy Hudson, "The Lessons of the Maritime Strikes," *Communist* 16 (Mar. 1937): 235.

68. Robert H. Zieger, "The Popular Front Rides Again," *Political Power and Social Theory* 4 (1984): 299, Taft, "Strife in the Maritime Industry," p. 224.

69. Schwartz, *The March Inland,* pp. 11–14, 19, 80, 94–95, 98.

70. Ibid., pp. 79, 84; *San Francisco Chronicle,* Dec. 20, 1936, p. 7.

71. Bernstein, *Turbulent Years,* pp. 626–28; Galenson, *The CIO Challenge to the AFL,* pp. 383–84; *Voice of the Federation,* Oct. 1, 1936, p. 2.

72. Lapham, "Pacific Maritime Labor Conditions as They Affect the Nation," in Lapham, "An Interview on Shipping," p. 420.

73. Schwartz, *The March Inland,* pp. 110–11; *Voice of the Federation,* May 21, 1936, p. 8; June 18, 1936, p. 8; July 2, 1936, p. 5; Aug. 6, 1936, p. 4; Goldblatt quoted in Schwartz, *The March Inland,* p. 133.

74. David F. Selvin, *Sky Full of Storm: A Brief History of California Labor,* rev. ed. (San Francisco: California Historical Society, 1975), p. 52. Goldblatt, *Working Class Leader in the ILWU,* pp. 162–63, 168.

75. Carey McWilliams, *The Education of Carey McWilliams* (New York: Simon and Schuster, 1979), pp. 83–84. Rose Pesotta, an organizer for the International Ladies' Garment Workers' Union in 1934, affirmed that the "general strike in 'Frisco gave tremendous momentum to unionism all along the West Coast." Pesotta, *Bread upon the Waters,* p. 90.

8. AFL versus CIO: "We found brother slugging brother"

1. Galenson, *The CIO Challenge to the AFL,* p. 15.

2. Bernstein, *Turbulent Years,* p. 404; Galenson, *The CIO Challenge to the AFL,* p. 12.

3. *Report of Proceedings of the Fifty-Seventh Annual Convention of the American Federation of Labor,* Denver, Oct. 4–15, 1937, p. 10.

4. Galenson, *The CIO Challenge to the AFL,* pp. 383, 393.

5. Boyer, *The Dark Ship,* p. 226; *Voice of the Federation,* July 14, 1938, p. 5, July 7, 1938, p. 3.

6. Christopher L. Tomlins, *The State and the Unions: Labor Relations, Law, and the Organized Labor Movement in America, 1880–1960* (New York: Cambridge University Press, 1985), p. 148; Bernstein, *Turbulent Years,* pp. 697–99.

7. Taft, "Strife in the Maritime Industry," p. 224; Clark Kerr and Lloyd Fisher, "Conflict on the Waterfront," *Atlantic Monthly* 184 (Sept. 1949): 22.

8. Sailors' Union of the Pacific, Emergency Committee, "Report [on] Charter Revocation," [May? 1936], in ILWU files relating to seamen and maritime unions, carton 12; *Voice of the Federation,* Mar. 12, 1936, pp. 1, 6; Ivan Hunter to William Green, Apr. 3, 1936, in ILWU files relating to seamen and maritime unions, carton 12; *Seamen's Journal,* Apr. 1936, pp. 95–98, 101–3, 135–37; June 1936, pp. 1–2; Goldberg, *The Maritime Story,* pp. 146, 149.

9. *Voice of the Federation,* July 23, 1936, p. 5; July 30, 1936, p. 5.

10. *Daily Worker*, Nov. 26, 1935, pp. 1, 6; *Maritime Worker*, Aug. 10, 1936, p. 2; *Voice of the Federation*, July 23, 1936, p. 5.

11. Hudson, "The Lessons of the Maritime Strikes," p. 240; *Voice of the Federation*, Dec. 24, 1936, p. 4.

12. *Voice of the Federation*, Aug. 20, 1936, p. 4.

13. Ibid, Aug. 6, 1936, p. 5; Aug. 13, 1936, p. 5; Dec. 24, 1936, p. 4; De Caux, *Labor Radical*, p. 234.

14. *West Coast Sailors*, May 25, 1937, p. 2.

15. Boyer, *The Dark Ship*, p. 147. On the alleged relationship between Joe Curran and Tommy Ray, William McCuistion testified that "since the spring strike of 1936 [Ray] has been more or less constantly with Joe Curran. In other words, Joe Curran cannot make a speech before he talks to Tommy. It is common knowledge on the waterfront that Joe Curran has not got the ability to write the speeches that he makes, and that he is Tommy Ray's stooge." Dies Committee, *Hearings*, 11: 6571. See also King et al., *We Accuse*, pp. 171–72, for a highly skewed portrait of "Commissar Thomas (Tommy) Ray, . . . the Party big gun on the waterfront."

16. Bernstein, *Turbulent Years*, p. 584; Galenson, *The CIO Challenge to the AFL*, pp. 435–36; Goldberg, *The Maritime Story*, pp. 165–66; *Proceedings of the Third Annual Convention of the Maritime Federation of the Pacific Coast*, Portland, Oregon, June 7-July 9, 1937, Morning Session, June 21, 1937, p. 9; "Statement of Mrs. Elinore M. Herrick, Regional Director of the Second Region, National Labor Relations Board, New York, N.Y.," in U.S. Congress, Senate, Committee on Commerce and Committee on Education and Labor, *Amending the Merchant Marine Act of 1936*, 75th Cong., 3d sess., 1938 (Washington, D.C.: Government Printing Office, 1938), pp. 866–67, 872.

17. *Voice of the Federation*, Mar. 25, 1937, p. 6.

18. Mers, "One Step at a Time, Many Backward," pp. 431–33.

19. *Proceedings of the Third Annual Convention of the Maritime Federation of the Pacific Coast*, Afternoon Session, June 21, 1937, p. 8; Bernstein, *Turbulent Years*, p. 285; "Statement of Mrs. Elinore M. Herrick," p. 876; Galenson, *The CIO Challenge to the AFL*, p. 436; Edward Levinson, *Labor on the March* (New York: Harper and Brothers, 1938), p. 261. In 1939 Philip Taft stated that the "National Maritime Union has attempted to bring about more cordial relations, mutual recognition of respective membership, and cooperation; but the Sailors' Union of the Pacific has persistently rebuffed these peaceful overtures." Taft, "Strife in the Maritime Industry," p. 231.

20. Mark Levinson and Brian Morton, "The CIO, John Lewis, and the Left: An Interview with Philip Van Gelder," *Dissent* 32 (Fall 1985): 460–63; B. Carwardine to P. H. Van Gelder, May 3, 1937; Philip H. Van Gelder and John Green to John L. Lewis, May 7, 1937; John Brophy to H. R. Bridges, Mar. 30, 1937, in Congress of Industrial Organizations, Records, 1935–56, box A7–27 (folder on "Marine and Shipbuilding Workers of America, Industrial Union, 1950"), Department of Archives and Manuscripts, Catholic University of America, Washington, D.C. On the Communists', and Bridges's, reluctance to abandon the AFL, see Cochran, *Labor and Communism*, pp. 345–47.

21. [Benjamin Carwardine], "Survey and Criticism of the West Coast Labor Situation as It Affects the CIO," appended to Carwardine's "Brief History of the Industrial

Union of Marine and Shipbuilding Workers of America in San Francisco Bay," in Industrial Union of Marine and Shipbuilding Workers of America Papers, University of Maryland, College Park. I am indebted to Richard Boyden for making his copy of the Carwardine material available to me. *Voice of the Federation,* Apr. 22, 1937, pp. 1, 4; June 3, 1937, pp. 1, 4.

22. Bob [Stowell] to Whitey, [June 1937]; Bob [Stowell] to Harry [Lundeberg], June 10, 1937; June 3, 1937; June 15, 1937; all in SUP Central Archive, E. R. Stowell correspondence, 1937.

23. Bob [Stowell] to Harry [Lundeberg], June 25, 1937, in ibid.

24. Goldberg, *The Maritime Story,* p. 155; Lapham, "An Interview on Shipping," pp. 106–7. *Voice of the Federation,* Nov. 19, 1936, p. 8; Bob [Stowell] to Whitey, [June 1937], in SUP Central Archive, E. R. Stowell correspondence, 1937.

25. Bernstein, *Turbulent Years,* p. 585; Cochran, *Labor and Communism,* p. 97.

26. Brophy, *A Miner's Life,* p. 275; *Proceedings of the Third Annual Convention of the Maritime Federation of the Pacific Coast,* Afternoon Session, June 9, 1937, pp. 15, 18, 25, 33–34.

27. H. Lundeberg to E. R. Stowell, July 5, 1937, in SUP Central Archive, E. R. Stowell correspondence, 1937.

28. Harry Lundeberg to John L. Lewis, June 11, 1937, in SUP Central Archive, Stowell's Report—Lewis Committee—CIO Maritime Conference, 1937; Brophy, *A Miner's Life,* p. 275; John L. Lewis to Harry Bridges, June 12, 1937, in ILWU Archives, History file, folder on "switch to CIO, 1936–1938"; "Report of H. R. Bridges on C.I.O. Maritime Conference," [July 1937], in ibid.

29. Frances Perkins, "The Reminiscences of Frances Perkins," Oral History Collection, Columbia University, 1955, vol. 7, p. 282; E. R. Stowell to Harry Lundeberg, July 8, 1937, in SUP Central Archive, E. R. Stowell correspondence, 1937; Mervyn Rathborne, "An Open Letter to the Membership of the I.L.A. from the C.I.O.," in ILWU Archives, History file, folder on "switch to CIO, 1936–1938."

30. Bob [Stowell] to Harry [Lundeberg], June 29, 1937, in SUP Central Archive, E. R. Stowell correspondence, 1937.

31. Bob [Stowell] to Harry [Lundeberg], July 4, 1947, in ibid.

32. Brophy, *A Miner's Life,* pp. 274–75; John Brophy to Dorothy Day, July 10, 1937, in CIO Records, Central Office Correspondence, box A7–A2, folder on "John Brophy."

33. Brophy, *A Miner's Life,* p. 275; Goldblatt, *Working Class Leader in the ILWU,* p. 159; Carwardine, "Survey and Criticism of the West Coast Labor Situation as It Affects the CIO"; Neuberger, "Bad-Man Bridges," p. 199.

34. Mervyn Rathborne to John L. Lewis, July 14, 1937, and Aug. 27, 1937, in CIO Records, box A7–28, folder on "Maritime Union of America, National."

35. J. W. Engstrom to John L. Lewis, July 30, 1937; John Brophy to J. W. Engstrom, Aug. 11, 1937; San Francisco Bay Area District Council #2, Maritime Federation of the Pacific Coast, resolution, [June 1936]; V. J. Malone to John L. Lewis, Aug. 23, 1937, in CIO Records, box A7–28, folder on "Maritime Union of America, National"; *Voice of the Federation,* Aug. 19, 1937, p. 3.

36. Tomlins, *The State and the Unions,* p. 177; *I.L.A. 38-79 Bulletin,* Aug. 11, 1937, p. 2; *West Coast Sailors,* July 23, 1937, p. 3.

37. Sailors' Union of the Pacific, "To the Membership of the Sailors' Union of the Pacific: Steady as She Goes," in Scharrenberg papers, carton 1.

38. Lampman, "Collective Bargaining of West Coast Sailors," pp. 201–2. The Sailors' Union accused the NLRB of "holding an election without the SUP ever being notified by the Shepard Line or the NLRB, and the SUP not even appearing on the ballot." *West Coast Sailors,* May 6, 1938, p. 3.

39. When the San Francisco police discovered several cartons of baseball bats in Lundeberg's car, he claimed: "This is a Communist plot. Those bats were placed in the car after it was parked here." Years later he admitted, "I had fifty ballbats in the tire compartment of my car. . . .[A] cop seen them so I said it was a dam' Communist plant to discredit loyal American sailors." *San Francisco Chronicle,* Apr. 19, 1938, p. 4; Westbrook Pegler, "Dump or Be Dumped," *Los Angeles Examiner,* Aug. 29, 1956, xerox in ILWU files relating to seamen and maritime unions, carton 13.

40. *San Francisco Chronicle,* Apr. 19, 1938, pp. 1, 4; *San Francisco Examiner,* Apr. 19, 1938, pp. 1, 4; Galenson, *The CIO Challenge to the AFL,* p. 693 (n. 38); Lampman, "Collective Bargaining of West Coast Sailors," p. 204.

41. [Sailors' Union of the Pacific], "To the Membership of the Sailors' Union of the Pacific: The Undisputed Facts," in Scharrenberg papers, carton 1. On the Tacoma ILA and its support for the SUP in the Shepard line beef, see Magden and Martinson, *The Working Waterfront,* pp. 126–27.

42. [SUP], "The Undisputed Facts," Scharrenberg papers; *West Coast Sailors,* May 13, 1938, p. 2; June 3, 1938, p. 4; Richard L. Neuberger, "Labor's Overlords," *American Magazine* 125 (Mar. 1938): 16.

43. *Labor Herald,* May 12, 1938, p. 1; *West Coast Sailors,* June 24, 1938, p. 1; Lampman, "Collective Bargaining of West Coast Sailors," p. 206.

44. Harry Lundeberg to William Green, Nov, 21, 1938, and July 7, 1939; William Green to Harry Lundeberg, Mar. 5, 1940, and Aug. 2, 1940, in ILWU files relating to seamen and maritime unions, carton 13; *Report of Proceedings of the Fifty-Eighth Annual Convention of the American Federation of Labor,* Houston, Oct. 3–13, 1938, pp. 435–36.

45. Harry Lundeberg to William Green, July 7, 1939, in ILWU files relating to seamen and maritime unions, carton 13. See also Harry Lundeberg to William Green, Nov, 26, 1940, in ibid.

46. "Report by Harry Lundeberg to President Green," Feb. 1, 1940, in ILWU files relating to seamen and maritime unions, carton 13.

47. *Voice of the Federation,* Dec. 1, 1938, pp. 2, 4, Apr. 20, 1939, p. 5.

48. Goldberg, *The Maritime Story,* pp. 167–68; "Report on Harry Lundeberg," in ILWU files relating to seamen and maritime unions, carton 13; Ruth Sutherland, *Treacherous Passage* (San Francisco: National Union of Marine Cooks and Stewards, n.d.), pp. 19–27. For an account of the McCuistion trial and the events that led up to it, see the *New Orleans Times-Picayune,* Jan. 22–24, 1941. See also Herbert Resner to H. R. Bridges, June 4, 1942, and Herbert Resner to Arthur J. Mandell, June 4, 1942, in ILWU files relating to seamen and maritime unions, carton 13. Resner was Bridges's attorney at the time. He was convinced that the accused men were guilty and that Lundeberg was implicated in their activities. His letter to Bridges stated that "tie[ing] Lundeberg into this thing . . . is our ultimate objective."

49. Bernstein, *Turbulent Years,* p. 576; Harry Lundeberg to William Green, Nov. 26, 1940; Harry Lundeberg to William Green, July 7, 1939; "Report by Harry Lundeberg to President Green," Feb. 1, 1940, in ILWU files relating to seamen and maritime unions, carton 13.

50. Gorter and Hildebrand, *The Pacific Coast Maritime Shipping Industry,* vol 2, p. 251; Lampman, "Collective Bargaining of West Coast Sailors," p. 207.

51. *Voice of the Federation,* Oct. 31, 1935, p. 4; *West Coast Sailors,* July 23, 1937, p. 2; Oct. 15, 1937, p. 3; July 8, 1938, p. 4; Record, "Ideologies and Trade Union Leadership," pp. 47–48; Lampman, "Collective Bargaining of West Coast Sailors," pp. 208–9.

52. Al Burton, "In the Shadow of the Blackjack," *American Socialist* 2 (Mar. 1955): 13.

53. *West Coast Sailors,* July 15, 1938, p. 3; *Voice of the Federation,* Sept. 8, 1938, p. 2; Nov. 17, 1938, p. 2; Dec. 8, 1938, pp. 1, 5; Arthur H. Landis, *The Abraham Lincoln Brigade* (New York: Citadel Press, 1967), pp. 558–59. The quote about isolating "the Stalinist infection" is from Ralph Chaplin, *Wobbly: The Rough-and-Tumble Story of an American Radical* (Chicago: University of Chicago Press, 1948), p. 379. Chaplin served a brief stint as editor of the *Voice of the Federation.* His account of the West Coast waterfront is an amalgam of fact, fantasy, and outright distortion.

54. [Morris Watson], "No Colored Allowed to Work Here," pt. 1, p. 1, and pt. 3, p. 3, in ILWU files relating to seamen and maritime unions, carton 13.

55. Goldberg, *The Maritime Story,* p. 207; Herbert Hill, *Black Labor and the American Legal System: Race, Work, and the Law* (1977; reprint ed., Madison: University of Wisconsin Press, 1985), pp. 228, 220; Richard Boyden interview with Frank Barbaria, Sept. 17, 1984.

56. Isserman, *Which Side Were You On?,* pp. 142, 278 (n. 53); Hill, *Black Labor and the American Legal System,* pp. 223–24, 230, 233; Stan Weir, "The Informal Work Group," in Alice and Staughton Lynd, *Rank and File: Personal Histories by Working-Class Organizers* (Boston: Beacon Press, 1973), p. 188.

57. Hill, *Black Labor and the American Legal System,* pp. 227, 230–31; *Report of Proceedings of the Fifty-Eighth Annual Convention of the American Federation of Labor,* p. 458; Burton, "In the Shadow of the Blackjack," p. 12; Larrowe, *Harry Bridges,* pp. 349–50. See also Tomlins, *The State and the Unions,* pp. 158–96 for an extended discussion of the AFL's critique of the National Labor Relations Board.

58. Hill, *Black Labor and the American Legal System,* pp. 224, 234; [Watson], "No Colored Allowed to Work Here," pt. 2, p. 4, and pt. 3, p. 2; *Washington Post,* Sept. 7, 1947, p. 6B.

59. *San Francisco News,* Aug. 30, 1952; [National Union of Marine Cooks and Stewards], "SUP Rank and File 100% With MCS—But Take a Look at Their 'Leader' " (leaflet, [1952]), in NUMCS Records, carton 17.

60. "The Maritime Unions," p. 134; Gorter and Hildebrand, *The Pacific Coast Maritime Shipping Industry,* vol. 2, p. 138.

61. Burton, "In the Shadow of the Blackjack," p. 12; *San Francisco Chronicle,* July 19, 1949, and *Shipping News,* May 26, 1952, xerox of both articles in ILWU files relating to seamen and maritime unions, carton 13.

62. *West Coast Sailors,* Jan, 28, 1938, p. 3; May 13, 1938, p. 2; Jan. 6, 1939, p. 2; Oct. 18, 1940, p. 1; Oct. 25, 1940, p. 1; *San Francisco News,* July 20, 1952, xerox of article in ILWU files relating to seamen and maritime unions, carton 13.

9. Porkchops and Politics: Unions and the Popular Front

1. *San Francisco Examiner,* Oct. 14, 1935, p. 4A; Lapham, "Pacific Maritime Labor Conditions as They Affect the Nation," in Lapham, "An Interview on Shipping," p. 420; Kerr and Fisher, "Conflict on the Waterfront," p. 18; Tomlins, *The State and the Unions,* p. 156.

2. On the constraints that a wider union membership imposed, see Friedlander, *The Emergence of a UAW Local,* pp. 115–31; and Max Gordon, "The Party and the Polling Place: A Response," *Radical History Review,* no. 23 (Spring 1980): 131–32.

3. Klehr, *The Heyday of American Communism,* pp. 178, 187; "Review of the Month," *Communist* 15 (Jan. 1936): 8; Earl Browder, "The Party of Lenin and the People's Front," *Communist* 15 (Feb. 1936): 129. In the *New Masses,* Communist spokesman Mike Gold was already sounding a more conciliatory note. Although advocating the formation of a farmer-labor party, he declared, "Such a new party . . . might not even nominate a presidential candidate to oppose Roosevelt. But . . . it could have a tremendous pressure value on President Roosevelt, after his re-election." Michael Gold, "No Blank Check for Roosevelt," *New Masses* Jan. 21, 1936, p. 6.

4. Klehr, *The Heyday of American Communism,* pp. 207, 210; Clarence A. Hathaway, "The 1938 Elections and Our Tasks," *Communist* 17 (Mar. 1938): 215; Waltzer, "The Party and the Polling Place," p. 115.

5. *Voice of the Federation,* July 28, 1938, p. 8.

6. Ibid., Mar. 23, 1939, pp. 1, 4; July 20, 1939, p. 1; July 21, 1938, p. 8; Sept. 7, 1939, p. 4. On Bridges's first deportation hearing, and the cast of characters who promoted it, see Larrowe, *Harry Bridges,* pp. 133–216.

7. *Voice of Federation,* Nov. 10, 1938, p. 3; Mar. 30, 1939, p. 4; Mar. 9, 1939, p. 1; Sept. 8, 1938, p. 5; July 7, 1939, p. 7; Sept. 7, 1939, p. 1; July 13, 1939, p. 3.

8. Ibid., Aug. 26, 1938, p. 1.

9. The unions claimed eighty-five thousand marchers; the bitterly antiunion Industrial Association estimated "approximately 30,000." The *Chronicle* characterized the marchers as "a mighty tide of moving humanity that flowed unceasingly for more than five hours." *San Francisco Chronicle,* Sept. 6, 1938, pp. 1, 4. *Voice of the Federation,* Sept. 8, 1938, p. 6; May 4, 1939, p. 4.

10. Frost, *The Mooney Case,* pp. 477–85; *Voice of the Federation,* Jan. 12, 1939, p. 5; Nov. 17, 1938, p. 3.

11. *Voice of the Federation,* Oct. 27, 1938, p. 3; Sept. 7, 1939, p. 2; Nov. 10, 1938, pp. 1, 3.

12. "Review of the Month," *Communist* 16 (Sept. 1937): 782–83; William Z. Foster, "New Methods of Political Mass Organization," *Communist* 18 (Feb. 1939): 144.

13. "Review of the Month," *Communist* 16 (Aug. 1937): 684; Melvyn Dubofsky and Warren Van Tine, *John L. Lewis: A Biography* (New York: Quadrangle/New

York Times Book Co., 1977), pp. 314–15; "Review of the Month," *Communist* 16 (Sept. 1937): 781.

14. Waltzer, "The Party and the Polling Place," pp. 113, 115; Browder, "The American Communist Party in the Thirties," p. 237; E. Wight Bakke, *Citizens without Work* (New Haven: Yale University Press, 1940), p. 53; Charney, *A Long Journey*, pp. 60, 77.

15. Irving Howe, *Socialism and America* (New York: Harcourt Brace Jovanovich, 1985), pp. 73–86; Gordon, "The Party and the Polling Place: A Response," pp. 133–34; Hugh T. Lovin, "CIO Innovators, Labor Party Ideologues, and Organized Labor's Muddles in the 1937 Detroit Elections," *Old Northwest* 8 (Fall 1982): 223–43; Daniel Nelson, "The CIO at Bay," pp. 565–86, quoted on pp. 571, 576.

16. Matthew Josephson, *Sidney Hillman: Statesman of American Labor* (Garden City, N.Y.: Doubleday, 1952), pp. 398–400; "The Coming Labor Party," *Nation*, Apr. 15, 1936, pp. 468–69; Earl Browder, "New Developments and New Tasks in the U.S.A.," *Communist* 14 (Feb. 1935): 114; Klehr, *The Heyday of American Communism*, p. 220.

17. Charney, *A Long Journey*, pp. 122–23; Klehr, *The Heyday of American Communism*, pp. 395, 397, 400.

18. Richmond, *Long View from the Left*, p. 201; author's interview with Bill Bailey; *Voice of the Federation*, Sept. 28, 1939, p. 4.

19. *Voice of the Federation*, Oct. 5, 1939, pp. 4, 7; Oct. 19, 1939, p. 1.

20. Ronald L. Filippelli, "UE: An Uncertain Legacy," *Political Power and Social Theory* 4 (1984): 229, 225; "Statement Issued by San Francisco Bay District Council #2 of the Maritime Federation of the Pacific Coast to: Honorable Franklin D. Roosevelt," Jan. 22, 1936, attached to F.D.R. Memorandum for the Secretary of Labor, Jan. 27, 1936, in FDR Official File; Adamic, *My America*, p. 371; Eggleston quoted in Larrowe, *Harry Bridges*, pp. 126–27.

21. Glazer, *The Social Basis of American Communism*, p. 114; Jack Stachel, "Build the Party for Peace, Democracy, and Socialism!," *Communist* 17 (Mar. 1938): 223–24; Klehr, *The Heyday of American Communism*, pp. 240–41.

22. *Voice of the Federation*, Mar. 4, 1937, p. 5; Ferguson's testimony is in Dies Committee, *Hearings*, 4: 2919–41; Kempton, *Part of Our Time*, p. 99; Starobin, *American Communism in Crisis*, p. 39.

23. Lapham, "An Interview on Shipping," p. 96; Galenson, *The CIO Challenge to the AFL*, p. 445; Larrowe, *Harry Bridges*, p. 255; Kerr and Fisher, "Conflict on the Waterfront," p. 21.

24. "History of [the Marine Cooks and Stewards'] Union," p. 45, in NUMCS Records, carton 2; Record, "The Rise and Fall of a Maritime Union," pp. 85, 92.

25. John Gladstone to author, Nov. 3, 1986; Isserman, *Which Side Were You On?*, p. 142.

26. Schmidt, *Secondary Leadership in the ILWU*, p. 228; Northrup, *Organized Labor and the Negro*, p. 153. See also Quin, *The Big Strike*, p. 51, and Karl G. Yoneda, *Ganbatte: Sixty-Year Struggle of a Kibei Worker* (Los Angeles: Asian-American Studies Center, University of California, Los Angeles, 1983). Yoneda was the first Japanese-American admitted to the San Francisco longshore local, in 1936.

27. Larrowe, *Harry Bridges*, pp. 285, 367–68; Pilcher, *The Portland Longshoremen*, pp. 67–76.

28. Adamic, *My America*, p. 378; Roger Keeran, *The Communist Party and the Auto Workers Unions* (Bloomington: Indiana University Press, 1980), p. 190; Harvey Klehr, "American Communism and the United Auto Workers Union: New Evidence on an Old Controversy," *Labor History* 24 (Summer 1983): 409.

29. Kerr and Fisher, "Conflict on the Waterfront," p. 18; Gorter and Hildebrand, *The Pacific Coast Maritime Shipping Industry*, vol. 2, pp. 234, 258.

30. SFBA DC#2, MFPC, "Minutes," Apr. 21, 1936; [Harry R. Bridges et al.], *Town Meeting* (n.p. [1938?]), p. 6; De Caux, *Labor Radical*, p. 301.

31. Galenson, *The CIO Challenge to the AFL*, p. 391; Schmidt, *Secondary Leadership in the ILWU*, pp. 136–37.

32. *San Francisco Examiner*, Dec. 18, 1938, p. 10; Dec. 20, 1938, p. 7; Dec. 21, 1938, p. 1.

33. *San Francisco Chronicle*, Dec. 21, 1938, p. 1; Larrowe, *Harry Bridges*, pp. 131–32; Liebes, "Longshore Labor Relations on the Pacific Coast," pp. 186a–90.

34. *Voice of the Federation*, Nov. 2, 1940, pp. 1, 4; James McGregor Burns, *Roosevelt: The Lion and the Fox* (New York: Harcourt, Brace and World, 1956), p. 442; Dubofsky and Van Tine, *John L. Lewis*, p. 360; Samuel Lubell, "Post Mortem: Who Elected Roosevelt?," *Saturday Evening Post*, Jan. 25, 1941, p. 9. See also Irving Bernstein, "John L. Lewis and the Voting Behavior of the C.I.O.," *Public Opinion Quarterly* 5 (June 1941): 233–49.

35. Klehr, *The Heyday of American Communism*, pp. 174–75, 187; Harry R. Bridges to John L. Lewis, Feb. 3, 1936, in CIO Records, folder on "Maritime Union of America, National"; R. B. Hudson, "The Fight of the Seamen for Militant Unionism," *Communist* 15 (Mar. 1936): 223.

36. *Voice of the Federation*, Nov. 9, 1940, p. 1. Joe Curran, president of the NMU, also joined in the attack on Roosevelt and the New Deal, declaring, "The NMU can safely say that we have gotten absolutely nothing from the Roosevelt administration. On the contrary, we have spent most of our time . . . fighting the attempts of the Roosevelt administration to destroy us." He predicted that if FDR were elected for a third term, "the progressive unions would be smashed." Ibid., p. 5.

37. Ibid., p. 2; Nov. 2, 1940, pp. 1, 2.

38. Byron Darnton, "The Riddle of Harry Bridges," *New York Times Magazine*, Feb. 25, 1940, p. 5; Larrowe, *Harry Bridges*, p. 126; *Voice of the Federation*, Nov. 9, 1940, p. 2.

39. Isserman, *Which Side Were You On?*, p. 146; Larrowe, *Harry Bridges*, p. 254; Cochran, *Labor and Communism*, pp. 211, 214; Harry Henderson and Sam Shaw, "Readin', Writin', and No Strikin'," *Collier's*, Apr. 21, 1945, pp. 22–23.

40. Larrowe, *Harry Bridges*, pp. 255–56; Starobin, *American Communism in Crisis*, pp. 59, 77, 91, 273n.; Kampelman, *The Communist Party vs. the C.I.O.*, p. 202. The shipowners' view of Harry Bridges was not altered by his class collaborationist proposals during the war. Until 1948, and in some cases longer, they remained convinced that he was a dangerous radical. As the *Pacific Shipper* put it, "The responsibility for West Coast shipping's 14 years of labor strife lies primarily with the left-wing unions captained by Harry Bridges." Gorter and Hildebrand, *The Pacific Coast Maritime Shipping Industry*, vol. 2, p. 218.

41. Schmidt, *Secondary Leadership in the ILWU*, p. 139; Darnton, "The Riddle of Harry Bridges," p. 5.

Conclusion: "Labor on the March"—How Far?

1. Levinson, *Labor on the March*, p. 236; Bernstein, *Turbulent Years;* Ann Banks, *First-Person America* (New York: Alfred A. Knopf, 1980), p. 67; Jeremy Brecher, Jerry Lombardi, and Jan Stackhouse, *Brass Valley: The Story of Working People's Lives and Struggles in an American Industrial Region* (Philadelphia: Temple University Press, 1982), p. 178.

2. Nelson, "The CIO at Bay," p. 583; Cowley, *The Dream of the Golden Mountains,* p. 316. For an excellent survey of the literature on the CIO and the American working class in the 1930s, see David Brody, "The CIO after 50 Years: A Historical Reckoning," *Dissent* 32 (Fall 1985): 457–72.

3. Dubofsky, "Not So 'Turbulent Years'," pp. 5–20; Nelson Lichtenstein, *America's War at Home: The CIO in World War II* (New York: Cambridge University Press, 1982), pp. 13–14.

4. *Voice of the Federation,* Dec. 21, 1938, p. 4; July 7, 1939, p. 1. For discussions of the parochial character of shop-floor militancy, see especially Daniel Nelson, "Origins of the Sit-Down Era," pp. 198–225, and Lichtenstein, "Auto Worker Militancy," pp. 335–53.

5. Gorter and Hildebrand, *The Pacific Coast Maritime Shipping Industry,* vol. 2, pp. 137–38; Harvey Swados, "West-Coast Waterfront—The End of an Era," *Dissent* 8 (Autumn 1961): 449; Stan Weir, "The Informal Work Group," in Lynd and Lynd, *Rank and File,* pp. 182–83.

6. *Voice of the Federation,* July 7, 1939, p. 1; *I.L.A. 38–79 Bulletin,* Aug. 11, 1937, p. 1.

7. *West Coast Sailors,* Oct. 18, 1940, p. 3.

8. Westbrook Pegler, "A Fighting Unioneer," *Los Angeles Examiner,* Aug. 30, 1956, xerox of article in ILWU files relating to seamen and maritime unions, carton 13; "Ten Who Deliver," *Fortune* 34 (Nov. 1946): 151; Larrowe, *Harry Bridges,* p. 111.

9. Philip Van Gelder to John Brophy, Mar. 25, 1937, in CIO Records, box A7-27, folder on "Marine and Shipbuilding Workers of America, Industrial Union, 1950"; Trimble, "Harry Bridges," p. 7.

10. *Report of Proceedings of the Fifty-Eighth Annual Convention of the American Federation of Labor,* p. 376; De Caux, *Labor Radical,* pp. 381, 301; Dorothy Day to John Brophy, July 5, 1937, in CIO Records, Central Office Correspondence, box A7-A2, folder on "John Brophy"; Swados, "West-Coast Waterfront—The End of an Era," p. 459; Carwardine, "Survey and Criticism of the West Coast Labor Situation as It Affects the CIO"; *Justice,* July 1, 1938, xerox of article appended to Wm. Gately to Editor, "Justice," July 15, 1938, in Brophy papers, box 6, folder on "Calif.—1938, CIO."

11. Murphy quoted in ILWU, *The Everlasting Bridges Case* (San Francisco: International Longshoremen's and Warehousemen's Union, 1955), p. 5; Harvey Schwartz, "Harry Bridges and the Scholars: Looking at History's Verdict," *California History* 59 (Spring 1980): 72; Daniel Bell, "The Racket-Ridden Longshoremen," *Dissent* 6 (Autumn 1959): 417–29.

12. *Report of Proceedings of the Fifty-Eighth Annual Convention of the American Federation of Labor*, p. 373; Mary Heaton Vorse, *Labor's New Millions* (New York: Modern Age Books, 1938), p. 277.

13. Christopher L. Tomlins, "AFL Unions in the 1930s: Their Performance in Historical Perspective," *Journal of American History* 65 (Mar. 1979): 1021–42.

14. Goldberg, *The Maritime Story*, p. 179; Galenson, *The CIO Challenge to the AFL*, p. 441.

15. *Pacific Coast Longshoreman* quoted in Magden and Martinson, *The Working Waterfront*, p. 126.

16. *Los Angeles Times*, June 16, 1940, p. 20.

17. Carwardine, "Survey and Criticism of the West Coast Labor Situation as It Affects the CIO"; Thompson, *The Making of the English Working Class*, p. 12.

Bibliography

Archival Collections

Brophy, John. Papers, 1917–63. Department of Archives and Manuscripts. Catholic University of America, Washington, D.C.

Congress of Industrial Organizations. Records, 1935–56. Department of Archives and Manuscripts. Catholic University of America, Washington, D.C.

Denman, William. Correspondence and Papers, c. 1900–59. Bancroft Library, University of California, Berkeley.

Federal Emergency Relief Administration. State File (Maryland). RG 69, National Archives, Washington, D.C.

International Longshoremen's and Warehousemen's Union. Archives. Anne Rand Research Library, San Francisco.

———. Subject files relating to seamen and maritime unions, c. 1936–76. Bancroft Library, University of California, Berkeley.

Lannon, Al. Papers, c. 1930–68. In author's possession, courtesy of Albert Lannon, Jr.

Lubin, Simon Julius. Correspondence and Papers, 1912–36. Bancroft Library, University of California, Berkeley.

Macarthur, Walter. Correspondence and Papers, c. 1905–44. Bancroft Library, University of California, Berkeley.

Maritime Federation of the Pacific Coast. Files, 1935–41. International Longshoremen's and Warehousemen's Union, Anne Rand Research Library, San Francisco.

Mason, Redfern. Correspondence and Papers, c. 1895–1939. Bancroft Library, University of California, Berkeley.

National Union of Marine Cooks and Stewards. Records, c. 1935–55. Bancroft Library, University of California, Berkeley.

Neylan, John Francis. Correspondence and Papers, c. 1911–60. Bancroft Library, University of California, Berkeley.

Olander, Victor A. Papers, 1898–1942. Chicago Historical Society Library.

Roosevelt, Franklin D. Papers as President, Official File, 1933–45. Franklin D. Roosevelt Library, Hyde Park, N.Y.

Sailors' Union of the Pacific. Central Archive. Sailors' Union of the Pacific Headquarters, San Francisco.

San Francisco Labor Council, AFL-CIO. Correspondence and Papers, 1906–65. Bancroft Library, University of California, Berkeley.

Scharrenberg, Paul. Correspondence and Papers. Bancroft Library, University of California, Berkeley.

Taylor, Paul S. Material relating to agricultural and maritime strikes in California, 1933–42. Bancroft Library, University of California, Berkeley.

Government Documents

Congressional Sources

U.S. Congress. House. Committee on Merchant Marine and Fisheries. *Hearings on Bills Relating to the Rights and Duties of Seamen.* 54th Cong., 1st sess., 1896. Washington, D.C.: Government Printing Office, 1896.

————. House. Special Committee on Un-American Activities. *Investigation of Un-American Propaganda Activities in the United States: Hearings before a Special Committee on Un-American Activities* [Dies Committee]. 76th Cong., 1st sess., vol. 11. Washington, D.C.: Government Printing Office, 1940.

————. Senate. Committee on Commerce and Committee on Education and Labor. *Amending the Merchant Marine Act of 1936.* 75th Cong., 3d sess., 1938. Washington, D.C.: Government Printing Office, 1938.

————. Senate. Committee on Interstate and Foreign Commerce. *Waterfront Investigation: New York–New Jersey; Interim Report of the Committee on Interstate and Foreign Commerce.* 83d Cong., 1st sess. Report no. 653. Washington, D.C.: Government Printing Office, 1953.

————. Senate. Subcommittee of the Committee on Education and Labor. *Report, Violations of Free Speech and Rights of Labor* [La Follette Committee]. 77th Cong., 2d sess. Report no. 1150. Washington, D.C.: Government Printing Office, 1942.

Other Government Publications

Albrecht, Arthur Emil. *International Seamen's Union of America: A Study of Its History and Problems.* Bulletin of the United States Bureau of Labor Statistics, Miscellaneous Series, no. 342. Washington, D.C.: Government Printing Office, 1923.

Immigration and Naturalization Service. Department of Justice. *In the Matter of Harry Renton Bridges: Memorandum of Decision.* File no. 55973/217. Washington, D.C.: Government Printing Office, 1941.

Landis, James M. *In the Matter of Harry R. Bridges: Findings and Conclusions of the Trial Examiner.* Washington, D.C.: Government Printing Office, 1939.

United States Maritime Commission. *Economic Survey of the American Merchant Marine.* Washington, D.C.: Government Printing Office, 1937.

U.S. National Longshoremen's Board. "Proceedings before the National Longshoremen's Board . . . to Arbitrate Controversies between the Waterfront Employers and the International Longshoremen's Association, Local 38, of the Pacific Coast District." San Francisco, Aug. 8–24, 1934. Copy in Bancroft Library, University of California, Berkeley.

Works Progress Administration. *The Law in Action during the San Francisco Longshore and Maritime Strike of 1934*. Work Project no. 1950. Written and prepared under the direction of Herbert Resner. Berkeley, 1936.

Union Convention Proceedings

American Federation of Labor. *Report of Proceedings of the Annual Convention,* 1937–38.

Congress of Industrial Organizations. *Proceedings of the Constitutional Convention,* 1938–39.

International Seamen's Union of America. *Proceedings of the Annual Convention,* 1900–1936.

Maritime Federation of the Pacific Coast. *Proceedings of the Annual Convention,* 1935–41.

———. *Proceedings of the Special Convention,* San Francisco, Nov. 12–22, 1935.

Maritime Newspapers, Journals, and Bulletins

Foc'sle Head, San Francisco.
The Hook, New York.
ISU Pilot, New York.
Marine Workers Voice, New York.
Maritime Worker, San Francisco.
Pacific Coast Longshoreman, San Francisco.
Pacific Seaman, San Francisco (later published as *American Seaman*).
Pilot, New York.
Seamen's Journal, San Francisco (published as *Coast Seamen's Journal* until 1918).
Seamen's Lookout, San Francisco.
Voice of the Federation, San Francisco.
Waterfront Worker, San Francisco.
West Coast Sailors, San Francisco.

Other Newspapers

Daily Worker, New York.
Labor Clarion, San Francisco.
Los Angeles Times.
New Orleans Times-Picayune.
New York Times.
San Francisco Chronicle.
San Francisco Examiner.
San Francisco News.
Voice of Action, Seattle.
Western Worker, San Francisco.

Oral History Material

Interviews Conducted by Author

Austin, Ken. Emeryville, Calif., Oct. 3, 1981.
Bailey, Bill. San Francisco, Calif., Jan. 24, 1979.
Boano, Dan. San Diego, Calif., Feb. 25, 1979.
Bridges, Harry. San Francisco, Calif., Oct. 6, 1981.
Cullinan, George. New York, N.Y., Dec. 12, 1979.
Darcy, Sam. Harvey Cedars, N.J., Dec. 19, 1979.
Gladstone, John. Miami, Fla., Oct. 21, 1979.
Hudson, Roy. San Francisco, Calif., Oct. 29 and Nov. 23, 1981; Apr. 1, 1982.
J. R. (name and place withheld at interviewee's request), May 28, 1979.
Johnson, Harold. San Francisco, Calif., Aug. 4, 1984.
Johnson, Miriam Dinkin. San Francisco, Calif., Aug. 2, 1984.
Kagel, Sam. San Francisco, Calif., July 18, 1984.
Kendall, Jim. San Francisco, Calif. (telephone interview), July 16, 1981.
Lynch, Barney. Miami, Fla., Oct. 20, 1979.
Lynch, Greta. Miami, Fla., Oct. 20, 1979.
McCarthy, Bill. Grass Valley, Calif., Sept. 30, 1980.
McElroy, Bob. New York, N.Y., May 31, 1979; Feb. 3 and Aug. 19, 1981.
Olsen, John P. San Francisco, Calif., Oct. 22, 1981.
Paton, Frank, San Francisco, Calif. (telephone interview), Sept. 21, 1981.
Postek, Stanley. New York, N.Y., Dec. 12, 1979.
Quittenton, Al. San Bruno, Calif., May 11, 1981.
Ray, Thomas. New York, N.Y., Nov. 27, 1978; May 31, 1979.
Richmond, Al. San Francisco, Calif., Nov. 2, 1978; Sept. 17, 1982; Apr. 6, 1983.
Rubin, Charles. Ramona, Calif., Oct. 6, 1979.
Schmidt, Henry. Sonoma, Calif., Oct. 14, 1981.
Stack, Joe. Woodside, N.Y., Nov. 26, 1978.
Stack, Walter. San Francisco, Calif., Sept. 21, 1979.

Other Oral History Material

Barbaria, Frank. Interviewed by Richard Boyden, San Diego, Calif., Sept. 17, 1984.
Curran, Joseph. "The Reminiscences of Joseph Curran." Columbia University, Oral History Collection, 1964.
Land, Emory Scott. "The Reminiscences of Emory Scott Land." Columbia University, Oral History Collection, 1963.
Lapham, Roger. "An Interview on Shipping, Labor, San Francisco City Government, and American Foreign Aid." Conducted by Corinne L. Gilb. University of California, Berkeley, General Library, Regional Cultural History Project, 1957.
"Henry Melnikow and the National Labor Bureau: An Oral History." Interview conducted by Corinne Lathrop Gilb. Institute of Industrial Relations, University of California, Berkeley, 1959.
Perkins, Frances. "The Reminiscences of Frances Perkins." Columbia University, Oral History Collection, 1955.
St. Sure, J. Paul. "Some Comments on Employer Organizations and Collective Bargaining in Northern California since 1934." Interview conducted by Corinne

Gilb. Institute of Industrial Relations Oral History Project, University of California, Berkeley, 1957.

Scharrenberg, Paul. "Reminiscences." Bancroft Library, University of California, Berkeley, 1954.

Books

Adamic, Louis. *My America, 1928–1938*. New York: Harper and Brothers, 1938.

Ameringer, Oscar. *If You Don't Weaken*. New York: Henry Holt, 1940.

Anderson, Perry. *Arguments within English Marxism*. London: Verso, 1980.

Auerbach, Jerold S. *Labor and Liberty: The La Follette Committee and the New Deal*. New York: Bobbs-Merrill, 1966.

Avrich, Paul. *Kronstadt 1921*. Princeton: Princeton University Press, 1970.

Axtell, Silas B., comp. *A Symposium on Andrew Furuseth*. New Bedford, Mass.: Darwin Press, 1948.

Bakke, E. Wight. *Citizens without Work*. New Haven: Yale University Press, 1940.

Banks, Ann. *First-Person America*. New York: Alfred A. Knopf, 1980.

Barnes, Charles B. *The Longshoremen*. New York: Survey Associates, 1915.

Bedford, Ian, and Ross Curnow. *Initiative and Organization*. Melbourne: F. W. Cheshire, 1963.

Bell, Thomas. *Out of This Furnace*. 1941. Reprint. Pittsburgh: University of Pittsburgh Press, 1976.

Bernstein, Irving. *The Lean Years: A History of the American Worker, 1920–1933*. Boston: Houghton Mifflin, 1960.

———. *Turbulent Years: A History of the American Worker, 1933–1941*. Boston: Houghton Mifflin, 1970.

Bessie, Alvah. *Men in Battle*. 1939. Reprint. San Francisco: Chandler and Sharp, 1975.

Bodnar, John. *Workers' World: Kinship, Community, and Protest in an Industrial Society, 1900–1940*. Baltimore: Johns Hopkins University Press, 1982.

Boyer, Richard O. *The Dark Ship*. Boston: Little, Brown, 1947.

Brecher, Jeremy. *Strike!* San Francisco: Straight Arrow Books, 1972.

Brecher, Jeremy, Jerry Lombardi, and Jan Stackhouse. *Brass Valley: The Story of Working People's Lives and Struggles in an American Industrial Region*. Philadelphia: Temple University Press, 1982.

Brody, David. *Labor in Crisis: The Steel Strike of 1919*. Philadelphia: Lippincott, 1965.

———. *Steelworkers in America: The Nonunion Era*. Cambridge, Mass.: Harvard University Press, 1960.

———. *Workers in Industrial America: Essays on the 20th Century Struggle*. New York: Oxford University Press, 1980.

Brophy, John. *A Miner's Life*. Edited and supplemented by John O. P. Hall. Madison: University of Wisconsin Press, 1964.

Burns, James McGregor. *Roosevelt: The Lion and the Fox*. New York: Harcourt, Brace and World, 1956.

Camp, William Martin. *San Francisco: Port of Gold*. Garden City, N.Y.: Doubleday, 1947.

Carr, E. H. *Twilight of the Comintern, 1930–1935*. New York: Pantheon, 1982.

Chaplin, Ralph. *Wobbly: The Rough-and-Tumble Story of an American Radical.* Chicago: University of Chicago Press, 1948.

Charney, George. *A Long Journey*. Chicago: Quadrangle Books, 1968.

Claudin, Fernando. *The Communist Movement: From Comintern to Cominform.* New York: Monthly Review Press, 1975.

Cochran, Bert. *Labor and Communism: The Conflict that Shaped American Unions.* Princeton: Princeton University Press, 1977.

Conlin, Joseph Robert. *Bread and Roses Too: Studies of the Wobblies.* Westport, Conn.: Greenwood Press, 1969.

Cowley, Malcolm. *The Dream of the Golden Mountains: Remembering the 1930s.* New York: Viking Press, 1980.

Cross, Ira B. *A History of the Labor Movement in California*. Berkeley: University of California Press, 1935.

Dallek, Robert. *Franklin D. Roosevelt and American Foreign Policy, 1932–1945.* New York: Oxford University Press, 1979.

Daniel, Cletus E. *Bitter Harvest: A History of California Farmworkers, 1870–1940.* Ithaca: Cornell University Press, 1981.

Daniels, Roger. *The Politics of Prejudice: The Anti-Japanese Movement in California and the Struggle for Japanese Exclusion.* Berkeley: University of California Press, 1962.

De Caux, Len. *Labor Radical—From the Wobblies to CIO: A Personal History.* Boston: Beacon Press, 1970.

Dennis, Peggy. *The Autobiography of an American Communist: A Personal View of a Political Life, 1925–1975.* Westport, Conn.: Lawrence Hill; Berkeley, Calif.: Creative Arts, 1977.

Draper, Theodore. *American Communism and Soviet Russia.* New York: Viking Press, 1960.

———. *The Roots of American Communism.* New York: Viking Press, 1957.

Dubofsky, Melvyn. *We Shall Be All: A History of the Industrial Workers of the World.* New York: Quadrangle/New York Times Book Co., 1969.

Dubofsky, Melvyn, and Warren Van Tine. *John L. Lewis: A Biography.* New York: Quadrangle/New York Times Book Co., 1977.

Dunn, Robert W. *The Americanization of Labor: The Employers' Offensive against the Trade Unions.* New York: International Publishers, 1927.

Edwards, Richard. *Contested Terrain: The Transformation of the Workplace in the Twentieth Century.* New York: Basic Books, 1979.

Eliel, Paul. *The Waterfront and General Strikes, San Francisco, 1934: A Brief History.* San Francisco: Hooper Printing Co., 1934.

Fine, Sidney. *Sit-Down: The General Motors Strike of 1936–1937.* Ann Arbor: University of Michigan Press, 1969.

Fingard, Judith. *Jack in Port: Sailortowns of Eastern Canada.* Toronto: University of Toronto Press, 1982.

Foner, Eric. *Free Soil, Free Labor, Free Men: The Ideology of the Republican Party before the Civil War.* New York: Oxford University Press, 1970.

———. *Politics and Ideology in the Age of the Civil War.* New York: Oxford University Press, 1980.

Foster, William Z. *Pages from a Worker's Life*. New York: International Publishers, 1939.

Friedlander, Peter. *The Emergence of a UAW Local, 1936–1939: A Study in Class and Culture*. Pittsburgh: University of Pittsburgh Press, 1975.

Frost, Richard H. *The Mooney Case*. Stanford, Calif.: Stanford University Press, 1968.

Galenson, Walter. *The CIO Challenge to the AFL: A History of the American Labor Movement, 1935–1941*. Cambridge, Mass.: Harvard University Press, 1960.

Glaberman, Martin. *Wartime Strikes: The Struggle against the No-Strike Pledge in the UAW during World War II*. Detroit: Bewick Editions, 1980.

Glazer, Nathan. *The Social Basis of American Communism*. New York: Harcourt, Brace and World, 1961.

Goldberg, Joseph P. *The Maritime Story: A Study in Labor-Management Relations*. Cambridge, Mass.: Harvard University Press, 1958.

Goldblatt, Louis. *Working Class Leader in the ILWU, 1935–1977*. Interview conducted by Estolv Ethan Ward. Berkeley: Regional Oral History Office, Bancroft Library, University of California, 1983.

Gordon, David M., Richard Edwards, and Michael Reich. *Segmented Work, Divided Workers: The Historical Transformation of Labor in the United States*. New York: Cambridge University Press, 1982.

Gornick, Vivian. *The Romance of American Communism*. New York: Basic Books, 1977.

Gorter, Wytze, and George H. Hildebrand. *The Pacific Coast Maritime Shipping Industry, 1930–1948*. Vol. 2: *An Analysis of Performance*. Berkeley: University of California Press, 1954.

Hareven, Tamara K., and Randolph Langenbach. *Amoskeag: Life and Work in an American Factory City*. New York: Pantheon, 1978.

Harris, Joe. *The Bitter Fight: A Pictorial History of the Australian Labour Movement*. Brisbane: University of Queensland Press, 1970.

Harris, William H. *The Harder We Run: Black Workers since the Civil War*. New York: Oxford University Press, 1982.

Hill, Herbert. *Black Labor and the American Legal System: Race, Work, and the Law*. 1977. Reprint. Madison: University of Wisconsin Press, 1985.

Hinton, James. *The First Shop Stewards' Movement*. London: George Allen and Unwin, 1973.

Hobsbawm, Eric. *Labouring Men: Studies in the History of Labour*. New York: Basic Books, 1964.

Hohman, Elmo P. *History of American Merchant Seamen*. Hamden, Conn.: Shoe String Press, 1956.

———. *Seamen Ashore: A Study of the United Seamen's Service and of Merchant Seamen in Port*. New Haven: Yale University Press, 1952.

Howe, Irving. *Socialism and America*. New York: Harcourt Brace Jovanovich, 1985.

Isserman, Maurice. *Which Side Were You On? The American Communist Party during the Second World War*. Middletown, Conn.: Wesleyan University Press, 1982.

Jensen, Vernon H. *Lumber and Labor*. New York: Farrar and Rinehart, 1945.

Johns, Orrick. *Time of Our Lives: The Story of My Father and Myself*. New York: Stackpole, 1937.

Joll, James. *The Anarchists*. Boston: Little, Brown, 1964.

Josephson, Matthew. *Sidney Hillman: Statesman of American Labor*. Garden City, N.Y.: Doubleday, 1952.

Kampelman, Max M. *The Communist Party vs. the C.I.O.: A Study in Power Politics*. New York: Frederick A. Praeger, 1957.

Keeran, Roger. *The Communist Party and the Auto Workers Unions*. Bloomington: Indiana University Press, 1980.

Kempton, Murray. *Part of Our Time: Some Monuments and Ruins of the Thirties*. New York: Simon and Schuster, 1955.

King, Jerry, Ralph Emerson, Fred Renaud, and Lawrence McRyn. *We Accuse (From the Record)*. New York: n.p., 1940.

Klehr, Harvey. *The Heyday of American Communism: The Depression Decade*. New York: Basic Books, 1984.

Knight, Robert Edward Lee. *Industrial Relations in the San Francisco Bay Area, 1900–1918*. Berkeley: University of California Press, 1960.

Krebs, Richard [Jan Valtin]. *Out of the Night*. New York: Alliance Book Corp., 1941.

Landis, Arthur H. *The Abraham Lincoln Brigade*. New York: Citadel Press, 1967.

Larrowe, Charles P. *Harry Bridges: The Rise and Fall of Radical Labor in the United States*. New York: Lawrence Hill, 1972.

———. *Shape-up and Hiring Hall: A Comparison of Hiring Methods and Labor Relations on the New York and Seattle Waterfronts*. Berkeley: University of California Press, 1955.

Laurie, Bruce. *Working People of Philadelphia, 1800–1850*. Philadelphia: Temple University Press, 1981.

Lawrenson, Helen. *Stranger at the Party: A Memoir*. New York: Random House, 1975.

Leuchtenburg, William E. *Franklin D. Roosevelt and the New Deal, 1932–1940*. New York: Harper and Row, 1963.

Levenstein, Harvey A. *Communism, Anticommunism, and the CIO*. Westport, Conn.: Greenwood Press, 1981.

Levinson, Edward. *Labor on the March*. New York: Harper and Brothers, 1938.

Lichtenstein, Nelson. *Labor's War at Home: The CIO in World War II*. New York: Cambridge University Press, 1982.

London, Jack. *John Barleycorn*. 1913. Reprint. New York: Greenwood Press, 1968.

Lowitt, Richard, and Maurine Beasley, eds. *One Third of a Nation: Lorena Hickok Reports on the Great Depression*. Urbana: University of Illinois Press, 1981.

Lynd, Alice, and Staughton Lynd. *Rank and File: Personal Histories by Working-Class Organizers*. Boston: Beacon Press, 1973.

McKay, Richard C. *South Street: A Maritime History of New York*. New York: G. P. Putnam's Sons, 1934.

McWilliams, Carey. *The Education of Carey McWilliams*. New York: Simon and Schuster, 1979.

———. *Factories in the Field: The Story of Migratory Farm Labor in California*. 1939. Reprint. Santa Barbara, Calif.: Peregrine Publishers, 1971.

Madison, Charles A. *American Labor Leaders: Personalities and Forces in the Labor Movement*. 2d ed. New York: Frederick Ungar, 1962.

Magden, Ronald, and A. D. Martinson. *The Working Waterfront: The Story of Tacoma's Ships and Men.* Tacoma, Wash.: International Longshoremen's and Warehousemen's Union, Local 23, 1982.

[Mann, Tom]. *Tom Mann's Memoirs.* With a preface by Ken Coates. 1923. Reprint. London: MacGibbon and Kee, 1967.

Marot, Helen. *American Labor Unions.* New York: Henry Holt, 1914.

Marquart, Frank. *An Auto Worker's Journal: The UAW from Crusade to One-Party Union.* University Park: Pennsylvania State University Press, 1975.

Matles, James J., and James Higgins. *Them and Us: Struggles of a Rank-and-File Union.* Englewood Cliffs, N.J.: Prentice-Hall, 1974.

Meacham, Standish. *A Life Apart: The English Working Class, 1890–1914.* Cambridge, Mass.: Harvard University Press, 1977.

Melville, Herman. *Redburn, His First Voyage.* 1849. Reprint. London: Penguin, 1976.

Minton, Bruce, and John Stuart. *Men Who Lead Labor.* New York: Modern Age Books, 1937.

Montgomery, David. *Workers' Control in America: Studies in the History of Work, Technology, and Labor Struggles.* New York: Cambridge University Press, 1979.

Moore, Barrington, Jr. *Injustice: The Social Bases of Obedience and Revolt.* White Plains, N.Y.: M. E. Sharpe, 1978.

Morgan, Murray. *The Last Wilderness.* New York: Viking Press, 1955.

Morris, Richard B. *Government and Labor in Early America.* 1946. Reprint. New York: Octagon Books, 1965.

Moss, Bernard H. *The Origins of the French Labor Movement, 1830–1914: The Socialism of Skilled Workers.* Berkeley: University of California Press, 1976.

Mulzac, Hugh. *A Star to Steer By.* New York: International Publishers, 1963.

Naison, Mark. *Communists in Harlem during the Depression.* Urbana: University of Illinois Press, 1983.

Nelson, Steve, James R. Barrett, and Rob Ruck. *Steve Nelson, American Radical.* Pittsburgh: University of Pittsburgh Press, 1981.

Northrup, Herbert R. *Organized Labor and the Negro.* New York: Harper and Brothers, 1944.

O'Connor, Harvey. *Revolution in Seattle: A Memoir.* New York: Monthly Review Press, 1964.

Olmsted, Frederick Law. *The Cotton Kingdom: A Traveller's Observation on Cotton and Slavery in the American Slave States.* 1861. Reprint. Edited, with an introduction, by Arthur M. Schlesinger. New York: Alfred A. Knopf, 1953.

O'Neill, Eugene. *The Long Voyage Home: Seven Plays of the Sea.* New York: Modern Library, 1946.

Painter, Nell Irvin. *The Narrative of Hosea Hudson: His Life as a Negro Communist in the South.* Cambridge, Mass.: Harvard University Press, 1979.

Parker, Carleton H. *The Casual Laborer and Other Essays.* 1920. Reprint. Seattle: University of Washington Press, 1972.

Pells, Richard H. *Radical Visions and American Dreams: Culture and Social Thought in the Depression Years.* New York: Harper and Row, 1973.

Perkins, Frances. *The Roosevelt I Knew*. New York: Viking Press, 1946.

Perlman, Selig. *A Theory of the Labor Movement*. 1928. Reprint. New York: Augustus M. Kelley, 1968.

Perlman, Selig, and Philip Taft. *History of Labor in the United States*. Vol. 4.: *Labor Movements*. New York: Macmillan, 1935.

Perry, Louis B., and Richard S. Perry. *A History of the Los Angeles Labor Movement, 1911–1941*. Berkeley: University of California Press, 1963.

Pesotta, Rose. *Bread upon the Waters*. New York: Dodd, Mead, 1944.

Pilcher, William W. *The Portland Longshoremen: A Dispersed Urban Community*. New York: Holt, Rinehart and Winston, 1972.

Quin, Mike. *The Big Strike*. Olema, Calif.: Olema Publishing Co., 1949.

Raskin, Bernard. *On a True Course: The Story of the National Maritime Union of America, AFL-CIO*. New York: National Maritime Union of America, 1967.

Richmond, Al. *A Long View from the Left: Memoirs of an American Revolutionary*. Boston: Houghton Mifflin, 1973.

Riesenberg, Felix, Jr. *Golden Gate: The Story of San Francisco Harbor*. New York: Tudor Publishing Co., 1940.

Rubin, Charles. *The Log of Rubin the Sailor*. New York: International Publishers, 1973.

Rudé, George. *Ideology and Popular Protest*. New York: Pantheon, 1980.

Saxton, Alexander. *The Indispensable Enemy: Labor and the Anti-Chinese Movement in California*. Berkeley: University of California Press, 1971.

Schatz, Ronald W. *The Electrical Workers: A History of Labor at General Electric and Westinghouse, 1923–60*. Urbana: University of Illinois Press, 1983.

Schmidt, Henry. *Secondary Leadership in the ILWU, 1933–1966*. An oral history conducted 1974–81 by Miriam F. Stein and Estolv Ethan Ward. Berkeley: Regional Oral History Office, Bancroft Library, University of California, 1983.

Schneider, Betty V. H. *Industrial Relations in the West Coast Maritime Industry*. Berkeley: University of California, Institute of Industrial Relations, 1958.

Schwantes, Carlos A. *Radical Heritage: Labor, Socialism, and Reform in Washington and British Columbia, 1885–1917*. Seattle: University of Washington Press, 1979.

Schwartz, Harvey. *The March Inland: Origins of the ILWU Warehouse Division, 1934–1938*. Los Angeles: University of California, Institute of Industrial Relations, 1978.

Selvin, David F. *Sky Full of Storm: A Brief History of California Labor*. Rev. ed. San Francisco: California Historical Society, 1975.

Spero, Sterling D., and Abram L. Harris. *The Black Worker: The Negro and the Labor Movement*. New York: Columbia University Press, 1931.

Standard, William L. *Merchant Seamen: A Short History of Their Struggles*. New York: International Publishers, 1947.

Starobin, Joseph R. *American Communism in Crisis, 1943–1957*. Cambridge, Mass.: Harvard University Press, 1972.

Stein, Miriam Feingold, interviewer-editor. *The Shipboard Murder Case: Labor, Radicalism, and Earl Warren, 1936–1941*. Berkeley: Regional Oral History Office, Bancroft Library, University of California, 1976.

Steinbeck, John. *Of Mice and Men*. New York: Covici Friede, 1937.

Stolberg, Benjamin. *The Story of the CIO*. New York: Viking Press, 1938.

Swanstrom, Edward E. *The Waterfront Labor Problem: A Study in Decasualization and Unemployment Insurance*. New York: Fordham University Press, 1938.

Taylor, Paul S. *The Sailors' Union of the Pacific*. New York: Ronald Press, 1923.

Terkel, Studs. *Hard Times: An Oral History of the Great Depression*. New York: Pantheon, 1970.

Thompson, E. P. *The Making of the English Working Class*. New York: Pantheon, 1963.

―――. *The Poverty of Theory and Other Essays*. New York: Monthly Review Press, 1980.

Todes, Charlotte. *Labor and Lumber*. New York: International Publishers, 1931.

Tomlins, Christopher L. *The State and the Unions: Labor Relations, Law, and the Organized Labor Movement in America, 1880–1960*. New York: Cambridge University Press, 1985.

Trachtenberg, Alan. *The Incorporation of America: Culture and Society in the Gilded Age*. New York: Hill and Wang, 1982.

Tridon, Andre. *The New Unionism*. New York: B. W. Huebsch, 1913.

Turner, Ian. *Industrial Labour and Politics: The Dynamics of the Labour Movement in Eastern Australia, 1900–1921*. Canberra: Australian National University, 1965.

Tyler, Robert L. *Rebels of the Woods: The I.W.W. in the Pacific Northwest*. Eugene: University of Oregon Books, 1967.

Vorse, Mary Heaton. *Labor's New Millions*. New York: Modern Age Books, 1938.

Ward, Estolv E. *Harry Bridges on Trial*. New York: Modern Age Books, 1940.

Weintraub, Hyman. *Andrew Furuseth: Emancipator of the Seamen*. Berkeley: University of California Press, 1959.

Williams, Raymond. *Marxism and Literature*. New York: Oxford University Press, 1977.

Winter, Ella. *And Not to Yield: An Autobiography*. New York: Harcourt, Brace and World, 1963.

Wood, Peter H. *Black Majority: Negroes in South Carolina from 1670 through the Stono Rebellion*. New York: Alfred A. Knopf, 1974.

Yoneda, Karl G. *Ganbatte: Sixty-Year Struggle of a Kibei Worker*. Los Angeles: University of California, Los Angeles, Asian-American Studies Center, 1983.

Zobel, Hiller. *The Boston Massacre*. New York: W. W. Norton, 1970.

Pamphlets

[American League against War and Fascism (Los Angeles Committee)]. *California's Brown Book*. Los Angeles: American League against War and Fascism, 1934.

[Bridges, Harry R., et al.]. *Town Meeting*. N.p., [1938?].

Browder, Earl. *Lincoln and the Communists*. New York: Workers' Library, 1936.

―――. *Who Are the Americans?* New York: Workers' Library, 1936.

Dana, Richard Henry, Jr. *Cruelty to Seamen: Being the Case of Nichols and Couch*. 1839. Reprint. Berkeley: privately printed, 1937.

Dunne, William F. *The Great San Francisco General Strike: The Story of the West Coast Strike—the Bay Counties' General Strike and the Maritime Workers' Strike*. New York: Workers' Library, 1934.

Furuseth, Andrew. *The Shipowners and the I.W.W.* San Francisco: Pacific District Unions of the I.S.U. of A., n.d.

————. *A Sound Warning and the Shipowners' Queer Policies.* N.p., [1921?].

Harrison, Gregory. *Maritime Strikes on the Pacific Coast: A Factual Account of Events Leading to the 1936 Strike of Marine and Longshore Unions.* Statement before the United States Maritime Commission, at San Francisco, Nov. 2, 1936. San Francisco: Waterfront Employers Association, 1936.

Hedley, George P. *The Strike as I Have Seen It.* An address before the Church Council for Social Education, Berkeley, July 19, 1934. N.p., [1934].

Hudson, Roy B. *True Americans: A Tribute to American Maritime Workers Who Fought for World Democracy in the Trenches of Spain.* New York: Waterfront Section, Communist Party, 1938.

————. *Who Are the Reds?* New York: Workers' Library, 1937.

[Hurst, William A., and Lynn Mah.] *Waterborne Trade of California Ports.* San Francisco: Federal Reserve Bank of San Francisco, 1951.

Industrial Workers of the World. *Exposed by the Marine Transport Workers Industrial Union No. 510 of the I.W.W.* Chicago: I.W. of the W., [1922?].

————. *The Lumber Industry and Its Workers.* 3d ed. Chicago: I.W. of the W., [1922?].

————. General Defense Committee. *California the Beautiful and the Damned.* Chicago: General Defense Committee, n.d.

International Longshoremen's and Warehousemen's Union. *The Everlasting Bridges Case.* San Francisco: International Longshoremen's and Warehousemen's Union, 1955.

[International Longshoremen's Association, Local 38–79]. *The Maritime Crisis: What It Is and What It Isn't.* San Francisco: International Longshoremen's Association, Local 38–79, [1936].

————. *The Truth about the Waterfront: The I.L.A. States Its Case to the Public.* San Francisco: ILA Local 38-79, [1935].

Joint Marine Modesto Defense Committee. *The Modesto Frame-up.* San Francisco: Joint Marine Modesto Committee, [1936].

Marine Workers Industrial Union. *The Centralized Shipping Bureau.* New York: Marine Workers Industrial Union, 1934.

————. *Four Fighting Years: A Short History of the Marine Workers Industrial Union.* New York: Marine Workers Industrial Union, [1934].

————. *The Point Gorda Strike: Report of Ship Delegate George Clark at the National Committee Meeting of the Marine Workers Industrial Union.* New York: Marine Workers Industrial Union, [1932?].

National Maritime Union of America. *Two Years: A Record of Struggle and Achievement of the East Coast Seamen.* New York: NMU of A, 1939.

National Seamen's Union of America. *The Red Record: A Brief Resume of Some of the Cruelties Perpetrated upon American Seamen at the Present Time.* San Francisco: Coast Seamen's Journal, [1895?].

Pell, Mike. *Six Seamen: Different Men under Different Systems.* New York: International Publishers, 1933.

Petersen, Walter J. *Marine Labor Union Leadership.* San Francisco, 1925.

Roth, Almon E. *"Men and Ships": A Clinical Study in Human Relationships on One of the World's Most Turbulent Waterfronts*. Speech to the Rotary International Convention, San Francisco, June 23, [1938].

—————. *Merchant Marine Labor Problems on the Pacific Coast*. An address before the Commonwealth Club of California, Jan. 28, 1938.

Schneiderman, William. *The Pacific Coast Maritime Strike*. San Francisco: Western Worker Publishers, 1937.

Scribner, Tom. *Lumberjack*. Davenport, Calif.: Redwood Ripsaw, 1966.

Sparks, N. *The Struggle of the Marine Workers*. New York: International Publishers, 1930.

Sutherland, Ruth. *Treacherous Passage*. San Francisco: Education Department, National Union of Marine Cooks and Stewards, CIO, n.d.

Tank, Herb. *Communists on the Waterfront*. New York: New Century Publishers, 1946.

Waterfront Employers' Union. *"Full and By": A Message from the Waterfront Employers' Union*. San Francisco: [Waterfront Employers' Union], Office of the Secretary, 1921.

Waterfront Workers' Federation. *The Longshoremen's Strike: A Brief Historical Sketch of the Strike Inaugurated on June 1, 1916, in Pacific Coast Ports of the United States*. San Francisco: Waterfront Workers' Federation, 1916.

Articles and Essays

Adamic, Louis. "Harry Bridges Comes East." *Nation*, Dec. 26, 1936, p. 753.

—————. "Harry Bridges: Rank-and-File Leader." *Nation*, May 6, 1936, pp. 576–80.

Argersinger, Jo Ann E. "Assisting the 'Loafers': Transient Relief in Baltimore, 1933–1937." *Labor History* 23 (Spring 1982): 226–45.

Ashleigh, Charles. "The Floater." *International Socialist Review* 15 (July 1914): 34–38.

Auerbach, Jerold S. "Progressives at Sea: The La Follette Act of 1915." *Labor History* 2 (Fall 1961): 344–60.

Baker, Ray Stannard. "A Corner in Labor: What Is Happening in San Francisco Where Labor Holds Undisputed Sway." *McClure's Magazine* 22 (Feb. 1904): 366–78.

Bell, Daniel. "The Racket-Ridden Longshoremen." *Dissent* 6 (Autumn 1959): 417–29.

Bercuson, David Jay. "The One Big Union in Washington." *Pacific Northwest Quarterly* 69 (July 1978): 127–34.

Bernstein, Irving. "John L. Lewis and the Voting Behavior of the C.I.O." *Public Opinion Quarterly* 5 (June 1941): 233–49.

Bittelman, Alex. "The Supreme Court, the New Deal and the Class Struggle." *Communist* 14 (July 1935): 579–603.

Bodnar, John. "Immigration, Kinship, and the Rise of Working-Class Realism in Industrial America." *Journal of Social History* 14 (Fall 1980): 45–65.

Boryczka, Ray. "Militancy and Factionalism in the United Auto Workers, 1937–1941." *Maryland Historian* 8 (Fall 1977): 13–25.

A British Marine Officer. "Can America Produce Merchant Seamen?" *Atlantic Monthly* 104 (Dec. 1909): 798–807.

Brody, David. "The CIO after 50 Years: A Historical Reckoning." *Dissent* 32 (Fall 1985): 457–72.

Browder, Earl. "The American Communist Party in the Thirties." In *As We Saw the Thirties: Essays on Social and Political Movements of a Decade,* edited by Rita James Simon, pp. 216–53. Urbana: University of Illinois Press, 1967.

———. "New Developments and New Tasks in the U.S.A." *Communist* 14 (Feb. 1935): 99–116.

———. "The Party of Lenin and the People's Front." *Communist* 15 (Feb. 1936): 120–29.

———. "The Struggle for the United Front." *Communist* 13 (Oct. 1934): 951–55.

Brown, Donald Mackenzie. "Dividends and Stevedores." *Scribner's* 97 (Jan. 1935): 52–56.

Buhle, Paul. "Historians and American Communism: An Agenda." *International Labor and Working-Class History,* no. 20 (Fall 1981): 38–45.

———. "Jews and American Communism: The Cultural Question." *Radical History Review,* no. 23 (Spring 1980): 9–33.

Burke, Earl. "Dailies Helped Break General Strike." *Editor and Publisher,* July 28, 1934, p. 5.

Burton, Al. "In the Shadow of the Blackjack." *American Socialist* 2 (Mar. 1955): 11–15.

Cantwell, Robert. "War on the West Coast: I. The Gentlemen of San Francisco." *New Republic,* Aug. 1, 1934, pp. 308–10.

Carlson, Oliver. "The San Francisco Waterfront." *Nation,* Jan. 22, 1936, pp. 105–6.

Chiles, Frederic. "General Strike: San Francisco, 1934—An Historical Compilation Film Storyboard." *Labor History* 22 (Summer 1981): 430–63.

"The Coming Labor Party." *Nation,* Apr. 15, 1936, pp. 468–69.

Critchlow, Donald T. "Communist Unions and Racism: A Comparative Study of the Responses of the United Electrical Radio and Machine Workers and the National Maritime Union to the Black Question during World War II." *Labor History* 17 (Spring 1976): 230–44.

Cronin, James E. "Labor Insurgency and Class Formation: Comparative Perspectives on the Crisis of 1917–1920 in Europe." In *Work, Community and Power: The Experience of Labor in Europe and America, 1900–1925,* edited by James E. Cronin and Carmen Sirianni, pp. 20–48. Philadelphia: Temple University Press, 1983.

Darcy, Sam. "The Declining American Federation of Labor." *International Press Correspondence,* Aug. 28, 1930, p. 835.

———. "The Great West Coast Maritime Strike." *Communist* 13 (July 1934): 664–86.

———. "The San Francisco Bay Area General Strike." *Communist* 13 (Oct. 1934): 985–1004.

———. "The San Francisco General Strike—1934." *Hawsepipe* 2 (Sept.–Oct. 1982): 1, 7–9.

Darnton, Byron. "The Riddle of Harry Bridges." *New York Times Magazine,* Feb. 25, 1940, pp. 5, 21.

Davin, Eric Leif, and Staughton Lynd. "Picket Line and Ballot Box: The Forgotten

Legacy of the Local Labor Party Movement, 1932–1936." *Radical History Review*, no. 22 (Winter 1979–80): 43–63.

Davis, Mike. "The Barren Marriage of American Labour and the Democratic Party." *New Left Review*, no. 124 (Nov.–Dec. 1980): 43–84.

———. "The Stop Watch and the Wooden Shoe: Scientific Management and the Industrial Workers of the World." *Radical America* 9 (Jan.–Feb. 1975): 69–95.

Dawley, Alan, and Paul Faler. "Working-Class Culture and Politics in the Industrial Revolution: Sources of Loyalism and Rebellion." *Journal of Social History* 9 (Summer 1976): 466–80.

De Ford, Miriam Allen. "San Francisco: An Autopsy on the General Strike." *Nation*, Aug. 1, 1934, pp. 121–22.

DeLottinville, Peter. "Joe Beef of Montreal: Working Class Culture and the Tavern, 1869–1889." *Labour/Le Travailleur*, no. 8/9 (Autumn-Spring 1981–82): 9–40.

Draper, Theodore. "American Communism Revisited." *New York Review of Books*, May 9, 1985, pp. 32–37.

———. "Communists and Miners, 1928–1933." *Dissent* 19 (Spring 1972): 371–92.

———. "The Popular Front Revisited." *New York Review of Books*, May 30, 1985, pp. 44–50.

Dreiser, Theodore. "The Story of Harry Bridges." *Friday*, Oct. 4, 1940, pp. 2–7, 28.

Dubofsky, Melvyn. "Not So 'Turbulent Years': Another Look at the American 1930s." *Amerikastudien* 24 (Jan. 1979): 5–20.

Durein, Theodore. "Scabs' Paradise." *Reader's Digest* 30 (Jan. 1937): 19–21.

Egolf, Jeremy R. "The Limits of Shop Floor Struggle: Workers vs. the Bedaux System at Willapa Harbor Lumber Mills, 1933–35." *Labor History* 26 (Spring 1985): 195–229.

Eliel, Paul. "Labor Peace in Pacific Ports." *Harvard Business Review* 19 (Summer 1941): 429–37.

———. "Labor Problems in Our Steamship Business." *Yale Review*, 2d series, 26 (Spring 1937): 510–32.

Ficken, Robert E. "The Wobbly Horrors: Pacific Northwest Lumbermen and the Industrial Workers of the World, 1917–1918." *Labor History* 24 (Summer 1983): 325–41.

Filippelli, Ronald. "UE: An Uncertain Legacy." *Political Power and Social Theory: A Research Annual* 4 (1984): 217–52.

Fingard, Judith. " 'Those Crimps of Hell and Goblins Damned': The Image and Reality of Quebec's Sailortown Bosses." In *Working Men Who Got Wet*, edited by Rosemary Ommer and Gerald Panting, pp. 323–33. St. John's: Maritime History Group, Memorial University of Newfoundland, 1980.

Fischer, Lewis R. "A Dereliction of Duty: The Problem of Desertion on Nineteenth Century Sailing Vessels." In *Working Men Who Got Wet*, edited by Rosemary Ommer and Gerald Panting, pp. 53–70. St. John's: Maritime History Group, Memorial University of Newfoundland, 1980.

Foster, William Z. "New Methods of Political Mass Organization." *Communist* 18 (Feb. 1939): 136–46.

———. "Syndicalism in the United States." *Communist* 14 (Nov. 1935): 1044–57.

Fraser, Steve. "Dress Rehearsal for the New Deal: Shop-Floor Insurgents, Political

Elites, and Industrial Democracy in the Amalgamated Clothing Workers." In *Working-Class America: Essays on Labor, Community, and American Society,* edited by Michael H. Frisch and Daniel J. Walkowitz, pp. 212–55. Urbana: University of Illinois Press, 1983.

Fredrickson, George M., and Christopher Lasch. "Resistance to Slavery." In *American Slavery: The Question of Resistance,* edited by John H. Bracey, Jr., August Meier, and Elliott Rudwick, pp. 179–92. Belmont, Calif.: Wadsworth Publishing Co., 1971.

Gold, Michael. "No Blank Check for Roosevelt." *New Masses,* Jan. 21, 1936, p. 6.

Goodey, Chris. "Factory Committees and the Dictatorship of the Proletariat (1918)." *Critique,* no. 3 (Autumn 1974): 27–47.

Gordon, Max. "The Party and the Polling Place: A Response." *Radical History Review,* no. 23 (Spring 1980): 130–35.

"The Hard Lot of the Sailor." *Survey,* May 13, 1911, pp. 266–67.

Harrison, Charles Yale. "Stalin's American Merchant Marine." *American Mercury* 51 (Oct. 1940): 135–44.

Hathaway, Clarence A. "The 1938 Elections and Our Tasks." *Communist* 17 (Mar. 1938): 208–19.

Healey, Dorothy. "False Consciousness and Labor Historians." *Political Power and Social Theory: A Research Annual* 4 (1984): 281–88.

Henderson, Harry, and Sam Shaw. "Readin', Writin', and No Strikin'." *Collier's,* Apr. 21, 1945, pp. 22–23.

Hohman, Elmo P. "American Merchant Seamen." *Industrial and Labor Relations Review* 15 (Jan. 1962): 221–29.

Hopkins, William S. "Employment Exchanges for Seamen." *American Economic Review* 25 (June 1935): 250–58.

Hudson, R. B. "The Fight of the Seamen for Militant Unionism." *Communist* 15 (Mar. 1936): 220–29.

———. "The Lessons of the Maritime Strikes." *Communist* 16 (Mar. 1937): 229–40.

———. "New Developments in Organizing the Marine Industry." *Communist* 16 (Nov. 1937): 1016–22.

———. "The Work of the Marine Union." *Party Organizer* 7 (May–June 1934): 26–30.

Hunter, George McPherson. "Destitution among Seamen." *Survey,* Aug. 3, 1912, pp. 610–18.

Hyman, Richard. Foreword to the 1975 edition of *The Frontier of Control: A Study in British Workshop Politics,* by Carter L. Goodrich. 1920. Reprint. London: Pluto Press, 1975.

"Interview with Herbert Gutman." *Radical History Review,* no. 27 (May 1983): 202–22.

Isserman, Maurice. "The 1956 Generation: An Alternative Approach to the History of American Communism." *Radical America* 14 (Mar.–Apr. 1980): 43–51.

———. "Three Generations: Historians View American Communism." *Labor History* 26 (Fall 1985): 517–45.

Johnson, Richard. "Three Problematics: Elements of a Theory of Working-Class Culture." In *Working-Class Culture: Studies in History and Theory,* edited by J.

Clarke, C. Critcher, and R. Johnson, pp. 201–37. New York: St. Martin's Press, 1980.

Jones, Alfred Haworth. "The Search for a Usable Past in the New Deal Era." *American Quarterly* 23 (Dec. 1971): 710–24.

Josephson, Matthew. "Red Skies over the Waterfront." *Collier's,* Oct. 5, 1946, pp. 17, 88–90.

Kahn, Lawrence M. "Unions and Internal Labor Markets: The Case of the San Francisco Longshoremen." *Labor History* 21 (Summer 1980): 367–91.

Kerr, Clark, and Lloyd Fisher. "Conflict on the Waterfront." *Atlantic Monthly* 184 (Sept. 1949): 17–23.

Kingsdale, Jon M. "The 'Poor Man's Club': Social Functions of the Urban Working-Class Saloon." *American Quarterly* 25 (Oct. 1973): 472–89.

Klehr, Harvey. "American Communism and the United Auto Workers Union: New Evidence on an Old Controversy." *Labor History* 24 (Summer 1983): 404–13.

La Monte, Robert Rives. "The New Socialism." *International Socialist Review* 13 (Sept. 1912): 212–16.

Larrowe, Charles P. "The Great Maritime Strike of '34: Part I." *Labor History* 11 (Fall 1970): 403–51.

———. "The Great Maritime Strike of '34: Part II." *Labor History* 12 (Winter 1971): 3–37.

Laski, Harold. "The Problem of the General Strike." *Nation,* Aug. 15, 1934, pp. 178–80.

"The Last Serfs." *Nation,* Feb. 2, 1927, pp. 107–8.

Lemisch, Jesse. "Jack Tar in the Streets: Merchant Seamen in the Politics of Revolutionary America." *William and Mary Quarterly,* 3d ser., 25 (July 1968): 371–407.

———. "Listening to the 'Inarticulate': William Widger's Dream and the Loyalties of American Revolutionary Seamen in British Prisons." *Journal of Social History* 3 (Fall 1969): 10–29.

Levenson, Lew. "California Casualty List." *Nation,* Aug. 29, 1934, pp. 243–45.

Levinson, Mark, and Brian Morton. "The CIO, John Lewis, and the Left: An Interview with Philip Van Gelder." *Dissent* 32 (Fall 1985): 460–63.

Lichtenstein, Nelson. "Auto Worker Militancy and the Structure of Factory Life, 1937–1955." *Journal of American History* 67 (Sept. 1980): 335–53.

———. "The Communist Experience in American Trade Unions." *Industrial Relations* 19 (Spring 1980): 119–31.

"Longshore Labor Conditions in the United States—Part I." *Monthly Labor Review* 31 (Oct. 1930): 1–20.

"Longshore Labor Conditions in the United States—Part II." *Monthly Labor Review* 31 (Nov. 1930): 11–25.

Lovin, Hugh T. "CIO Innovators, Labor Party Ideologues, and Organized Labor's Muddles in the 1937 Detroit Elections." *Old Northwest* 8 (Fall 1982): 223–43.

Lubell, Samuel. "Post Mortem: Who Elected Roosevelt?" *Saturday Evening Post,* Jan. 25, 1941, pp. 9–11, 91–94, 96.

Lynd, Staughton. "The Possibility of Radicalism in the Early 1930's: The Case of Steel." *Radical America* 6 (Nov.–Dec. 1972): 37–64.

McFee, William. "Seagoing Soviets." *Saturday Evening Post,* Sept. 21, 1940, pp. 27, 83–88.

"Marine Subsidies." *Fortune* 16 (Sept. 1937): 65–67, 180–84.

"The Maritime Unions." *Fortune* 16 (Sept. 1937): 123–28, 132, 134, 137.

Miller, Raymond Charles. "The Dockworker Subculture and Some Problems in Cross-Cultural and Cross-Time Generalizations." *Comparative Studies in Society and History* 11 (June 1969): 302–14.

Mills, Herb. "The San Francisco Waterfront: The Social Consequences of Industrial Modernization." In *Case Studies on the Labor Process,* edited by Andrew Zimbalist, pp. 127–55. New York: Monthly Review Press, 1979.

Montgomery, David. "Strikes in Nineteenth-Century America." *Social Science History* 4 (Feb. 1980): 81–104.

Naison, Mark. "Communism and Harlem Intellectuals in the Popular Front: Anti-Fascism and the Politics of Black Culture." *Journal of Ethnic Studies* 9 (Spring 1981): 1–25.

———. "Harlem Communists and the Politics of Black Protest." *Marxist Perspectives* 1 (Fall 1978): 20–50.

"Nationality of Members of the International Seamen's Union of America." *Monthly Labor Review* 12 (Feb. 1921): 430–31.

Nelson, Bruce. "Immigrant Enclaves versus Class Consciousness: Miners and Steel Workers in Pennsylvania, 1900–1940." *Reviews in American History* 11 (Dec. 1983): 576–81.

———. " 'Pentecost' on the Pacific: Maritime Workers and Working-Class Consciousness in the 1930s." *Political Power and Social Theory: A Research Annual* 4 (1984): 141–82.

———. "Unions and the Popular Front: The West Coast Waterfront in the 1930s." *International Labor and Working-Class History,* no. 30 (Fall 1986): pp. 59–78.

Nelson, Daniel. "The CIO at Bay: Labor Militancy and Politics in Akron, 1936–1938." *Journal of American History* 71 (Dec. 1984): 565–86.

———. "Origins of the Sit-Down Era: Worker Militancy and Innovation in the Rubber Industry, 1934–38." *Labor History* 23 (Spring 1982): 198–225.

Neuberger, Richard L. "Bad-Man Bridges." *Forum* 101 (Apr. 1939): 195–99.

———. "Labor's Overlords." *American Magazine* 125 (Mar. 1938): 16–17, 166–70.

O'Connell, John A. "Transforming a Company Union." *American Federationist* 37 (Jan. 1930): 61–62.

"Once upon a Shop Floor: An Interview with David Montgomery." *Radical History Review,* no. 23 (Spring 1980): 37–53.

Peterson, Larry. "Revolutionary Socialism and Industrial Unrest in the Era of the Winnipeg General Strike: The Origins of Communist Labour Unionism in Europe and North America." *Labour/Le Travail,* no. 13 (Spring 1984): 115–31.

Poole, Ernest. "The Ship Must Sail on Time." *Everybody's Magazine* 19 (Aug. 1908): 176–86.

Pouget, Emile. "Syndicalism in France." *International Socialist Review* 15 (Aug. 1914): 100–105.

Preston, William. "Shall This Be All? U.S. Historians Versus William D. Haywood *et al.*" *Labor History* 12 (Summer 1971): 435–53.

Prickett, James R. "New Perspectives on American Communism and the Labor

Movement." *Political Power and Social Theory: A Research Annual* 4 (1984): 3–36.

Radosh, Ronald. "The Corporate Ideology of American Labor Leaders from Gompers to Hillman." In *For a New America: Essays in History and Politics from "Studies on the Left," 1959–1967*, edited by James Weinstein and David W. Eakins, pp. 125–52. New York: Vintage Books, 1970.

Record, Jane Cassels. "The Rise and Fall of a Maritime Union." *Industrial and Labor Relations Review* 10 (Oct. 1956): 81–92.

Reed, Mary. "San Pedro." *Nation*, July 9, 1924, pp. 45–46.

Rogin, Michael. "Voluntarism: The Political Functions of an Antipolitical Doctrine." *Industrial and Labor Relations Review* 15 (July 1962): 521–35.

Rosenberg, William. "Workers and Workers' Control in the Russian Revolution." *History Workshop Journal*, no. 5 (Spring 1978): 89–97.

Rosenzweig, Roy. "Organizing the Unemployed: The Early Years of the Great Depression, 1929–1933." *Radical America* 10 (July–Aug. 1976): 37–60.

———. " 'United Action Means Victory': Militant Americanism on Film." *Labor History* 24 (Spring 1983): 274–88.

Schatz, Ronald. "Union Pioneers. The Founders of Local Unions at General Electric and Westinghouse, 1933–1937." *Journal of American History* 66 (Dec. 1977): 582–602.

Schwartz, Harvey. "Harry Bridges and the Scholars: Looking at History's Verdict." *California History* 59 (Spring 1980): 66–79.

Schulberg, Budd. "Joe Docks: Forgotten Man on the Waterfront." *New York Times Magazine*, Dec. 28, 1952, pp. 3–5, 28–30.

Seeley, Evelyn. "War on the West Coast: II. Journalistic Strikebreakers." *New Republic*, Aug. 1, 1934, pp. 310–12.

"Seven Seamen." *Fortune* 16 (Sept. 1937): 121–22, 130–32.

Shields, Art. "The San Pedro Strike." *Industrial Pioneer*, June 1923, pp. 14–18.

"The Shop Paper—An Organ of Struggle." *Party Organizer* 6 (Feb. 1933): 76–78.

Sinclair, Upton. "Protecting Our Liberties." *Nation*, July 4, 1923, pp. 9–10.

Sirianni, Carmen. "Workers' Control in Europe: A Comparative Sociological Analysis." In *Work, Community, and Power: The Experience of Labor in Europe and America, 1900–1925*, edited by James E. Cronin and Carmen Sirianni, pp. 254–310. Philadelphia: Temple University Press, 1983.

Smith, Steve. "Craft Consciousness, Class Consciousness: Petrograd 1917." *History Workshop Journal*, no. 11 (Spring 1981): 33–56.

Stachel, Jack. "Build the Party for Peace, Democracy, and Socialism!" *Communist* 17 (Mar. 1938): 220–41.

Stedman-Jones, Gareth. "History and Theory." *History Workshop Journal*, no. 8 (Autumn 1979): 198–202.

———. "Working-Class Culture and Working-Class Politics in London, 1870–1900: Notes on the Remaking of a Working Class." *Journal of Social History* 7 (Summer 1974): 460–508.

Susman, Warren. Introduction to *Culture and Commitment, 1929–1945*, edited by Warren Susman, pp. 1–24. New York: George Braziller, 1973.

Swados, Harvey. "West-Coast Waterfront—The End of an Era." *Dissent* 8 (Autumn 1961): 448–60.

Symes, Lillian. "After EPIC in California." *Nation*, Apr. 22, 1936, pp. 509–11.
———. "California, There She Stands!" *Harper's* 170 (Feb. 1935): 360–68.
Taft, Philip. "The Unlicensed Seafaring Unions." *Industrial and Labor Relations Review* 3 (Jan. 1950): 187–212.
———. "Strife in the Maritime Industry." *Political Science Quarterly* 54 (June 1939): 216–36.
Taylor, Frank J. "Roughneck Boss of the Sailors' Union." *Saturday Evening Post*, Apr. 18, 1953, pp. 22–23, 180–84.
Taylor, Paul S. "Eight Years of the Seamen's Act." *American Labor Legislation Review* 25 (Mar. 1925): 52–63.
———, and Norman Leon Gold. "San Francisco and the General Strike." *Survey Graphic* 23 (Sept. 1934): 405–11.
"Ten Who Deliver." *Fortune* 34 (Nov. 1946): 146–51.
Terry, John. "The Terror in San Jose." *Nation*, Aug. 8, 1934, pp. 161–62.
Thomas, Herman "Dutch." "Seamen Ashore." *Hawsepipe* 1 (Nov.–Dec. 1981): 9–10.
———. "Seamen Ashore: Waterfronts of the World." *Hawsepipe* 1 (Mar.–Apr. 1982): 1, 15–16.
Thompson, E. P. "Eighteenth-Century English Society: Class Struggle without Class?" *Social History* 3 (May 1978): 133–65.
———. "The Moral Economy of the English Crowd in the Eighteenth Century." *Past and Present*, no. 50 (Feb. 1971): 76–136.
Tomlins, Christopher L. "AFL Unions in the 1930s: Their Performance in Historical Perspective," *Journal of American History* 65 (Mar. 1979): 1021–42.
Trimble, Peter. "Harry Bridges." *Frontier* 2 (Jan. 1951): 5–7.
"The U.S. Merchant Marine." *Fortune* 16 (Sept. 1937): 61, 163–69.
"Upton Sinclair Defends the Law." *Nation*, June 6, 1923, p. 647.
Verba, Sidney, and Kay Lehman Schlozman. "Unemployment, Class Consciousness, and Radical Politics: What Didn't Happen in the Thirties." *Journal of Politics* 39 (May 1977): 291–323.
Vorse, Mary Heaton. "The Pirates' Nest of New York." *Harper's* 204 (Apr. 1952): 27–37.
Waltzer, Kenneth. "The Party and the Polling Place: American Communism and an American Labor Party in the 1930s." *Radical History Review*, no. 23 (Spring 1980): 104–29.
West, George P. "After Liberalism Had Failed." *Nation*, May 30, 1923, p. 629.
———. "Andrew Furuseth and the Radicals." *Survey*, Nov. 5, 1921, pp. 207–9.
———. "Andrew Furuseth Stands Pat." *Survey*, Oct. 15, 1923, pp. 86–90.
———. "California Sees Red." *Current History* 40 (Sept. 1934): 658–62.
———. "Labor Strategist of the Embarcadero." *New York Times Magazine*, Oct. 25, 1936, pp. 7, 17.
Wetjen, Albert Richard. "Ships, Men and the Sea." *Collier's*, Mar. 7, 1925, pp. 24–25.
"Who Owns the San Francisco Police Department?" *Nation*, Aug. 29, 1934, pp. 228–29.
"With Matson down to Melbourne." *Fortune* 16 (Sept. 1937): 101–6, 170–74.
Zelnik, Reginald E. "Passivity and Protest in Germany and Russia: Barrington

Moore's Conception of Working-Class Responses to Injustice." *Journal of Social History* 15 (Spring 1982): 485–512.

Zieger, Robert H. "The Limits of Militancy: Organizing Paper Workers, 1933–35." *Journal of American History* 63 (Dec. 1976): 638–57.

——. "The Popular Front Rides Again." *Political Power and Social Theory: A Research Annual* 4 (1984): 297–302.

Dissertations and Theses

Burki, Mary Ann. "Paul Scharrenberg: White Shirt Sailor." Ph.D. dissertation, University of Rochester, 1971.

Francis, Robert Coleman. "A History of Labor on the San Francisco Waterfront." Ph.D. dissertation, University of California, Berkeley, 1934.

Hield, Wayne Wilbur. "Democracy and Oligarchy in the International Longshoremen's and Warehousemen's Union." M.A. thesis, University of California, Berkeley, 1950.

Lampman, Robert James. "Collective Bargaining of West Coast Sailors, 1885–1947: A Case Study in Unionism." Ph.D. dissertation, University of Wisconsin, 1950.

Liebes, Richard Alan. "Longshore Labor Relations on the Pacific Coast, 1934–1942." Ph.D. dissertation, University of California, Berkeley, 1942.

Nelson, Joseph Bruce. "Maritime Unionism and Working-Class Consciousness in the 1930s." Ph.D. dissertation, University of California, Berkeley, 1982.

Prickett, James. "The Communists and the Communist Issue in the American Labor Movement, 1920–1950." Ph.D. dissertation, University of California, Los Angeles, 1975.

Randolph, Robert Eugene. "History of the International Longshoremen's and Warehousemen's Union, 1945–1951." M.A. thesis, University of California, Berkeley, 1952.

Record, Jane C. "Ideologies and Trade Union Leadership: The Case of Harry Bridges and Harry Lundeberg." Ph.D. dissertation, University of California, Berkeley, 1954.

Robinson, Robert McClure. "A History of the Teamsters in the San Francisco Bay Area, 1850–1950." Ph.D. dissertation, University of California, Berkeley, 1951.

Weintraub, Hyman. "The I.W.W. in California, 1905–1931." M.A. thesis, University of California, Los Angeles, 1947.

Unpublished Manuscripts and Papers

Bailey, Bill. "The Kid from Hoboken." San Francisco, 1980. In author's possession.

Cherny, Robert W. "Securing 'Industrial Freedom': The American Plan in San Francisco." Paper delivered at the annual meeting of the Organization of American Historians, Los Angeles, Apr. 1984.

Egan, Michael. " 'That's Why Organizing Was So Good'; Portland Longshoremen, 1934: An Oral History." Senior thesis, Reed College, 1975.

Gill, Peter B. [with Ottilie Dombroff Markholt]. "The Sailors' Union of the Pacific from 1885 to 1929." Seattle, 1942. Copy in Bancroft Library, University of California, Berkeley.

Katzman, David M. "Black Longshoremen." Paper delivered at the annual meeting of the Organization of American Historians, San Francisco, Apr. 1980.

Kimeldorf, Howard. "Reds or Rackets: The Making of Radical and Conservative Unions on the Waterfront." Manuscript accepted for publication by the University of California Press.

Lane, Tony. " 'Philosophical Anarchists': British Merchant Seamen and Their Attitudes to Authority, 1850–1910." London, n.d. In author's possession.

Lannon, Albert, Jr. "Red Diaper Baby: A Personal Political Memoir." N.p., n.d. In author's possession.

Mers, Gilbert. "One Step at a Time, Many Backward." Houston, 1983. Autobiography scheduled for publication by Singlejack Books, San Pedro, Calif.

Record, Jane Cassels. "The San Francisco Waterfront: Crucible of Labor Factionalism." University of California, Institute of Industrial Relations, Berkeley, 1952.

Schwartz, Stephen. "The Year 1934: A Chapter from the History of World Labor." San Francisco, n.d. In author's possession.

Index

A Note on the Author

Bruce Nelson received his B.A. from Princeton University and his M.A. and Ph.D. from the University of California at Berkeley. He has published articles and reviews in *International Labor and Working-Class History, Labor History, Political Power and Social Theory,* and *Reviews in American History.* He teaches in the Department of History at Dartmouth College.

Books in the Series
The Working Class in American History